Mayaya Rising

Mayaya Rising

Black Female Icons in Latin American and Caribbean Literature and Culture

D A W N D U K E

LEWISBURG, PENNSYLVANIA

Library of Congress Cataloging-in-Publication Data

Names: Duke, Dawn, 1965– author.
Title: Mayaya rising : Black female icons in Latin American and Caribbean literature and culture / Dawn Duke.
Description: Lewisburg, Pennsylvania : Bucknell University Press, [2023] | Includes bibliographical references and index.
Identifiers: LCCN 2022012799 | ISBN 9781684484386 (paperback ; alk. paper) | ISBN 9781684484393 (hardback ; alk. paper) | ISBN 9781684484409 (epub) | ISBN 9781684484416 (mobi) | ISBN 9781684484423 (pdf)
Subjects: LCSH: Women, Black, in literature. | Latin American literature—Women authors—History and criticism. | Latin American literature—Black authors—History and criticism. | Caribbean literature—Women authors—History and criticism. | Caribbean literature—Black authors—History and criticism. | Latin America—Civilization—African influences. | Caribbean Area—Civilization—African influences. | LCGFT: Literary criticism.
Classification: LCC PQ7081.5 .D85 2023 | DDC 860.9/352208996—dc23/eng/20220831

LC record available at https://lccn.loc.gov/2022012799

A British Cataloging-in-Publication record for this book is available from the British Library.

References to internet websites (URLs) were accurate at the time of writing. Neither the author nor Bucknell University Press is responsible for URLs that may have expired or changed since the manuscript was prepared.

♾ The paper used in this publication meets the requirements of the American National Standard for Information Sciences—Permanence of Paper for Printed Library Materials, ANSI Z39.48-1992.

www.bucknelluniversitypress.org

Distributed worldwide by Rutgers University Press

Manufactured in the United States of America

I dedicate this book to Meighan Duke, Norma Jackson,
Abigail Peazer, Rosamunde Renard, Christine Mariner,
Sandra Cummings, and Eleanor Duke, examples
of assertive and confident Guyanese women.

Contents

Mayaya Rising

Introduction

THE FUNDAMENTALS OF GLORY

With words of wisdom, leading Afro-Cuban poet Georgina Herrera (1936–2021) provides us with a clear perspective of the Black woman's intellectual mission and unsettling journey as she was forcibly abducted from her home in Africa and obligated to make her way across the Atlantic into the Americas:

> La mujer negra, en la literatura oral que trajo desde África,
> que resistió en su memoria la travesía brutal . . .
> es de una variedad y riqueza sin límites.

> [The Black woman, within the oral literature she brought from Africa,
> that endured the brutal crossing in her memory . . .
> is of limitless variety and richness.][1]

It is a significant piece of writing and part of her essay "Oriki por las negras viejas de antes" [Oriki for old Black women from before], published in *Afrocubanas: Historia, pensamiento y prácticas culturales* [Afro-Cuban women: History, thought, and cultural practices; 2011], a groundbreaking collection of texts from leading writers, scholars, and activists compiled by Daisy Rubiera Castillo and Inés María Martiatu Terry.[2] In a compressed yet effective manner, Herrera's words create a dynamic portrayal that displays the reverence she feels obligated to bestow on the Black female subject. In light of her distinction as an expert in poetic creativity and language, Herrera best captures the essence of what is at the core of such subjectivity—history, gender, Negritude, and writing. In tone, message, and purpose, her verses feed my study with relevant categories of analysis.

Afro-descendant women writers from Latin America and the Spanish Caribbean have always anchored their contemplations and their works in personal experiences related to family, community, and even national settings, as these stimulate their poetic creativity. Such a high level of sensitivity to the social milieu impacts the direction of their literary journeys and drives them to capture and interpret actions, connections, and relationships that are an integral part of their lives. One particular journey has resulted in legendary portrayals of those female subjects who have impacted and transformed narratives of history and their communities. I seek to describe this phenomenon and the way it has, over time, counteracted an existing problem. Who are the female icons of African ancestry in the Spanish- and Portuguese-speaking Americas? What mechanisms are in place to identify, establish, and maintain the glorification and indisputable recognition of Black women in Latin American and Caribbean societies? My argument is that litera- ture by Afro–Latin American women writers, such as those at the center of this study, is the stimulus driving and ultimately sustaining the ever-increasing prom- inence and recognition of exemplars in the region. Three case studies highlighting the achievements of specific Black women are the core of this work. Through these female achievers, I will be able to provide a wealth of cultural information that gains meaning in relation to each female endeavor.

The lives and contributions of Teodora and Micaela Ginés compose my first case study. They were sisters and talented musicians, originally enslaved but later freed, whose presence and artistic skills continue to be a source of inspiration and pride in Cuba and the Dominican Republic. The adequate reconstruction of their origins and life stories requires a focus on the cities of Santiago de Cuba, Cuba, and Santo Domingo, the Dominican Republic; the revered musical genre *el son cubano* [the Cuban *son*]; and the epic poem *Yania Tierra: Poema documento* [Yania earth: Document poem], first published in 1981 by renowned Afro-Dominican poet Aída Cartagena Portalatín. The second case study immortalizes the life work of the iconic Ivy Elizabeth Forbes Brooks (or Elizabeth Forbes Brooks), affectionately known as Miss Lizzie, the matriarch of *palo de mayo* [May Pole] in Bluefields, Nicaragua. The impact of her artistic legacy is still being felt today and has entered history by way of her 2011 biographical and community memoir, *Memorias de Miss Liz- zie: Danzas, música y tradiciones de Bluefields* [Miss Lizzie's memoirs: Dances, music, and traditions of Bluefields]. A backdrop of Afro-Nicaraguan, Creole, Garifuna, and Atlantic coastal cultural contexts supports my aim of creating syn- ergy among Miss Lizzie, Creole grassroots heritage, and Creole literary writings available in anthologies associated with the Caribbean Nicaraguan community of Bluefields, the town she calls home. The third case study references the icono- graphic *palenqueras* of Cartagena, Colombia, whose historical and contemporary imaging and ongoing advocacy have inspired unique anthologies and dictionaries today recognized as creative endeavors by Afro-Colombian and *palenquera* women writers, community leaders, scholars, and activists.[3]

This book takes a woman-centered path in the way it focuses exclusively on female endeavors specific to Latin America within a feminist analytical framework. It is designed to join a stellar group of interdisciplinary published studies, as it sits at the intersection of history, heroism, gender, and literature.[4] Its difference is in the cultural information it provides, much of which is relatively unknown to a North American audience. It draws exclusively on lived achievements and is intentionally transnational in approach (Cuba, the Dominican Republic, Nicara- gua, and Colombia), arguing that the need for more visible Black female icons is a regional shortfall. It is singular in the way it focuses exclusively on Spanish- and Portuguese-speaking territories as well as in the way it creates synchrony between progressive social activism and a militant literary voicing, thereby securing the establishment of a community of writers and leaders in perfect harmony. This text does not present a comparative agenda—that is, comparing U.S., Latino, and Latin American production—which appears to be a trending characteristic for studies in this area; rather, the selection, presentation, and analysis of the three very different case studies serve to confirm how the issue of recognition affects Latin American nations. My discussion provides a strong argument as to why every country in the region should be committed to publicly lauding the amazing creative production of Afro-descendant women. The pattern against which I move is the consistent ignoring and general lack of awareness that such women endure in spite of the way their actions transformed and continue to build their communities and national cultures.

Increasingly during the last four decades, women writers have spent their time perfecting symbolic representations or characterizations, presenting them as the ideal tools with which to promote glowing portraits of select icons who continue to leave their mark on the region's history and culture. This study embraces these tools as strategies of analysis that will support the identification, rationale, and awarding of distinguished figures. Identifying acts of heroism in order to promote the revitalization of the historical presence and significance of the female subject is a constant mechanism of critical literary analysis. In particular, both Paula Sanmartín's *Black Women as Custodians of History* (2014) and Marta Moreno Vega, Marinieves Alba, and Yvette Modestín's *Women Warriors of the Afro-Latina Diaspora* (2012) expand on the idea of heroism in relation to an aggressor—a rebel, a warrior, or a fighter—even as they attest to the complex subjectivities within the realm of Afro-descendant women.[5] Moreno Vega, Alba, and Modestín's specific approach is to record individual testimonies. B. Christine Arce's *Mexico's Nobodies: The Cultural Legacy of the Soldadera and Afro-Mexican Women* (2017) is of a similar intent in that revolutionary warfare is the locus in discovery, occupied by women soldiers and poor camp followers. These largely Black and mulatto women emerge in a historical counternarrative produced by Arce that works to unearth the race and gender biases of their era. She proposes rebel, warrior, and soldier depictions that reconfigure historical representations and potentially facilitate the application of other kindred roles to this exercise in reconstruction—queen, general, leader, griot, healer, activist, elder, guide, advisor, ruler, politician, matriarch, monarch, insurrectionist, freedom fighter, and guardian of tradition and legacy. Her aim echoes Sanmartín's: "Because black women's identity is rooted in their historical experience, the analysis of slave women's history is fundamental to contemporary culture's images of black women and the latter's present position in society."[6]

The idea of heroism in the traditional sense—that is, in alignment with political nation-building agendas—is not accommodating to the iconic female figures that lived during enslavement and beyond. As cultural protagonists, their bravery and sacrifice involved acting against officialdom, order, and institutions of power; their only path to freedom was rebellion. Sanmartín uses the term "law breaker" to describe this countertrajectory that guaranteed immortalization within the legacies of resistance and revolution in the Americas, although such confrontation simultaneously secured her systematic exclusion from her nation's canonical archives.[7] This is where our memory of such bravery is in jeopardy. Arce's *soldadera* and Afro-Mexican women study works to overcome the challenges of remembrance and naming; paying homage to early ancestors requires the confirmation of their names, their actual existence, and their involvement in key happenings.[8] In a similar direction, Monique-Adelle Callahan's *Between the Lines: Literary Transnationalism and African American Poetics* (2011), a comparative examination of poems and narratives by Cristina Ayala (Cuba), Auta de Souza (Brazil), and Frances Harper (United States), nurtures notions of revival and historical reinsertion through the idea of naming, which she defines as "the act of applying a name to a physical or imagined body," thereby solidifying our knowledge of the said individual, whether ancestral or contemporary.[9]

This line of argumentation regarding heroism supports the politicized agenda of historical reconfiguration and re-presentation today. My intention is to contribute to this ongoing task, albeit a bit differently, for I seek to reconcile the past with the present by offering updated readings of how iconic women—their experiences, their life projects, and their critical and effective collaborative efforts with institutions of power—attest to the monumental challenges they face and their outstanding capacity to work through (even within) systems that often prove hostile and unsupportive in order to achieve their goals. In this sense, the kinds of outstanding work and initiatives on display in the three case studies are less about women as "bearers of culture and tradition," or their acts of rebellion, and more about their impressive undertakings as guardians of legacies and nations.[10] Analytical perspectives on heroism tend to be historical in nature, which is where this study differs, as I seek to present a more culturally driven analysis. My principal motivation is woman-centered, expressive of a deep interest in capturing and transmitting the uniqueness of that individual experience in all its dimensions, working toward the creation of a truly iconic profile. Moving forward beyond the description of historical rebelliousness, those in the spotlight are contributors, builders of legacies and enduring positive benefits for their communities. They create unique narratives, engage the power structures of their time fearlessly, and spend their lives fully involved in projects devised to benefit many others. The transition from cultural portrayal to literary configuration and interpretation is a natural one, serving to confirm triumph and success.

The elaborate discussions I develop about each case study take up most of this text and aim at emphasizing the long-term impact of cultural representations while providing paths that are redemptive in nature and that lead to glory. For various reasons, women often fall short of receiving well-earned praises and distinguished accolades, while those who do are disproportionally fewer in number. One striking characteristic that the three case studies share is the way their stories or narratives of successful endeavors have to compete with other national phenomena: the Ginés sisters, Miss Lizzie, and the *palenqueras* become present primarily through *el son cubano*, the *palo de mayo*, and Palenque de San Basilio and its hero, Benkos Biohó, respectively. This marks in a positive way our ability to glorify them even as it mars our direct and immediate access to them, as first we have to go through the aforementioned cultural and historical phenomena. Visibility, accessibility, and recognition are results that can prove difficult to attain given the complex and ambiguous relations such women have with their nation-states as well as those difficulties and distractions that shroud and potentially downplay or even distort their achievements. These challenges also make them more vulnerable to universal doubting and denial, as their relevance and worthiness repeatedly come into question. Mapping their profiles may prove troubling, largely due to our inability to confirm their historical relevance by way of concrete evidence or to cultural trends and views that deem them less worthy of veneration. This particular direction that negatively impacts how they are perceived is reversible if we envision their successes and achievements from within aesthetic and scholarly enterprises strategically arranged to capture and display their experiences. This process inevitably relies on experts capable of designing enterprises that will counteract specific problems such as the dearth of women icons, nonpresence, denial, and silencing.

The identification of a bond between literature and worthy endeavor is a direct result of initiatives and agendas related to historical reaffirmation, experiential writing, and a feminist response to Negritude. With this in mind, this introduction debates the nature of this bond within three frameworks: (1) "I, Black woman, have a history," a concept associated with poet and activist Alzira Rufino; (2) Conceição Evaristo's paradigmatic frame of reference, *escre(vivência)* (understood as "written-lived experience"); and (3) Negritude from a Black feminist perspective, associated with Inés María Martiatu Terry and other authors. I espouse these three notions for providing a methodology of assessment that could be a guide to identify those unique makers of history as worthy of long-term distinguished acknowledgment. Further, in relation to the three case studies, these paradigms provide a base for constructing measures and methodologies to ensure their well-deserved placements as heroines within their nation's narratives, histories, and cultural settings.

A Mulher Negra Tem História

The Black woman has a history is a phrase that dates back to possibly the mid-1980s and represents a movement that expanded into several Afro-Brazilian women's groups and entities (Geledés, Criola, and Casa de Cultura da Mulher Negra) as they started campaigns and research in response to the query, Who are our famous Black female ancestors? This questioning is not unique to Brazil but rather reflective of a Latin American concern about the recognition and prominence of Black, brown, and other women of color. A similar motivation inspired this study. The results are visible in the way the three case studies have uncovered valuable information pertaining to the life experiences of the women icons who are central to each case study. Legends, heroism, spirituality, sacrifices, triumphs, the foundation of nations, and ancestrality are all themes that have a place within their life's work. Increasingly, recent interdisciplinary studies from within North American academia have compensated for the shortfalls in the visibility of notable Afro-diasporic female figures. Sanmartín describes how narratives and poems are driving the rediscovery of mythical and ancestral individuals in a process of constant unearthing of more information, and even other historical figures, thereby reinforcing the urgency for further research to undo centuries of "discontinuities and ruptures."[11] Her intention mirrors that of Flora González Mandri, whose text *Guarding Cultural Memory: Afro-Cuban Women in Literature and the Arts* (2006) serves as a site of convergence for Black women's creativity in art, film, and the word. By emphasizing the artistic and intellectual production of María Magdalena Campos-Pons, Excilia Saldaña, Gloria Rolando, and Nancy Morejón, she captures their intention to control and determine the images and representations of themselves (and women like them). Their discourses, lodged in modernity, reject and defy traditional imaging, issue new forms of cultural perceptions regarding enslavement, and ground themselves in oral and written narratives of remembrance. Their artistry is fundamental in its interdisciplinarity and capacity to envision and populate the unwritten past. González Mandri's focus on the writers themselves differs from my objective in *Mayaya Rising*, which aims to create a correspondence between writers and these outstanding national figures. Regardless, González Mandri's design functions well and complements my intentional recognition of the Ginés sisters as Original Mothers, my description of Miss Lizzie's resurrection of the goddess Mayaya as it relates to her adherence to the May Pole traditions, and my retelling of the *palenquera* legend about Catalina Loango (also written as Luango). Each occurrence gains meaning as a realistic, concrete phenomenon (not myth or fiction) and represents belief systems that serve as stimuli for the nation's Black women poets. They, in turn, do their part to solidify the global cause of reaffirming the female historical presence at the very heart of the Afro–Latin American woman's identity, writing, and agency.

Today, replacing systematic erasure is at the core of strategies meant to enlighten us about unknown and forgotten actors and endeavors—as a case in point, the lives and trajectories of the Ginés sisters. How can we find our way back to them? How can we reinstate their legacy? There is a transregional campaign taking place as Afro-descendant women from Latin America and the Caribbean are making a concerted effort to claim attention in their nations' mainstream societies. Conceptualizing the iconic figure is about the heroic individual, but it is also about groups of Afro-descendant women of cultural worth who share a common characteristic. Scholars of Afro-Latina and Afro–Latin American women and their writings, many from North American academia, and writers currently residing in Latin America have, in ever-increasing numbers, made it their obligation to reconstruct and reconfigure the female presence and endeavors throughout history. These two groups create enclaves of theoretical discourses that move in and out of history, literature, culture, and politics. Their main purpose is to write the subject back into the historiographies of Latin American nations while simultaneously creating an aesthetic of art, beauty, and social consciousness.

Arce's *Mexico's Nobodies* provides an example of research that has successfully identified and captured the nuances of the *soldaderas* as active, conscious collaborators of war.[12] The use of a generic term or reference to identify a grouping is a mechanism I have also adopted, as confirmed by my discussion about the *palenqueras*, who are known for their roles in women-centered activism as strong, proud advocators of their origins and protectors of their economic enterprises. Drawing attention to significant and active/activist groups while counteracting the disfigurement of life stories is an ongoing strategy in research dedicated to uncovering the Black female trajectory through time. Self-identifying as a comparative scholar, Sanmartín observes the African American writer's intent to secure women's rightful place historically, especially since their profiles suffer distortions and displacements into the realm of the imaginary—in other words, in myth, fiction, even spirituality.[13] Her study highlights literary representations of the historic roots of struggle and resistance in the United States and Cuba, using *Incidents in the Life of a Slave Girl* (1861), by former African American slave Harriet Jacobs; *Dessa Rose* (1986), by African American writer Sherley Ann Williams; *Reyita, sencillamente: Testimonio de una negra cubana nonagenaria* [Simply Reyita: Testimonial narrative of a nonagenarian Black Cuban woman; 1996], written and transcribed by Afro-Cuban writer, historian, and researcher Daisy Rubiera Castillo from her interviews with her mother, María de los Reyes Castillo Bueno, or Reyita; and a selection of poems from contemporary Afro-Cuban poets Nancy Morejón and Georgina Herrera. She argues that the writers participate via self-inscription by positioning themselves as subjects of their pasts and producers of discourses that describe their trajectories.

I have always been inspired by literary contemplations and creations from Brazil; indeed, I firmly view that country's Afro-descendant women writers as leaders, at the forefront when it comes to designing mechanisms for poetic innovation and aesthetic analysis, genres and skills they have truly mastered. The best critical essays and concepts to use when engaging writings from Latin America are the ones that writers themselves design and promote. This somewhat subjective and self-glorifying path came to be in large part due to one particular detail—that is, until the twenty-first century, there were not many critical essays on Black women's writings in the Spanish- and Portuguese-speaking Americas, and those available were products from the writers themselves. Today, the area is exploding with new and dynamic studies available in virtual and hard copies, theses and dissertations, documentaries, and intellectual social media platforms.

As discussions surrounding the case studies will confirm, there are multiple paths to appreciating the expanse of female achievements. History and myth (including spirituality) are targets of several studies that provide theoretical paradigms, specifically North American scholarship of the twenty-first century and critical essays by writers who indulge in creative self-assessment, thereby registering their social consciousness and literary journeys. While I reference recent

scholarship by academics, my main purpose is to feature philosophical contemplations coming from major regional writers who have addressed the issues pertinent
to this study.

Poet, essayist, and community leader Alzira Rufino is valuable for the way
she represents the connection among Afro-descendant feminism, grassroots
militancy, and poetry; her anthology of poems *Eu, mulher negra, resisto* [I, Black
woman, resist] coincides perfectly with the short historical compilation she coordinated, *Mulher negra tem história* [The Black woman has history], which were
published in 1988 and 1986, respectively. These two productions continue to have
ripple effects as concepts, textual militancy, and poetry. They illustrate changes
in mindset, set in motion movements of self-repositioning, and serve as the basis
for the creation of initiatives (social, political, cultural, and artistic), the results of
which are ongoing. During the late 1980s and early 1990s, in her capacity as the
director of the Coletivo de Mulheres Negras da Baixada Santista [Black Women's
Collective of the Baixada Santista] and founder of the nongovernmental organization A Casa de Cultura da Mulher Negra [Black Women's House of Culture],
Rufino dedicated her resources to recuperating the history of Afro-Brazilian
women. Arising out of this endeavor was *Mulher negra tem história*, a biographical
collection of great women who left their mark on various aspects of cultural life
and fought against enslavement, racism, and social injustice.[14] Firmina dos Reis is
one of the thirty women presented as icons and heroines of this Brazilian experience. Anastácia, Aqualtune, Brandina, Clementina de Jesus, Francisca, and Luiza
Mahin are among the pretwentieth-century leaders who emerge from obscurity
in this grassroots effort among women of the same community seeking to fill a
void of historical magnitude. At the very core of this enterprise are the woman-
centered liberating concepts such as *da senzala ao quilombo* [from slave quarters
to maroon settlement], *de mucama a empregada doméstica* [from enslaved house-
maid to domestic servant], and *de escrava a Ialorixá* [from slave to Candomblé
high priestess].[15] Rufino stands at the intersection of creative writing, women's
movements, and historical redefinition, confirmed in the way her compilation of
famous Black women in history finds reflection in her 1988 anthology of poems
Eu, mulher negra, resisto, in homage to Luiza Mahin; Winnie and Nelson Mandela;
liberation; the warrior woman; two orishas, Oxum and Iansã; among others. This
exercise in critical *écriture* positions such writers as both creative and philosophical
producers who, sensing their country's reticence, are driven to design discourses
that highlight the deeper ideological agendas behind such poetic production.

No less striking are the accomplishments among Cuban women writers, where
we also can argue in favor of linking history, literature, and advocacy. Historicizing art and activism summarizes the motivation behind *Magín: Tiempo de contar
esta historia* [Magín: Time to tell this story], a 2015 publication by Daisy Rubiera
Castillo and Sonnia Moro that provides historical perspective with regard to the
roots of women's activism in Cuba not necessarily located within the revolutionary
agenda. In her introduction to *Magín*, Sara Más defines the nature of this movement: "Un grupo muy diferente a los que habitualmente se conformaban por esta

geografía: sin normas ni reglamentos, completamente informal, particularmente
espontáneo, creativo, participativo, con sentido de pertenencia, pero a la vez abierto" [A very different group from those that usually make up this geographical
space: without rules or regulations, completely informal, particularly spontaneous,
creative, participative, with a sense of belonging, but at the same time open].[16]

In addition, "Magín" was the name of choice for the Association of Women
Communicators formed during the 1990s, whose story is only now being told.
A group effort, the resulting publication, *Magín: Tiempo de contar esta historia*,
is a dynamic text about the history of the movement, a collection of memorable
episodes, memoirs, and personal stories recounting, among other things, the
life-changing effect of such a gathering on the women involved.[17] Poet Georgina
Herrera describes the impact of this movement:

> I'm part of a non-official women's organization, of women in the media, called
> MAGIN. It's called MAGIN from "iMAGINation," intelligence. Since it's a
> nongovernmental organization, it has gained a lot of prestige nationally and
> internationally, over and above the FMC. When I joined the group, I gained this
> vision of gender in a way that opened my horizons for approaching the women's
> problem. If I had known this years ago, things would have been different. Intu-
> itively, I acted in a given way, but that's not the same. One thing is empiricism
> and another the truth. That's why as women we are very stimulated by MAGIN,
> but up until now it has no legal status. We receive a lot of material on Latin
> America, . . . Women thought we were all equal but we're not, we're talking
> about differences. I'm fascinated by MAGIN and what it's doing.[18]

Magín impacted Herrera profoundly, as it elevated her understanding of racism's
continuing presence in spite of the revolution, an awareness that determined the
direction of her career paths in media and literature.

As Rubiera Castillo and Moro clarify, *magín* means "intelligence" and was
created based on two words, *imagen* [image] and *imaginación* [imagination].[19]
From within this space, there emerged projects, one of which was called "Historia
de mujeres con y sin historia" [History about women with and without history],
a core enterprise providing a purpose and vision around which they organized
meetings, readings, publications, and sessions dedicated to sharing their lives and
realities.[20] "Cubanas de esencia y presencia" [Cuban women of essence and pres-
ence] represents another important endeavor to produce a dictionary featuring
major professionals in the area of communications dating back to the nineteenth
century, which connected with the movement's active agenda to build social awareness about widespread sexism and discrimination.[21]

Rubiera Castillo brings her expertise as an essayist and producer of *testimonios* [testimonial narratives] to bear on *Magín* through her strategy of providing
chronicles of the past, perspectives on race, and descriptions of women's lives. This
work sits at the junction of creative and intellectual writing and, similar to her two
testimonio masterpieces, *Reyita, sencillamente: Testimonio de una negra cubana
nonagenaria* [Simply Reyita: Testimonial narrative of a nonagenarian Black Cuban

woman; 1996] and (with Georgina Herrera) *Golpeando la memoria: Testimonio de una poeta cubana afrodescendiente* [Striking memory: Testimonial narrative of an Afro-descendant female Cuban poet; 2005], registers her commitment to historical reconsiderations. By way of literary critique and philosophical support, besides *Magín* and *Afrocubanas*, she has published various studies located at the intersection of race, gender, religion, and writing.[22]

Rubiera Castillo's literary agenda includes projects that are, by design, recuperative, into which she embeds messages about legacy, human value, and identity construction. Such scholarship is particularly valuable and strategic when it comes to writing and historical visibility in relation to the Afro-Cuban female experience. Her critical positioning supports my process of (re)presenting the Ginés sisters gloriously, within a context that reflects uncertain and debatable separations between myth and reality, truth and fiction, history and oral traditions, and the word and the text. Her essay "El tiempo de la memoria" [The time of memory; 2005] describes her creative process and proves useful for understanding the motivations and strategies that underpin her projects.[23] She defines memory as the driving principal upon which she designed her two *testimonios*, *Reyita, sencillamente* and *Golpeando la memoria*. Here is a space that is all about remembrances [*recuerdos*], those stories and oral narratives that we heard as children and that we learned to envision as tales about our ancestors and about ancient times, imagining a world of myths and legends. Remembrances can also be associated with actual historical fact—for example, accounts and stories during the time of slavery that are specific to individual lives and experiences and take shape through oral narrations based on personal reminiscences.[24]

The ultimate aim driving Rubiera Castillo and Martiatu Terry's collection of essays, *Afrocubanas*, is "avivar la memoria histórica" [to fuel historical memory] to affirm the Afro-Cuban woman's image, production, subjectivity, value system, and knowledge. This edited volume provides analytical perspectives: first, about the qualitative effects of long-term repression, and second, about counternarratives and initiatives of active resistance. Writers such as Ana Maria Gonçalves, Rufino, Herrera, and Rubiera Castillo appear as creators and protagonists of their own discourse, a textual strategy woven into the fabric of their production that changes our perspective of similar women in history. The value of this methodology is in the way it ensures the voicing of women. "Avivar la memoria" is a way of keeping the focus on this subject while building appreciation and understanding of Rubiera Castillo's trajectory over time.[25]

Afro-Cuban poet Georgina Herrera contributes to this volume of essays by confirming that the Black woman did not have the opportunity to leave her footprint (or handprint) on written history. She was a migrant who did not travel of her own free will. She was unable to enjoy the changing landscapes to broaden her understanding and appreciation of other cultures freely and openly. Most importantly, she was forbidden to write. Memory conjures images of entrapment as her physical being found itself caught between Africa and the Americas, forcibly detained inside a vessel on the high seas and in a desperate struggle to comprehend this hellish fate and continue living. Strange and ominous sounds and smells, lamentations, whippings, and illnesses overwhelmed her psyche, marking her and her offspring forever. Denied her dignity and classified as less than human, it seemed that she was destined for absolute erasure, but this is not what transpired; instead, she somehow activated her will to survive and her mental powers that allowed her to remember, envision, and recount tales of freedom, leading to what we imagine today as an oral literature and oral traditions from Africa.[26] Herrera then talks about the "imposible literatura escrita por la mujer negra de antes" [impossible literature written by Black women way back then] and reflects on how much time has passed and how things have changed.[27] Women have learned to read and write, are attending university, and are world travelers. Many are now famous, others less so; however, increasingly, they know and are aware of one another, which is a vital part of the ongoing struggle that is, like these women, in constant motion, a light that keeps going and coming. Her symbolism in many ways aligns perfectly with such writers' relationship with the written word, especially in terms of their overall ability to prosper from their artistry.

In a similar fashion, as chapters 1 and 2 of this book will illustrate, in spite of existential indignities and forgetting (are they myth or reality?) and by virtue of their unforgettable talent, our ability to imagine (image) the Ginés sisters has survived the passage of time. This path reminds us also of *Golpeando la memoria*, a detailed narration, testament to Herrera's family legacy, and proof of such literary inheritance. In this *testimonio*, Herrera recalls her grandfather, whose convincing storytelling fascinated both her and her mother as an interweaving of history and myth, a web of truth and fabrication that enriched their lives even as it frustrated other family members.[28]

Recuerdos, or memories, defy forgetting and stand the test of time while supporting acts and ideas in favor of recuperation and preservation. Orality resists or even overcomes the passage of time, for the more these stories are told, the more they create their own time and, eventually, their own space. They become part of a time that is special because of its timelessness. Rubiera Castillo spent many hours interviewing her mother, Reyita, and Herrera; consequently, she uses this expertise to explain the fluidity of the narratives that emerged. The story retold is never the same because it constantly moves—changes its direction, its details, its nature, even its speed. Every version is unique, a substitution. Understanding speed is important, as it refers to the length of time in which the tale is told and provides images of how much time has passed in terms of the events in the story. Panoramic happenings such as battles or political episodes go by faster than events that are emotional and personal. While interviewing, Rubiera Castillo observed that the storyteller's use of time is varied and complex; sometimes in the oral rendition, she tells the conclusion first; the events in the tale are not necessarily told in a chronological way even as they connect with one another in a format that the listener understands. The speaker deliberately causes a constant rupturing of time even as her analyses and comparisons are consistent, full of wisdom, and grounded in the past.[29] Transferring this process into written word represents the creation of one more version while we lose the fascinating experience of actually listening to it being told.

Memory as a sphere of endeavor needs to design and manage its own time and space. As Rubiera Castillo and Herrera explain, an important feature is its ability to incorporate rituals during certain periods and at certain events, and this is where it expands to include various participants, groups, and communities: "Es el momento de la memoria colectiva, cuando entra en contradicción con la memoria individual, cuando entra en contradicción entre la verdad y la mentira" [It is the moment of collective memory, when it contradicts individual memory, when it creates contradiction between truth and lie].[30] This is the juncture of emission, transfer, and sharing of memories, when it expands outward and belongs to everyone, initiating a collective experience that becomes legacy. Such a universal gesture guarantees memory's continuity through the generations. Rubiera Castillo confirms that the community's capacity to remember is vital. How a community sustains and transmits its recollections as well as how and what its members forget make up the raw material for the history (stories) they transmit to their descendants.

This legacy never goes away; rather, it is reinforced even more by writings today, even those belonging to the younger generation of authors. Representative of this group is Puerto Rican writer Yolanda Arroyo Pizarro, whose collection of essays *Tongas, palenques y quilombos: Ensayos y columnas de afroresistencia* [Maroon settlements: Essays and columns of Afro-resistance; 2013] deconstructs historical paradigms forcefully, calling them out as deficient and exclusionary by design. Within rubrics such as "Hablar de las ancestras" [Speaking of female ancestors], "Mujeres esclavas en Mayagüez, 1872" [Slave women in Mayagüez, 1872], "Rio Piedras 2013, sede del Women Warriors of the Afro-Latina Diaspora" [Rio Piedras 2013, site of the women warriors of the Afro-Latina diaspora], and "Lesbianas" [Lesbians], Arroyo Pizarro traces the Afro-descendant woman's journey from Africa to the Americas into the contemporary period.[31] *Tongas, palenques y quilombos* is a diverse collection of verses, anecdotes, reflections, historical data, personal militancy, interviews, and contemplations about gender and sexuality. It is a critical collection of the underlying motivations and precepts driving some of this author's best literary production—*Caparazones* (2010), *Saeta, the Poems* (2011), *Las negras* (2012), and *Violeta* (2013). It offers clarification about how she processes history and how she positions herself in relation to Africa, Puerto Rico, the female condition, and her origins.

In a similar trajectory, younger twenty-first-century writers are leading the charge when it comes to claiming history. From Brazil and Costa Rica, Mel Adun's "Zamani: Mulheres que contam, transforman e fazem história" [Zamani: Women who narrate, transform, and make history; 2016], Débora Almeida's "Se não for a minha história, eu não vou contar: Por uma representação negra" [If it is not my story, I will not tell it: In support of Black representation; 2016], and Shirley Campbell's "Letras e vozes da diáspora negra" [Literature and voices of the Black diaspora; 2017] are critical essays that bear marks of the previous generations of writers who inspire them as they carve out their own paths of historical and literary interpretation. Considered a driving force in the production and publication of prose, poetry, and children's literature in Salvador da Bahia, Adun addresses the mythical and spiritual bond with the motherland of Africa, made manifest in the presence of deified ancestors and Yoruba-originated orishas.

Faith and religious belief systems do play an influential role in two of the three case studies. Faith and creativity complement each other in cultural analyses that characterize experiences specific to Latin America and the Caribbean. Studies continue to hypothesize about the indelible bonds between women and orishas such as Yemayá and Oshun, whose power and influence within the pantheon of gods in Cuba and Brazil are well recorded: here is a mechanism that sustains symbolic connections with the original motherland even as it attests to that intricate and intimate part of their identity as women of African ancestry. Vanessa K. Valdés's *Oshun's Daughters: The Search for Womanhood in the Americas* (2014) and Solimar Otero and Toyin Falola's *Yemoja: Gender, Sexuality, and Creativity in the Latina/o and Afro-Atlantic Diasporas* (2013) are two critical works that construct comparative narratives of gendering and Afro-centered religious belief. *Oshun's Daughters* argues that African-based religious manifestations, when incorporated into literature from Brazil, Cuba, and the United States that feature contemporary forms of womanhood, have allowed for the development of differential configurations. Valdés's contribution is to unite major works by a diverse group of women writers in English, Portuguese, and Spanish that clearly develop this pattern in relation to their configurations of events and experiences. What is also noteworthy is that these are not only Afro-Latin American writers; rather, they are reflective of the major literary genres associated with women's writings in the Americas today—African American, Afro-Hispanic, Latino, Cuban, Afro-Brazilian, and so on. The writers in focus are Audre Lorde, Sandra María Esteves, Ntozake Shange, Cristina García, Loida Maritza Pérez, Nancy Morejón, Daína Chaviano, Helena Parente Cunha, Sônia Fátima da Conceição, and Conceição Evaristo.

Adun extends the value of this discussion on faith and spirituality by confirming the nature of belief as it pertains to Brazil's African city, Salvador da Bahia. Community figures, or *Yalodés*, are griots of myths originating in Africa that are narrated to children and adolescents. The *Yalodé* is usually one of the founding members of the *terreiro de candomblé* [Candomblé temple or compound of worship] who serves as the custodian of the community's past as well as its spiritual leader. Adun speaks to the oral nature of such religious practices, originating in Africa and associated with centuries-long prohibitions placed on writing and reading.

In this world, as occurs in two of the three case studies, myth as oral tradition becomes a place of historical preservation, historical construction, building knowledge, invention, and imagination. As I will discuss, the goddess Mayaya (the Nicaraguan case study) and the legendary ancestor Catalina Loango (the Colombian case study) exist in a kind of pseudohistorical, imaginary way, occupying roles that inspire and bridge the divide between this world and the next. Glory, pride, and hope take shape in this space, for the community griot's task is to be dynamic, interesting, and in keeping with the times. Adun's discussion reinforces this legacy. The *Yalodé*'s style of remembering is singular, at times playful even as it is the basis for the enduring nature of their myths. Myths can become real, almost pseudohistorical in nature, because of who listens; it is always a community event during which different generations build their collective memory. Working within the context of Afro-Brazilian spirituality, Adun defines myth as the telling of a sacred story connected to origins, ancestry, and ancient times. As this reality is no more, it is perceived as transcendence, having moved into the realm of the supernatural. The spoken myth is the ideal medium for describing what happened and how things came to be. Itself a collective voicing that travels through the generations, it gives meaning to existence and human actions.[32]

Writer, actor, and playwright Débora Almeida is all for an appreciation of African ancestral legacy. As a twenty-first-century Black Brazilian of consciousness, she gazes on today's world as her space of inspiration and recognizes the transformative power of writing, especially when the text is the product of a voice from within that experience. She insists on the need to narrate and cherish all facets of history—that is, its grief and bitterness but also its joys and accomplishments. Africa, enslavement, *quilombos* [maroon settlements], and reparations define the nature of her discourse, which reflects her comprehension of history's impact and the value of an awareness that origins and heritage do build a strong sense of pride and personal confidence. To this end, Almeida insists on prioritizing Africa as the ultimate source of human life. She emphasizes the importance of the writer's role in this process of enlightenment, in which history is defined as millennia, mythology, ancient empires, and resistances. She endorses the need for Afro-Brazilian voices to be prominent when recounting their history.[33]

I close this section with words from renowned Costa Rican poet Shirley Campbell, whose critical essay "Letras e vozes da diáspora negra" [Literature and voices from the Black diaspora], is part of the Brazilian publication *Griôs da diáspora negra* [Griots of the Black diaspora], edited by Ana Flávia Magalhães Pinto, Chaia Dechen, and Jaqueline Fernandes, a collection that addresses memory in relation to writing in the African diaspora and its connection to African literature. Her essay contemplates African writing as unique because it came into being through memory or remembering. This indicates that within African cultures, the function of literature is to preserve culture and history. The channeling of ancestral and mythical wisdom and learning was accomplished by oral traditions and is therefore also the foundation of said literature in Latin America and the Caribbean. Campbell views this millennial connection to memory as enriching and valuable not only because it participates in a process of historical reconstruction but also because memory is not repetition but rather more of a reuniting with crucial moments of the past using current values and stable, yet open, recollections.[34]

ESCRE(VIVÊNCIA): I WRITE THEREFORE I AM. I AM WHAT I WRITE.

This second concept has to do with formulating the narratives of life. Who should write these narratives and how can they write them? Marques Samyn explains it well: "O gesto em que uma mulher negra toma em suas mãos um lápis ou uma caneta, ou leva às teclas seus dedos, produzindo um discurso literário a partir de suas vivências, é sempre um ato subversivo e revolucionário" [The gesture with which a Black woman takes a pencil or a pen in hand, or places her fingers on the keys, producing a literary discourse based on her experiences, is always a subversive and revolutionary act].[35] Revelations of glory require identifying within this universe of feminism, intellectual thought, and aesthetic production those markers or ideas that are universally applicable and inspiring in an all-encompassing way. The term *glory* is strong, vital, and inspired by Conceição Evaristo's strategic theoretical design. Indisputably positioned as Brazil's most recognized Black woman writer, Evaristo is today accredited with being the creator of the literary paradigm known as *escre(vivência)*, a term she coined that refers to written-lived experience. It proposes a state or place of experiential writing and stands out as a concept that aptly describes Afro–Latin American women's writings of today that began as *vivências*, or life experiences, and then transitioned to narratives, which is the path of all three case studies. It provides a systematic definition and understanding of the ultimate intention and purpose of such production; the term speaks to the process that I will explain as "I write therefore I am. I am what I write." The act of writing is to exist and to draw on all experiences in order to design portrayals that speak to their trajectories as Black women through time and space. Evaristo herself is an example of someone constantly put to the test, having to overcome adversities that gain global dimension as her fame increases. She had to confront the trauma and challenge of artistic rejection in August 2018 as one of the nominees shortlisted to fill a position that became available in the Brazilian Academy of Letters. She garnered widespread support, clocking some forty thousand signatures, and subsequently was not nominated, the vote instead favoring world-famous filmmaker Carlos (Cacá) Diegues. As the dream of finally seeing a second Afro-Brazilian writer inducted into this prestigious literary circle is squashed, once again must the Brazilian populace face its nemesis, rooted in a racialized self-rejection as a people of African ancestry while largely driven by the fantasy of a racist-free democracy to which a segment of the population still clings. The political implication of nominating such a writer is that such a decision would have solidified and legitimized Afro-Brazilian literature. Evaristo's climb to glory and consolidation as a Black literary philosopher (the distinguished creator of *escre[vivência]*), at least for now, will not cushion her from the brutality of institutional racism, white supremacy, and politicized literary conservatism that firmly shores up the status quo as it pertains to the world of literature; on the contrary, as she continues to climb the ladder of success and fame, accompanying her ever so closely are those adversarial challenges and racist positionings that continue to impact Brazil's national cultures and narratives of identity.[36]

In her role as writer and analyst, Evaristo finds that literature emerges as a privileged space for the symbolic production and reproduction of meaning. As proof of its power, persuasion, and influence, she points to the historical trajectory of literature that, over time, has designed characters and protagonists clearly marked by negative differentiations. While in many ways reflective of historical experience, such discourses are also fictional, imaginary, disassociated with the female figure, and uninterested in elevated or inspirational portrayals such as mother or matriarch. In this specific discursive design, the African or Afro-descendant character is portrayed as the antimuse, while particular kinds of Euro-descendant subjects are promoted as ideal aesthetic archetypes. Evaristo confirms that the repositioning of such a discourse becomes possible by way of an active critical engagement with concepts of womanhood and value. A transformed vision of women's roles in the family is a crucial starting point:

> É preciso observar que a família representou para a mulher negra uma das maiores formas de resistência e de sobrevivência. Como heroínas do cotidiano desenvolvem suas batalhas longe de qualquer clamor de glórias. Mães reais e/ou simbólicas, como as das Casas de Axé, foram e são elas, muitas vezes sozinhas, as grandes responsáveis não só pela subsistência do grupo, assim como pela manutenção da memória cultural no interior do mesmo.

> [It must be noted that for the Black woman, the family represented one of the greatest forms of resistance and survival. As heroines of the quotidian, they construct their battles far away from any clamor for glory. Real and/or symbolic mothers such as those of the Houses of Axé, they were and are, often solely, the ones largely responsible not only for the livelihood of the group, but also for the maintenance of cultural memory within it.][37]

Evaristo's words exemplify the types of charged, inspirational counterdiscourses associated with women writers such as those highlighted in this study and the way in which they smoothly align their literary projects of reconfigurations. She perceives the place from which writing occurs as their place in life itself, their "lugar da vida."[38] By way of homage to those who paved the way for her, Evaristo remembers the giants of literary production in Brazil—Maria Firmina dos Reis, Carolina Maria de Jesus, Geni Guimarães, Miriam Alves, Lia Vieira, Celinha, Roseli Nascimento, Ana Cruz, and Mãe Beata de Iemonjá—as those who speak and write in displays designed as strategic countervoicing, whose aim is to engage with the spheres of power and use their skills at literary devices to so do: "Pode-se concluir que na *escre(vivência)* das mulheres negras, encontramos o desenho de novos perfis na literatura brasileira, tanto do ponto de vista do conteúdo, como no da autoria" [One can conclude that in the lived and written experiences of Black women, we encounter designs of new profiles in Brazilian literature, from the point of view of content as well as authorship].[39]

Evaristo's belief in the transformative power of literary discourse is confirmed in the literary alliances she has built over the years. Such alliances are visible in the way she has collaborated by contributing her time and introductory remarks to special publications, products associated with community projects that allow women to write, and social causes meant to transform their lives. Four of her essays attest to this commitment: the introduction to *Oro obinrin: 1 prêmio literário e ensaístico sobre a condição da mulher negra* [Oro obinrin: First literary and essay prize on the state of black women; 1998]; "Conversa com o leitor da construção de *Becos*" [Conversation with the reader about the construction of Becos; 2006]; "Apresentação" [Introduction], in *Olhares diversos: Narrativas lésbicas, contos* [Diverse gazes: Lesbian narratives, short stories; 2008]; and "Prefácio: Em legítima defesa" [Preface: In legitimate defense], in *Escritos de uma vida: Sueli Carneiro* [Writings about a life: Sueli Carneiro; 2018]. She works to clarify the direction and purpose behind each creative piece. "Conversa com o leitor da construção de *Becos*" introduces her chronicle-novel *Becos da memória*, in which her final thoughts reiterate the nature of her relationship with literature as one in which memory, testimony, and fiction converge.[40]

In the introduction to her anthology of short stories, *Insubmissas lágrimas de mulheres* (2011), Evaristo declares, "Gosto de ouvir" [I like to listen] as she emphasizes the enormous pleasure of capturing stories even if they provoke tears.[41] Emotional responses are an integral part of the journey into the lives and experiences of the characters, both real and invented, that populate this anthology of short stories. She confesses that these stories are not hers alone; rather, they exist on a continuum that runs from invention to experience. It is all part of the same movement: "Invento? Sim, invento, sem o menor pudor. Então, as histórias não são inventadas? Mesmo as reais, quando são contadas. Desafio alguém a relatar fielmente algo que aconteceu" [Do I invent? Yes, I do without the slightest shame. So, are stories not invented? Even the real ones are, when narrated. I challenge anyone to narrate faithfully something that happened]. Emotion is part of her creative trajectory, which starts from listening to tales at times so unbelievable, it is difficult to imagine they are real. In the process of literary creation, pieces of the original version are lost, and this is where the imagination takes over. As actual lived experience becomes compromised, writing becomes central and deepens the bond between what is lived and what is written. This writer reaffirms the consistency of her mission, which is to sketch her *escre(vivências)*—that is, her lived-written experiences.[42] This approach is at the root of the literary sphere she has created that is now quite crowded with anthologies, novels, translations, critical essays, interviews (written texts and on YouTube), awards, and images of her.[43]

Evaristo's paradigm emerges as an asset to this study, providing an explanatory base and justification for the way the main figures in the three case studies serve as inspiration for the woman-centered literary agendas with which they bond—that is, the Ginés sisters' interaction with Portalatín's *Yania Tierra*; Miss Lizzie's relationship with Creole women's writings from Bluefields, Nicaragua; and the *palenqueras'* connection with poetry that self-defines as *palenquera*. All three linkages are envisioned as movement, a smooth transition from a state of lived experience to a state of existential representation in writing. Evaristo's paradigm grounds the planned methodological objectives of this work, these being to design possible paths to highlight Afro-feminine initiatives and to illustrate how it can potentially be done in spite of underlying doubts and difficulties. Her two essays—"Gênero e etnia: Uma escre(vivência) de dupla face" [Gender and Ethnicity: A Two-Sided

Experiential Writing] and "Da grafia-desenho de minha mãe, um dos lugares de nascimento de minha escrita" [Regarding the script-design by my mother, one of the birthplaces of my writing; 2007]—match the spirit of this project in the way they describe her feisty relationship with writing.[44] "Da grafia-desenho" is particularly symbolic in the way it speaks to a conglomeration of various elements—writing, the earth, maternal love, ancestry, mothering, and childhood memory. She describes her childhood recollection of when, for the first time, she witnessed the gesture of writing, and it was from her mother. Gathering her skirt, her mother got down on the ground and drew a large sun in the dirt. Evaristo perceived in this gesture her mother's emotional outpouring. Now, years later, she has arrived at a deeper understanding regarding the power of her mother's creation, for it was not meant to be merely an act of imitation or representation; rather, it became what she drew. Her gesture in the earth was a summons in her time of need and despair, as their lives were riddled with cold, hunger, and poverty. Her writing in the dust was their lives, her way of creating hope, of seeing writing as hope even as her image exposed her daughter to the inextricable bond between life's challenges and writing itself. This fusing of life to writing is particularly valuable in understanding how the art of writing—as occurs with Miss Lizzie, the *palenqueras*, and the Ginés sisters—is fundamental to describing the context as well as creating and sustaining the momentum of each iconic portrayal.

Evaristo's profound relationship with words began as a growing childlike awareness of them as elements belonging to the world of washerwomen, located somewhere in the kitchen and back room of their employers' mansions. She watched and learned, innocently interpreting as natural the dirt, grime, and menstrual blood that stained the clothes even as she mentally recorded the lists of items that always had to be accounted for as inventory. These women toiled and served as her first teachers; they taught her to read and write using any reading material or writing paper they could find. Today, she attributes her artistry in fiction to the eclectic mass of readings to which she was subjected while growing up. Within this space of women, she learned the value of family and its stories. Today, she is convinced her writing reflects the accumulation of words, storytelling, tales, secrets, whisperings, and noises of love and pain that surrounded her during childhood. Particularly enticing were the women's conversations that Evaristo describes as defense mechanisms but also as remedies. These moments gave them respite from a difficult reality marked by *machista* [sexist] domination in the form of their *patrões* [employers] and by financial constraints. Inspired by these *vivências*, she molds her characters into expressive human subjects, the majority of whom are women.

Evaristo writes in homage to these women who populated her life, for it is through them that she learned to harvest words. She had a childhood surrounded by stories and storytellers and was introduced to the joys of listening to and narrating life. As an adolescent, reading and writing offered solace and respite from difficulties even as they made her face and participate in the space to which she belonged. As a result, she learned to embrace this space, even play and transform it, re-creating it constantly to make other worlds that engage and include her perspectives as a Black woman and as a Black woman writer. *Escre(vivência)* as writing and as being is particularly significant, for as production coming from such a human subject, it will also create discomfort and challenge injustice.[45]

APPROPRIATING NEGRITUDE: A WOMAN-CENTERED ENTERPRISE

The final concept supports the ideological agenda and direction of this study, for it is entirely about Black women's lives and achievements and their reflection in literary production. Across the Latin American region, women writers who display a clear Afro-descendant agenda have embraced Negritude, the paradigmatic movement and concept launched by Aimé Césaire (Guadeloupe, 1913–2008), Léopold Sédar Senghor (Senegal, 1906–2001), and Léon Damas (French Guiana, 1912–78) to explain their pride and allegiance to their own ancestral Blackness even as they (women writers) have provoked its decentering by challenging its deficiencies when it comes to engaging with Afro-feminine *écriture*. Within this discussion, Negritude functions as a poetic movement of the 1930s, as an aesthetic, and as an endeavor of politicized consciousness with far-reaching results. It was and remains a product of writers among whom it thrives as a mechanism of identity assertion and pride. Aimé Césaire, considered the father of Negritude, used the term for the first time in his epic poem *Cahier d'un retour au pays natal* [Return to my native land], originally published in 1939. Césaire's literary alliances with Léon Damas and Léopold Sédar Senghor produced poetry, literary critiques, and politically driven essays that together established Negritude as the bedrock of an enriching Black Arts movement that continues to inspire the literary world.

Negritude (uppercased) as a generic concept and a specific artistic movement as well as *negritude* (lowercased), envisioned as Blackness, complement each other and support *Mayaya Rising*'s direction and purpose. The advent of this movement during the 1930s provided an understanding of historical alienation, colonialization, destitution, and marginalization as Black global experiences, particularly referencing the Americas, Europe, and Africa. It rose to a political banner, a confrontational stance to colonial rule, and merged with independence struggles in Africa and the Caribbean. It changed how colonized peoples thought about and envisioned their future. The space used to launch the initiative was poetry, as these three poets philosophically created verses grounded in notions of beauty and value, thereby providing all peoples in Africa and the Americas with self-directed cultural understanding while fueling literary production for decades to come. To date, Aimé Césaire and his wife, Suzanne, are prominent names in the surrealist movement and in Caribbean literature. Negritude stands as their life's work and continues to influence generations of writers.[46]

Since 1975, Afro–Latin American women's writings have more than compensated for Negritude's shortfalls. These women continue to create their own discursive spheres of engagement with said concept within which to interact philosophically and aesthetically with the universe as they envision its possibilities. They have co-opted its agenda; they have actively attacked its original generic formation;

they have ruptured, penetrated, dissected, and divided it among themselves in acts of metaphysical enrichment that impel us to see Negritude as heterogeneous plurality, as a multitude of Afro-descendent identities, measures, movements, and initiatives they instigate and sustain by way of their ongoing efforts to reinforce a valuing of women's contributions. The most effective measure has been the way female authors from different territories have channeled their creative energies toward producing critical essays that address their issues with Negritude's exclusive nature and subsequent ignoring of women's writings, while simultaneously, these authors have absorbed the richness of its purpose and intentions into their own intellectual and literary endeavors.

There is no doubt that international (primarily North American) scholars of Latin America continue to grapple with the philosophical configurations of Blackness as identity as it relates to the region. Arce uses the term "metonymic freezing" and openly reveals the difficulty she faces when grappling with such an elusive configuration of what it means to be a woman, or Indigenous, or Black in Mexico.[47] She cites Peter Wade and Christina Sue's views in support of this dilemma in a comparative analysis that reveals overall discomfort with race formulations and beliefs in Latin America and seems to fall victim to the same trope as other similar scholars who make comparisons with the apparent standard formula—that is, the United States' binary race structure.[48] In *Yemoja*, the edited volume by Otero and Falola, Elizabeth Pérez, in her chapter, "Nobody's Mammy: Yemayá as Fierce Foremother in Afro-Cuban Religions," claims, "Blackness as a quintessentially modern, gendered category of identity for which pigmentation and phenotype act as unstable signifiers. While underscoring Blackness as constituted within communities through shared experiences of racialization, usually entailing exposure to discriminatory practices, I also wish to emphasize the local modalities of Blackness found throughout the Afro-Atlantic world. The multiplicity and 'slipperiness' of 'Black' can be said to mirror that of Yemayá herself."[49] The tendency is to regard Latin America's version of Blackness as problematic given its apparent indecisive nature and unwillingness to self-define with precision, as does the North American version. I sense a certain frustration and desire in texts such as Arce's and Pérez's as they push back against such instability and are close to imposing an African American vision of racialized history and identity. Within *Mayaya Rising*, I have had to reconcile the two positions, comfortably so, given that both configurations coexist within the region. The two formerly enslaved musicians in a European-structured orchestra, the Creole identity of Bluefields (with its European/African/Indigenous roots), and the *palenquera* economic enterprise are results of a diverse and cultural multiplicity of identities and human encounters, although, as these case studies will confirm, they are all fundamentally proud and expressively focused on being ancestrally African, ancestrally Black. Precision is therefore possible and emerges in the way these communities embrace and protect this intrinsic part of their overall identity.

How do some of the region's outstanding literary and militant female voices navigate issues related to the Black Arts movements and the diversity implied in

Latin America's version of Blackness? Renowned Cuban writer, patron of the arts, feminist, and literary and cultural analyst Inés María Martiatu Terry, affectionately known as "Lalita" (1942–2013), wrote the prologue to *Afrocubanas*, in which she revisits twentieth-century experiences and confirms that the various Negritude movements, with rare exceptions, have generally tended to ignore or exclude contributions by women. She refers to the stereotypical distortions that were a part of the Cuban *Afronegrismo* movement during the 1920s and 1930s, followed by North American Black Power activism of the 1960s and 1970s, both of which, even at their most inspirational moments, relegated women to secondary roles as the spotlight continued to shine exclusively on male endeavors both in writing and in action. Well into the 1990s, organized activism tended to keep themes situated at the intersection of women, gender, race, and sexuality outside of their main agenda. Under the umbrella of universal representation, male-dominated leadership customarily set agendas that dealt with certain matters from a supposedly neutral (inclusive) stance, when in fact, decisions were more than likely to be determined by a predominantly male leadership, often to the detriment of women's issues. Within the sphere of activism, both Afro-descendant women and men rejected feminism as a suitable paradigm given its association with the mainstream (predominantly white) women's movement, which further explains the difficulties faced by women of color. Change came when women embraced the idea of autonomy and acquired leadership skills. Martiatu Terry describes the inclusion of Afro-descendant women's agendas as having a transformative impact on Black activism and on the mainstream feminist movement. During the mid-1980s, the increasing need for female leadership and the rise of those willing to serve in that capacity transformed women's advocacy by creating many women's groups while forcing feminism to recognize the need for deep structural adjustments and greater inclusivity—in Martiatu Terry's words, the need to "ennegrecer el feminismo" [Blacken feminism]. The creation of a female-centered and female-led sphere provoked the dawning of a new perspective, one meant to "feminizar la negritud" [make Negritude more woman-conscious], revealing her vision regarding the potential of this artistic concept and its capacity to reflect and serve women's issues once certain adjustments are made.[50]

Martiatu Terry's explanation is applicable to activists and authors across Latin America who engage in critical writing. Aída Cartagena Portalatín's *Culturas africanas rebeldes con causa* [African cultures, justifiably rebellious; 1986], Esmeralda Ribeiro's "A escritora negra e seu ato de escrever participando" [The Black women writer and her act of writing as a participant; 1987], Miriam Alves's *BrasilAfro autorrevelado: Literatura brasileira contemporânea* [Afro-Brazil self-revealed: Contemporary Brazilian literature; 2010], Mayra Santos-Febres's *Sobre piel y papel* [On skin and paper; 2005], Yolanda Arroyo's *Tongas, palenques y quilombos: Ensayos y columnas de afroresistencia* [Maroon settlements: Essays and columns of Afro-resistance; 2013], and Shirley Campbell's "Letras e vozes da diáspora negra" [Literature and voices of the Black diaspora; 2017] are indicative of conceptual appropriations of Negritude (as an aesthetic movement) and negritude (as expressive of a racialized identity of Blackness). Each writer varies in her proximity to Negritude's original design. While they do pay homage to this concept as a highly respected foundational paradigm whose influence is ongoing and at the base of their creativity, they bring their own critical perspective to bear on its nature and vision. Finding the movement specific to global patriarchal and colonial systems of power, they prefer to debate, even question, its problematic portrayals and expectations that are potentially rigid or narrow, or they challenge its presumption of a neutrality capable of serving the interests of both sexes equally when, in fact, poetry by male writers does not include an awareness of gender as an important experiential characteristic.

Women writers will continue to engage Negritude as an umbrella under which they design a compelling counternarrative comprising dual (race and gender), triple (race, class, and gender), and multiple (intersectional) possibilities. The dominant discourse of Africanizing or darkening the nation and its canon that is Negritude's goal is simultaneously supported and pushed off-balance by advocating for the inclusion of womanism (*mujerismo* and *mulherismo* in Spanish and Portuguese, respectively) as an essential criterion for determining canonical selections.[51] This appropriation of Negritude redirects cultural discourses away from unilateral, male-oriented agendas toward female-focused, more dynamic, potentially multifaceted portrayals. It also complements plans to define a literary movement that is specific to Latin America, even as the writers engage with and are deeply inspired by international (primarily North American) personages and their frames of reference: Angela Davis (Black Panthers, Black Power, Black Is Beautiful, and her ongoing advocacy against Black incarceration), bell hooks (*Ain't I a Woman? Black Women and Feminism* [2015]), and Kimberlé Crenshaw (Intersectionality). In the 1970s through the 1990s, the imaging of Blackness such as the enduring Afro hair style, Afrocentric and African attire, Pan-Africanism, and an intellectual interest in African history and philosophy were supported by a somewhat limited availability of Black and feminist-centered publications translated into Spanish and Portuguese in places like Brazil, Colombia, Costa Rica, Panama, and Cuba.

A writing that is reflective of Negritude is one way of defining Mayra Santos-Febres's collection of essays and memoirs *Sobre piel y papel* (2005). A collection of short chapters, her reflections seem random and disconnected, moving in many different directions all at once in a dynamic display of her world of emotions, literary creativity, and views on a number of aspects related to defining who she is and what is most interesting in her world. Her contemplations situate themselves within the rubrics of Negritude, womanism, Caribbeanness, postmodernity, nationhood, sexuality, and writing, with her narrating voice emerging as the only stabilizing force that unifies this diverse agenda. She appears to have positioned herself at this junction as she works to engage her reader in a conversation that is philosophical in tone but very immediate and based on lived (and written) experiences.

I sense that Santos-Febres appreciates Negritude as an identity concept even as she appropriates and engages with it on her own terms. She imposes her own personality, thereby facilitating her evaluation of Negritude's usefulness and its flaws. Her analysis of topics related to racism and identity is nurtured by a feminine perspective. In the chapter "Por boca propia," she confronts the issue of preferential skin color and the cultural phenomenon of having a multitude of terms or local expressions to describe shades and tones of nonwhiteness while whiteness remains nameless as the privileged norm, the archetype, and the perfect state of being to which everyone should aspire, since it symbolizes access, well-being, comfort, and prosperity. The terminology used to describe skin colors is at the core of racial prejudice, for it is deeply divisive, creates controversy, and manifests a divide in which Puerto Ricans either reject any kind of affiliation with African-originated identity or, in denial, avoid engaging with it as difference and pretend it does not exist. In her opinion, both are problematic postures; it has become especially important to engage with the topic as identity, legacy, and national history.

Santos-Febres defines the discourses of race and racism in Puerto Rico as comprising three discussions: abolitionism, Negritude, and a critical analysis of racial formations. She views Negritude as a productive paradigm that continues to generate historical and geographical discourses. However, she does not embrace it fully; rather, she is critical of its specific focus, deemed too narrow, since it has created fixed profiles of what it means to be a Black woman or a Black man.[52] For Santos-Febres, Negritude

> implica que todos los negros y las negras, por obra y gracia del color de piel, nacemos fuertes, sensuales, fiesteros, violentos, primitivos. . . . Como si la concentración de melanina determinara un tipo de comportamiento. Y peor aún, como si ser negro fuese lo único que somos. Pone demasiada atención en un sólo aspecto de nuestra experiencia, que es mucho más compleja que la de la raza.

> [implies that all Black men and women, by dint and grace of the color of our skin, are born strong, sensual, partying, violent, primitive. . . . As if the concentration of melanin determined a type of behavior. And worse, as if being Black were all we are. It focuses too much attention on a single aspect of our experience, which is much more complex than race.][53]

Santos-Febres projects such subjects as multifaceted, dynamic human beings who are much more than just that beautiful skin color and whose nationalities, age, sexuality, professions, and humanity are considerations that cannot be excluded from subjective processes seeking to define who they are and who they can be. Her definition of Negritude coincides with Crenshaw's concept of Intersectionality in the way it resists potentially static or categorical frames of reference and goes on to explain the energetic and ever-changing nature of her literary production as well as her preferences when it comes to describing Puerto Ricans: "En un país como el nuestro, donde hay tanta mezcla racial, delimitar 'quien es' y 'quien no es' puede convertirse en un laberinto sin salida" [In a country like ours, where there is so much racial mixture, defining "who is" and "who is not" can become a labyrinth with no exit].[54] Later, she situates Negritude within a metaphor in which it becomes symbolic of society's relationship with its Afro-descendant citizens. "¿Ser una negra pública?" is a chapter that positions such identity as "performance," bearing both positive and negative weight in society.[55] It generates constant tensions that performers of color (its citizens) have to endure, oftentimes as a lifelong dilemma that many cannot fathom. How can we freely address the topic of race in public without such tensions? How can citizens openly and naturally be themselves if it is always a problem to reference their racialized state of being? The difficulty and stress make silence the preferred option to the point where publicly saying or using certain words or having certain conversations is just avoided, "como si con el silencio pudieran aclarar el color de su piel" [as if by remaining silent, they could whiten their skin color].[56]

Santos-Febres recalls being a young girl moving in the opposite direction of those who avoided such self-affirmation. She deliberately sought out such words and was able to find them in literature, with effort, by pushing past comical and derogatory phrases or stereotypical characterizations like blackface or the mystical African queen.[57] Then there was the challenge of poets who refused to include themes of race for fear of being identified permanently and professionally in a racialized way—that is, as an Afro–Puerto Rican poet. Santos-Febres identifies this as an explicit example of the negative effect produced by performative tension, "el de aceptar que la 'especialidad' de un negro se limita a la 'experiencia' de su raza" [of accepting that the "specialization" of a person is limited to the "experience" of his or her race].[58] For Santo Febres, Negritude's value is in the way it pushes against the silence that racism favors and often achieves. It encourages public demonstrations, presence, and visibility in moves that force reassessment and valuing. More importantly, it releases the ever-tightening valve of race-based tensions that overwhelm performers who do not feel free to express themselves and be whoever or whatever they would like to be. Blackness [*negritud*] is but one part of what it means to be a person of color.[59] In a later chapter addressed to Isabelo Zenón Cruz, Santos-Febres urges her people to be bold, to be publicly Black in spite of the high cost, as a way of effecting positive change.[60]

As a creative writer and academic, Santos-Febres is very clear in her detailed analysis and arguments regarding the racist configurations visible throughout the centuries-long trajectory of the island's literary production.[61] Among others, she has identified the systematic invisibility of Afro–Puerto Rican history, presence, and culture; the reductive folklorization and problematic fixation on the dark-hued body; and the positioning of Negritude and the African-originated world at the fringes of human knowledge. Instead of rupturing this model of cultural representation, many local Afro-descendant writers and intellectuals opted for silence, thereby sustaining Puerto Rico's incompleteness (she uses the word *enfermedad* [illness]) while helping to advance the preferred agenda of a Creole harmony.[62] A cultural analyst, Santos-Febres pens essays that are succinct and direct, planned attacks meant to rupture the idiosyncrasies that prevent her culture from embracing its true self.

Afro-Brazilian writers have been engaging with concepts associated with Negritude as an inspirational aesthetic movement for decades. During the early 1980s, Miriam Alves and Esmeralda Ribeiro initiated activities of critical writing in support of their politicized literary agenda. Such activity resulted in one of the most substantive and rewarding enterprises launched and sustained by the original members of Quilombhoje during the 1970s.[63] Alves and Ribeiro then joined Geni Guimarães and were recognized as some of the first women writers to publish in the first five volumes of the now highly successful *Cadernos Negros* series; today, alongside Conceição Evaristo, they are the globally recognized giants of Brazil's contemporary cohort of Black women writers, which has expanded exponentially and is probably now the largest in Latin America. An important literary direction within this genre of writing is paying homage to historical and contemporary icons.

Alves has, since the 1980s, written critical essays that accompany her prolific and ongoing creative writing, now in its novels-producing phase.[64] She defines literature as a pathway to intelligence.[65] It is her view that practicing literature automatically becomes a social commitment, the reason being that oftentimes, their work will contain information that others may not wish to hear or are afraid of hearing. Such literature creates a rupturing just by moving against typically derogatory imaging and promoting an expressiveness that only they as writers can create because of who they are, where they are currently located, and how they feel. This idea permeates Alves's critical thinking to date: "Nas várias abordagens teóricas, depoimentos, textos poéticos e ficcionais, a escrita da mulher passa a violar este silenciamento" [In the various theoretical approaches, statements, poetic and fictional texts, women's writings proceeds to rupture this silence].[66]

Alves is the Afro-Brazilian woman writer who very early recognized the need and value of producing literary criticism designed to accompany the overall production of creative writing that was, until the late 1990s, practically ignored by the literary academy and academia. Her *BrasilAfro autorrevelado* fuels her distinction as an engaged writer whose focus is on the female condition. *BrasilAfro* refers to two waves that merge: literary voices that manifest a spirit of militancy and a literary voicing that is sufficiently widespread to create discomfort and provocation.[67] Alves usually grounds her analyses in historical processes as proof of exclusion and intolerance. She reiterates the value of militancy in Brazil as a countermeasure to historically imposed brands of inferiority and stigmas.[68] Moving beyond such debilitating impositions requires cultural rerouting, and this is where the role of literature proves transformative, as it provides opportunities for creating new agendas in which said subject has a voice and is the protagonist of her own history and destiny.[69]

Alves envisions writing as constructing worlds in which she is an agent who apprehends, discusses, and directs. Writing creates presence, a new kind of appearing grounded in the art of poetry but also in the self-affirming language of literary criticism.[70] It is a process that Alves values, aligning its rise and expansion in Brazil with the *Cadernos Negros* series even as she critiques the series and its decisions during the early years for sidelining the topic of women's writings in their literary debates and discussions. A major concern among the few women writers back then, it was ignored by the male writers who dominated in numbers and controlled the discussions. Even as they continued to be ignored, women writers never abandoned their position, and as their skills, production, and knowledge accompanied the ever-expanding activism of the 1980s, they were emboldened to demand equal share and attention at major Black arts caucuses and meetings.[71] Alves's essay is significant in the way it confirms the existential synchrony between conceptualizations and actual creative writing. She closes her work with biographies of herself, Celinha, Esmeralda Ribeiro, Geni Guimarães, Conceição Evaristo, Ruth Souza Saleme, and Cristiane Sobral.[72]

As part of an original group of four women writers whose legacies precede the 1980s (Guimarães, Ribeiro, Alves, and Evaristo), Esmeralda Ribeiro has spent decades involved with and at the helm of *Cadernos Negros*.[73] Inaugurated in 1978 with the publication of its first anthology of poems, *Cadernos Negros 1*, and existing under the guidance and protection of a company of writers that self-identify as Quilombhoje, this publication series, without missing a year, today stands as the oldest and most distinguished literary collection in Latin America. In partnership with chief editor Márcio Barbosa, Ribeiro has taken the collection to new heights, securing its place in the Brazilian national literary realm, each production a space renewed yearly and exclusively dedicated to writers of African ancestry. Within the sphere of this collection, creative writing has always been accompanied by published and unpublished literary critiques, *saraus* [soirees], book launchings, book fairs, group discussions, poetry recitations, *rodas de poesia* [poetry circles], and debates on what constitutes literature, the canon, and literariness, among other topics. By offering another kind of enriching experience for the Brazilian readership as it slowly transitions toward a historical appreciation of its African ancestry, the series finds itself at the forefront of the nation's all-consuming battle to define and embrace its ancestral identity. According to the editors, "These words of testimony give continuity to the stories of our *griots*."[74] The first volume was published rudimentarily in 1978, the end product of youthful ideals and lively enthusiasm by a new and vibrant generation of writers in São Paulo who perceived their slim chances of being published in the local presses. This initiative continues to date, retaining the original spirit seen in the way each production features a range of well-known and new writers. When introducing the special volume published in homage of their thirtieth anniversary, Ribeiro and Barbosa used the words *multifaceted* and *diverse*.[75] They state, "Os *Cadernos* têm suas ondulações, suas diferenças internas, textos que podem evocar opiniões variadas e desiguais" [*Cadernos* have their ripples, their internal differences, texts that can evoke varied and uneven opinions].[76]

Ribeiro's trajectory as critic is well established, as is her position as one of the leading voices on literary Negritude; her critical writing is a reflection of this crucial role.[77] She also has contributed introductory remarks to various anthologies and compilations.[78] She actively engages the uneven divide between male and female writers within their own writing community, Quilombhoje. Her 1987 essay, "A escritora negra e seu ato de escrever participando" [The Black woman writer and her act of writing as a participant], confirms the inevitable linkage between art and politics as writers like herself are driven to challenge the established hierarchy that automatically relegates them to the second tier simply because of their gender.[79] Ribeiro actively critiques certain poems, working their inner flaws or contradictions and the ways in which they impact the woman writer's political agenda and awareness campaign. She identifies emotional messages within poems by women, recognizes the need for expressions of sentiment, and contemplates how they work alongside militant postures and declarations of women's rights. We are in the 1980s, and writing declares its agenda and commitment to never disconnect from national reality and, as Ribeiro declares, to remain conscious of the "realidade negra universal" [universal Black reality].[80] Here, Ribeiro is citing lines taken from "Um sol guerreiro" [A warrior sun], one of Celinha's poems dedicated to the children assassinated in Atlanta during the civil rights era. The art of writing represents both liberation and trap, a warning visible in Miriam Alves's poem "Cuidado! Há navalhas" [Careful! There are razors].[81] Alves warns about the danger of "palavras de concessões" [words of concession], for they can turn against their creator, shrouding the past, forcing her denial, and suppressing her very being.[82] Ribeiro confirms that for Black women writers, there is limited or no financial benefit to writing, and they are so few in numbers that anonymity is the norm, while fame is but a distant dream.[83]

Looking ahead, Ribeiro's gaze remains on the dual reality of the Black woman writer, marked by her identity as a woman of African ancestry and as a member of a society absorbing the blows of political and socioeconomic injustice and inequality. Her critical essay "Dois textos para autocontemplar-se" [Two texts to contemplate oneself; 2016] reaches back to the iconic slum dweller–writer Carolina Maria de Jesus, placing her bestseller, *Quarto de despejo* [Child of the dark; 1960], alongside three contemporary short narratives: "Obsessão" [Obsession; 1993], by Sônia Fátima da Conceição; "*Cagüira: 'Tears of the Soul'*" (1999), by Ruth Souza; and "Por que Nicinha não veio?" [Why didn't Nicinha come?; 1993], by Lia Vieira.[84] Ribeiro's essay reaffirms the themes and ideological intentions of these three writers and how they coincide with the precepts of Negritude. Overall, Ribeiro describes and uses this textual space with conviction, determined to overcome and defiantly break away from debilitating concepts that work against a strong sense of pride in one's identity.

The Chapters

Mayaya Rising presents an introduction, part 1 (chapters 1 and 2), part 2 (chapters 3 and 4), part 3 (chapters 5 and 6), and a conclusion. Two chapters are dedicated to each of the three case studies; the initial chapter establishes the context, displays the social and cultural settings pertaining to the iconic figure, and facilitates familiarity with the feminist direction of the text. The following chapter seals the connection between the person(s) in the limelight while presenting and analyzing select literature by women writers that either displays or complements the distinguished profiles that have emerged.

Both chapter 1 ("Teodora and Micaela Ginés: Myth or History?") and chapter 2 ("The Invention of History through Poetry: A Dominican Initiative") contemplate the roots of Cuban music as a fascinating story about the lives and expertise of two formerly enslaved sisters. Cuban scholars including Alejo Carpentier and Alberto Muguercia y Muguercia as well as Afro-Dominicans Aída Cartagena Portalatín (poet) and Celsa Albert Batista (historian) debate the existence of Teodora and Micaela Ginés, who, enslaved in 1503, might actually be the first figures known for their talents in music and are slated as possible founders of the popular grassroots Cuban music known as *el son cubano*. Portalatín describes them as the Original Mothers, foundational figures who are absent from the archives of both nations, and includes them in her nationalist poem, *Yania Tierra*, an epic piece that rewrites Dominican history from a female historical perspective. Dominican literature confronts Cuban scholarship, as the latter denies that the Ginés sisters ever existed and refutes the claim that they are an integral part of the story surrounding the creation of the first Cuban *son*, "El son de la Ma' Teodora." Chapter 1 describes *el son cubano* as traditional grassroots music originating in the countryside, in Oriente province on the eastern part of the island. The debate about the origins of this musical genre among local musicologists, historians, and writers is quite lively and takes us in multiple directions while stimulating constant research and rewriting of the genre's origins and history, consequently provoking a reconsideration of the nation's colonial and postcolonial trajectories. Today, the Cuban debate is ongoing, while the Dominican claim to *son* remains unresolved. Portalatín's epic poem complements her nation's claim even though her work is driven not by this agenda but rather by a desire to write a Dominican, woman-centered version of her country's history, one that includes the Ginés sisters.

Part 2, "A Nicaraguan Case Study," comprises chapter 3 ("Tracing the Dance Steps of a 'British' Subject: Miss Lizzie's *Palo de Mayo*") and chapter 4 ("From 'Mayaya las im key' to Creole Women's Writings"). Miss Lizzie's *palo de mayo* [May Pole] and writings by Creole women poets are brought together in a discussion that privileges this centuries-old tradition, its matriarchal protector, and Creole female *écriture* in terms of the way they project what is most sacred for their community—Caribbean identity and political autonomy on Nicaragua's Atlantic coast. Through Miss Lizzie (Elizabeth Forbes Brooks), *palo de mayo* is symbolic of cultural heterogeneity in the neighborhood of Beholden, located in the town of Bluefields, Nicaragua. A focus on Miss Lizzie's matriarchal profile offers insight into the way music, Caribbean-based (West Indian) folklore, and poetry sustain the notion of her as the leading and stabilizing force in a community impacted by modernization. The literary and biographical texts paying homage to this icon are "Mrs. Lizzie," by Ninozka Chacón, and *Memorias de Miss Lizzie: Danzas, música y tradiciones de Bluefields*, by Elizabeth Forbes Brooks. Ms. Lizzie stands for pride, historical memory, and Afro-Nicaraguan legacy even as her *palo de mayo* dances are also symbolic of historical change and identity crisis. The Creole, Garifuna, and coastal writings used in this study are available in four anthologies: *Poesía atlántica* (1980), *Antología poética de la Costa Caribe de Nicaragua* (1998), *Bluefields en la sangre* (2011), and *Antología poética "Afrocarinica"* (2011). The history of Bluefields, the origins of *palo de mayo*, Miss Lizzie's choreography, community activism, and the goddess Mayaya appear as some of the most popular themes in this Creole Nicaraguan poetic production. Writers self-identify in terms of race, geography, and ethnicity (Creole, Garifuna, mestiza, Bluefieldian, and so on), inserting their identity and origins into the picture and guiding the reader in terms of their focus and poetic purpose. Within the context of Nicaragua, where such expression is relatively unknown, isolated, and even questioned in terms of its validity as to what constitutes national identity, Creole poets are making a clear and proud statement of their place and value as legitimate citizens and as writers. Equally notable is their insistence on publishing in multiple languages—Creole, Spanish, English, and even the Garifuna and Indigenous languages.

The final case study unfolds in chapter 5 ("Rituals of *Alegría* and *Ponchera*: The Enterprising *Palenqueras*") and chapter 6 ("*Palenquera* Writings: A Twenty-First-Century Movement"). These chapters contemplate the difference between the exotic, tropical images of *palenquera* women as colorful street vendors that are marketed in Cartagena, Colombia, and across the globe and their ancestral legacy as solidified in Palenque de San Basilio; *cimarronaje* [marronage]; the mythical figure of María Lucrecia; the *lumbalú*, or ritual for the dead; and famous *palenqueras* including Catalina Luango, Graciela, and Cha-Inés. Literature transcends the social sphere in terms of justice and recognition, for *palenquera* poetry has become a space of preservation and appreciation. The literary and cultural texts I engage are María Teresa Ramírez's three *palenquera* anthologies, *Flor de palenque* [Palenque flower; 2008], *Abalenga* [Star; 2008], and *Mabungú triunfo: Poemas bilingües, palenque-español* [Triumph: Bilingual poems, Palenque-Spanish; 2013]; Mirian Díaz Pérez's anthology *Tejiendo palabras con libertad / Binda ndunblua ku bindanga* [Knitting words with freedom; 2013]; Solmery Cásseres Estrada's *Diccionario de la lengua afropalenquera-español* [Dictionary of the Afro-Palenquero-Spanish language; 2009]; and *Lengua ri Palenge: Jende suto ta chitiá; Léxico de la lengua palenquera* [Lexicon of the palenquero language; 2008], compiled by Rutsely Simarra Obeso, Regina Miranda Reyes, and Juana Pabla Pérez Tejedor. These two chapters describe the *palenqueras*, revisit the emblematic status of Palenque de San Basilio, introduce testimonies by women who are working to protect and preserve this legacy and its language, and confirm how poetic production by *palenquera* writers continues to be inspired by centuries-old practices and value systems such as the *kuagros* and the *lumbalú* ritual.

By way of a conclusion, I revisit each case study, locating them within a structured plan that exploits the symbolic-real dimension found in literature in order to promote an agenda of homage and glory, one intended to compensate for historical shortfalls by confirming the wonderful life stories waiting to be uncovered, rediscovered, and written (back) into existence.

PART I

A Cuban/Dominican Case Study

CHAPTER 1

Teodora and Micaela Ginés

MYTH OR HISTORY?

Cuban scholars Alejo Carpentier (1904–80) and Alberto Muguercia y Muguercia (1928–87) as well as Afro-Dominican poet Aída Cartagena Portalatín (1918–94) and historian Celsa Albert Batista debate the existence of sisters Teodora and Micaela Ginés. Probably enslaved in 1503, they might actually be the first female figures known for their talents in music and the possible founders of the popular grassroots musical genre *el son cubano*.[1] Positioned as women of African ancestry, Teodora and Micaela were reported to have lived during the early 1500s, those formative decades of the first Spanish settlements in the Americas, on the islands of Hispaniola and Cuba. The controversy surrounding the original composers and the origins of the first Cuban *son*, the "Son de la Ma' Teodora," continues to be important scholarship among Cuban musicologists and historians today.[2] This song, recognized as the foundation of Cuban popular music, may well have been the composition of Teodora. What begs discussion is the way this particular detail is meaningful not only to the legacy of these two musicians but also to the idea of Afro-descendant women as worthy contributors to the early histories of Cuba and the Dominican Republic.

Situated among the leading Afro-Dominican scholarly voices to date, Portalatín and Albert Batista coincide in the way they use their expertise to make a case for Teodora and Micaela, the first Afro-descendant female figures in the Dominican Republic on record for their excellence and talent in music. Both Caribbean countries have thus embraced and to some extent mythologized them even, as with passing time, proving their actual existence is increasingly difficult. The Ginés sisters are unique because they continue to exist at the border of history and legend, fiction and nonfiction. Limited and varying references to them in historical and anthropological studies have inspired national imagination and led to stories about their lives in association with the cities of Santo Domingo and Santiago de Cuba.

Dominican literature faces off against Cuban historical scholarship, as the latter has deeply questioned if the sisters ever existed and disputes the claim that they are an integral part of the story surrounding the creation of what may be the first

Cuban *son*, the "Son de la Ma' Teodora." Inevitably, this is a transatlantic story at the heart of the formation of the Americas that involves the recognition of these sisters as migrating subjects whose footprints are implanted in West Africa, the Dominican Republic, and Cuba. Over time, they have emerged as literary icons, a process that took centuries to achieve, especially since it requires unraveling their depiction as the most lowly of creatures who came into the Americas under the status of merchandise, a condition of their enslavement. According to poetic versions of history, contemplating them as instigators with roles in the foundation and settlement of the Americas has allowed them to thrive and prosper in the region's memory, a counterpoint to the precarious nature of historical records given that there was, at the time, absolutely no interest in registering their existence. How do you go about constructing a narrative of such African female experience when all attempts seem fated to appear as a blend of questionable history, myth, and fiction? How much can we prove? It requires working with traces, residuals of information, resulting art forms such as *el son cubano*, and evidence of historical human action that affected society for the long term. Literary representations of historical existence speak louder—more boldly than slim historical written archives—and are ready to pay homage to such potential founders of the nation.

Arguments in support of the idea that these sisters may have played a role in the origins of the musical form called *son* as it exists in both Cuba and the Dominican Republic are a vital part of this story, even as it is difficult to confirm what actually happened. The reconstruction that takes place entails returning them to life literarily, since both the historical debate in Cuba and the limited archival information in the Dominican Republic have created a situation that favors abandoning the possibility of their existence. The literary sphere, however, has them enshrined in Portalatín's *Yania Tierra: Poema documento*. The proposal here is to describe the unpredictable process of historical reconstruction, on the one hand, and reveal the unquestioning faith in the idea of their actual existence, on the other, as it appears in poetry. It is in literature that they will prosper, a way of counteracting the inevitable fallout that transpires every time an attempt is made to historically claim their existence and contributions. My plan in this first case study is not to prove anything; rather, I will reflect on this particular story as a fascinating way of retaking their legacy, a teaching moment that offers insight into these African women's journeys through these two Hispanic Caribbean islands at the beginning of colonial rule. The process is more important, for we can imagine the possibility of constructing a historical voicing for them first by systematically counteracting the very situation that is seeking to wipe them from history and second by analyzing poetic verse. Portalatín's poem insists on enshrining them forever as part of the Dominican nation's traumatic legacy, especially as it relates to colonization, the Black experience, and the Dominican Republic's relationship with Haiti.

The idea of a lost story feeds Portalatín's poetic intentions. The deeper purpose is to declare that Dominican Afro-descendants have not forgotten such stories, for even as they are not told today, they remain an important part of the collective memory, a connection to the ancestors. The many stories, historical and mythical, remain with families and communities, surviving as connections to ancestral beliefs, spiritual practices, traditions, knowledge, and Africa.[3] Portalatín's investigations into these sisters led her to call them the Ginés sisters from Santiago de los Caballeros (in the Dominican Republic), musicians who by their talent and insistence broke through barriers in both Cuba and the Dominican Republic. Portalatín creates epic versions of these female figures. The grandiose nature of the poem is in keeping with Dominican historical trajectory from conquest, colonization, and slavery into modernity, consistently paying homage to all women, both triumphant and oppressed, throughout the centuries. The female figure is both past and present, representing one experience as well as countless others like herself, and is a consistent instigator who firmly establishes her deep-rooted historical worth and registers her leadership role within the poetic space. Through the power of Portalatín's verses and her intentional process of feminist historicizing, such a figure is alive, active, present, and now an integral part of not only the literary canon but also the historical consciousness in both nations.

A large part of the research surrounding the Ginés sisters focuses on them as inhabitants of Cuba and is deeply significant, for as popular Cuban belief and recorded history have insisted over the centuries, they are among the island's first authentic musicians. At the very least, they appear to be the two important Afro-Cuban musicians actively practicing their trade during that first century immediately following Columbus's arrival in Santo Domingo. Even as Cuba claims them as its own, they seem to have migrated to Cuba from Santo Domingo, making the Dominican claim on *son* equally legitimate. Available records seem to have no secure information about their birthplace, dates of birth, or true origins. They appear in several twentieth-century publications, such as Natalio Galan's *Cuba y sus sones* [Cuba and its sones; 1983], that recount the history of that musical genre. Galan presents them as free Black Dominican women, instrumentalists and members of a small orchestra appearing in 1562 to be the first irrefutable indication of a Cuban popular musical group that entertained the public at all kinds of secular and religious events.[4] This is the beginning of a legacy of musical artistry and, most importantly, developments surrounding the famous "Son de la Ma' Teodora." The design and influences of African and European origins in this first *son* are well debated. Galan, as with other historians of music of our modern era, does not question the existence of these two women. He presents and situates them as peripheral to the matter at hand—that is, the roots and development of the musical genre.

Teodora Ginés appears in historical studies about music because of her connection to this first *son* by name. She is a veritable icon and appears among musical greats in the *Diccionario de la música cubana biográfico y técnico* [*Biographical and Technical Dictionary of Cuban Music*; 1992] by Helio Orovio. Interestingly enough, she and her sister do not appear in Alicia Valdés's *Diccionario de mujeres*

notables en la música cubana [Dictionary of notable women in Cuban music; 2011].
Orovio's dictionary entry recognizes Teodora Ginés as a legendary figure within
Cuban musical historiography. It describes her and her sister's roots in the Dominican city of Santiago de los Caballeros and recognizes them both as musicians. It
indicates that Teodora is attributed as having created the famous *son*, a piece of
history reviewed and negated by Muguercia y Muguercia, who claims that there is
not enough evidence to prove such a theory.[5]

According to Orovio, the original assertion that Teodora composed the first
son cubano was initially made by renowned Cuban composer, music director, and
violinist Laureano Fuentes Matons in his book *Las artes en Santiago de Cuba* [The
arts in Santiago de Cuba] and by Cuban professor and historian Antonio Bachiller
y Morales in *Cuba primitiva* [Primitive Cuba]. Orovio works to verify the origins
of the "Ma' Teodora" *son*, asserting that it could not have possibly been a production dated before the nineteenth century. His dictionary entry includes a musical
score of this *son*.[6] Historical scholarship is generally skeptical and cannot, in its
current path, pay homage to the sisters. Instead, we will probably need to rely on
the elaborate poetic counterargument that Portalatín provides in *Yania Tierra*, the
perfect detour away from the potential erasure being proposed by such historical
scholarship.

EL SON CUBANO: A TRADITIONAL ART FORM
AND GRASSROOTS MOVEMENT

Esta canción la cantaban un hombre y una mujer que daban vueltas en forma de
espiral, "buscándose" sin encontrarse, hasta que en un momento dado el hombre
daba media vuelta y se encontraba con la mujer, entonces la ceñía por la cintura y
"contoneándose" al son de los tres últimos octosílabos, caían rendidos.

[A man and a woman would sing this song while spinning in spirals, "seeking"
without finding each other, until in a given moment the man would make a
half turn and find the woman, then he would take hold of her by the waist and,
"moving their shoulders and hips" to the sound of the last three octosyllables, they
would fall.]

—Tomás Fernández Robaina, "Sobre Alberto Muguercia"

In Cuba, the debate continues surrounding the true origins of *el son cubano*. In the
Diccionario enciclopédico de la música en Cuba, volume 4, leading Cuban musicologist Radamés Giro describes *son* as a musical genre for singing and dancing. A
soloist and four-part choir compose the vocal components, while over the centuries, a multitude of instruments have been used to provide music for dancing,
including the guitar, bass, bongo, *botija*, *marímbula*, *tumbadora*, and trumpet.[7]
Similar to other Caribbean and Latin American musical genres, *el son cubano* is
the product of the convergence of two main ethnocultural roots, the African
and the European, a process of centuries that continues, filled with tensions and

conflicts. During the era of conquest and initial settlement, Africans arriving to the island from Africa and Spain brought with them patterns of singing and rhythms, arguably making Cuba the best-defined cradle from which the genre later expanded to other parts of Spanish America. The story of *son*'s origins and development is the story about the creation of Cuba, and it folds into the traditions, religious belief systems, and practices that forged this nation's identity.

As a poetic expression, *el son cubano* remains etched in history thanks to the illustrious pen of Nicolás Guillén (1902–89), Cuba's preeminent literary voice of the twentieth century. During our discussion on May 18, 2017, in Havana, Radamés Giro described Guillén as the "poeta del son" [*son*'s poet] and insisted that Guillén's *negrista* and Afro-Cuban poetry of the 1930s nourished the nation's music during the early decades of the twentieth century and did much to transform society's overall appreciation of grassroots musical genres. Local scholarship on the history of *música popular cubana* [popular Cuban music] dedicates itself to uncovering its formation and trajectory as part of the broader historical and national agenda dedicated to defining and understanding Cuban nationhood. Guillén's Afro-Cuban anthologies, *Motivos de son* (1930), *Songoro cosongo* (1931), and *West Indies Ltd.* (1934), set the tone for rather controversial portrayals of Blacks even as they emerged as vital manifestations of the nation's preoccupation with its racial identity and ethnicity during the modern era. *Motivos de son* may have been inspired by the music he enjoyed, which included groups such as the Sexteto Habanero.[8] In a similar fashion, Danilo Orozco comments,

> La personalidad creativa del poeta Nicolás Guillén, con una obra incipiente y prometedora por aquellas décadas iniciales del siglo, en un momento dado se ve atraída por las expresiones y proyecciones del flujo de sones que, en su caso, le llegaba a través de los mencionados modelos o cánones de Matamoros, Piñeiro, y el conocido movimiento de los sextetos y septetos, donde a su vez, recordemos, de alguna manera se concentraban ciertas resultantes de procesos con sus rasgos y códigos representativos.

> [The poet Nicolás Guillén, with his creative personality and nascent and promising work during those initial decades of the century, found himself at a certain point attracted by the expressions and influences of the abundance of *sones* that reached him through the aforementioned models and canons of Matamoros, Piñeiro, and the famous movement of the Sextets and Septets, which, let's not forget, somehow conserved certain vestiges of processes with their representative characteristics and codes.][9]

Thanks to Guillén, during the early twentieth century, the nation homed in on *son*, which became a kind of genesis not only for this poet but also for the construction of a modern-day discourse combining music, identity, and nationhood. Within this context, envisioning the first *son* in relation to the most humble figures—enslaved and freed women—is provocative, begs consideration, and produces changes in the direction and process of historical discourse.

Orozco discusses the clear presence of *son*'s traits in different spheres of human endeavor, whether artistic or intellectual. He describes Guillén's verses as direct and vigorous. Their tone confirms a commitment to social realism even as the use of movement, song, and rhythmic devices provokes changes in the mood—playful, serious, musical, light, heavy, and so on.[10] Guillén's lyricism emerges from that musical space and, in turn, contributes to the genre in a process of spontaneous giving-back that subsequently encourages the renewal of national interest in this antique musical modality and initiates philosophical discussions that are ongoing. His initial period of creativity coincided with a moment of reflection and reconsideration about the value of *lo popular* [the social masses] and *Afro-negrismo* [Afro-literary and artistic Blackness] occurring within a group of artists and intellectuals.[11] Racial discrimination and social inequalities provided a concrete backdrop upon which he fed. They showed him the model and provided the codes—vocabulary, rhythm, sonority—he needed to design his characters, create contrasts, and invent language and sounds that are emblematic of his work. Orozco describes Guillén as having the ability to use poetry to capture and give back certain sociocultural forms of comportment and points of view, emotions, and lyrical-cultural traits that together resulted in a *negrista* poetry, or poetry of *son*.[12] It is a trend Guillén would take forward into later anthologies as a seasoned poet. Guillén's trajectory occurred with Cuban music composers as well as other *negrista* poets, including José Zacarías Tallet, Alfonso Camín, Alfonso Hernández Catá, and Ramón Guirao.[13]

Can we truly establish a connection between the musical genre as it is envisioned today and what many see as the first *son* popularly associated with "Ma' Teodora"? Cuban historians and musicologists who have written on the origins of the genre have expressed a wide range of views regarding the roots of popular Cuban music. Controversy surrounds the exact time of its invention, the original musical forms, which *son* was actually the first, and the exact time that the art form made its appearance in Havana. There seems to be consensus that it emerged in the countryside, within the province broadly known as Oriente, situated on the eastern side of the island; however, this is where the consensus ends.[14] The choice of Oriente has everything to do with the prestige of Santiago de Cuba as the seat of government during the colonial era, as opposed to Havana, as well as the more Afro-centered, Afro-diasporic ethnic and cultural composition of that eastern region and its difference from the rest of the island.[15]

During the early centuries, the Oriente was known for agricultural production on a smaller scale, featuring tobacco, coffee, and subsistence farming; there were fewer large-scale slave plantations. Over time, fewer Yoruba and Congolese slaves were imported from Africa; instead, enslaved peoples were transported to Cuba from Haiti, Jamaica, and other parts of the Caribbean under British colonization. Some obtained their freedom, and by way of miscegenation, a creolized society emerged that was rather different from the established colonial and hierarchical racial culture visible in Havana and Matanzas. It is within this blended culture that the Oriente's musical forms would take shape. The popular and intellectual acceptance that *el son cubano* originated in the Oriente is also due to the ongoing preference for traditional music there.[16] Peter Manuel's study points to the genre's evolving forms and the way they provided structure and stylistic base for salsa. He presents sufficient bibliography that supports the idea of the genre's consolidation around 1910–20.[17] In his view, the genre is not specifically defined but rather seems to be part of a broad range of other forms of music with which it intertwines—*nengón*, *kiribá*, *sucu-sucu*, *changüí*, and others—making it a fertile art in terms of its musical affiliations.[18] Manuel seeks the exact moment in which the term *son* is used in a clear and decisive way to mark the genre, and he concludes that even with sporadic usage over time, it is difficult to reach any decisive conclusions: "'*Son*' is mentioned in neither the 1849 nor the 1875 editions of Esteban Pichardo's Magisterial dictionary of Cuban Spanish nor can it be found in such otherwise musically informative and relevant works such as Cirilo Villaverde's 1839/1882 novel *Cecilia Valdés*, Antonio Bachiller y Morales' *Cuba primitiva* (1883), or Laureano Fuentes Matons's *Las artes en Santiago de Cuba* (1891), which cites other genres such as *bolero* and *danzón*. The term appears once ambiguously in Emilio Bacardí's *Crónicas de Santiago de Cuba* (1891)."[19]

The connection that was created between *son* and the Oriente region is also a legacy rooted in oral tradition, available among elderly musicians from the provinces who spoke of genres such as *son*, *montuno*, and *son montuno*, which were still surviving at the turn of the twentieth century. Manuel confirms that literature on Cuban music has many references to the "Son de la Ma' Teodora," which first appeared so named in Fuentes Matons's *Las artes en Santiago de Cuba*, later becoming very popular in the early twentieth century; however, even Fuentes Matons called it a *canción* [song] and not *son*. Manuel can only speculate that local musicians in the rural spaces may have been using the term to refer to a simple refrain, informal verses inserted in their songs, or typical percussion (bongo) patterns repeated throughout the renditions.[20] Both Manuel and Emilio Grenet will work on the *son* during its most popular moments of the twentieth century. Grenet is representative of the most commonly held view that while *son* became well known during the twentieth century, it has a deep past, attributed to the first decades of colonization, inextricably linked to Micaela and Teodora. Grenet continues that "Ma' Teodora" played the *vihuela* between 1568 and 1592, singing popular songs while she also played the *bandola* in the town of Baracoa, identified by musician and composer Eduardo Sánchez de Fuentes as the birthplace of the truly Cuban *son*.[21]

The earliest forms of *son* seem to have employed mostly instruments from Europe, with more local percussion artifacts being introduced over the centuries. The basic components are voice and guitar. Over time, several versions of guitar-like instruments adopted from Spain, as well as other instruments, have been associated with this musical genre—*guitarra*, *bandurria*, *vihuela*, *tiple*, *botija*, *marímbula*, and *bongó*.[22] An examination of the history of *son* confirms that there have been modifications to the guitar and other string instruments used in performances over the centuries. The *bandurria* is a plucked chordophone from

Spain, similar to the cittern and the mandolin that make up an important part of traditional music forms in various parts of Spain. It continues to be visible in Latin America. The original version had three strings, gaining a fourth during the Renaissance period and up to ten during the Baroque era. At one point, it was very similar to the Portuguese guitar. The *vihuela* (*viola* in Italy and Portugal) is like a guitar with six double strings; however, over time, several kinds of *vihuelas* emerged. An old instrument, its roots are in Aragón, in northeastern Spain, and it was well used in the fifteenth century, although its wide usage is known to have faded by the sixteenth. The *tiple* follows this pattern. While the word means "treble" or "soprano," it was also used for specific instruments—in this case, a small chordophone belonging to the family of guitars.

Meanwhile, the *botija* and *marímbula* provide rhythm. The *botija* is a percussion instrument whose roots lie in the quotidian. *Botija* means "earthenware jar or jug," and it was transformed to have two openings and used in *son* orchestras as a bass instrument, probably appearing during the late nineteenth century. The two openings, one on top and one on the side, were usually filled with varying levels of water for different pitches. The openings were then blown into to produce different bass notes, with or without a reed. Cuban composer and musicologist Argeliers León confirms that another strategy was to cover and uncover the openings with the palm of the hand to create rhythmic effect.[23] The use of this rustic instrument came to an end during the early 1900s, replaced by the double bass. The *marímbula* is a plucked box. A sound hole is carved into the center of a wooden box and a series of metal strips are placed across the hole and attached to one end of the resonating box. Victoria Eli Rodríguez and Zoila Gómez García discuss the Bantu roots of this instrument. The strips are tuned to different pitches, producing a musical bass line. The *marímbula*'s roots lie in African-originated instruments, and this version is associated with the province of Oriente during the nineteenth century, from where it spread to other parts of the Caribbean. The instrument was central to traditional forms of Afro-Cuban music such as *changüí* and *son*.[24]

Finally, we have the *bongó*, a pair of open-bottomed drums of different sizes, popularly known as *macho* (smaller) and *hembra* (larger). Its history accompanies that of the *marímbula* in region and historical period; it is also associated with the popular music forms of *son*, *nengón*, and *changüí*. The *bongó* increased its popularity during the 1900s and, with *son*, migrated to the capital, where, like the latter, it laid the base for orchestra and big band music that made the Havana nightlife of the 1940s and 1950s world famous. Today, the Cuban bongo is played all over the world.[25] *el son cubano* combines voice with these instruments. The vocal rendition emerges in the form of *estribillo* [chorus] and *copla* [couplet]. The lyrics could appear as octosyllabic verses that are descriptive improvisation. One possible format is that of interplay between a main singer and a chorus of voices that respond to the main singer's call or question. The choral response will always be short and repetitive—a few words or a short phrase. This call-and-response technique has been connected to African-originated singing patterns. The singing and dancing connect with the instrumental renditions, and they join to make manifest the harmonious and rhythmic nature of the art form that points to its roots on the African continent.[26]

Peter Manuel's study of the *son* takes into account its richness in terms of what he calls its "extra-musical associations," which make it "a quintessential expression of Cuban identity."[27] This commentary mirrors the views from various scholars on the topic, such as Helio Orovio and Radamés Giro, who indicate that the roots of music in Cuba are in the fusion of elements from African and Spanish cultures, since practically no aspects of the Indo-Cuban aborigine legacy survived.[28] Robin D. Moore comments on its deep and little-known roots even as he recognizes its indelible connection with the rural eastern provinces long before transitioning into the capital, Havana.[29] Giro describes the advent of the genre as emerging from a context of diversity and conflict that led to a "criollismo musical" [musical creolization], a musical form not exclusive to Cuba, occurring with similar characteristics in other Caribbean and Latin American countries.[30] Giro does, however, present Cuba as the place where *son* found its widest, most definitive expression; established its deepest roots; and went on to influence multiple subsequent genres locally and regionally. Rodríguez and Gómez García reiterate the need to consider the prolonged and complex processes of interaction among the Hispanic and African cultures that would have resulted in the emergence of new forms.[31] Manuel's study of the *son* in its primitive form identifies it as a production of the late nineteenth-century Oriente countryside that took hold of Havana in the early twentieth century.[32] Manuel briefly refers to the "Son de la Ma' Teodora," commenting on the many references to it in Cuban musical scholarship; however, he does not discuss said *son* as possibly the first evidence of this musical form. This vision of the *son* as anything but a sixteenth-century phenomenon associated with the "Ma' Teodora" rendition also appears in Argeliers León's work *Del canto y el tiempo* [Of song and time], a study that associates its emergence with the Spanish *copla* and *estribillo* of the eighteenth century.[33] Differently, Rodríguez and Gómez García cite Orozco, who viewed the *son* as effectively originating in the nineteenth century, a product of that defining period of nationhood.[34]

These studies point to a confluence of views with respect to origins and musical associations. While the general agreement seems to be that *el son cubano* is a fusion of musical contact between the two dominant cultures, no consensus is possible in terms of a specific time period for its emergence. Among Cuban ethnomusicologists of revolutionary scholarship, there seems to be minimal preoccupation with creating or sustaining a scholarly consensus on the matter of *son*'s origins and developments beyond accepting Oriente as its place of origin. It is a field crowded with solid intellectual input and engagement. At the center of this debate is the "Son de la Ma' Teodora," which drives the imagination of the nation in terms of traditional music that is truly Cuban and its ethnoracial and cultural origins. A lively feud continues between the island and the Dominican Republic regarding origins and ownership of the musical genre itself. Overall, the preferred direction is to propose that the genre is a product of merging influences, thereby shying away from its potential Africanization even as the African contribution is recognized.

As has transpired with other art forms, it is symbolic of Cuba's mulattoness—or to use a more Caribbean expression, creolization.

ALEJO CARPENTIER'S CREATION OF CUBAN HISTORY

Carpentier's *La música en Cuba* (1946) is one of the highly respected national studies on the history of this artistic form. He describes the status and role of the first Africans who arrived on the island during the sixteenth century, a period that coincides with Micaela and Teodora. Africans were in Cuba by 1513 and found themselves at the lowest level of the social hierarchical structure, a position even beneath that of the subjugated Indigenous peoples. Upon arrival, Spanish men took and violated Indigenous women and bore mestizo children while adopting repressive measures against Black and mulatto women who, for example, were prohibited from dressing like white women. At the same time, Carpentier claims that the situation of Africans was not as bad then as during later decades, when the slave industry became an immensely lucrative business that led to the rise of a truly prosperous class that took pride in its family name, wealth, land, and property. Carpentier's commentary about the subhuman conditions Africans faced, minimizing the horrors of enslavement during the initial years of the settlement in comparison to the later centuries, has the effect of shrouding the debilitating experience from its inception. He emphasizes the precariousness of life in the new settlement and the resulting fact that settlers were heavily dependent on one another other for survival, irrespective of their ethnic origins.[35] Elements such as diseases, pirates, and food shortages impacted the size of the population, and on occasion, Blacks constituted a majority: "Había días de angustia en que el blanco se veía obligado a hacer causa común con su siervo. Casos hubo en que el heroísmo de un negro arrancara gritos de admiración a los blancos" [There were days of anguish when the white man found himself obligated to serve the same cause as his slave. There were cases in which the heroism of a Black man evoked shouts of admiration from the whites].[36]

The situation of enslaved women on the island during the sixteenth and early seventeenth centuries confirms that the initial stages of social settlement were difficult, requiring them to perform a wide range of tasks of the domestic kind and also in the public sphere. They were vendors in the food business and managed inns and taverns. They worked as cleaners and launderers, even performing companionship services, including prostitution. Evidence points to the hiring out system, another source of potential self-remuneration. This social structure confirms the budding colony's heavy dependence on such laborers; as a result, they had considerable mobility and autonomy.[37] The value of the enslaved woman in the building up of Cuban city life is a relatively new discourse. Recent scholarship confirms the existence of free and freed women, some of means, although records do tend to identify specific individuals—only refer to a widespread phenomenon.[38] A distinction is made between free women and those who were manumitted, with information indicating that it was easier for African women to gain manumission (three-quarters of Africans freed were women), while among criollos, or Cuban-born slaves, the percentages between men and women were relatively equal.[39] Specific mention is made of enslaved women who, upon gaining manumission, were able to enrich themselves, even acquire slaves.[40] "Black women transgressed social conventions and displayed their riches in public. When authorities tried to force free Blacks to participate in public festivities, they proudly refused, using the very conventions of gender and honor that local elites claimed to be theirs."[41] Overall, the majority remained subjugated, and the social environment remained specific in terms of their status as enslaved persons and a class of lesser human beings, valuable as merchandise, exclusively alive for their labor. While historical study cannot itemize subjectively what they endured, literary reconstruction does—specifically, writings about the Black experience. As humans in challenging circumstances, over time they learned to create opportunities to ensure their own survival, maybe even enjoy occasional autonomy. This eclectic environment could serve to explain the role of the Ginés sisters as musicians, accounting for their apparent freedom of movement and the long-term exploitation of their talent.

Alejandro de la Fuente mentions forms of socialization and entertainment. These included religious ceremonies, public processions, and festivities involving the entire community of masters and slaves. Blacks had their own parties and dances that speak to processes of cultural adaptation and assimilation with certain retention and re-creation of African customs and practices.[42] The rudimentary nature of life in this new place meant that music was practically nonexistent—or at the least, a very poorly executed art form. There was a shortage of instruments and musicians; oftentimes in Santiago de Cuba, any musician not part of the religious congregation was called up to provide the music needed during mass, a situation that continued until the end of the sixteenth century.[43] Santiago de Cuba appears as the first town to have an orchestra, and this is where Carpentier's version of the circumstances surrounding Micaela and Teodora Ginés begins. While Havana of the 1550s did not possess professional musicians, Santiago de Cuba already had a small orchestra comprising two flutists, a violinist from Seville called Pascual de Ochoa, and two free Black Dominican women who were sisters, Micaela and Teodora. The orchestra was created primarily to perform at parties, but it was also used in churches. In 1553, Havana was declared the official town of residence for the governors of the colony, and such an expansion of the city's importance motivated the disbandment of the orchestra as Pascual de Ochoa and Micaela made the decision to move to Havana in search of betterment. By the end of the century, they became part of a quartet that included a Spanish violinist from Málaga, Pedro Almanza, and a clarinet player from Lisbon, Jácome Viceira. This group provided primarily secular entertainment, performing at dances and parties for which they were paid in cash and food. They also serviced church events, such as festivities and processions in homage to religious celebrations and the saints.[44] Carpentier points out that the economic circumstances of such musicians were never good, as confirmed by a January 10, 1597, report from the Havana town council granting a request from the quartet that they be paid a salary by the city on the condition that they performed for public events when needed.[45]

Based on Carpentier's study, Micaela appears as the first woman to participate in an orchestra in Havana. His study also presents Teodora, probably her sister, as the first woman to participate in the first known orchestra in Santiago de Cuba. Both women were influential in the formative years of Cuban music simply by virtue of their talent. They benefited from the embryonic nature of the society and its shortage of musicians, a circumstance that, according to Carpentier, would have allowed them to overcome the discriminatory barriers placed against Blacks generally, as they sat beside Spanish and Portuguese musicians and performed on European instruments. Carpentier uses this situation to make the problematic declaration that the shortage of skilled musicians excluded the possibility of racial discrimination, and he goes on to cite José Antonio Saco, Cuba's renowned eighteenth-century historian and sociologist, who supported this theory by confirming that music was the sphere where it was not unique to see whites, mixed-race peoples, and Blacks in orchestras.[46] One can question the implication behind this statement, for the fact that they were allowed to participate in the orchestras did nothing for their status as enslaved women in colonial Cuba; their presence in the orchestra did not translate into an automatic erasure of their status as sub-human. Their talent set them apart; however, their role as valuable performers would not have undermined in any way the existing status quo within which their social circumstance and identity were irreversible. If anything, their delegation to such duty, which was never designed to recognize their distinction as musicians, ensured their continued classification as women in bondage. Their worth remained connected to those of their kind—that is, their status as a commodity. Music (using instruments from Europe) is the historical mechanism that confirmed their fixed and defined roles in the established system.[47]

Even as he focuses on a more contemporary period, Robin D. Moore reflects on the social structure and the ways in which human initiative can potentially circumvent situations of oppression and subordination: "Controversies over minority culture in ethnically and racially divided societies often reflect judgments as to whether such practices conform to established notions of collective identity. The expression of minorities can be perceived (and function) as a form of symbolic resistance, a challenge to the imposed culture of the majority. Alternatively—and this is especially true in the case of syncretic forms—subaltern culture can be accepted and appropriated by others in an attempt to play down social differences and to symbolically reintegrate the disenfranchised into the region or nation."[48] Teodora's participation in this orchestra, when placed alongside the first *son* that bears her name, works as a mechanism for marking her in a concrete way as its creator. Her role becomes charged with ideological implications, for it facilitates her positioning as a founding figure responsible for initiating a national notion of self, today defined as the very core of Cuba's transcultural identity—*el son cubano*. This way of envisioning her compensates for her historical voicelessness (she plays music; she never speaks or pronounces historically) and works to showcase her endeavors and talent. Even as she plays only European instruments, when we transition to include the "Son de la Ma' Teodora," such inclusion forces a shift away from European genres toward an aesthetic that seems to engage with African artistry (style, rhythms, instruments) while featuring the enslaved woman's experience. In this case, she must toil as a musician, for it is her existential role within the context of the Americas.

Unlike her sister, Teodora remained in Santiago. Carpentier advises that she was a "negra horra" [freed Black woman]; however, there are no details about to how she secured her freedom. He marks the word *Má* as indicative of her advanced age, explaining that this may have been the reason why she did not make the trip to Havana. *Má* also leaves the impression of a motherly and wise figure who is valuable to her community. Carpentier does not question the existence of these two women and seamlessly presents Teodora as the composer of this famous *son*. He values it as the single item of music that points to the origins of the island's national musical production and as the rendition that illustrates what Cuban popular music was like in the sixteenth century. He confronts it as a production exhibiting Spanish influences and takes up the challenge of interpreting its structure in order to discover its roots. He proposes that it emerged spontaneously, an expression of a musical phenomenon that has survived the passage of time and is specific to Cuba.[49]

Fuentes Matons, Orovio, and Carpentier display the earliest known musical score in their works, currently preserved in the Chiqui Gómez Lubián Library of the Central University of Villa Clara.[50] The lyrics are simple and direct, focusing on the figure of an older female subject who is engaged in a basic activity associated with the domestic sphere and normally carried out by slaves. The simple form of the verses and direct language makes the song seem folkloric in structure, reminiscent of popular songs that describe or tell stories about daily life among the simple folk and popular masses:

¿Dónde está la Má Teodora?
Rajando la leña está.
¿Con su palo y su bandola?
Rajando la leña está.
¿Dónde está que no la veo?
Rajando la leña está.
Rajando la leña está.
Rajando la leña está.
Rajando la leña está.

[Where is Ma' Teodora?
She is chopping firewood.
With her walking stick and her *bandola*?
She is chopping firewood.
Where is she for I do not see her?
She is chopping firewood.
She is chopping firewood.
She is chopping firewood.][51]

The simplicity of the musical line, its connection to the quotidian, and the fact that it is an integral part of Cuba's oral tradition may explain why it stood the test of time. Carpentier describes it as a "primitivo antillano," the word *primitivo* pointing to the African-originated influences and *antillano* representing a Caribbean Hispanic legacy of mixtures. It is his way of confirming harmony among structure, the rudimentary nature of the tune, and basic activities to which the verses speak.[52] He aligns the melody with the "romance extremeño," a song whose characteristics retain elements from a regional language form called *extremeño* spoken in the northeast of Extremadura and south of Salamanca in Spain: "En lo que se refiere a la melodía, el *Son de la Má Teodora* guarda el más estrecho parentesco a las de todo un grupo de romances extremeños" [With reference to the melody, the *Son de la Má Teodora* bears a close similarity to those of a group of *romances* from Extremadura].[53] This *son* does distance itself from its Iberian Peninsula origins by design, bearing all the vocal habits and musical intonation of the region and its way of life. At the same time, Carpentier confirms that there is no way of knowing whether Má Teodora herself knew any *romances extremeños* or consciously appropriated the style and melody. In his analysis of the verses, Carpentier observes that the rhythm of the phrases approximates classical Hispanic models, thereby aligning them to the *coplas*.[54]

Carpentier's study shows the multitextured nature of the rhythm and verses, highlighting the influences and subsequent modifications that could have resulted in such structures. He considers that a good portion of the melody may have come from a *romance extremeño* called "Delgadina." He is careful to point out that it would be impossible to say for sure that the "Ma' Teodora" *son* consciously mimicked or used the melody from "Delgadina," which was very popular at the time. He prefers to believe that it was influenced by music that was circulating and created a similar version using a variety of influences available in Cuba, including imported forms coming from African-originated musical and dance influences in Argentina and Chile.[55]

The song speaks to the expertise of this musician even as it sets the persona right back into the category of laborer whose job it is to cut firewood. Her role as a musician appears alongside her socioeconomic category as a lowly laborer. According to the lyrics, partygoers are looking for her to entertain them with music; however, she cannot perform because she is out chopping firewood. She is a musician-entertainer and at the same time performs this laborious, backbreaking work. She has to chop the wood, no doubt used for cooking. The *son* is a window into the quotidian of the simple folk; it displays their lifestyle through music and lyrics, bringing it onto center stage.

Carpentier proposes an interpretation of the verses that provides an interesting juxtaposition of two universes—the arena of manual labor and the sphere of performance. He interprets "rajar la leña" [to cut firewood] to mean "estar en un baile" [to be at a dance].[56] He observes that the choral response, "She is cutting wood," is actually a symbolic way of saying that she is working, doing her job as a musician by providing entertainment. He calls it an ironic allusion to the notion of work; in this case, she is stimulating fun and frolic. He explains that this is an idiomatic substitution that created a completely new form of representation in Cuban popular music. Tasks such as chopping firewood, hunting boars, skimming lard, and harvesting sweet potatoes were central to the lives of country folk. The insertion of these activities into music emphasized these daily routines and provoked the appearances of nuances whereby they took on a life of their own in popular music, becoming useful as idiomatic replacements when referring to other things.[57] Similar argumentation is later adopted by professor of Dominican folklore Flérida de Nolasco, who in her 1956 study *Santo Domingo en el folklore universal* [Santo Domingo in universal folklore], sees "Rajando la leña está" [She is cutting firewood] as a chorus response that, evenly interspersed throughout the song, is really a popular expression for "tocando en el baile está" [she is playing an instrument at the dance].[58]

Building on the original Carpentier legacy, the unquestioning stance of accepting this Cuban *son* as Teodora's creation or as directly connected with her is visible in contemporary literary studies done by Roberto González Echevarría and Vera Kutzinski. A product of *taíno* (Arawak), Spanish, and African elements, González Echevarría references this *son* as Teodora's creation—one she performed during the second half of the sixteenth century. He describes her as an Afro-Dominican woman originally from Santiago de los Caballeros in the Dominican Republic. In his explanation of the repetitive and rhythmic call-and-response technique of the ballad, this critic aligns the verse "Rajando la leña está" to literally mean "She's splitting the logs," which, within Cuban linguistic nuance, must be further interpreted as "cutting the rug"—in other words, dancing.[59]

González Echevarría is particularly keen on clarifying African and Spanish structural influences in relation to Teodora's instruments. He translates "su palo y su bandola" as "her staff and her guitar," even though he does use the word *bandola* as well, and describes them as African and Spanish Caribbean instruments used in folk music.[60] The structure of the verses reminds him of the Spanish ballad. At the same time, the dialogic nature of the relationship between Teodora as lead singer and the chorus that responds to her calls or prompts while she moves around dancing is reminiscent of chants and rhythms associated with Africa. González Echevarría calls attention to the connections among daily life, the rhythm or the beat, and the nature of the lyrics that usually have more than one meaning: "One can almost hear Teodora's staff hit the ground on 'Rajando la leña está.' And the brief alliteration in the middle of the line (la leña) adds to the rhythmic effect.... The ritual turns into a joyous repetition and affirmation of an answer for which there is no longer a question."[61]

The direction of this critic's primarily musical interpretation proves interesting for the way it allows Teodora to exist within and beyond the song. The inclusion of dancing as a way of understanding the message behind the lyrics keeps the past alive and values the ideas of tradition and heritage in association with this *son*. Further, this idea of deep roots, tradition, and African legacy is legitimized by the word *Ma'* (taken from "Ma' Teodora"), which begs the maternal interpretation even though it is not expanded upon. At best, we can imagine that the verses respectfully summon an older, loving female figure who, by design, brings a certain ancestral value to the performance: "Teodora is memory incarnate."[62] González Echevarría finds in the verses enough musical and poetic stimulation to encourage a deeper questioning of the design of this female figure. Flowing through the music are interrogations of who she was and what her life was like. It becomes possible to read symbolic trends in Caribbean identity, a space in which work such as chopping firewood for the stove becomes a source of inspiration and cultural representation through song and dance, a reenactment of life's daily chores. As González Echevarría explains, "Ma' Teodora is turning her subservient, uprooted self into a joyful mode of being; she is transforming toil into dance."[63] Within this context, her elderly status gains value, representative of physical endurance and the labor-intensive legacy of an enslaved people: she is the *son*.

Literary scholar and professor Vera Kutzinski describes this song as the mother of the Cuban *son* that has local significance as the inspirational source of Nicolás Guillén's musical poems.[64] She varies a bit in her interpretation of the reference to cutting wood, seeing it instead as dancing. She uses the call-and-response technique of the verses to confirm how the figure of Ma' Teodora, embedded as she is within such musical poetic structure, lapses into silence and invisibility: "It is her dancing that defines her as absence; she does not exist outside of the syncretic *son* that supposedly originated with her. Because of Ma Teodora's conspicuous textual invisibility, it is relevant to note that there has been serious doubt among musicologists about the actual origins of this prototypical Cuban dance, which has been linked with and named after the Black Dominican dancer Teodora Ginés."[65] Intellectual preoccupations with historical validity in relation to this *son*'s origins in the sixteenth or nineteenth century contrast with widespread popular belief in said music's iconic status and legacy as a first, truly Cuban grassroots manifestation directly associated with an older (albeit respectable) woman. It is important to note here that Ma' Teodora does seem to barely sidestep the categorization of the Black Mammy. She was never a wet nurse, always a musician; based on the lyrics, we can speculate that she also did some kind of domestic (kitchen) labor. The *son*'s popularity among the masses is secure and well, an interesting phenomenon within which it is possible to observe a certain battle between objective intellectual probing and sentimental public opinion that favors clinging to its iconic illusion. Kutzinski's concern with our inability to perceive Ma' Teodora within the confines of this music, which is where she is supposed to exist simply by recognition or name, reiterates the challenge that this Black female subject faces within the confines of historical discourse: "Her sole shapes are the cross-cultural rhythms of the '*son*,' presumably the earliest known product of Cuba's *mestizaje*. Indeed, the perpetual quest for tradition in this *son* is premised on her (textual) displacement."[66] The troubling process of historical (imagined?) reconstruction seems to indicate that legitimizing and referencing the Black female figure as an original forbearer is incompatible with the process of recuperating the nation's cultural legacy. Kutzinski deduces that the idea of Ma' Teodora's existence as an actual person is reduced, relegated to the level of the mythical or the imaginary; this is a marginalizing process that must inevitably take place so that the "masculine structures of cultural memory" used to design the historical trajectory of the Cuban *son* can have center stage.[67] It is a process of imposed silencing and nonrecognition that legalizes her erasure from this part of the nation's cultural discourse. In fact, Ma' Teodora's presence may actually be a liability.

Kutzinski's interpretation of Ma' Teodora's cultural value serves as a good basis for critiquing the controversial Muguercia article. However, while one can appreciate the debilitating effect on Ma' Teodora's erasure, it is precisely such effacing that seems to have provoked the construction of a contemporary literary profile gaining much leverage for the way it is successfully writing her back into existence as a creator of the nation. The strategic endeavor to place this figure outside of and beyond history has led to poetic devices re-creating this subject in a glorified form that goes far beyond the specificities of factual evidence that historians cherish. In this new medium or larger universe, her mythological existence takes center stage, and her eulogized representation as the inventor of the Cuban *son* is assured.

While we may encounter some difficulty capturing the nuanced meanings of the words in this *son*, popular belief interprets the verses as referring to a woman who cannot be found because she is at a party enjoying herself. Within popular social imaginary, she is a *gozadera* [fun-loving person] who likes to sing and dance. This reading is widely appreciated, as it allows Cubans to see themselves reflected in her. They are innovative, musical, loud, confusing, fun-loving, and yes, they have parties—a broad, sweeping characterization that fuels a false sense of familiarity and national unity even though it may not necessarily be so perfect, so true. While the legacy of such generalizations are fraught with potential stereotypical representations, they feed the popular imaginary of the masses in terms of how they see themselves and how they treasure the ideas behind this piece of music. The references to laborious daily chores—she is nowhere to be seen because she is out cutting wood—may also serve as symbolically synonymous with a woman who fights for survival, who is strong and prepared to face difficulty. Another potential direction is to view the lyrics as empowering, capable of giving her leadership qualities by associating such action with forms of organized resistance and activism against oppression. The range of interpretive possibilities, from actual wood splitting to serious acts of resistance and rebellion, expand the music's potential as a historical Cuban representation and allow the interpretive mechanisms that naturally exist in these verses to spring forth on their own accord, especially if we introduce those multiple, colorful, and contrasting aspects that many see as defining what it means to be Cuban. The dramatic change comes when, in order to contemplate such a configuration, history and fiesta merge and become redeposited back into this female figure as the source, the one who makes things happen.

Carpentier's historical study is the only one that describes Teodora as a producer of popular songs. He affirms that the call-and-response format between a soloist and a chorus can be traced back to the singing games in Africa, although he cannot confirm that the said structure rests exclusively on these African musical displays.[68] His examination of this *son* confirms its transcultural composition, an amalgamation of Hispanic meters, melodies, and instruments with ancient oral African traditions. Its popularity endured, and it survived until the first part of the nineteenth century, appearing in carnivals in San Juan and Santiago.[69] The particular story arising out of this *son*—even in its current, disputed form—is revelatory of the path of Hispanization that African descendants such as Micaela and Teodora were forced to follow. Their roles as musicians in an orchestra confirm their successful acculturation to the Hispanic colonial structure. Carpentier's view that Teodora was a composer of this *son* confirms his belief in her creativity and indicates initiative on her part, as (maybe unknowingly) she found a way to incorporate elements of her musical legacy into the popular songs she composed, the music she performed, and the art forms she had to learn to call her own. The recognition of African-stylized elements confirms the initiative of those first inventors of Cuban music who, by incorporating their own musical traditions, transformed musical sounds from instruments like the *bandola* into rhythm or from the guitar into percussion.[70]

Elena Pérez Sanjurjo's *Historia de la música cubana* appears among recent reputable historical studies that unquestioningly consume and reiterate this version of the Ginés sisters. Pérez Sanjurjo declares that Teodora was the author of this first *son* ever known and written.[71] She is working with information gleaned from Sánchez de Fuentes, who went on to argue that this first *son* was influenced by the aborigine cultures of the time, an idea that Pérez Sanjurjo admits is difficult to prove.[72] She draws attention to the merging between Spanish song and African rhythm, valuing this characteristic as the point of departure for Cuban popular music. The call-and-response format in the *son* between soloist and chorus is a reminder of Yoruba religious chants. At the same time, she does indicate that due to the presence of multiple cultures, it is somewhat difficult to determine the exact sources that ultimately had an impact on the *son*'s structure. She confirms the dissolution of the orchestra and Micaela's departure to Havana, a journey that Teodora declined to make due to the precarious nature of travel in those days and the suggestion that she was not strong enough for the journey. Thus they separated, "Micaela cantando y Teodora tocando su 'bandola,' como dice el *Son* de que hablamos" [Micaela singing and Teodora playing her "*bandola*," according to the *Son* about which we are speaking].[73] Teodora continued her musical career as an orchestra player, living a long life and attaining status as somewhat of a celebrity, confirmed in the lyrics of the "Son de la Ma' Teodora" that emerged during her lifetime and remain with us to this day.[74]

THE HAVANA CONTROVERSY

The idea that Cuban popular music originated in the sixteenth century in association with Ma' Teodora has been solidly challenged by renowned Cuban musicologist Alberto Muguercia y Muguercia in his famous article "Teodora Ginés ¿Mito o realidad histórica?"[75] His argumentation has had an enormous, maybe even devastating impact on studies about music in Cuba, oral folklore, and popular belief. In a detailed article that highlights the flaws existing in renowned historical scholarship, he sets out to question the validity of this *son*, until that moment recognized and assumed as the first of its kind. While he does not say that this *son* has its roots in popular culture, he does insist that it could not have originated that early in Cuba's history, during those formative years of settlement, colonization, and initial cultural contact. Even as he cannot offer an exact date of origin, his findings seem to indicate that its roots are more recent, during the nineteenth century. The challenge that faces us is to understand the trajectory of this piece that characteristically seems to be traditional and folkloric—a part of oral tradition, its survival assured by recitations and performances through the generations.[76] While the Muguercia challenge presents itself as rigorous historical research, its detailed questioning of all previous historical studies and refusal, in this particular case, to acknowledge the role of orality as a legitimate tool for proving legacy has had a severe impact on the legacy of the Ginés sisters as the founding figures of Cuban popular music. His postulations stand in stark contrast to poetic illustrations glorifying the genre and embracing it as part of *el proceso*—that is, the Cuban revolutionary process.

As occurs with oral legacies, references to Ma' Teodora were embraced and associated with Teodora Ginés, a spontaneous connection that exists historically and in popular imagination, grounded in the historical data previously presented. Muguercia's new challenge, in its quest for greater historical accuracy, negatively affects the ideological value weighted in the *son* itself as well as in the historical possibility of the existence of these two female figures. The potential debunking of popular widespread belief in all aspects of this story has an impact on projects that seek to reinsert the said female figures as active initiators and participants in processes of national formation in Latin America—more specifically, in this nation that has produced the only two narratives by enslaved men.[77] A closer examination of the Muguercia text reveals its worth and promise in its intent to closely micromanage the accumulation of knowledge, even as, in the final analysis, it represents a specific research direction that circumvents efforts to solve the process of female historical invisibility; on the contrary, in this case, it will only increase the inclination toward denial. Historical archival work is accompanied by an unwillingness to trust earlier documentation, claiming it to be too distant, vague, and rudimentary or impossible to verify. This renders all references to such female subjects as problematic even when music seems to have left traces of evidence.

Today, the Muguercia text has built a case against earlier historical documentation by renowned historians that viewed the "Son de la Ma' Teodora" as Teodora's composition. "Muguercia y el fin de un mito" [Muguercia and the end of a myth] is the title of a newspaper article that appeared in the Dominican online newspaper *Hoy*.[78] It summarizes how this scholar fiercely challenges the veracity of a document known as the "Crónica de Hernando de la Parra" [Chronicle of Hernando de la Parra] available in *Las artes en Santiago de Cuba* (1893), a product of the distinguished nineteenth century musician and researcher Laureano Fuentes Matons.[79] Fuentes Matons's version is part of a larger study that focuses on the history of music in Santiago de Cuba, and he based his reconstruction of the sixteenth-century musical scene on annotations supposedly belonging to a certain Don José de la Cruz Fuentes that read,

> En 1580, apenas había en Santiago de Cuba dos o tres músicos tocadores de pífanos; un joven natural de Sevilla nombrado Pascual de Ochoa, tocador de violín, que había venido de Puerto Príncipe con unos frailes dominicos, y dos negras libres, naturales de Santo Domingo, nombradas Teodora y Micaela Ginés; tocadoras de bandola.

> [In 1580, there were only two or three musicians, flutists, in Santiago de Cuba; a young native of Sevilla named Pascual de Ochoa, a violin player who had arrived from Port-au-Prince with some Dominican friars and two free Black women from Santo Domingo named Teodora and Micaela Ginés, *bandola* players.][80]

Not long after, Pascual de Ochoa departed for Havana, and the two Dominican-born *bandola*-playing sisters separated, as Micaela also moved to Havana, leaving Teodora in Santiago, where, along with a few other instrumentalists, she entertained locals. A 1598 description of Havana by Don José María de la Torre confirms that at that time, there were four musicians who, for a fee, played for all events and entertained the town. They were Pedro Almanza, a violinist from Málaga; Jácome Viceira, a clarinet player from Lisbon; Pascual de Ochoa, a violinist from Seville; and Micaela Ginés, a free Black woman and *bandola* player from Santiago de los Caballeros.[81] This constitutes the last available information about Micaela. Teodora remained in Santiago de Cuba and continued to practice her profession as a musician who played several instruments, providing entertainment for dances as needed. The annotations go on to infer that Teodora lived to a ripe old age and became somewhat of a celebrity by virtue of the first *son* bearing her name.

On the last page of his controversial study, Muguercia lays out a table that presents the original materials associated with the controversy. They are (1) "Crónica de Hernando de la Parra," the primary historical document; (2) Laureano Fuentes Matons's *Las artes en Santiago de Cuba* (1893); (3) Emilio Bacardí Moreau's *Crónicas de Santiago de Cuba* (1908); and (4) Alejo Carpentier's *La música en Cuba* (1946). This controversy has become very public primarily because Muguercia's position within the legacy of musicology in Cuba. Originally from Santiago de Cuba, he was born on February 22, 1928, and died on October 22, 1987. A famous musicologist, he dedicated his life to recovering and restoring numerous original popular Cuban musical scores as well as biographical and sociological information about local composers and musicians. He labored long and arduously at the José Martí National Library in Havana. He continued to be greatly respected for his accomplishments during the last two decades of his life as an excellent researcher and promoter of the musical arts. His life's work as a researcher of

Cuban music began in 1969, when he started to work in the field, eventually becoming known for using the interview as his main investigative technique. His study "Teodora Ginés ¿Mito o realidad histórica?" [Teodora Ginés: Myth or historical reality?], published in 1971 and at the center of this discussion, led to his national recognition in 1974 as recipient of the Pablo Hernández Balaguer Musicology Award. His use of actual testimonials and genuine musical scores representing the best of Cuban popular music has helped create valuable national archives of cultural information. In spite of his many health problems, he carried out hundreds of interviews focusing on music from the eastern part of the island, known for its many distinctive variations of the Cuban *son*. He has left behind an invaluable legacy of scripts, interviews, songs, recordings, and music. The archive, known today as the Colección Muguercia, is currently available at the Biblioteca Nacional de Cuba José Martí in the León Muguercia Music Room (a space that is also dedicated in honor of Argeliers León Pérez), where he held conferences, courses, and interviews and wrote various published and unpublished studies and papers. The collection contains books, brochures, academic papers, journals, recordings in film and tapes, and numerous photographs.[82]

The fine line between myth and reality is being tested in an interesting way with regard to Teodora and Micaela Ginés. In 1893, a well-known musician from Santiago de Cuba, Fuentes Matons, wrote about the arts in that town and, as part of his study, mentioned that the origins of traditional music forms rest with the figure of a woman called Teodora Ginés, who, according to his research, actually existed.[83] He set the stage for what is today a national treasure and a symbol of the valuable contribution music originating in Santiago de Cuba has made to the national milieu.[84] Muguercia's article criticizes the way in which Cuban historiography has throughout the twentieth century allowed such an affirmation to go unchallenged. His own view differs, and he has strongly asserted that the arguments used in the Fuentes Matons's text offer no irrefutable proof of Teodora's existence.[85] In his drive to confirm authenticity and historical veracity, he questions the validity of specific historiographical data in existence today, particularly since the information rests on origins that have not been tested and adequately verified, resulting, in his view, in a series of myths that live on as an indelible part of Cuba's historical traditions.[86] He therefore sets out to prove the arbitrary nature of Fuentes Matons's assertions:

> Es nuestro propósito demostrar en el presente trabajo la ilegitimidad de toda una serie de inferencias y de asociaciones arbitrarias e intencionadas realizadas en torno a la existencia de dos mujeres, Teodora y Micaela Ginés, *sobre las cuales no existen documentos originales fidedignos del siglo XVI que corroboren su paso por nuestra historia colonial.*

> [It is our intention to demonstrate in the present study the illegitimacy of a series of arbitrary and intentional inferences and associations raised surrounding the existence of two women, Teodora and Micaela Ginés, *about whom there are no original reliable documents from the sixteenth century that corroborate their passage through our colonial history.*][87]

This musicologist confirms that throughout the 1800s, various publications insisted that both women resided in Cuba between 1580 and 1598. Micaela's name appears for the first time in a volume edited by José Joaquin García under the title *Protocolo de antigüedades, literatura, agricultura, industria, comercio, etc.* [Protocol of antiquities, literature, agriculture, industry, commerce, etc.], published in Havana in 1845. This *Protocolo* seems to comprise a series of publications produced during that year. It is here that her name appears within a text known to date as "Crónica de Hernando de la Parra," of unknown authorship.[88] Muguercia indicates that García was working on dance, music, and entertainment during that initial epoch and included the "Crónica" because it offered details on the existence of a quartet that performed using classical European instruments. The "Crónica" states, "Son estos músicos, Pedro Almanza, natural de Málaga, violin; Jácome Viceira, de Lisboa, clarinet; Pascual de Ochoa, de Sevilla, violon; Micaela Gínez, negra horra, de Santiago de los Caballeros, viguelista" [These musicians are Pedro Almanza, native of Málaga, violin; Jácome Viceira from Lisbon, clarinet; Pascual de Ochoa from Sevilla bass violin; Micaela Gínez, a free Black woman from Santiago de los Caballeros, vihuela player].[89] He confirms that this single detail available in the "Crónica" was reproduced by other nineteenth-century historians of music, including Torre, Bachiller y Morales, Ramírez, López Prieto, Mitjans, and finally Fuentes Matons, the latter having the distinction of being the last musicographer of the 1800s to do so and who fully based his argumentation on García's *Protocolo*.[90]

Muguercia strategically undermines the validity of information contained in the García publications by way of a series of postulations, all based on other studies subsequently published beginning in the 1920s. He supports his plan of questioning the existence of these two women by insisting that twentieth-century studies done by Manuel Pérez Beato and José Juan Arrom are flawed, as they were unable to locate the persons mentioned in the García publication in any of the currently available municipal and parochial documents.[91] He then insists that subsequent historians such as José María de la Torre were deceived by García's document, parts of which de la Torre cites in his work, *Lo que fuimos y lo que somos, o La Habana antigua y moderna* [What we were and what we are, or old and modern Havana; 1857]. Finally, he is adamant that that the event at which said musicians were performing does not appear in a consistent and completely verifiable way in any records, and therefore it is difficult to corroborate if, when, and in what form it occurred. The problem appears to emerge from an inability to find said names in primary documents from the 1500s and an inability to establish if they did indeed perform in the comedy and street festivities in 1597 and if, in fact, 1597 was the year of the events under scrutiny.[92]

Muguercia calls attention to the rather rustic, unsophisticated nature of society at the end of the sixteenth century, emphasizing the rough culture and limited sophistication of the Indigenous inhabitants (referring to the original peoples and new arrivals), a detail that would have directly influenced the nature of the street celebrations and festivities at the time in Havana.[93] These were the kind of events in which the said quartet would no doubt have performed at a time known for its lack of resources, typical of a population whose settlement was in its formative stages.[94] He painstakingly seeks out information about the kind of public festivities that would have been occurring at that time, between 1570 and 1610, and is able to identify several Catholic celebrations as well as events organized by Blacks as attested to by other details available in legal documents from the time. This, alongside evidence of a limited economy and precarious commerce, confirms the difficulties the inhabitants of San Cristóbal de La Habana faced during those trying times.[95] The rather grave reality of a difficult existence was the backdrop against which these musicians entertained the masses, a service for which they demanded payment, wine, and food—their way of earning their keep.

While this quartet may well have been known as the first Cuban orchestra of the sixteenth century, there is some difficulty confirming the identities of the four musicians.[96] As mentioned earlier, the "Crónica de Hernando de la Parra," published by García in *Protocolo*, is the first time that the name Micaela Ginés appears, and this also warrants some questioning. Muguercia then focuses on the instruments that were used, questioning aspects related to invention and availability—for example, the idea that the violin was one of the instruments used by the quartet given that said instrument acquired its contemporary form and dimension in Italy between 1700 and 1720. The sixteenth century was cited as the embryonic period of the violin, meaning that in 1598, Pedro Almanza, the alleged violinist of the group, could have been playing any instrument, but not the violin. In discussing instrument invention and usage, Muguercia undermines the view of Cuba's first orchestra by confirming inconsistencies with regard to the other two instruments—the bass violin and the clarinet. He argues that the vihuela is the only instrument that corresponded to the period in discussion, implying that the person who wrote the "Crónica" was not well versed in the history of musical instruments. He questions the quality of García's work, drawing our attention to the author's prologue and his apparent "falta de seriedad," or lack of scholarly precision, seen in the way García brought under one umbrella such dissimilar topics as literature, agriculture, industry, commerce, and the arts, among others.[97]

Muguercia encounters evidence to support the view that 1893 was the year when the idea emerged that Teodora Ginés and Ma' Teodora were one and the same. She was part of Fuentes Matons's *Las artes en Santiago de Cuba*, published that year, the very period when the story became part of the national imaginary. It appears that Fuentes Matons changed the original orthography from "Ginez," as it first appeared in the "Crónica," to "Ginés."[98] Muguercia challenges the spontaneous nexus between the verse "¿Dónde está la Ma' Teodora?" and the evocation of the person of Teodora Ginés in *Las artes en Santiago de Cuba* and states that this is the source mentioned in all subsequent references and citations, which offers no possibility of confirming if indeed the former has anything to do with the latter. He challenges the historical authority established by Fuentes Matons on this matter, who, as it appears, never really presented proof of his conclusions. Fuentes Matons indicates that Teodora Ginés must have died during the mid-1600s; because of her advanced age, she needed a walking stick but never once abandoned her role as a vihuela player. He proposes for our consideration, in the form of a question, the immortalization of Teodora, a native of Santiago de los Caballeros, as the first musical celebrity of Cuba, a personage from those initial precarious years of colonial establishment and therefore formative period for a tradition of music and performance on the island. He defends such contemplation as worthy, requiring the acceptance of Teodora as a naturally talented musician, probably self-taught, and herself a maestro or teacher.[99]

Muguercia describes the information that Fuentes Matons published as inauthentic and false, pointing out that the document to which the latter refers constantly has never been seen by anyone. He emphatically declares that Micaela Ginés was an invention:

¿Cómo admitir entonces la veracidad de un documento que aparece misteriosa-mente en el siglo XIX y que recoge información de aquella época relativa a estos personajes apócrifos? (Documento que, por demás, no ha sido visto nunca por nadie, obrando tan sólo el testimonio de Fuentes Matons, quien afirma que éste perteneció a su padre).

[How to admit, then, the veracity of a document that appears mysteriously during the nineteenth century and retains information of that era in relation to these apocryphal persons? (A document that, additionally, has never been seen by anyone, based exclusively on the testimony of Fuentes Matons, who declares that it belonged to his father.)][100]

He could not understand how Fuentes Matons's father, alive during the second half of the eighteenth century, would have had such a document in his possession or be familiar with such facts that reportedly occurred some two centuries before. He seriously doubts the preservation of information across multiple generations. In his view, inconsistencies abound in relation to the way an association emerged between the person and the song, this occurring in the midst of very little solid information about the song's creator, origins, and location. He regards these circumstances as incomplete—mere speculation that, at best, should be taken as a clue in the investigation and never as a medium for confirming historical facts.[101]

In Muguercia's quest for the truth, he delves deeper into twentieth-century documentation that has insisted on repeating the Fuentes Matons information unquestioningly, proving, in his view, the compilation of decades of additional unverifiable information. He cites Bacardí Moreau as the first historian to do this, who, in addition to describing the orchestra in which Teodora and Micaela played, added that they also performed in churches, with there being no indication of the source of this information.[102] Max Henríquez Ureña and Alejo Carpentier are on the receiving end of similar criticism, two icons of Cuban letters whose writings never question Teodora's existence and position her musical production at the source of traditional forms originating in Santiago de Cuba.[103] Carpentier's major accomplishment, La música en Cuba, is not immune to attack, accused of presenting such imaginative information as "que en las Iglesias cantaban negras" [Black women sang in the churches],[104] justifying their employment in this role as symptomatic of the colony's shortage of skilled personnel in further support of his unquestioning belief in the Teodora legacy. Muguercia overturns these postulations simply by emphasizing the unavailability of documentation from the 1500s that could validate these statements. Carpentier's total reliance seems to have been on previous documentation such as that published by Bacardí Moreau:

> Este historiador reproduce la noticia en forma semejante a como lo hiciera Don Emilio Bacardí, señalando, además, algo que ha sido reiterado con suma frecuencia antes y después de publicado su libro: nos estamos refiriendo a la relación paternal que se ha venido estableciendo entre ambas mujeres cuando se afirma que eran hermanas.

> [This historian reproduces the information in a manner similar to that of Don Emilio Bacardí, pointing out, additionally, a detail that has been reiterated with great frequency before and after the publication of his book; we are referring to the paternal relationship established over time between both women when we affirm that they are sisters.][105]

Their status as siblings is not found in the Fuentes Matons text, meaning that it could have been a subsequent addition. Carpentier's work on Teodora is grounded less in Cuban historiography and more in prior publications, a detail that Muguercia uses to deduce that any primary sources Carpentier may have used did not, in fact, offer further clarification about the relationship between the women. As evidence of Carpentier's reliance on previously published details, Muguercia cites a section of the Carpentier text that repeats information about the circumstances that made the sisters part ways during the early 1550s: Micaela decided to join another member of the orchestra, Pascual de Ochoa, and move to Havana in search of betterment, while Teodora remained in Santiago.[106] Muguercia continues to focus on the flaws that exist in Carpentier's premises, the main one being that the arguments presented lack solid support and provide no evidence to confirm their veracity. At one point, Carpentier presumes that Blacks would have suffered less or minimal racial discrimination if they were musicians, citing the scarcity of individuals with such abilities, forcing Africans, Afro-descendants, and whites to perform together side by side in orchestras. Muguercia worried that in making such a claim, Carpentier was blending nonverifiable data with historical scenarios that surely occurred much later, during the nineteenth century.[107]

The next challenge in Muguercia's argument is Carpentier's unquestioning acceptance that Ma' Teodora was in fact Teodora Ginés, as the word *Ma* is in reference to her advanced age and a way of expressing affection for a woman who became so well known in the community for her songs and music. Carpentier aligns her with this singular musical piece, identifying her as the composer of the only remaining evidence indicative of what music may have been like during the 1500s and early 1600s. Muguercia is critical of the fact that Carpentier provided additional data by assuming that this *son* was from the sixteenth century. The Fuentes Matons study only went so far as to say that the famous *son* was composed shortly after her death at a very old age, close to the mid-1600s.[108] Carpentier's words seem to imply that she was also the composer of the *son*: "La trovera de Santiago había asimilado lo que entonces se escuchaba en la isla, y lo devolvía a su manera" [The musician from Santiago had assimilated what people were listening to at the time on the island, reproducing it in her style].[109] Preoccupied that perhaps Carpentier had discovered additional information about which he was unaware, Muguercia meticulously reviewed the known and available sources but discovered no new details. The use of the word *son* to describe the song is also a point of contention. The word *son* seems to have been used broadly during the nineteenth century to refer to various rhythms in song, instrumental music, and dance enjoyed by the masses. Muguercia's own investigation identified at least three different meanings or situations to which the term applied. Until 1920, it represented a specific musical rhythm. It served as a reference for small orchestras that played *sones* or other kinds of popular dance music in Havana. In the Pinar del Río province, it referred to a party.[110]

Carpentier is the cultural personality who has most insisted on the Ma' Teodora legacy, a situation that does nothing to remove the remaining problem of limited primary documentation and information. In light of the precarious historical evidence, the question remains of how to sustain the hypothesis in favor of her existence. Even more deeply problematic is her prestigious legacy that, at the very best, relies totally on a single document—the "Crónica de Hernando de la Parra"—about which little is known. It is clear that Muguercia is not willing to trust the historical process of preservation and documentation in this particular case. Carpentier's project (perhaps a production stimulated by his authorship and literary imagination) is responsible for the glorification of the "Ma' Teodora" *son* far beyond realistic available historical data, to the point where popular belief in the value of this music seems irreversible. Further, Carpentier's homage to the Parra document established widespread belief in Micaela and Teodora's actual existence, which implies that any argumentation capable of debunking the existence of one potentially reverses the possibility of the other's existence. Muguercia continues to find inconsistencies in Carpentier's *La música en Cuba* and seems convinced that the author did not, in fact, have access to the "Crónica" document. He closes his deliberations on this topic by expressing the need for a national repositioning to avoid falsely led homage:

> Ya que nos aproximamos al año 1980 y bien podría ocurrírsele a cualquiera festejar el cuatricentenario de Teodora Ginés, cuando es lo cierto que hace tan sólo setenta y ocho años se obtuvieron las primeras noticias acerca de esta negra liberta dominicana, manumitida no se sabe cómo, que viajó de "Santiago de los Caballeros" a "Santiago de Cuba" no se sabe cuándo.

> [Since we are approaching 1980 and it could occur to someone to celebrate the four hundredth anniversary of Teodora Ginés, when surely it was only

seventy-eight years ago that we received the initial information about this free Black Dominican woman, manumitted we don't know how, who traveled from "Santiago de los Caballeros" to "Santiago de Cuba" we don't know when.][111]

The final part of Muguercia's study delivers oral testimonies from seven of the oldest surviving residents of Santiago de Cuba, born during the late nineteenth century, and focuses on their lifelong connections to traditional music. Their testimonies support the direction of this study in relation to the dire shortage of trustworthy, concrete information and the lack of clear evidence that Ma' Teodora's *son* was widely popular and familiar to many. Their words further encourage Muguercia to conclude that by the end of the 1800s, this *son* was no longer regularly performed in the streets. While these witnesses did have substantial contact with music since childhood, none of those interviewed had heard the song outside of their homes.[112] The *son*'s popularity endured for two centuries; however, by the nineteenth century, the period corresponding to the infancy and life of Fuentes Matons until his death in 1898, it had grown old and was no longer known or heard.[113] Muguercia claims to have stumbled across another version of said *son* in use during the nineteenth century by way of information passed down through the generations. This inspired him to declare, "Según la arbitraria asociación establecida entre este canto y la persona de Teodora Ginés, el mismo se origina a raíz de la muerte de ésta (siglo XVII)" [Based on the arbitrary association established between this song and the person of Teodora Ginés, the former originates with the death of the latter (seventeenth century)].[114] He is clear in his skepticism of the claim that the original lyrics of the *son* presented by Fuentes Matons could have survived the passage of two centuries without suffering modifications. He ponders what motivated Fuentes Matons to create the legend of Teodora Ginés.[115] He imagines that the stimulus must have been old regional songs originating in Santiago and taken to Havana, all part of his larger enterprise to preserve and record Santiago's musical legacy. Muguercia attributes such fixation on the idea that this was the very first *son*. While scholarly motivation produces great information and raises concerns, it does not seem to guide us to any particular conclusion. In the end, Muguercia's greatest contribution may be how he questions the widespread popular belief that Teodora Ginés and the *son* are connected in some way and that she may have been the *son*'s composer. His in-depth examination of historical records and methodical compilation of information confirms his dedication to the topic; however, we can still question his arguments and reasons in light of his apparent unwillingness to consider oral traditional forms of cultural knowledge at the grassroots level, which is where this *son* took shape.

This exhaustive work done by Muguercia has been valuable in tracing the development of historical writing as it relates to this *son* and is good at revealing the cumulative nature of historical research—its faults, its often precarious paths, and most importantly, its underlying subjective nature. Information was added by historians that to date cannot be proven and emerges as imaginative reconstructions of what may have transpired. While the Muguercia essay is very thorough, questions remain. Did it succeed in proving that these women did not exist, that they were not musicians, and that they had nothing to do with the origins of this *son*? Is a fixation on these female figures external to their possible configuration as talented, productive, and creative individuals? The dramatic challenge that this renowned musicologist has left his people may have undermined prior research on the origins of *son*, but it is even more debilitating for processes seeking to revalue such female subjects. It is troubling to find out that such legitimizing research potentially leads to invisibility, even erasure, in the name of accuracy. Even if Teodora were an integral part of the original orchestra, her underprivileged status as enslaved, African-descent, merchandise, and female automatically rendered her a nonperson and therefore unworthy of any historical written registration. All existing texts that include her do so in passing, for the focus is on the history of *son*. The early references that survived the passage of the centuries include her because there was literally no choice; she was a member of the orchestra whether by virtue of her talent or because of the shortage of capable musicians during those foundational years of colonial settlement.

Musicologist Radamés Giro offers an interesting appraisal of Muguercia's article. His main argument is that Muguercia's essay is scientifically flawed because he develops his refutations using the same source that Carpentier and others used—that is, Fuentes Matons's *Las artes en Santiago de Cuba*. The process of refuting a theory relies on one's ability to seek out and present new sources of information that collide with or challenge said theory. Muguercia offers a strong critique; however, he does nothing to cancel prior historical findings, nor does he solve the problem of determining the origins of the first *son* and its relationship with the sisters. He also did not present new knowledge or findings. Cuba's musicology experts are specialists who have different interests and are not always in debate with one another. There was no response or challenge to Muguercia's essay, and subsequently, very little was written on the topic. Two recent essays are María Antonieta Henríquez's "Otras disquisiciones sobre la tonada Ma' Teodora" [Other disquisitions on the Ma' Teodora tune], originally published in 2002, and Danilo Orozco's "Nexos globales desde la música cubana con rejuegos de son y no son" [Global connections from Cuban music with interplays of *son* and not *son*], published in 2014.[116] Neither essay challenges the Muguercia position; both focus rather on scientific analyses and structure and argue in support of a global and eclectic vision of the genre.

This type of historical analysis and processing is critical if we are to find a way to introduce the possibility of female value and glory in a region that does not provide a single enslaved female autobiographical narrative. The difficulty of working with these kinds of sources lies in the lack of strategic focus on this figure (historical texts make only cursory mention of the Black female, providing thereby no possibility for positive attributions, usually focusing instead on something or someone else). In the case of Micaela and Teodora, while shortfalls exist regarding their enslaved status during early Spanish colonial settlement, we can assume that they had worker status and would probably have been engaged in other kinds of manual and slave labor besides playing in the orchestra. Our understanding of the cruel and grueling nature of slavery would incline us to believe that their status as musicians offered respite from hardship, drawing them away from the horrible reality of enslavement that was the only available social and economic condition for all Africans and their direct descendants. We can perhaps imagine the extent to which music offered them a reprieve and provided some emotional and physical solace even as it did not necessarily protect them from the harsh reality that was theirs as oppressed subjects. How, then, can the appreciation of these possible historical icons proceed? The glimpses that this historical data provide, problematic as they may be, combined with a belief in the value of oral traditions, in this case kept alive by popular belief about the origins and value of this first *son*, have laid the foundation and provided certain legitimacy for the process that took place in modernity—that is, the feminist-based appropriation of the information and presentations (even inventions) of "historical" and literary versions of it. Interestingly enough, such literary activity originates in the Dominican Republic, possibly the land of their birth.

CHAPTER 2

The Invention of
History through Poetry

A DOMINICAN INITIATIVE

It is an interesting development that Dominican poetry recognizes and values Teodora and Micaela Ginés as two of the nation's first settlers and talented pioneers probably responsible for laying the foundations of Dominican music—that is, the *son*. As Karoline Bahrs states, "En la República Dominicana no se abandonó la idea de haber sido la cuna de una música tan importante como el son" [In the Dominican Republic, they have not abandoned the idea of being the cradle of music as important as the *son*].[1] Aída Cartagena Portalatín's symbolic celebration of the Ginés sisters in her poem *Yania Tierra: Poema documento* becomes a significant tool; it sits within a broader plan of historical gendering that serves multiple purposes such as allowing the sisters to exist textually, creating a feminine version of national history, and confirming the kind of woman-centered patriotism that underpins specific interests of developing an alternative discourse. Poetry is moving differently from the cultural context visible in the dispute between Cuba and the Dominican Republic as to which country has the right to claim the *son* as its own. Debates and research continue in which understanding the origins of "Son de la Ma' Teodora" have priority; this points to an unresolved part of history regarding the sisters and their contributions to establishing the roots of this popular local genre in both countries. The desire remains to discover and understand the formation of each nation's music (the base of national sovereignty) and to confirm, as close as possible, its composers. To date, most of the research in relation to the *son* has been done in Cuba.

THE DOMINICAN CLAIM

The registering of *son* and its origins in the Dominican Republic takes place within a structure that, overall, is not very forthcoming with regard to the contributions Africans and Afro-Dominicans have made to nation building. While there is some interest in claiming that *son* originated in the Dominican Republic, the association of such origin with enslaved women and their potential iconization is not a preferred topic of discussion or debate. Within local academia, three researchers have left their mark on topics of nationhood, identity, Afro-Dominican historical trajectory, and literature: Carlos Andújar, known for *Identidad cultural y religiosidad popular* [Cultural identity and popular religiosity] and *La presencia negra en Santo Domingo* [Black presence in Santo Domingo]; Carlos Esteban Deive, who wrote *Los guerrilleros negros* [The Black guerrillas]; and Odalís G. Pérez, author of *La ideología rota* [Broken ideology].[2] Along with Celsa Albert Batista and Pura Emeterio Rondón, these researchers address race, discrimination, gender, and identity even as their scholarship associates *dominicanidad* [Dominicanness] with *mulataje* [mulattoness].[3]

The process is different in literary writing, as poetic invention and interpretation of the Ginés sisters facilitate their association with talent, creativity, distinction, and matriarchal lineage. Such inventiveness also works to compensate for the fact that so little is known about their birthplaces or origins. To make up for this shortfall, the poem conflates the geographical locations associated with these heroines; in other words, instead of multiple locations, they merge into one. The Caribbean is the island of Hispaniola; Hispaniola, in turn, is the Dominican Republic—indeed, this is a purposeful coalescing that suits the nationalistic agenda of the poet. *Yania Tierra* is a manifestation of Portalatín's love for her motherland and her desire to illuminate Dominican female initiatives; it facilitates her vision of her country as the prototype, a kind of epicenter whose centuries-long trajectory will repeat itself in the historical experience of the region.[4]

Within a society that has a conflictive relationship with its Afro-descendant legacy, due in part to its political relationship with Haiti, it is a challenge to find scholarship that will singularly describe Dominicans as a people of African ancestry. Denial, distancing from similarities with Haiti, and a preference for identity as mulattoness in Dominican culture counteract the development of African-originated female characters as nation builders. The Afro-descendant male figure emerges as spoken for, permanently etched in a distant and forgotten past, lodged within a discourse of coloniality and never conceived as a contemporary subject, while the female figure is marked by absence. Marisel Moreno speaks to this difficulty and finds in Afro-Dominican women's writings an enclave of change, one that resituates such a subject by making her "un agente libre que logra 'burlarse' de los sistemas que la oprimen" [a free agent who manages "to make fun" of the systems that oppress her].[5]

The association of the Ginés sisters with the Dominican Republic and their role as architects of popular Dominican music will not receive much attention; of greater importance is defending the argument that Santo Domingo (not Santiago de Cuba) is *son*'s place of origin. Andújar's *De cultura y sociedad* [On culture and society] confirms the underlying national trauma surrounding the topic of racial identity in relation to Haiti. In a later study, Andújar declares, "El pueblo dominicano ha sufrido un lento y progresivo proceso de alienación respecto a su identidad étnico-cultural" [The Dominican people have suffered a slow and progressive process of alienation with respect to their ethnocultural identity].[6] He purports that the ideological denial of African-originated cultural elements, as well as the cultural distortion that emerged when the Dominican people turned away from this segment of their past, led to a situation in which the authentic cultural representation of self was replaced by one that is fictitious. Upon arrival, Africans were made to repress and reject their forms of expression even as they were overwhelmed with new and hostile conditions and made to assimilate to the alienating dominant culture. Andújar comments on the current trends of suppressing this historical fact, including the way such suppression removes possibilities of determining African contributions to nation building as well as acknowledging the African-based ethnic component that is the foundation of today's mulatto and criollo societies. While Andújar moves beyond the traditional contemplation of highlighting their contributions to music and religion, his list is still very much in the artistic-cultural realm. His discourse contemplates the arriving Africans neither as the economic and social builders of the new colonies nor as skilled human beings who brought their own sources of knowledge and creativity.[7]

Discussions on the topic focus on the African figure within the sphere of marronage, rebellion, music, dance, and religion. Studies about slavery and African cultural expressions in the Dominican Republic today seem to depend heavily on the early twentieth-century findings of Cuban scholars like Fernando Ortiz. Further, as with Andújar's *La presencia negra en Santo Domingo*, explanations appear limited as they relate to topics of resistance. Andújar and Carlos Esteban Deive seem to avoid engaging too deeply with the lasting implications of the Haitian Revolution, primarily its effects on Afro-Dominicans and the permanent legacy of their nation, which found itself under Haitian rule between 1822 and 1844. Further, their insistence on identifying the Dominican Republic as a mulatto nation crowds their approach, producing affirmations that move toward the notion of fusion and harmonious miscegenation. In the end, the impression is that the contributions of Africans were, at best, rudimentary. Philosophical thought, ancestral knowledge, medicinal knowledge, knowledge of the land, and scientific thought are never mentioned. The notion of the African as leader, teacher, or philosopher is never present. The discourse of the Black subject in the Dominican Republic is dominated by visions of a victimized creature in the past and an economically disadvantaged person in the present. This portrayal of historical passivity in relation to the enslaved is ruptured by the single heroic male figure of African ancestry in Dominican territory—Sebastián Lemba (d. 1547?). Lemba stands alongside the remaining Latin American warrior and maroon heroes, including Zumbi dos Palmares of Brazil, Esteban Montejo of Cuba, and Benkos Biohó of Colombia, even as he is the ancestral insurrectionist and leader of Hispaniola's maroons whose story remains relatively unknown.[8]

While deliberations about maroon initiatives and resistance are crucial for constructing a more fulfilling and complete history of the Americas, we cannot rely solely on these narratives if we are to envision and be inclusive of female endeavors. News of the Ginés sisters appears in Flérida de Nolasco's *Santo Domingo en el folklore universal* [Santo Domingo in universal folklore], an early study that seeks to establish the roots, formation, and development of Dominican music. In her chapter "Las danzas a través de nuestra historia" [Dances throughout Our History], de Nolasco writes about the Ginés sisters in relation to dance and music, confirming that available information starts in 1580, identifying the sisters as Black women, natives of Santiago de los Caballeros who were able to gain their freedom and then migrate to Cuba.[9] Teodora became one of four musicians available in Havana and either served as the inspiration for or composed a song for dancing, a musical score that has since been published many times and that, according to famous Dominican intellectual, literary critic, and writer Pedro Henríquez Ureña, is similar in structure to the Argentine milonga, a music and dance form bearing some of the basic elements of the tango.[10] Based on Benigno Gutiérrez's *Arrume folklórico de todo el maíz* [Folkloric arrangement of all the corn], de Nolasco refers to a popular dance with an accompanying song that is analogous to the music and lyrics of "Son de la Ma' Teodora."[11] De Nolasco's discovery supports Peter Manuel's view that *son* is a Latin American phenomenon and should therefore be taken as a broader reference within which *el son cubano* is just one version. Manuel focuses on the *son jalisciense* of Central Mexico to make his point.[12] De Nolasco's discovery is a song called "La Guacamaya," originally from Antioquia, a department located in the central northwestern part of Colombia. As can be observed in the following verse, the song's rhythm aligns fully with that of "Son de la Ma' Teodora":

¿Onde está la Guacamaya?
  En Palenque está.
¿Onde está que no la veo?
  Volando va.

[Where is the Guacamaya?
  She is in the bush.
Where is she for I do not see her?
  Fleeing she goes.][13]

The *guacamaya* is a colorful blue, yellow, and red macaw, and in Colombia, the word *palenque* means "maroon community" as well as "bush," "forest," and "shrubs." The possible double entendre in the rendition is not lost. Equally interesting is the way that the music, in rhythm and structure, is similar to the "Ma' Teodora" rendition. De Nolasco confirms that identifying the "Ma' Teodora" composition has more value historically, one that surpasses its role within the realm of folklore. At the same time, the elements of adaptation, variation, and mobility that mark folklore confirm this music's place as central to such deep traditions. She explains that while she was able to associate "La Guacamaya" with dance, she was unable to locate any evidence that associated any particular dance with the "Ma' Teodora" piece. De Nolasco unilaterally declares that these varieties of *son* were, without a doubt, originally from imperial Spain.[14]

Afro-Dominican poet Aída Cartagena Portalatín has played several roles in relation to the sisters, serving as historian, feminist advocate, and poet. She has produced a pseudohistorical narrative that provides the foundation for her literary endeavors. She makes a strong case for the sisters as historical icons worth remembering and uses Flérida de Nolasco, Alejo Carpentier, and Pedro Henríquez Ureña for many of her arguments. Inspired by Carpentier's *La música en Cuba*, she finds it easier to reconstruct topics about life and entertainment in Cuba than in Hispaniola. However, she does indicate that during the first phase of European settlement, the churches would have served as concert halls, and Blacks, carrying the legacy of music in their veins, would have therefore been drawn to those spaces.[15] She is emphatic in declaring the sisters a part of Hispaniola's history of enslavement and sets the tone of her essay by using the phrase "mercancia de ébano" [ebony merchandise].[16] The space in question is Santiago de los Caballeros, a city founded in 1495 on the banks of the Yaque del Norte River and home to these sisters until they were freed. She identifies them as Dominican, their forefathers having landed on the island from West Africa, victims of the slave trade. Carlos Larrazábal Blanco's *Los negros y la esclavitud en Santo Domingo* [Blacks and slavery in Santo Domingo] aids her reconstruction of the era and describes the business of exchanging gold for specific numbers of slaves, hundreds and thousands of them, specifically paying attention to the business transactions up to the beginning of the seventeenth century.[17] In *Las Ginés de Santo Domingo: Esclavas negras libertas y músicas* [The Ginés sisters of Santo Domingo: Freed Black slaves and musicians; 1975], the Ginés sisters are characterized as descendants of African ethnicities, the latter known for being gentle and intelligent. Even though Portalatín does admit that their names do not appear in any known archives, she assumes that they were baptized and given Hispanic names, a clear indication of their status as commodities for sale.[18]

Portalatín admits that the Dominican awareness of the sisters initially came from Cuba by way of the Fuentes Matons publication, and she reproduces this historical tale, adding that Cuban composer Eduardo Sánchez Fuentes attributes the unique nature of the Cuban *son* to specific Haitian influences in the Oriente province. There was in Hispaniola a code or royal decree that provided rules for manumission during the second half of the sixteenth century; Portalatín refers to the process in relation to the sisters while admitting that there is a lack of information regarding how they actually achieved freedom. She does speculate that they arrived in Cuba as free women or servants of some unknown master, or they may have used this destination in their quest for betterment.[19]

Contemplating the sisters as musicians is a detail that coincides with Portalatín's findings of at least twenty musicians from Spain who lived in Hispaniola during the sixteenth century, serving as organists, entertainers, instrumentalists, and teachers. Her research does lead her to make some emphatic statements—namely, that *son* existed in Cuba before the sisters and that Teodora is responsible for the oldest known version, to which many danced in Havana back then. She questions the tendency toward doubt and denial, claiming this first musical piece as a legacy of Blacks in the Americas, one that is exclusively theirs: "Todavía hoy el ritmo perdura en el negro, en su alma, en su cadera, en sus manos, en sus pies, en su voz, en el tambor. Todavía el negro de las Américas canta con el mismo timbre gutural y la pronunciación exagerada, a veces casi ininteligible" [Even today the rhythm lingers on in the Black man, in his soul, in his hips, in his hands, in his feet, in his voice, in the drum. The Black man of the Americas still sings with the same guttural tone and exaggerated, at times almost unintelligible, pronunciation].[20] Portalatín's *negrista* descriptions of this subject are, at best, reductive even as, within her era, they do display this poet's celebration and interpretation of Africa's legacy and the way it thrives to date.

FROM AÍDA'S POETRY TO CELSA'S SCHOLARSHIP: CREATING SPHERES OF FEMALE ENDEAVOR IN SANTO DOMINGO

The fundamental value of having the Ginés sisters appear in verses written by the nation's leading twentieth-century poet is in the generating of African and Afro-descendant heroines in Dominican history, where before, there were none. Their presence in poetry goes against the grain; it is an imposition on the nation's canon, which struggles with concepts or writings that have to do with African legacies. Literary notions that associate the female figure with historical glory and presence in roles such as *cimarrona* [fugitive slave woman], rebellion leader, or resistance fighter are contradictory to nationalistic sentiment and collide with definitions of the nation's identity, which molds itself on the premise of anti-Haitianness.

Developing a discourse of Afro-descendant female historical and literary representation in the Dominican Republic is a contemporary challenge. Aída Cartagena Portalatín and Celsa Albert Batista are two Afro-Dominican women of renown who have written about women and enslavement in the Dominican Republic. Albert Batista is a nationally known Afro-Dominican historian and professor who engages the topic in two short historical works: *Los africanos y nuestra isla* [The Africans and our island; 1989] and *Mujer y esclavitud en Santo Domingo* [Woman and slavery in Santo Domingo; 1990]. Her focus is on national genesis and the role of these women in nation building. These texts are the first two publications by an Afro-Dominican female academician to address the idea of Africa as having a positive and enriching legacy, to pursue historical ancestral reconstruction, and to do so in harmony with the idea of proud heritage, even as the Dominican insistence of its mulattoness continues to match that nation's reticence toward Haitian culture and ethnicity. *Los africanos y nuestra isla* contains the message of the African continent as home, a source of pride and memories of freedom. Albert Batista presents the history of enslavement within frames of suffering and sacrifice but also contribution and resistance.

In *Los africanos*, Albert Batista uses the term *mulatto* to describe the Dominican people as a strategy for critiquing popular and racist references such as "indio claro, indio oscuro, indio lavaíto, jabao, blanco jipato, blanco moreno" [fair Indian, dark Indian, washed Indian, fair-skinned/dark-skinned, pale-skinned/yellow, fair brown-skinned], terms that were invented to mask the direct ancestral connection to African peoples.[21] She critically rejects such references as discriminatory and clarifies how their usage locally confirms the enduring troubling consequences of policies and political strategies promoted by the state, such as whitening and a cultural disengagement with the African legacy. Albert Batista—unlike Blas R. Jiménez (1949–2009), the country's leading Afro-Dominican poet, scholar, essayist, and nationalist—embraces the concept of mulattoness as her people's identity without question.[22] The strategy of constructing commonalities and connections is further enhanced by her short presentation of Haiti and the idea of a shared legacy of colonization.[23] Her text highlights Afro-Dominican historical figures, closing with a reference to Micaela, an enslaved woman who may have been responsible for the establishment of the first medical services on the newly occupied island in 1503 and who does not appear to be connected in any way to the Ginés sisters. *Mujer y esclavitud en Santo Domingo* presents a chart that provides details about the economic activities in which women were engaged. These two musicians would have fallen into the category of *esclava de tala*—that is, an enslaved woman of African or American origin whose tasks included fieldwork, street commerce, domestic service, and the production of basic goods and services.[24]

Albert Batista's engagement of this legacy is matched only by the literary homage paid to the Ginés sisters in Portalatín's poetry. Dominican poetic space finally includes them, successfully improving on their ongoing doubtful status in the Cuban cultural imaginary. Portalatín's writing moves against Cuban intellectual debates; instead of wiping the sisters from the nation's history, the author designs them poetically so as to place them among the first female nation builders. In poetry, the sisters are the center, the origin, the creators—the very core of Dominicanness. This Dominican-driven inspirational literary proposal, working against Cuban refutation and rehistoricizing, redeems these female figures even as these two contrasting positions and processes confirm the difficulty of mapping their legacy exclusively based on historical writing. They do not make an appearance in Cuban literature.

Through her poetry, Portalatín will write women back into history, claiming them as part of her island's consolidation and expansion while ensuring their perpetuity in her anthology *Yania Tierra*. She is distinctive as the poet who resuscitates the sisters and places them on pedestals in her epic poem that pays homage to the nation's women, whose sacrifices and endeavors are barely known. Portalatín is, for many, the major poet of the twentieth century in the Dominican Republic. She retains the profile of a feminist writer who very early on pushed herself to excel beyond her male peers, for which she remains the country's stalwart example of poetic creativity, versatility, and intellectual dynamism.[25] She was born in Moca on June 18, 1918, and died in the capital, Santo Domingo, on June 3, 1994. Cocco de Filippis describes her as the spiritual mother of twentieth-century Dominican poetry by women, leading the way in finally breaking her literary silence by way of a production about her own reality, in her own words.[26] Besides renowned poet and novelist, she was a veritable patron of the arts, analyst of literature and art, editor and novelist, specialist in African and Black literature, and the only Dominican known to have participated in the surrealist movement in Paris.[27] The initial prominent phase of her literary career coincided with the latter decades of the Trujillo regime and dictatorship (1930–38, 1942–61). She was part of the literary movement known as Poesía Sorprendida [Surprised Poetry], the leading literary society at the time, later perceived as an early twentieth-century literary genre. Between 1943 and 1947, she became the editor of the movement's publication bearing the same name. It was during this time that she produced her first anthologies: *Víspera del sueño* [Eve of the dream] and *Del sueño al mundo* [From dream to the world], soul-searching works that reflect on the value of the written word and her role as a poet in Dominican society.[28]

The emergence of this movement requires an understanding of its historical precedents. The literary period that largely influenced Portalatín's aesthetic formation runs from 1930 to 1958 and coincides with the race-based and anti-Haitian ideology emanating from the Trujillo regime.[29] Prior to the 1930s, literary developments were largely independent of political persuasions, and the fields of poetry, journalism, the historical novel, intellectual discourses, and short narratives maintained productivity relatively separately from recurring social, military, and political developments. At the same time, the practice of literary production tended to be an activity of the privileged classes of intellectuals and educated elite, meaning that oftentimes, literary productions lacked class-conscious reflections. In 1930, there emerged a political stance in relation to the role of literature in the nation that came out in the form of essays, novels, and influential politicized propaganda. Joaquín Balaguer draws attention to Manuel Arturo Peña Batlle, Juan Bosch, and Pedro Mir as the influential thinkers and literary agents of the time who brought new critical interpretations of national history, identity, and aesthetic structuring that proved effective in providing the country with patriotically driven ideas.[30]

One can interpret these ideas as providing philosophical argumentation to counter the Haitian leadership and their vision of hegemonic structure in the form of a single united island state, a political agenda that fed on their historical role as victorious rulers of the island from 1822 to 1844. This was another important stage in the expansion of a firm and solid Dominican consciousness and a fierce spirit of nationalism that determined the country's development and political direction. A specific intention of favoring their own historical experience is visible in Portalatín's literary writings and explains the ambivalence therein, product of her situation as one of the first Dominican writers who researched and understood Negritude by way of the African liberation struggles of the 1960s and 1970s and who appreciated the legacy while simultaneously repelling the idea of Haitian historical and political dominion over her beloved nation. The Ginés sisters appear as heroines in *Yania Tierra*, as Portalatín's increased awareness of Afro-Dominicanness will inspire her to claim them as the nation's own.

Portalatín's writing is variegated, following a wide range of genres and interests; indeed, Sherezada (Chiqui) Vicioso, upon investigation, confirms the poet's sense of social consciousness in her collection *La tierra escrita* (1967) together with her nationalistic and female-focused agenda in *Mi mundo el mar* (1953). *Una mujer está sola* (1955) is central to this agenda, as confirmed in the poem bearing the same name. Later, *Yania Tierra* (1981), both epic and feminist, climaxes as a forceful manifestation that is proudly patriotic and fiercely woman-centered.[31] Clementina R. Adams identifies the Dominican Republic as a space with a substantive literary tradition of writing among women and places Portalatín within a group of eight women writers whose Afro-Dominican themes and interpretations of their country's history and reality confirm their resolve, purpose, and willingness to face head-on the more challenging issues related to their nation's political and social upheaval.[32] Gendering their nation are Aurora Arias, Ángela Hernández, Ida Hernández Caamaño, Jeannette Miller, Carmen Sánchez, Dulce Ureña, and Vicioso.[33]

Portalatín initiates the process of redirecting her culture's perception of the woman's universe, and one component of this reconfiguration is the inclusion of the Afro-Dominican legacy in all its aspects. Her initial sources of inspiration were beyond the island, found in experiences related to African independence struggles and the American civil rights movement and manifested concretely in poems such as "Otoño negro" [Black autumn], "Mi madre fue una de las grandes mamás del mundo" [My mother was one of the great moms of the world], "Memorias negras" [Black memories], and "Réquiem por la paz de la ONU" [Requiem for U.N. peace].[34] Her verses and narratives display actual historical figures and emphasize their identities and their moments of trauma and tragedy—Colita-Aurora, Donna Summer, her mother, the Sharpeville massacre, the 16th Street Baptist Church bombing, and the Ginés sisters.[35] The descriptions and experiences are violent, heavy, and traumatic, closely connected with racial discrimination and historical silencing. Her writing becomes more concrete with a narrating, prose-like style that is visible even in her poetry. While her heroines are North American or South African, they are also Dominican. Who does she envision her heroines to be and why? This soul-searching question registers her anguish as she seeks to identify this trajectory and value it within the broad and dynamic artistic portrayal she is creating of the Dominican space and the Americas.

Portalatín's anthologies of the 1950s, *Mi mundo el mar* [My world the sea] and *Una mujer está sola* [A woman is alone], serve as the blueprints for contemporary Dominican women's writings.[36] This is the launching of her singular literary style as well as the consolidation of a genre of women's literature in the Dominican Republic. According to Vicioso, afterward, Portalatín's style and approach change radically during the period coinciding with the peak of the Trujillo dictatorship and beyond—that is, during the 1960s and into the 1980s:

> Publica *La voz desatada* (1962), *La tierra escrita* (1967), *Yania Tierra* (1981), y *La casa del tiempo* (1984), libros que el bloqueo radical de la entonces joven poesía, enarbola como símbolos de ruptura con la tradición literaria femenina porque Aída "trueca el verso complicado por uno simple que pueda calar en las masas." Renuncia el intimismo, declarándose partidaria de una "poesía objetiva"; reniega de la poesía "subjetiva" que invade la realidad y aboga por una poesía de "utilidad social."

[She publishes *La voz desatada* (1962), *La tierra escrita* (1967), *Yania Tierra* (1981), and *En la casa del tiempo* (1984), books that the radical block of the then new poetic movement brandish as symbols of a rupture with the feminine literary tradition because Aída "replaces complex verses with simple ones that can leave a lasting impression on the masses"; she renounces intimism, declaring herself a supporter of "objective poetry"; she rejects "subjective" poetry that invades reality and advocates for a poetry of "social usefulness."][37]

In December 1961, she launched two journals: the first, *Brigadas Dominicanas* [Dominican brigades], a series of ten publications that continued until March 1963, the second, *Colección Baluarte* [Baluarte collection], a series of twelve publications. They displayed a combative literature in resistance to the Trujillo dictatorship, a production of militant literature that Portalatín managed to sustain during hostile times.[38]

Dominican literary critics display restraint when characterizing Portalatín as a Black writer. Odalís G. Pérez defines her artistry as Caribbean and Dominican and views her African and Afro-Dominican essays and poems as nourishment for that objective.[39] Vicioso explains that while Portalatín is venerated as the authority on feminine poetic discourse, no attention is given to her poems that illustrate the experiences of Blacks on the island and in the United States, nor is there consideration of her cultivation of Negritude as poetic rebellion. This apparent invisibility begins to unravel in the face of Portalatín's short narrative "La llamaban Aurora (Pasión por Donna Summer)" [They called her Aurora (Passion for Donna Summer)] and her book-length essay *Culturas africanas rebeldes con causa* [African cultures, justifiably rebellious]. The *dedicatoria* [dedication] sets the tone of and intention for the work:

Dedicatoria
   Con el sentimiento de la sangre mulata que corre por las venas de los dominicanos auténticos, DEDICO esta obra a TEODORA y MICAELA GINES, negras esclavas libertas de Santiago de los Caballeros, las dos primeras mujeres músicas en La Habana y en Santiago de Cuba.

—A.C.P.

[Dedication
   With the sentiment of the mulatto blood that runs in the veins of true Dominicans, I DEDICATE, this work to TEODORA and MICAELA GINES, freed Black slave women from Santiago de los Caballeros, the first two women musicians in Havana and Santiago de Cuba.

—A.C.P.][40]

These words confirm Portalatín's curiosity about the lives of women in history and her desire for a deeper understanding of the African and transcontinental experience. Her words "mi camino a la Negritud" [my path to Negritude] confirm her vision of this as a journey of enlightenment.[41] *Culturas africanas* comprises a

series of short texts, overviews of the main protagonists in the African independence struggles of the 1960s and 1970s, declarations about Negritude and Pan-
Africanism, and poetic excerpts from African writers and is, in style, a collection
of memoirs that reveal a wealth of knowledge and appreciation gained by direct
contact with Africa and its poetic, historical, and political experiences. It represents
Portalatín's message of the need for fuller recognition of this legacy within her
nation, and this collection seems to provide ample opportunity for debate and discussion. It pays homage to a wide range of fighters, revolutionaries of the weapon
and the pen. They are poets and politicians, thinkers and martyrs. Her first main
essay is about Léopold Sédar Senghor, who she discovers as a poet-warrior and
Negritude's main advocate on the African continent. Images and ideas that are
indicative of his absolute commitment to his people, sovereignty, and the ideals
of freedom are embedded in his verses.[42] Portalatín's *Culturas africanas* also contemplates Aimé Césaire, Nelson Mandela, Agostinho Neto, and Patrice Lumumba
through their verses as heroes of greater causes.[43] In this collection, Portalatín
processes her understanding of Africa through narratives and poetry by African
writers and through their national experiences in politics and persecution.

Working toward a more global understanding of identity, the second section of
Culturas africanas contemplates twentieth-century North American experiences
of segregation, on the one hand, and poetic redemption, on the other. Portalatín
finds in the Harlem Renaissance profound and enriching expressions of reality
and identity, and she uses examples of musicians, movements, and artistic, experiential struggles for advancement, including Josephine Baker, the blues, jazz, and
the magazine *Fire*. Words also matter, for she includes Countee Cullen, Claude
McKay, James Weldon Johnson, and Richard Wright in her quest to imagine and
reconstruct the noteworthy actions of that era such as resistance writing and the
establishment of a renowned African American literary legacy.[44] Frantz Fanon,
Jacques Roumain, Jean Price-Mars, René Depestre, and Jacques Stephen Alexis
allow an exploration of Black resistance from the Caribbean perspective and lead
Portalatín into the critical mass of production associated with Negritude. It is
within this context that she also describes the Spanish Caribbean poetic movement
negrismo.[45] Her contemplations continue in a way that brings together Black Arts
endeavors in the Caribbean and in Africa, including Haiti's vodun; Cuba's Nicolás
Guillén and Wilfredo Lam; the magazine *Tropiques*, edited by Aimé Césaire; and
African theater as a space of protest. Portalatín uses the idea of theater to voice
her own concern about female inclusion: "Además, el teatro es un medio de
comunicación de protesta abierto a todas las mujeres que se saben discriminadas,
pero que también reconocen su capacidad como seres humanos" [Besides, theater
is a medium of communication for protest, open to all women who experience
discrimination, but who also recognize their capacity as human beings].[46] For her,
true artistry is in poetry, as she closes this section of her work with the concept
of "poetas de sangre negra" [poets of Black blood], alluding to their commitment
to a poetic rendering of their experiences while reminding all that the blood of

Afro-descendants also runs red. She selects "De profundis," a poem by Philippe Thoby-Marcelin from Haiti:

> De hoy en adelante quiero cantaros a vosotros:
> revolucionarios, fusilamientos, matanzas,
> ladrido koko-makoko en negros hombros,
> gemido de lambí y mística lujuria de vodú
> éxtasis religioso tres veces lírico.

> [From today onward I wish to sing to you all:
> revolutionaries, shootings, killings,
> *koko-makoko* barking on Black shoulders,
> *lambí*'s groaning and vodun's mystical yearning
> religious ecstasy thrice lyrical.][47]

In the last section of *Culturas africanas*, Portalatín leaves Africa, returns to her island space, and with her final set of reflections, focuses on the Ginés sisters by way of two essays: "Teodora y Micaela Ginés, esclavas libertas nacidas en Santiago de los Caballeros en textos de Alejo Carpentier y Pedro Henríquez Ureña" [Teodora and Micaela Ginés, freed slaves born in Santiago de los Caballeros in texts by Alejo Carpentier and Pedro Henríquez Ureña] and "Teodora Ginés, ¿mito o realidad? Investigación sin respuesta de Alejo Carpentier; Trabajo de Alberto Murguecia Murguecia" [Teodora Ginés, myth or reality? Research without an answer by Alejo Carpentier; A paper by Alberto Murguecia Murguecia].[48] Portalatín confirms just how much the valiant struggles in Africa have inspired her to reflect on the Latin American condition, leading to her awareness of peoples whose freedom still has to be won.[49] An important part of this drive is to seek out and appreciate one's roots, which, for her, translates into another opportunity to remember two enslaved women, later freed, with an emphasis on their Dominican identity, valuing them for the way their musical talents allowed them to work and move beyond oppression to leave their mark on history.[50] She elaborates on these icons to create the idea of a new beginning in a motherland that is not African; rather, it is one that is here and now composed of who and where they are as Dominicans. Portalatín reflects on enslavement and writes to destabilize patterns of envisioning these people as passive masses "que tenían alma, orgullo, personalidad y que incorporaron a la vida americana elementos valiosos" [who had soul, pride, personality, and incorporated valuable elements into American life].[51] She posits a series of questions that reflect the historical mood today in terms of the difficulty of accessing further intimate details about past female experiences:

> ¿Qué aportan esas negras dominicanas? ¿Qué pensamientos agitaban los cerebros de aquellas horras o libertas? ¿Inician ellas la liberación de la mujer entre las mujeres de su raza? ¿Se niegan a acogerse a la manumisión conforme se establecía sobre el comportamiento de las mujeres horras en las Ordenanzas

del Cabildo de Santo Domingo, de 1528 a 1786, vigentes por muchas décadas, recogidas finalmente en el Código Negro Español para el Gobierno político, moral y económico de la Española?

[What do these Black Dominican women contribute? What thoughts stirred the minds of these freed or liberated women? Do they initiate female liberation among the women of their race? Are they refusing to embrace manumission as instituted over the behavior of freed women in the Ordinances of the Santo Domingo Town Council of 1528 to 1786, in force for many decades, finally enshrined in the Black Spanish Code by the political, moral, and economic Government of Hispaniola?][52]

While the interest in the sisters arises from their legacy as possibly the first such musicians in the Americas, their ultimate value is in the fact that, as records seem to indicate, at the time of their performances, they were free. Portalatín gives them life; she emphasizes their mental capacity, establishes them as thinking human beings, suggests that they sought to assert their right to freedom, and imagines that they resisted the repressive measures in place at the time to control and limit professional activities by Blacks. She first wrote about them in 1975 in an article published in *El Urogallo* under the title "Las Ginés de Santo Domingo." Located in Santiago de los Caballeros, a city founded in 1495, she imagines that the sisters may have been born there, their ancestors among those brought over from West Africa and sold into slavery. They must have been baptized according to the laws of that severe period under the Inquisition, meaning that their family bore the name of their enslaver, Ginés, a common practice at the time. Portalatín seeks out connections and seems drawn to the story of these sisters. She recalls her father commenting on the fact that he did have clients with that last name, and she ponders on whether such clients were descendants of the original slaveholding family that so branded these two *bandola* players.[53]

Portalatín's article reproduces all the details surrounding the "Ma' Teodora" *son*—that is, the names of those involved (Laureano Fuentes Matons, Alejo Carpentier, Vicente Mendoza, José María de la Torre, Pedro Henríquez Ureña), the instruments that the sisters played, and their dislocations into Cuba and then between cities. Their profiles as entertainers and migrants match perceptions of them as independent and seekers of their own destiny; maybe sensing that they could potentially survive better in Cuba, they abandon Santo Domingo, perhaps their way of pushing back against the debilitating laws of the Spanish Black code designed to keep them in their place.[54]

Her essay retrieves *son* yet is different in the way it strives to lay claim to the Ginés sisters by confirming them as originally and truly Dominican. She includes the work done by Pedro Henríquez Ureña, the Dominican writer and intellectual who spent years living in Cuba and wrote about the sisters as part of his work on popular Antillean music. Portalatín's essay is also different because she seems inclined to produce historical narratives whose construction rests less on documented facts about the sisters and more on details of contextual design related to that era that have already been proven. She inserts the sisters into their context while never taking them for granted as passive, inert beings dependent on destiny.

THE GINÉS SISTERS: BEYOND HISTORY, INTO POETRY

The single major literary presentation of Teodora and Micaela's story appears in Portalatín's poem *Yania Tierra*, an epic rendition that chronicles the Caribbean–Hispaniola–Dominican Republic's historical trajectory from their 1492 birth into modernity. It begins as a strategic appropriation of our region's history, then navigates firmly toward the glorification of a woman-centered *dominicanidad*. In a chronological progression, the female experience drives the action from Iberian colonial status to island-based nationalism. *Yania Tierra* has become an archival space for preserving renowned and unknown Dominican women and their endeavors from discovery to modernity—this time through feminine and feminist lenses. The inclusion of the Ginés sisters, who function in mythical and historical circumstances within the poem, serves as a reminder of the symbolic establishment of the Original Mother reference and the way it redesigns the broad literary history of nations, known for their nationalistic agendas that, when converted into literary text, led to problematic representations, primarily the Black Mammy and the *mulata*.[55]

Nicole Roberts confirms modern Spanish Caribbean poetry as a space for understanding female endeavor and action through time. She retakes the popular literary line of reconstructing this female figure as Original Mother (or as grandmother) and includes those deep-rooted influences within the family and the community directly derived from that legacy.[56] The strategy of aligning the Original Mother figure with the nation is poetry's way of compensating for this historically denied role. In Spanish, the nation is idealized as *patria*, or fatherland, a specific reference to a patriarchal, male-focused space dominated by male presence and power. Roberts goes on to refer to a "culture of machismo" within which any female presence is, at best, secondary.[57] This examination of the role these sisters play in *Yania Tierra* refers to a particular twist or redirecting in which the idea of *patria* is subverted poetically to become *madre patria*, or motherland, by force of linguistic addition, since Spanish does not have a single feminine word or equivalent. The possibility of such a shift is somewhat effective through the idea of motherland; however, it is definitely more impressive and visual in poetic dramatization, which is what this epic poem engages successfully.

Within these verses, heroism appears multiethnic and feminine, with a controlling narrator who relies heavily on such qualities as endurance, survival, tolerance, and sacrifice to build a profile of her omniscient, all-encompassing icon, Yania, the earth. It is extended storytelling through poetry and is historical in nature, for it refers to real events, personages, names, dates, and places. The narrator role is shared between an ephemeral Yania López (also referred to as Yania Tierra in the poem), the personification of the *tierra* [land], or Mother Earth, and a sardonic commentator called Cojito [Cripple], whose role is to remind us of history's tropes, inconsistencies, ironies, and tragedies.[58] The narrator's intention is to promote a feminine perspective of the nation's historical, political, geographical, and religious trajectories through the centuries, and she accomplishes this goal through a discourse that emanates from a female-driven perspective. This textual voice focuses on experiences that are exclusively female, featuring famous Dominican women freedom fighters, martyrs known and unknown, who, by their actions and initiatives, fought for, died for, and built the nation. While women of all ethnic backgrounds appear, a substantial part of the poem focuses on the independence struggles of the nineteenth century and the anti-imperialist sentiment of the early twentieth.

The poem is chronological and historically driven, as years, personages, wars, and struggles are clearly outlined. The narration repeats the classic tale of the Americas—discovery, colonization, annihilation, enslavement, independence, neocolonialism, and imperialism—with the difference that it is all from a female perspective, taking into account all the women who lived, suffered, perished, and triumphed for the cause as patriots. The narrating voice achieves a transference of poetic energies and references from male-dominated action, mechanisms that reveal the voices, actions, ideas, bodies, and emotions of the numerous women, named and unnamed, whose stories and versions of the nation's glories and tragedies were never a part of the country's documented history.

How can one read the role of the female figure within the elaboration of historical and national identity that these verses propose? The subversion of historical male-dominated voicing becomes possible by way of the employment of Mother Earth, signifier of Indigenous and African female interactions at all levels, emphasizing mental, physical, and sexual trauma because of the invading, domineering, European male subject. The poetic enterprise has as its main anchor the *tierra*, the land, and personification allows this element to operate as the central humanizing presence destined to experience and bear all human enterprise and action whether in suffering or in celebration. The land is nurture, nature, maternal protection, womanhood, eternal witness, a feeling and thinking being, and an enduring victim that bears the brunt of all human endeavor. By a process of absolute personification, Yania is the very land that is possessed and dominated, and she does not remain silent. In the poem, compromising images of capture, subjugation, and rape illustrate historical processes of extreme violence and, by implication, direct the idea of Yania to include all women and especially the historical experiences of the *dominicanas*. Yania becomes the ultimate omniscient presence that is both absolute witness and absolute victim, for her destiny is to bear the complete exposure and be the receptor of the total sum of experiences that humanity carves out on her.

The narrator is in continuous indirect dialogue with her unfathomable interlocutor, Cojito, whose reactions appear throughout the text in uppercase and whose responses are the voice of social and moral consciousness that force us to contemplate humankind's destructiveness, weaknesses, vulnerabilities, and numerous indiscretions. Mariana Past describes Cojito as "a heroic but demoralized native prototype, insufficiently strong to effect social change."[59] He is, by virtue of physical deformity, helpless; his power and might are in his devastating words, through which he provokes and demands renewed consciousness. He remains at the level of commentator, a reminder of dramatic historic events; his responses are short, direct, unforgiving, and harsh, oftentimes a kind of reading between the lines displayed in tones of condemnation and disgust, punctuated with postmodern jargon.

The poem's design is chronological, following the paths of the three major Caribbean-Dominican ethnic groups: the Indigenous inhabitants, or *taínos*; the Spanish colonizers; and the African slaves. The female-focused interpretation of history has a debilitating effect on the overall images of male instigators, depicting them as violent and destructive beings—constant violators of land, cultures, and women—a clear subversion of the glorified conquistador as builder of empires in the Americas. At the same time, even while writing an epic poem in homage to the nation's brave women, at times, Portalatín seems incapable of doing what she set out to do—that is, ignore masculine historical action. This remains intact through moments of male bellicose vigor and victory that are enabled by female fighters, wives, daughters, and mothers possessing equal or more passionate convictions. Ideological shifts in several verses reveal the underlying difficulty of telling the female story, (her)story. This other story, when placed alongside that of her nation, creates a display of fusions and separations, one that seems to have more to narrate about Hispanic Dominican female legacy than those pertinent to the Indigenous and African women.

In light of this, Past's interpretation, which limits total empowerment to marginalized voices, seems accurate.[60] The value of this poetic rendition is its ability to make us rethink traditional historical versions of "Columbus discovered America" stories and, through Portalatín verses, realize that the sacredness of the history of the Americas is debunked simply because if female subjects had been the colonizers and had written those first chronicles, those stories would have been different. *Yania Tierra* boosts our ability to dignify the Afro-descendant woman by simple inclusion even as actual voicing (i.e., her ability to speak) is not guaranteed or successfully achieved. The poem does not resolve the tension between Dominicanness and Haitianness; it reinforces notions of Dominican sovereignty and does seem to situate the African and Indigenous female subjects within the past rather than envision them also as part of contemporary spaces.

Verses do not avoid illustrating the inherited Dominican difficulty of interfacing with Haiti while dealing with its own troubled inherited African identity, issues that work on two levels: first, the Haitian-Dominican (and/or Dominican-Haitian) experience in the Dominican Republic, and second, the Afro-Dominican legacy from slavery to modernity. Studies continue to reiterate the historical and ethnonational tensions that persist between these two countries.[61] Past identifies this legacy as an inescapable truth from which Portalatín is not immune. Past uses the words "enduring anxiety" to describe the problem that surfaces in *Yania Tierra* because of Portalatín's tones of nationalism.[62] Equally problematic is the continuing inability to recognize that Blackness and Haitianness are one and the same.

Past continues to criticize Portalatín for seeing the former as exclusively historical and the latter as political-territorial, this in spite of claiming that the land is also reflective of such heritage: "If she is sensitive overall to issues of slavery and race, and elsewhere recognizes the African roots of Dominican society, then why does her celebration of Yania, the 'mother' of Hispaniola, exhibit prejudice toward the border between the Dominican Republic and Haiti?"[63]

The narrating voice in *Yania Tierra* is firm and clear in its historical overview and patriotic sentiment, positions that, in Past's opinion, undermine Portalatín's distinction as a major Dominican literary voice capable of manifesting condemnation of the anti-Haitian sentiment for which her country is famous. No direct references to the country's relationship with Haiti appear in the poem; rather, patriotic gestures of love for land and nation abound. *Yania Tierra* is not a good place to confirm Portalatín's position regarding the relationship between the two countries. Nor can it serve to confirm the way said poet values Blackness or the African legacy that is undeniably an indelible part of her nation's ethnic and cultural composition. Her essays in *Culturas africanas* and her other literary pieces are testaments to her political racialized consciousness, and their inclusion in the analysis of this poem helps clarify the extent of her dedication to Africa and Black identity. Within the poem, emotional verses portraying love of the motherland inevitably bear politicized tones rejecting Haitian historical domination, the racialized effects of which we witness to date.

The ideological intention here is specific: it is woman-centered and feminist, part of a larger nationalist-driven sentiment to speak on behalf of all the ethnic groups of women who are subjects in Portalatín's epic poem. This poet seeks to subvert the vision of the nation as a male-dominated arena by replacing it with a female agenda and initiative. In this sense, the poetic process remains worthy, for it transfers woman from "other" to center. Portalatín's nationalistic agenda dictates that she will move subtly and openly against the enemies of her nation, and the two biggest ones are Haiti and the United States. Having said that, within the sphere of literary womanhood, she has revealed herself to be very much aware of how distinctive the experiences are for each ethnic group of women. *Yania Tierra* is not meant to focus on any one specific ethnic group of women; rather, it is a homage to them all, and as we proceed closer to modernity, it reflects the dominant role that Hispanic women (the poem identifies them as white) increasingly play from the nineteenth century forward. It is a projection whose subtext will confirm the historical disappearance of the *taína* [Arawak] woman figure by force of ethnic cultural annihilation and the exclusion of the Afro-descendant woman from the process of political formation and development. The narrating voice's identification of five ethnic classes of women lines up with the vision this nation has of its ethnic composition and uses Cojito, the cripple, to rejoice in and lament it:

GRITA EL COJITO CON ALEGRIA Y PENA
INDIAS / NEGRAS / BLANCAS / MESTIZAS /

MULATAS / LAS AMAN LA JUSTICIA Y EL
AMOR CON RESPETO ¡VENID!

[THE CRIPPLE CRIES WITH JOY AND SORROW
INDIAN WOMEN / BLACK WOMEN / WHITE WOMEN / MESTIZO
    WOMEN /
MULATTO WOMEN / JUSTICE AND LOVE WITH RESPECT
LOVE THEM. COME!][64]

The poem's free verse has no persistent pattern for arranging its stanzas. At times, there may even appear to be no stanzas, as the lines of verse follow each other without a sense of planned format or specific structure, continuing at least until that section of symbolic historical narrating comes to an end. Such a layout is purposeful, an integral part of configuring another historical perspective, one that is female-generated without being homogeneous—projecting from a multitude of places, events, and voices. A single female narrating voice guides the eclectic nature of the verses, within which we find two main processes: first, descriptions about all human activity on Yania's land, and second, the interpretation that Cojito gives to certain situations, the latter sections always appearing in uppercase writing. The historic and contemporary state of the Black woman's legacy appears intermittently, included in the African historical trauma. Each of the three female ethnic experiences is on an equal footing, a contribution to the overall national historical legacy. Past describes Portalatín as a Dominican mulatto feminist writer who brings these three female ethnic experiences into the fold equally and seems to be advocating for strength in numbers.[65] The narrating persona is the voice of Yania Earth as she condemns the spectrum of male racial types, inheritors of the earth, for not working hard enough to ensure peace and prosperity for all. She addresses them directly, blaming them for the shameful death of peace.[66]

In keeping with her vision of Dominicans as a multiracial people, Portalatín makes a distinction between Black and mulatto identities (she uses *mulatto* and *mestizo* interchangeably). She legitimizes Afro-Dominicanness as a separate eth-noracial identity that runs parallel to mainstream mulatto-Dominicanness, which she recognizes as the true national identity resulting from African and Hispanic ancestral fusions. Her rebuke blames all racial types who have inherited the earth for not being able to work together, although the deeper intent seems to be to launch the ultimate culpability of warfare and destruction on the overall dom-ineering male presence. The generalized yet targeted and generic "usted Señor Usted" [you Sir You] is clearly to lay blame, a direct move against white masculine historical power accused of simply not allowing peace to reign.[67] The encompassing intention of the message, while seeking to resolve the exclusion of African and Indigenous historical voicing by placing them next to each other, at least in this section, eradicates poetry's ability to openly declare the debilitating processes of subjugation suffered by these two peoples that rendered them absolutely excluded from power sharing. Blaming them for not collaborating with each other in the name of peace implies that they had opportunities to partake in decision-making, which they did not.

The enslavement of Africans along with the annihilation of the island's Indigenous populations constitute the dark stain that completely negates any historical value that could possibly be attributed to the original project of civilization. In scathingly ironic tones, the narrator debunks any historical intention of worth simply by confirming that the humanitarian cost far outweighed the benefits. Any original benevolent action was soon lost in the plunder and avarice to satisfy a thirst for material wealth. The depiction of those in bondage in the poem serves as adornment for the idea of Spanish colonizing power and enrichment. Supporting poetic condemnation of such materialism, numerical references appear in various moments in the poem representing statistics of ships, number of slaves, years, and European accumulated wealth. The separation of the numbers is intentional, as it reinforces the magnitude of specific events, years, and the vast number of human lives destroyed in the highly lucrative transatlantic enterprise.

The value of the numbers continues in the repeated presentation of "400" as a painful reminder that the process of territorial and ethnic subjugation lasted at least four hundred years.[68] On December 25, 1492, Christopher Columbus lost the largest of his three ships during his first voyage. The *Santa María* ran aground and sank on what is today known as Cap-Haïtien, Haiti. Verses scorn the European mania of painting nobility in all of its splendor and using images of enslaved women as part of its artistry. Such images reinforce the status of humans as commodities and confirm the cultivation of historical exoticism visible in paintings and early writings used to record the history of the Americas. The poem berates the colonizer's slave trading commerce as exploitative, an ambitious business enterprise specifically for self-aggrandizement and enrichment, even as it emphasizes the emotional impact on Mother Earth and on human lives:

ARDE LA TIERRA La Colonia . . .
EN la Plaza Mayor
Subastan a los esclavos negros
Los negociadores de vida

¡Puñetero negocio!

[THE LAND BURNS The Colony . . .
IN the Main Plaza
The merchants of lives
Auction off Black slaves

Filthy business!][69]

The imagery of slavery punctuates the text throughout, as further seen in "El negro explotado como bestia" [The Black man exploited like a beast].[70] The graphic reminders of enslavement's agony reproduce the colonizer's order of historical representation when it comes to the Afro-descendant legacy in the Americas. The extent to which female voicing resonates through these verses continues to be questionable.

The poetic version of the Ginés sisters' story begins in a fiery blaze as the narrating voice continues to strategically design images of trauma in relation to Africa's role in the configuration of the Americas. She equates her vision of the colony with hell on earth, effectively returning to her theme of the land that she describes as burning, on fire. Her imagery, by design, zooms in on the transatlantic commerce as maritime trafficking, and the system of enslavement moves full steam ahead, the driving force that will compel the African presence and suffering in the Americas. The main elements are there: Africa; the slave ships from Spain, Portugal, Holland, and England; and the vessels from Africa arriving in the colonies. The next image takes us to the main square, the venue for all the major slave auctions. No specific town is identified, as this event was, for centuries, an integral part of the daily routine among slave societies in the Americas. In short verses, two sets of participants appear, the slaves on the auction block and their captors, "los negociadores de vidas" [the merchants of lives].[71] The narrating voice expresses absolute disgust as she initiates the recognition of the legacy to which the Ginés sisters belong:

> ¡Puñetero negocio!
> Venden al abuelo y al padre de
> Teodora y Micaela Ginés
> Esclavas
> luego libertas en
> Santiago de los Caballeros
> Antes de 1580 residentes en Cuba
> Las dos primeras damas músicas
> en aquel territorio.

> [Filthy business!
> They sell the grandfather and father of
> Teodora and Micaela Ginés
> Female slaves
> later freed in
> Santiago de los Caballeros
> Residents of Cuba before 1580
> The first two lady musicians
> in that territory.][72]

The verses focus on confirming a legacy of three generations of enslavement as unsavory business during colonization. This is a story about those first generations of Africans and their direct descendants, the earlier periods of colonial occupation during the early sixteenth century. The sisters are the direct inheritors of the trauma into which they are born, appearing as children and grandchildren of slaves, their grandfather and father having suffered the humiliation of capture, the Middle Passage, and the auction block. The verses reconstruct where history does not, inventing a family line for them; they had parents, grandparents, and an original home, all of which they lost or never knew. The descriptions establish a clear paternal line from Africa and confirm their status as Dominican, born into slavery, residing there and later freed, all prior to 1580, evidence that Portalatín was inspired by available historical documentation. A loud silence appears in the absence of their mother and grandmothers, one that is a continuation of history's deficiency in relation to the African female and her immediate descendants. Even the artistry of creating verses could not design or imagine such a presence for the sisters. Portalatín, driven by available information, felt secure in establishing paternal lineage but had nothing to work with for a similar attempt on the maternal side.

In light of such initial difficulty, the sisters appear as accomplished achievers whose intriguing life stories are worthy of inclusion in the group of heroines assembled for this accolade. The quality of their role as musicians is further elevated because of their misfortune of being born into slavery. Information about their talent, training, and contact with music growing up has evaporated over time; however, we can imagine that talent was a factor in light of the rudimentary, rustic nature of colonial life during the sixteenth century. Poetic narration repeats their biographical information, associating Micaela with Havana and Teodora with the Oriente province while describing them as instrumentalists, players of the *bandola* and the vihuela. Poetry acknowledges as undisputed their talents and roles as performers and lines them up with the "Son de la Ma' Teodora," which is fully cited in Portalatín's poem.[73] This two-page segment is the only moment when the Black female subject appears in association with creativity and initiative, busy at positive human endeavor and a contributor to the birth of a new nation. The process of attributing some form of merit to their achievements is ongoing. Even as historic academic argumentations and cultural self-questioning continue, the prestige that these sisters possess remains simply because the idea of who they might have been has survived the test of time.

PART II

A Nicaraguan Case Study

In honor of Elizabeth Forbes Brooks,
affectionately known as Miss Lizzie (1922–2021)

CHAPTER 3

Tracing the Dance Steps
of a "British" Subject

MISS LIZZIE'S *PALO DE MAYO*

Nicaraguan literature pays homage to Elizabeth Forbes Brooks (Miss Lizzie) and
Mayaya, two feminine forces—one real, the other mythical, both deeply inter-
connected. Substantial credit goes to Miss Lizzie for taking the initiative in what
can be described as a modern-day resuscitation of the *palo de mayo* [May Pole] in
a way that has made it meaningful beyond mere entertainment and performance.
In carnival, music, dance, and poetry, Mayaya, the goddess of rain, harvest, and
fertility, emerges as an integral part of the *palo de mayo* performance ritual, the
latter restored to its former glory in large part due to Miss Lizzie. *Maestra* [school-
teacher], *palo de mayo* dance instructor, and storyteller, here stands Miss Lizzie, a
distinguished matriarch of Bluefields, the Caribbean Creole town situated on the
Atlantic coast of Nicaragua. Alfonso Malespín Jirón's description of her is justified:

> Es la dama de la cultura. Esbelta, derecha, derecha como una palmera que ha
> vencido los vientos del Caribe por más de ocho décadas, de caminar elegante,
> como la bailarina que realmente es, de ademanes que reflejan su educación
> anglosajona, dueña de un liderazgo comunitario a prueba de huracanes, esta
> maestra de generaciones es venerada en Bluefields como su mejor experta en
> asuntos del Palo de Mayo.

> [She's the lady of culture. Slender, erect, upright like a palm tree that has with-
> stood the winds of the Caribbean for more than eight decades, of elegant gait,
> like the ballerina she truly is, with mannerisms that reflect her Anglo-Saxon
> upbringing, possessing a community leadership capacity to withstand hurri-
> canes, this schoolteacher who taught generations is revered in Bluefields as their
> best expert on matters regarding May Pole.][1]

Miss Lizzie refers to the *palo de mayo* as part of Creole folklore and insists
that community efforts continue to recover and preserve its original forms.[2] For
decades, her innovative choreography found inspiration in original versions of the
May Pole, often quite different from contemporary dance styles and performances,

known for their excessive gyrations and sensuality of movement. I propose Miss Lizzie's *palo de mayo* as a site of identity formation, heritage transformation, and poetic innovation, one that adds another story to the emerging profile of the Afro-descendant woman in Latin America. By way of her efforts and enthusiasm, it became symbolic of inspirational creativity and historical revival while highlighting the founding neighborhoods of Cotton Tree, Pointeen, Old Bank, and Beholden that together constituted the original town of Bluefields.[3] Today, Bluefields remains the centerpiece of the region, an enclave of Anglophone and Afro–Caribbean Nicaraguan cultural identities and expressions.

Over time, a modern *palo de mayo* movement emerged under Miss Lizzie's guidance, and for more than forty years (starting during the 1960s), she was its driving force. She appears at the heart of this discussion as a medium, offering insight into the way the European May Pole ritual, Caribbean-based folklore, and Creole literary production have merged. She was at the center of the movement from the beginning, a matriarchal figure, guide, teacher, and potentially stabilizing force within a community that was deeply impacted by the pressures of modernization. As the symbolic original founder, her *palo de mayo* adaptations using Caribbean (Creole) songs, rhythms, dance, and percussion instruments rekindled her community's pride and provided guidance toward greater appreciation of their heritage at a time when many such customs and traditions were fading. Her efforts have served to remind the people of Bluefields and the surrounding municipalities of their Creole, West Indian, Caribbean, European, and African roots. Miss Lizzie managed to rally her community around an ancient practice and, through organized performances, gained substantial national attention. Arguably, she became a significant force, strategic for promoting reunification at a time when it was much needed. Her dance groups introduced Nicaragua to the fact that there was a diverse Caribbean culture within its territories. Miss Lizzie's *palo de mayo* proved powerful for the way it has supported the difficult task of easing tensions that have always existed among the Indigenous peoples, Creoles, Garifuna, and Afro-descendants of the autonomous Caribbean coast, on the one hand, and the nation's majority mestizo-Hispanic and Pacific coast population, on the other. Miss Lizzie's image and her Bluefieldian version of *palo de mayo* are alive and well thanks to a solid collection of literary anthologies, studies about the community, Miss Lizzie's biography, a short documentary, and her interviews. Central to this discussion is her memoir, *Memorias de Miss Lizzie: Danzas, música y tradiciones de Bluefields* (2011), as well as four Caribbean-Creole anthologies: *Poesía atlántica* (1980), *Antología poética de la Costa Caribe de Nicaragua* (1998), *Antología poética "Afrocarinica"* (2011), and *Bluefields en la sangre* (2011).[4]

What constitutes Afro-descendancy in a place like Bluefields? What references serve to understand Miss Lizzie's trajectory while creating the profile of a potential heroine whose legacy remains with her people? The town of Bluefields has a distinctive character due in part to a number of elderly personages whose lives are documented as dating back to the 1950s and earlier.[5] Miss Lizzie is a part of this legacy; indeed, older folk like Mrs. Rose recall her as a young, dedicated teacher who loved the art of dance. The respect and homage Miss Lizzie has received as one of the region's remarkable teachers is matched only by the way she remains the point of reference for all things *palo de mayo* in Bluefields. An image of her emerges— a woman of firm and disciplined nature, a dance and movement expert, an activist for children and youth, campaigning to keep them away from drugs and in school, among others. She was immediately recognized in the streets, umbrella in hand, agile step, always busy; indeed, everyone knew her. A full-time teacher at home and in her community, she encouraged constant learning and self-development and guided many students who later became pillars of their community.[6]

Miss Lizzie unveils the coast as a colonial subject in a postcolonial context. A proud British heritage speaker, she capably navigates multiple forms of being, the results of ongoing historical and migratory shifts. She is from the Caribbean coast; she is also Creole and Bluefieldian, dwells in the Beholden neighborhood, is a product of Nicaragua's Sandinismo, and loves her town and motherland. Bluefields and the surrounding region are home to a specific population identifying as Creoles. Lizandro Chávez Alfaro confirms that *Creole* refers to a person of African ancestry who speaks English.[7] They are descendants of enslaved Africans and British colonizers, a people who trace their roots back to the Caribbean islands while currently dwelling in a predominantly Hispanic and mestizo space.[8] Edmund Gordon recognizes their role as the "torchbearer of English civilization on the coast," positioned to take leadership in this Atlantic region.[9] While, for the purposes of this study, Miss Lizzie emerges as the driving force behind the preservation of *palo de mayo* in Bluefields, this art form is by no means attributed to one person. It unfolds as a collective phenomenon that has, over time, taken on a life of its own. Miss Lizzie stands for pride, memory, and Creole presence even as her *palo de mayo* provides a gateway to contemplate modern-day transformations and challenges. An aura of respect and appreciation has solidified images of her as the symbol of this particular place and identity, even as she cannot necessarily keep abreast with the inevitable changes and fissures that constitute life today.

Afro-Nicaraguan identity has become a theme in some of the town's best literary productions, mostly from Creole and Creole-identified writers who design verses about *palo de mayo*, Nicaraguan nationhood, West Indian legacy, Caribbean coastal autonomy, Christianity, and Black struggles—over all, a spirited literary display that reflects who they are as a people. Their specific trajectory as members of Atlantic coastal communities is in a relationship of tension-reconciliation with the central government in the capital, Managua. This did not necessarily change during the Nicaraguan Revolution. Studies confirm Sandinista efforts to rescind the isolating and marginalizing effects suffered by *costeños* [coastal dwellers] even as the latter take extreme pride in their cultural differences. For the Creole population, the larger objective of encouraging greater cultural understanding among peoples by way of the *palo de mayo* is underpinned by the Bluefieldian conviction of their deep, unique history and earned rights to cultural and political autonomy.[10] The Miss Lizzie *palo de mayo* phenomenon clearly illustrates this process of creolization, or the merging of contrasting cultural patterns that have shaped ancestral relationships originating in the Caribbean and their diaspora in places like Bluefields. Miss Lizzie's rekindling of community interest in May Pole dancing, known for its European origins and the way these blended with Caribbean folklore, reveals specific aspects about her lineage and family ties. Her personal trajectory and love of dancing, in relation to the region's ethnoracial diversity and political experiences, explain why she was successful.[11]

Guided by an innovative spirit and creativity, Miss Lizzie's *palo de mayo* illustrates what Gordon envisions as the two contrasting strands of Nicaraguan Creole identity useful for discerning the roots and evolution of a people with indelible ties to both strands—the Black and Anglophone.[12] The idea of Africa as the original motherland as well as the legacy of enslavement and its origins in Jamaica and other islands intertwine with British colonialism and North American capitalist-driven imperialism to create this heterogeneous, diasporic way of being. The *palo de mayo* was not exclusive to this area; it was practiced across Central America, South America, and the Caribbean in geographic locations that experienced some form of British imperial rule. The British presence on the Caribbean coast dates from 1633, when the first settlers arrived, to 1905, when Great Britain handed over administration of the region to U.S. companies, whose control lasted until 1930.[13] Miss Lizzie's efforts ensured the *palo de mayo*'s legitimacy and recognition as an authentic local cultural manifestation, especially during the Sandinista era and beyond. Government support of Miss Lizzie is clear in its endorsement of the bilingual publication *Memorias de Miss Lizzie: Danzas, música y tradiciones de Bluefields*: "The Government of Reconciliation and National Unity, through the Culture Institute of Nicaragua, INC in the framework of rescuing, validating, defending and promoting all of the traits of our identity and national culture, in its multiethnic expressions, languages and unique signs of the different people and races that constitute Nicaragua, is pleased to present the book, 'MISS LIZZIE MEMOIRS, Dances, music and traditions from Bluefields.'"[14]

This introductory acclaim is part of the official pronouncement prepared by Luis Enrique Morales Alonso, then codirector of the Nicaragua Institute of Culture, in recognition of the iconic status Miss Lizzie achieved; indeed, she became emblematic of Caribbean Nicaraguan traditions and the nation's diversity. The publishing of her memoir was a collaborative effort involving her family, key archivists and community intellectuals from Bluefields, collaborators, friends, and the Nicaragua Institute of Culture. Released in May 2011, it stands today as an official document of Creole heritage and is potentially indicative of a spirit of goodwill between the government and the Caribbean coast, a region that has always insisted on its cultural distinction and fought for its political autonomy. Miss Lizzie's efforts seem to have worked as a form of mediation, winning over both sides of this clear divide full of tensions and possibilities: "We fulfill this promise with affection and love for Miss Lizzie Nelson, an exemplary woman, teacher of generations, and for whom we thank God she is still with us; we love and watch over her because she is our LIVING HUMAN TREASURE of the Caribbean and all of Nicaragua."[15]

Another long-standing member of the English-speaking Creole community, Reverend Rayfield Hodgson Bobb, who in November 2010 served as the president of the Regional Atlantic Autonomous Region Council, describes Miss Lizzie as his teacher, friend, counselor, and neighbor over a forty-year period. He cherishes the publication in her honor as an achievement that goes far beyond mere individual recognition, for it represents efforts to preserve the culture of the Caribbean coast. The memoir describes community customs and traditions that support an appreciation of Miss Lizzie's contributions; Hodgson Bobb observes that her influences were far reaching in both autonomous regions, the north and the south. She has accomplished a great mission in life and continues to receive accolades from many of the thousands of students she has taught over her long career. Hodgson Bobb defines her role as ambassadorial in terms of its careful wisdom and deep knowledge of the region's Indigenous cultures.[16] Miss Lizzie's own words reveal her purpose and commitment: "A struggle and the efforts to rescue and preserve the traditions of our beloved city of Bluefields. . . . It is my deepest desire and my hope that this book, 'Dance, music and traditions of Bluefields,' be of great benefit to all our coast people of the Caribbean Coast of Nicaragua and especially to our youth with the aim of starting to feel the need to know our city of Bluefields as how it was before, and the traditions of our ancestors."[17]

Her pronouncement reflects the ongoing quest to preserve the Creole legacy. A loss of oral traditions such as storytelling and a prevailing disinterest in local history and the wisdom of the elderly, especially among the youth, are her motivating factors. Cotton Tree, her neighborhood, has seen many changes, some of which have merged with the influences of materialism and globalization that seem to encourage the abandonment of teachings from the past as well as ancestral traditions. In a later interview, she discusses this concern, associating it with a broader national misinterpretation of who they are as a people, especially given that her largely Hispanic nation struggles to understand the *palo de mayo*.[18] Hugo Sujo Wilson shares her preoccupation with cultural loss and confirms this as the primary reason behind his *Oral History of Bluefields*. A respected educator and renowned historian, his testimonies are valuable for understanding their legacy as Afro-descendants. Both representatives of a generation born during the early decades of the twentieth century, Miss Lizzie and Sujo Wilson have observed how more recent generations are distant from or unfamiliar with their history, rich customs and traditions, positive influences, and folklore. Many customs have disappeared from daily life and are now available only in the memories and memoirs of the older generations.[19]

Miss Lizzie's deep desire was for the residents of Bluefields to always be aware of their rich heritage of May Pole, Ribbon Pole, and ballroom dances; indeed, her memoir captures how she felt driven to bring these traditions forward into the modern day in spite of the cultural confrontations they were likely to provoke or the serious competition they faced as younger generations enjoyed different dance movements. She was on a mission of recovery and restoration, and as the leading dance instructor, she displayed insightfulness and wisdom, having lived through numerous transformations within the original neighborhoods. She remained alert to their deficiencies—poverty, isolation, poor infrastructure, and lack of educational opportunity, among others. Corrosive and damaging, these factors have tended to block the community's memory of its rich ancestral customs, reducing everyone's ability to envision prosperity. She decided that she wanted to combat these debilitating effects using dance: "This small contribution of cultural rescue is dedicated to all the ones that love to promote our culture, for them to know not only the dances but also the history of each one of them."[20]

Chávez Alfaro confirms that Creole speakers tend to adhere to the Protestant faith, an inheritance from British colonization.[21] The Anglican missionaries arrived around 1833, followed some sixteen years later by the Moravian missionaries transferred from Jamaica, who acculturated the local population in Bluefields, drawing them away from various African-based traditions and forms of expression that were deemed evil. Their task was twofold: disseminate the message of the Bible and, through schooling, establish English as the primary language.[22] They were successful in their mission of cultural assimilation, as by 1860, the level of education attained by Creoles made them the dominant community in the region.[23] Processes of religious indoctrination accompanied specific political strategies implemented to maintain the region under some form of Anglophone control. The 1860 Treaty of Managua, signed between Nicaragua and Great Britain, represented the official recognition of Nicaraguan sovereignty while preserving the historical rights of the Atlantic coast and the Indigenous Miskito peoples, even as the former colonizers retained control within this region. However, the governing body known as the Miskito Court, established to administer the area, had already begun to reflect Creole political and administrative dominance.[24] Studies describe attempts to remove the British presence and reclaim national control over the Caribbean coast, a region rich in natural resources. In 1894, government troops initiated the process of reincorporating the Caribbean lowlands, thereby preparing the way for increased North American investment and presence in the area. There was an armed uprising and resistance involving the Creole population of Bluefields that was quickly quelled. On October 29, 1894, the first municipal council of Bluefields was established, headed by two American businessmen, J. Weinberger as mayor and Samuel J. Weill as the first town councilor.[25]

Studies seem to indicate that the May Pole was first introduced in Bluefields, later transforming into a blend of different beliefs and practices that made the Nicaraguan version unique. An ancient European tradition, it probably made its way to the Mosquito coast between the seventeenth and nineteenth centuries, emerging during the early 1800s as the Creole population expanded. The economy of the Mosquito coast flourished during the 1830s, and following the 1834 emancipation of slaves in the British colonies, this culturally Anglophone, English-speaking community grew with the arrival of Black merchants from Jamaica and Afro-Caribbean migrants from the islands. May Day, the May Pole, and the Festival of May solidified and became traditions.[26] A change in perspective occurred in 1849, when the presence of the German Moravian Church had a negative impact on the celebrations. Both Moravian and Anglican doctrines sidelined Afro-descendant displays, labeling them as problematic and outside the moral and educational code of conduct established for their congregations.[27] Preachers discouraged the practices and influenced their transition away from the religious and into more secular spheres of traditions and customs associated with Blacks in the area.[28] Such religious imposition proved divisive, as many coastal dwellers abandoned traditional agricultural, medicinal, and ritual practices condemned by Moravians, while others did not. Other churches applied similar pressure for the next twenty-three years; the practice diminished to children's games and songs, disappearing almost entirely among adults. Pockets of resistance remained, as confirmed in a Moravian priest's letter written in 1874:

> Muchos cambios se han experimentado en la Mosquitia. . . . Anteriormente una costumbre inofensiva se mantenía en el mes de mayo. . . . De esta inocente práctica placentera ha derivado un baile en que participan jóvenes y adultos durante las noches de luna con una bullaranga pagana y conducta muy inapropiada lo cual debe ser completamente descontinuado.

> [Many changes have taken place on the Mosquito Coast. . . . Previously, a harmless custom used to be practiced in the month of May. . . . From this innocent, delightful practice, a dance has emerged among young people and adults on full moon nights, with a pagan, rowdy crowd and very inappropriate behavior, which should absolutely be discontinued.][29]

Those who resisted the church's efforts to eliminate the practice stood firm, clinging to their beliefs and becoming even more radical in their practices. The pagan beliefs and corporal movements that accompanied the original European practice as well as the versions that evolved in the Americas were used as building blocks for songs and dances that cultivated themes and at times frenetic movements associated with sexuality, lovemaking, and fertility. At the same time, there were adult groups that retained earlier versions of the May Pole by way of their formal dress, movements, and British English–inspired songs. From this moment onward, there were two visions of the *palo de mayo*: one that clung to the colonial legacy and another that thrived on creativity and improvisation.[30] The latter, more rebellious version would undoubtedly have been the one that chose to incorporate local Indigenous, traditional, and African elements into its design, finding favor among folk who were deferential to their ancestral origins. In her interview with Alfonso Malespín Jirón, Miss Lizzie helps us understand the successful survival of the dance insofar as she explains where the towns held their festivities. Normally, they chose open spaces that were close to the towns. In Bluefields, they used to gather in a place called Long Field, near the predominantly Creole neighborhood of Beholden, a site for community entertainment now only in the memories of elderly folk. Music was provided by three men playing the drum, the donkey jawbone, and the grater. Back then, there were no radios, so the villagers were summoned by word of mouth and arrived laden with fruit and alcohol. The festivity was not

without salacious dance moves. Miss Lizzie associates the birth and expansion of
the dance with Cotton Tree, the neighborhood that was home to some of the best-
known dancers, musicians, and personalities connected with the art. This practice
died when those open spaces became unavailable, as they were private property.
No other public venue remained available, not even in Beholden, the neighborhood
with the largest number of Blacks.[31]

Miss Lizzie's Memoir: In the Words of the Matriarch

Miss Lizzie's pronouncement is indicative of her passion for music and commitment to her people and their culture: "I especially dedicate this effort to . . . all
the dancers, along with my much dedicated musicians, because each one of them
mentioned here participated in one way or another in the dance and the fulfillment
of this rescue."[32] How did Miss Lizzie move against the tide and resuscitate this
dying legacy? How did she gain the trust and respect of others, become the voice
of her people, and assume a leadership role in Bluefields? Her memoir, *Memorias
de Miss Lizzie: Danzas, música y tradiciones de Bluefields*, reinforces the idea that
traditions are a part of who she is, and her achievements have to be understood
in close connection with her beloved Bluefields: "The friends who had knowledge
about the environment where I grew up, and about my dancing abilities stimulated
me to contribute with this document to rescue the almost forgotten traditions
of our ancestors."[33] She has received recognition at the highest level in her community, visible, for example, in the homage paid to her at the Universidad de las
Regiones Autónomas de la Costa Caribe Nicaragüense (URACCAN) campus.[34] A
portrait of her hangs in the library with the following caption: "Ivy Elizabeth Forbes
Brooks. 'Miss Lizzy Nelson.' Mujer Kriol de Bluefields (Nació en 1921). Profesora
de la Costa Caribe Nicaragüense. Promotora inolvidable de la revitalización de la
cultura e historia Kriola a través de la danza del palo de mayo y/o palo encintado"
[Ivy Elizabeth Forbes Brooks. "Miss Lizzy Nelson." Creole woman from Bluefields
(Born in 1921). Teacher from the Nicaraguan Caribbean Coast. Unforgettable
promoter of the revitalization of Creole history and culture by way of the May
Pole and/or Ribbon Pole dance].[35]

Miss Lizzie descends from a long and rich family legacy, herself prone to longevity; one of her grandmothers and a cousin lived to be more than one hundred
years old, while one of her previous dancing companions was a ninety-eight-year-
old relative. Professionally very successful, her career as a teacher at the Moravian
school spans at least four decades. Music and dance are in her blood, for she is the
daughter of a dancer with roots in Graytown and a Honduran guitar player whose
forefathers were Colombian. As an adolescent, she was surrounded by music at
home, and she dreamed of having her own dance group, which she accomplished
outstandingly well.[36] She confirms that she grew up in a home where music and
performance were a priority and with a mother who was a great influence on her
children because she had belonged to the British Dance Company and danced
the quadrille, a British square dance. Their home had a gramophone that played

records, and her father and brother played the guitar. She recalls that they also learned a Scottish dance that they called *chotize* and Danish polka.[37] She fell in love with the art and started performing at a young age, even though, oftentimes, her mother exercised tight control over her attendance at weddings, receptions, and parties, a fact that proved annoying. Very much aware of the expected norms of comportment for proper, well-raised young girls, her mother provided protection from the scandal and derogatory public opinion that went along with attending or dancing at public events. These restrictions fueled Miss Lizzie's determination to dance even more.[38]

Her passion for dance, Protestant upbringing, and Christian-based education resulted in Miss Lizzie's May Pole enterprise. A dignified presence, her professional code of conduct, combined with a deep understanding of her community, allowed her to perceive the *palo de mayo*'s potentially enriching effect. Her choreography revealed a plan that has contributed to the well-being of Bluefieldian life by connecting today's descendants to their forefathers and mothers. Miss Lizzie's strategy of preservation through teaching, mentoring, activism, and performance elevated her status to a local and international cultural envoy for the Atlantic coast who marketed the region's unique traits strategically. As one of the most respected elders of her community, she embodies the memory of her family and previous generations.[39] She became the symbol of the Caribbean coast, summoned to enlighten the rest of the country about her people through the beauty of the *palo de mayo*; in fact, her creative artistry attracted choreographers from the Pacific coast seeking her skills and knowledge about the secrets to executing this now famous coastal dance.[40]

As a strong and capable champion, Miss Lizzie expanded the reach and value of her undertaking, confirmed in the way it allowed her to execute, at multiple levels, a kind of advocacy that proved to be successful, touching many lives across the region.[41] She rose to prominence within a space that did not have many Afro-descendant female icons. Gordon complements this discussion historically by confirming that during the pre-Sandinista era, Creoles and other *costeños* were likely to suffer institutional racism and marginalization in government sectors and as professionals.[42] Particularly striking are their experiences as Creole English speakers; Deborah Robb Taylor, as well as Evett Keyla Herbbert Kelly and Thomas Hodgson, confirm the challenges women continue to face today as they strive for increased political prominence and leadership within their communities, for while the Creole community acknowledges male leadership, the same cannot be said for women.[43] Within the broader context of the nation, when compared with mestizo women, Creole women are more often targets of discrimination and sexism. Within their communities, they remain highly vulnerable to acts of machismo by Creole men as well as subject to narrow perceptions of their capacity to lead.[44]

Feminist, writer, and researcher on Creole women and development Socorro Woods Downs calls attention to the devastating impact that aspects such as negative views of Black women's hair, the subordinating effects of Moravian and Protestant religious doctrines, domestic violence, and the stigma of speaking

Creole have on women.[45] At the same time, she points out that women have always organized and created associations and entities that serve them well as safe spaces ideal for developing leadership skills, supporting one another through difficulties, promoting socioeconomic enrichment, and ensuring cultural preservation.[46] Gordon provides evidence of the mobilization of Creole women around themes of politics and identity by referring to the Young Women's Union, an organization in existence since the early 1900s and one of the few spaces for such interaction that was public and nonreligious.[47] In Miss Lizzie's case, she dealt with challenges that women have to face in order to overcome difficulties, earn community respect, and achieve results. Political and professional arenas in Bluefields continue to be male-dominated, meaning that a woman who desires to run for public office or develop a larger community-based project will confront opposition. As the town's *maestra* and connoisseur of the performing arts, she used her influence and creativity to persuade women and their families to join her endeavors.

The *palo de mayo* is in synergy with community pride; its antidiscriminatory spirit is especially meaningful for Creole women who continue to feel the effects of being viewed as secondary citizens. Early in their lives, girls and young women were educated by their mothers to accept that their role was to take care of their husbands and families, a restricted upbringing that prepared them for subordinate roles and domesticity and taught them to expect limited opportunities. It reduced their self-confidence and barred their access to a complete education. It also limited their chances of professional development and significantly reduced their participation in all forms of public life outside the domestic sphere.[48] Miss Lizzie's projects served to revitalize the historical and educational value of certain musical, instrumental, and dance patterns. Performances brought children, young girls, and women to center stage, proud representatives in displays that served to counteract negative perceptions, phobias, and experiences of discrimination. These transformative and far-reaching efforts provided a new sense of self-worth, potentially helping female participants overcome sensations of inferiority in relation to mestizo women in areas such as education, the workforce, political office, and other public spaces.[49]

Through Miss Lizzie, we are cognizant of the linguistic and educational fabric of this coastal region. Born in the neighborhood of Cotton Tree, Bluefields, on December 11, 1922, she identifies as a Creole with some Indian heritage who speaks English, Spanish, and some Miskito. Her great-grandmother was of the Rama peoples, while her great-grandfather was William Hodgson from England. The descendants of their eight children continue to reside in neighborhoods such as Beholden, Cotton Tree, and Old Bank. Miss Lizzie's mother was Frida Brooks, married to Lewis Forbes, a Colombian from Cartagena. Miss Lizzie herself married Cecil Edmund Nelson from Pearl Lagoon.[50] Her parents made their home in Cotton Tree near the cemetery that was the final resting place of the first Moravian missionaries.

Miss Lizzie's first wish was to be a nurse; however, the financial circumstances of her parents made this impossible. Under the guidance and encouragement of her teachers, she decided to pursue a career as a schoolteacher even though her first love was to teach dance. There were many young people in her neighborhood who could not afford the cost of attending high school, so she also started to offer private tutoring, converting her house into a classroom. She recalls that her career began in Pearl Lagoon, a town of just under nine thousand inhabitants in the municipality with the same name, located north of Bluefields. Similar to Bluefields, the inhabitants are largely Creole, with some Garifuna and Miskito populations. *Palo de mayo* was also a traditional celebration there. By 1942, Miss Lizzie was married, a mother and teacher earning one hundred córdobas a month. Between 1942 and the 1960s, she taught in various locations along the Atlantic coast—Puerto Cabezas, Las Minas, and Bonanza. However, she considered Bluefields her home, and in 1950, she eventually returned there to become a teacher at the Moravian school. The influential Moravian Church was the driving force behind many outreach programs and social gatherings. She sang in the choir, served as a Sunday school teacher, and was an organizer of church-based activities. She entered the Teaching Profession School program for training to become a high school teacher. In 1957, she became director of the Moravian Church Primary School in Las Minas, Bonanza, a position she held for six years.[51]

Miss Lizzie rose to become a respectable *maestra* who taught English to generations of her community's inhabitants. Her perception of language as identity mirrors her approach to the performing arts, and for more than forty years, she engaged them similarly. She confirms that the interesting language and communication circumstances of her people meant that she often taught using a foreign-language teaching methodology; the Caribbean English or Creole oral forms commonly used when speaking meant that her students needed training when it came to writing English. Bluefieldians are known to declare that they speak Creole, a way of situating and affirming their linguistic and ethnocultural identity first and foremost. Given that the primary form of communication in the home was Creole, their relationship with Spanish was unique, troubling, often distant, even unsettling. Miss Lizzie's expertise and awareness proved invaluable as the struggles in both languages meant that oftentimes, her students could not speak (and therefore be well educated) in either language. An additional benefit was her training to teach English as a second language to Creole- and Spanish-speaking students. She appreciated the situation of her community's English- and Creole-speaking children, many born into socioeconomic difficulty—a sturdy folk, stubbornly proud, spontaneously resistant to Hispanic acculturation, assertive of their own history, ethnicity, and family values. The display of cultural defiance is also a mechanism of self-protection and cultural preservation, driven, on the one hand, by linguistic challenges (interpreted as deficiencies, even backwardness) and, on the other, by proud difference. Literary renditions manifest such complex and volatile linguistic tensions in the way various languages appear on the poet's page, with Creole as the central medium used to express what is most meaningful. Miss Lizzie's lived experiences align with the cultural intentionality that underpins such multilingual writings. Creole Nicaraguan poetry finds its true form and identity in the presence of Garifuna, Indigenous, Creole, Spanish, and English verses, a truly multilinguistic universe. Poems represent the region's Afro-coastal inhabitants (Creole and Garifuna) in ways that match the intentions of the region's matriarch and teacher; she treasured the legacy even as she perceived the added value of a quality education, which is why for years she taught "standard English."[52]

The general trend was that Bluefields's inhabitants were likely to be continuous users of Creole, while those who were better educated would also work to ensure the dominance of the "standard," a tendency resulting from a colonial indoctrination of inferiority that linked the Creole language to Blacks, people of color, limited schooling, backwardness, poverty, and so on. The ultimate desire among Caribbean folk was to align themselves with what they saw as refinement and prosperity. This intrinsic divide within the Creole English-speaking community deepened as community values, education systems, and codes of conduct intertwined with imported Protestant (Anglican, Moravian) religious doctrines due to church leaders who, upon arrival, eradicated aspects of the local heritage that detrimentally impacted their agenda.[53] Today, an effective countermeasure is to proudly reclaim one's origins, centering language and oral traditions as vital to an Afro-descendant legacy whose roots are in the islands, especially Jamaica. This celebratory reclaiming is visible in Miss Lizzie's *palo de mayo* and verses from June Beer and Carlos Rigby that seek to undo divisions, encouraging a deeper appreciation of all things Creole as unique.

Miss Lizzie's trajectory, albeit artistic, had its own political agency; indeed, she lived through two crucial moments that impacted the Caribbean coast politically— the move away from a predominantly Anglophone societal structure and the advent of Nicaragua's Marxist ideology, Sandinismo. A collaborator, she remained steadfast in her resolve to preserve her community's legacy irrespective of exigencies, preferences, or pressures that, at times, did not coincide with her hometown reality. During the early 1960s, while in Pearl Lagoon, she received a letter about an initiative by members of her neighborhood, including Hugo Sujo Wilson, Frank Hodgson, and Fred Kirkland. They had formed an association called the Organización Progresista Costeña [OPROCO; Organization in Pro of the Atlantic Coast] for the purpose of defending their rights as Caribbean peoples and safeguarding and promoting their way of life. Their right to autonomous rule, proud affirmation of Caribbean ancestry inspired in an identity politics of Garveyism, and cautious allegiance to the new waves of revolutionary resistance taking hold of the country would compose their struggles henceforth.[54] The letter she received expressed objection to imitation dances being performed in the Pacific that were not quite authentic or original, and it proposed an intervention. This initial request for Miss Lizzie to prepare and take a dance group to León drew her into the fold of OPROCO's politicized agenda, making it another outlet for advertising who they were, even as OPROCO had very few female members.[55] This was an important opportunity, for it represented their first invitation to showcase their heritage. She recalls that through her association with this movement, she was able to take some of her young dancers to León in 1962 and then later to Corinto: "With this mentality and dream of rescuing our ancestors' values, I put all my body and soul in the formation and training of the groups of different ages: 9, 12, and 15 to 20 years old, groups of adults and teachers, without thinking about a salary, expenses, adequate locations, etc., but the people and organizations such as OPROCO, Lions' Club, the Priests (Hermanos), supported me to get the job done and fulfill with this important event that was about to be forgotten and eliminated."[56]

Her collaboration with the Marxist state during the 1970s and the backing she received over the years are recorded in her memoir. She was inspired by the revolution, and she confirms her collaborations with the process and the revolutionary government's support of her: "In the years 1979–1980, I was immersed in cultural activities. I had three groups of dancers. After the triumph of the Sandinista Revolution, the Minister of Culture called me. They wanted to open a Cultural Center and they wanted to know how my dance groups could contribute. . . . I was pleased and went to meet him immediately; but I told him that if they wanted to maintain the tradition they had to allow me to have my own musicians and they agreed."[57] During the Sandinista rule, she coordinated the regional dance group at the Ivan Dixon Cultural Center, a position she used to expand her country's knowledge and appreciation of the dance.[58] Josef Hurtubise explains that June Beer and Carlos Rigby were also allies to the nation's revolutionary process.[59] It was under Sandinista rule that an acknowledgment of the nation's diversity seemed to be a welcome consideration in the state's agenda. The Creole language gained prominence, driven by writers who used it strategically: "Cuando los poetas criollos nicaragüenses escriben en criollo basilecto marcadamente distintivo, ellos se involucran en una celebración de la lengua y la cultura, que es muy propia" [When Nicaraguan Creole poets write in markedly distinctive Creole, they become involved in a celebration of language and culture that is very much their own].[60] June Beer's "Resarrection a' da wud" is a good example of Creole verse:

«dem wah nat deh brada keepa
Is deh brada killa
dem da de same wan
Who meh spit in Jesus face
an stone 'im too, on 'I' way to Calvary»

[«Those who are not their brother's keeper
Are their brother's killer
those are the same ones
Who spat in Jesus's face
and stoned him too, on his way to Calvary»][61]

Improvisation, flexibility, and adaptability characterize the Creole language, an effective transmitter for ring songs, chants, folk songs, and recitations. Such movement occurs with verses and music describing the goddess Mayaya, where each rendition is an innovative way of retelling the story through the ages—indeed, a powerful oral legacy. Names or popular idiomatic expressions appear dynamic, in constant motion, and the community embraces and engages the linguistic and literary varieties and instabilities. Hurtubise imagines a Creole language continuum that displays greater or lesser proximity to so-called standard English depending on the oral preferences at the time.[62] A spontaneous oral attribute makes the writing come alive, as it seems designed for storytelling and music.

FROM MAY POLE TO *PALO DE MAYO*: HISTORICIZING RITUALS

The roots of the May Pole rest with certain pagan and ritualistic village practices in the countryside of Europe. Miss Lizzie's knowledge of this heritage comes from written history, memories, and oral narratives passed down from generation to generation. The month of May represents blossoming, fertility, and nature's awakening, in recognition of which there used to be a Bluefieldian custom of celebrating birthdays with May Pole dances. It was widespread practice for ladies to appear dressed in headscarves and long skirts while dancing around a select tree trunk. They would continue by removing the trunk or pole and proceeding to the next venue in a joyful, high-spirited procession of music and dance, arms outstretched, clasping hands as a show of friendship—a veritable street gathering and festivity around the May Pole theme. Miss Lizzie and Sujo Wilson reminisce about those colorful street bacchanals for which Caribbean-originated peoples in Nicaragua are known and indicate that these displays continue today, but only as staged performances.[63]

Riding on influences of the past, a legacy of her European and Afro-Caribbean ancestors, Miss Lizzie identifies the display as an old British custom that dates back to Celtic pagan dances and that could have been transported to the Caribbean coast of Nicaragua. She mentions that older folk sometimes said that the May Pole was brought over by Africans. That there are multiple historical legacies of these Creole peoples means that the oral versions of their histories often either do not coincide or are motivated by familial and community historical preferences as they privilege their African and Caribbean legacies. Courtney Morris examines the implications of such multiple negotiable identities for the professional development and historical profiling of women by focusing on Madame Maymie Leona Turpeau de Mena, who, like Ms. Lizzie, self-identified as Afro-Nicaraguan and was a global advocate of Garveyism.[64] Sujo Wilson, Antonia McCoy, and Johnny Hodgson Deerings are the community's authors whose studies map the origins of this phenomenon in Nicaragua. They offer multiple perspectives, and their collected works function as a base upon which to better understand Miss Lizzie's reasoning in the following statement: "But like many things of our culture here on the coast, we cannot say that one ethnic group made this or that. May Pole is the expression of a mixed ethnic community and this mix is our biggest heritage. All those people came here and we took their dances and danced them our way."[65] The Bluefieldian *palo de mayo* of today is a reincarnation of similar ancient European rites that paid reverence to rebirth, fertility, and carnal pleasures. The presence of the tree or pole sustains humankind's reverence for nature, while the circular formation of the dancers around it reflects the human belief in the cycle of life, death, and rebirth.[66]

Miss Lizzie's timely resurrection provides a bridge between an Anglophone Protestant church-based colonial past and a heterogeneous present. Hodgson Deerings places its roots around 1849 with the establishment of the Moravian Church in Bluefields.[67] The May dances were to celebrate the end of the dry season, welcome the rains, and initiate the planting season. Other historical studies and oral traditions describe them as parts of customs and festivities on the Caribbean coast dating back more than three centuries. As part of his study reconstructing Bluefields's oral history, while reminiscing about the "good old days," Sujo Wilson reminds us of the May Pole's long-standing association with the town's original neighborhoods of Old Bank, Beholden, and Cotton Tree. He describes the dances as the initial part of popular public entertainment that ended with parades through the streets in a display they called the *Tulululu*. Thomas Wayne Edison's study refers to them as informal events that happened without much planning, a natural part of the month's activities. In those days, the traditional drink with which the locals celebrated the May Pole was called pinky-pinky and Ani-sou. This was an alcoholic beverage made by boiling anise seed in water with added sugar, alcohol, and pink coloring, hence the name.[68]

Hodgson Deerings refers to various theories of origin and the resulting general confusion about the roots of this ritual.[69] The May Pole of the 1500s and 1600s in Europe retained its characteristic as a custom among peasants; indeed, such gatherings were quite boisterous and unruly, so much so that they were banned by a parliamentary decree in 1644 for being an abomination and heathenish, provoking superstitious and evil practices. They did make it across the Atlantic to the United States during the 1600s in spite of bans and seizures of poles and remained one of the components that sustained European cultural expression in the Americas.[70] This is a good example of what Anthony Aveni calls "the invention of tradition," for over time, it proved useful, supporting European authority and privilege in the early Americas.[71] The 1700s to the early 1900s witnessed a shift in terms of its appreciation. The expansion of the urban industrial labor force together with trade unionism, the Industrial Revolution, the Civil War in the United States, and the social reformism of Karl Marx redirected the way May Day was valued. Even though the practice became politicized as Labor Day as socialism took Europe and the Americas by storm, its original legacy survived within European Protestant churches as they evangelized places like Nicaragua.[72]

A church-based commemoration of the 1800s, the May Day holiday took place on the first day of May every year in Swedish and German towns. Origins of the festival date back centuries to Beltane, a warm-weather feast that inaugurated the second half of the Celtic year. The festive spirit paid homage to the end of the long, dark winter days, dramatically welcoming the new season and the general burst of activity that normally accompanies warmer weather.[73] Aveni informs that fourteenth-century Welsh townships developed the custom of uprooting a tree in the forest, taking it to their villages, erecting it in the town square, and garnishing it with herbs and flowers. With streamers hanging from the top, they danced around it, creating the first authentic May Pole. They appeared to have used a specific tree, the Hawthorn tree, which "symbolized the divine tree that connects the human and heavenly realms, and people would circle about it to bring on the same good luck Bel's fire once brought to their ancestors."[74]

The *palo de mayo* is the Bluefields version of what remains today of these ancient seasonal festivities. Suffice it to say, since there are no winters in Nicaragua, one can imagine that such climatic significance was replaced by an emphasis on the tropical rains associated with May (a consistent and reliable pattern before the advent of global warming). In Europe, the warmth of May contributed to this month being a dangerous one, a time when evil forces roamed and made even usually good folk indulge in mischief. With the spring bloom came peril, evil influences accompanying nature's rejuvenation. The young were seen as being particularly susceptible, their thoughts stimulated by the rich fertility from the earth that surrounded them, encouraging thoughts of lovemaking. Stories seem to indicate that youthful trips into the woods resulted in fourteenth-century Welsh celebrants establishing the practice of uprooting a tree and erecting it in their village centers. Aveni describes this as a vegetation ritual in which humans created a connection with the world of flora as the source of new life, with every yearly cycle involved in a process of regeneration that humankind itself repeats.[75] Themes of birth, rebirth, nature, sex, and fertility reemerged in Miss Lizzie's dance designs. She confirms her familial knowledge of the historical and mythical base of her chosen art form.[76] The roots of her interpretations may also lie south of Bluefields, in Graytown with her mother's family, whose surname is Brooks, as well as with her other Central American connections, for there were a lot of Honduran families in the area.[77]

European traditions explain the use of the pole. Dance, mischief, and matchmaking together give meaning to the relationship between human activities and the regenerative forces of nature in the spring and summer. Flowers, greenery, and fertility among farm animals coincide with young love, marriages, and enamored youth, all ideas in homage to mankind's connection with and established dependence on nature and his need for its continued well-being. Aveni's research on the deep European legacy of the ritual confirms that there were several May Day enactments, and the dances were done by the youth. The pole could be a tree or a young man covered in vegetation. Poles back then were huge tree trunks, and their relocation became a major event that often involved oxen to get them to town.[78] The intention behind the ritual was to evoke positive attributes of regeneration, fertility, spirituality, prosperity, and endurance. To date, in the spirit of ecological preservation, we continue to exalt and glorify trees. The act of knocking on wood to guarantee the continuance of good luck and favorable destiny transcends cultures across the Western world.

The use of the tree trunk is an open door for pagan, carnal, and gender symbolism. The mythological force that accompanied the use of this wooden pole meant that it was transformed into a threatening spirit of evil in the form of a witch's broomstick, a subsequent source of storytelling, myths, and historical tragedy that marked the European Middle Ages and beyond. The May Pole festivities were very much an activity of the youth, and the pole proved provocative, a source of innuendos and suggestions. The nightlight, music, scents of nature, and dancing around a tall and erect log no doubt "carry all the subtle undertones of a ploy for whipping young damsels into a sexual frenzy."[79] There has been ample discussion of the phallic symbolism of the May Pole. Philosophers from Freud to Hobbes have argued that the May Pole refers back to the Roman worship of Priapus, the god of male potency. Historians have no confirmation of this and, at best, point to coincidental connections between the May Pole custom and ancient times.[80] We inherited a centuries-long debate and its impact on Christian values in Western Europe and England even as the custom never died; on the contrary, it rose in popularity, was exported to Europe's colonies in the Americas, and became the centerpiece in subsequent May Day celebrations in churches. There is no denying the original pagan nature of May Pole dancing by way of both the chants that mystified and challenged nature's pureness as well as the associations with bark or wood. Also, the practice naturally connected to the deep-rooted fantasy and belief in witches thanks to the mythical value of the broomstick.[81]

Community historian Hodgson Deerings has worked to identify an African-originated line of succession with limited findings. He identified a publication located in the Centro de Investigación y Documentación de la Costa Atlántica [CIDCA; Center for Research and Documentation of the Atlantic Coast], which cites a theologian named Hernán Savery, in which connections are made between the Bluefields version of *palo de mayo* and a dance in homage to a West African Yoruba deity, Shango, as a spiritual legacy.[82] Unable to confirm such a theory, Hodgson Deerings goes on to cite Sujo Wilson, also a leading personage on Creole history, who observes that practitioners of *palo de mayo* in Bluefields do not consciously associate it with any form of African religious belief.[83]

The ritual served the islands and continental Caribbean settlements that overlook the Atlantic Ocean and Caribbean Sea. Hodgson Deerings reiterates that the tradition found its way to the Caribbean coast from Europe, where the festivity—in terms of its dishes, games, and dance patterns—seems to confirm British influences:[84]

El estudio de nuestra historia deja claro que el Palo de Mayo llegó a la actual Costa Caribe de Nicaragua desde Inglaterra . . . a través de su principal colonia británica en el Caribe que era Jamaica con la cual el Reino de la Mosquitia mantenía comunicación directa y muy estrecha desde 1655.

[The study of our history makes it clear that the May Pole arrived at today's Caribbean Coast of Nicaragua from England . . . by way of its main British colony in the Caribbean that was Jamaica, with which the Kingdom of Mosquitia maintained direct and close communication since 1655.][85]

He cautions that it would be speculative to identify exact dates, indicating a need for thorough research of German and Moravian documents from that era written in Old German.[86] Hodgson Deerings works to find duplicating influences in the flourishing tropical landscape of the region, where trees bloom during the rainy season, leading to thanksgiving through song and dance.

Hodgson Deerings identifies British pirates, entrepreneurs, and settlers whose presence inspired songs such as "London Bridge Is Falling Down," which joined with local ballads such as "There's a Brown Girl in the Ring" and other circle songs and games. Bluefields, Gray Town, San Andrés, Pearl Lagoon, and Corn Island are Central American settlements populated by migrants from Jamaica, the Cayman Islands, and Belize whose homegrown songs introduced new trends to their adopted lands, where they gained local flavor. "Donkey wan wata" [Donkey wants water] is Jamaican, while San Andrés may have been the place of origin of the popular "Mayaya las im key" [Mayaya lost her key]. Bluefields's own composer, Silvester Hodgson, produced "Sin Saiman sin mai love" [Without Simon without my love], "Judith drownded" [Judith drowned], and "Lanch ton ova" [Boat turned over]. These grassroots renditions are crucial to the solidification of Caribbean languages and heritage in Nicaragua. Manifestations of daily life, they continue to evolve as testimonial renditions and storytelling. Creole songs with adaptations in Spanish are characterized as belonging to everyone, oftentimes reflective of communities—their views, their opinions, and their reasoning. Daily actions, abuses, vices, and hypocrisy are favorite targets, making these songs tools of comedy, ridicule, morality, and instruction.[87]

THE JOY OF DANCE: FROM STREET TO STAGE

Miss Lizzie has childhood memories of witnessing May Pole and Ribbon Pole dances. Growing up, she would attend fundraising festivities at the Anglican school, where she saw the dances and loved them; they were compelling experiences that ultimately made her a respected guardian of customs and traditions in Bluefields. While still very young, she participated in Ribbon Pole dances, probably introduced into the neighborhood schools by migrants from Jamaica, the Cayman Islands, and Belize. She reminisces that as children, she and her fellow students would playfully imitate the adults, cutting their own tree, decorating it with fruits, and dancing around it.[88] The Ribbon Pole, a derivative of the May Pole, was for children or, as oral traditions explained, for those who come afterward. Drawing on these experiences, Miss Lizzie later taught other ring dances and their accompanying songs in Creole while organizing appearances at birthday parties, fairs, church gatherings, and other events. She guided the youth and children in the Ribbon Pole, teaching them to wrap, or, as they prefer to say, twine the pole. During formal presentations, usually only girls danced, and they would decorate their pole with fruits that they later consumed.

There is a divide between childhood play and adult entertainment. In the past, at gatherings and parties, adults danced polka, waltz, mento, mazurka, and *chotize*, Creole adaptations of European dances.[89] May Pole dancing took place at public events such as church fairs, although not exclusively; there were also festivities not connected to any church. Miss Lizzie recalls that at late-night events, the adults danced to the sound of drums and rhythmic percussion objects such as coconut graters, pots, and pans. The women, with their long dresses and hair wrapped in scarves, danced in circles.[90] She uses the term *May Pole* broadly, a way of referring to numerous dance formations—around a tree or pole, in pairs, everyone dancing as couples or separate, and in an arch dancing through the streets in a choreography known as *Tulululu*, an onomatopoeic expression imitating the commotion created by the percussion instruments that accompanied the frolicking. A folk song accompanies this dance called "Tulululu pass anda" [Tulululu pass under].[91]

These dance traditions were accompanied by specific songs that revealed "the life history of the people,"[92] medleys in Creole and English (today, some are in Spanish) of scandals, tales, beliefs, and aspects of daily life, at times weighted by a double entendre that was intended to be mischievous or serve as a teaching moment. Popular examples are "Mayaya Oh," "Ananci Oh," "Zion Oh," "Soup pan di table" [Soup on the table], "Hav somting don yanda" [Have something down yonder], "Reed Oh" [Read oh], "Two coco make one dumpling" [Two coconuts make one dumpling], "Take This Fruit and When It Done It Done," and "A way don, a way don, yu bobi jen away don" [Weigh down, weigh down, your breasts weigh down].[93] Miss Lizzie strongly encouraged preserving the underlying significance of these lyrics, pointing to the specific knowledge and value in each element of the *palo de mayo* ritual—the tree, month, fruits, dancers, and music—that allowed her to reinforce the distinction between this deep Creole custom and modern-day presentations that were purely entertainment. This particular distinction is discernable in Creole poetry, where verses depend heavily on techniques of oral expression and rhythmic patterns associated with these songs.

From 1945 to 1959 on the Pacific coast, there were inaccurate displays of these Atlantic coast dances.[94] Miss Lizzie's first group was formed during the 1960s with teenaged girls from the neighborhoods of Cotton Tree, Beholden, and Old Bank who gathered for practice in Fred Kirkland's yard. They became Miss Lizzie's Dance Group.[95] There are two opinions regarding when men began to participate. Hodgson Deerings indicates that when the British taught the steps, only girls were allowed to dance around the pole; therefore, some of them dressed in men's clothing.[96] Male participation came much later, during the 1980s, when occasionally, some of the musicians also entered the circle to dance. According to Miss Lizzie, her biggest challenge was to persuade men to dance on stage or to dance with the ladies, as traditionally, they provided musical accompaniment, playing drums, graters, pans, and everyday household objects.[97] Her tours to León and Corinto during the 1960s marked the first time that men and boys participated. Male dancers were fully integrated into the group by 1970, an innovation that facilitated elaborate choreography and dance moves for couples.[98] Determined to take the legacy forward and ensure its survival, Miss Lizzie insisted on the participation of both sexes.[99]

Hodgson Deerings gives a historical overview of what transpired during the 1960s and 1970s, pointing out that such a dance display was marginalized until

1979, viewed as Creole entertainment and reserved for specific bars, clubs, or private parties.[100] T. M. Scruggs discusses its presence on the Pacific coast, describing its transition from homegrown domestic and rustic percussion instruments to electronic instrumentation and the openly lascivious and sensual dance styles (distortions?) that became quite popular.[101] In Managua, certain establishments and private parties catered to a specific, largely Afro-Nicaraguan clientele who enjoyed this kind of socializing. Given the limited access to available large spaces, it would take place any time of year without the pole but with the added feature of electronic instruments. In the capital, these specific spaces, frequented by Blacks, were often marginalized; negative perceptions of them were driven by racism, a lack of understanding, and inaccurate information about Creole traditions, as urban inhabitants refused to associate with the *palo de mayo*, designating it a dance for Blacks. Between 1960 and 1990, there was cultural reticence and even pushback from the media; indeed, it took a while to build a broad national appreciation of the art. Miss Lizzie reflected on the difficulty of media coverage that commented negatively on the dance movements. Rather than provide insight into lesser-known cultural expressions, reporters favored sensationalism. With time, she was able to circumvent the negative commentary as opinions started to change after her dance group's stellar national and international performances, accompanied by workshops and seminars.[102] Eventually, misconceptions eroded. The rise of Sandinismo in 1979 and the ongoing government support during the 1980s led to the dance's formal recognition as part of the nation's folklore, a position reinforced with the advent of the annual Mayo-Ya festivities in Bluefields.[103]

Expertise established, the adolescent girls performed the Ribbon Pole dance for the first time at a fair in the town of León in 1967, a successful staging that inaugurated Miss Lizzie's favorable connections with the Pacific coast and the capital. Following this achievement in León, these younger dancers received invitations to perform across the country. They transitioned into a semiprofessional group and began to receive payments for their shows. Miss Lizzie's dancers and musicians performed before the 1972 earthquake and from 1973 to 1978 in Masaya, Estelí, Managua, Boaco, Corn Island, and various Central American towns, including Port Limón, Costa Rica, and San Andrés, Colombia. During the 1980s and 1990s, they performed in Mexico, China, Taiwan, the United States, Costa Rica, and Cuba. Performances in Mexico in 1991 and in Taiwan in 1998 were memorable; Miss Lizzie's group won first place and a trophy in a 1996 international festival in Mexico. Her dance groups sustained a high level of professionalism at events and venues as well as on television. She named her best group Hilda Ida in homage to two dancers, Angélica Hilda Dixon and Ida Baker.[104]

In recognition of Miss Lizzie's commitment to the region's heritage, the government named her a cultural delegate for the Autonomous Region of the Southern Atlantic. Director, choreographer, and overall organizer, she became responsible for all logistical and financial aspects of her enterprise; indeed, her drive, vigor, and creativity inspired many and did much to teach the community about its history while serving to inspire a sense of togetherness. She was able to receive financial support from the government to maintain three groups. *Palo de mayo* transitioned from a little-known, underappreciated manifestation to an enterprise symbolic of Nicaragua's national identity and diversity. Miss Lizzie's words are significant: "This is why many people do not understand up to now what is Autonomy. We have our way, we do it our way, this is ours! Not African, not British, not Indigenous, just 100% Costeño."[105]

The 1990s witnessed several changes and developments: the increasingly popular Caribbean carnival celebration for which Bluefields is now famous, the move away from grassroots percussion instruments and improvisation to electronic music and contemporary dance styles, and the fact that younger generations are less interested in history and traditions. These factors have worked against the continuation of the original May Pole choreography and musical renditions.[106] Miss Lizzie's art forms may be regarded today as conservative, old-fashioned, and remnants of earlier generations of Antillean immigrants, therefore no longer reflecting the social preferences of today's youth. While this may be so, there is no doubt of a positive effect on the many female participants who emerged from these experiences with a deep appreciation of their community, a strong sense of pride, and sensations of achievement and self-realization.

Currently, the dance is part of Afro-descendant memory associated with the Caribbean islands and the Atlantic coast of Central America. It requires specific choreography that has to be taught by experts like Miss Lizzie who understand the development of oral traditions. Today's performances have been known to include contemporary dance steps to hip-hop, rap, reggaeton, and other popular rhythms that accommodate sensational gyrating movements and attract the younger population. Concerned, Miss Lizzie perceived such entertainment as potential spheres of bad influence involving youth already suffering the debilitating effects of economic, educational, and financial difficulty; drugs; and alcohol. She reiterated her opposition to changes in the rhythms and lyrics of the earlier songs, transformed to include offensive, derogatory words, references, and sexual innuendos, some of which have become an integral part of Bluefields's festive processions.[107] Sujo Wilson and Robb Taylor confirm these transformations in two different studies, especially the graphic dance moves and their impact on society:

> The dance and the music have even extended to the Pacific region of Nicaragua. The dance has been exploited commercially and it has suffered changes throughout the years. At present there is a version that consists of very erotic movements and contortions of the body, considered by puritanic and snobbish people as obscene.[108]

> The Sandinistas promoted the event as a tourist attraction supporting local bands and dance groups, under Miss Lizzie's leadership. Miss Lizzie involved 70 year-old women to dance the old style, to teach the youth the real thing, but by 1993 she had lost much of her ground to a new style of May Pole which Otis reported as a dirty display of dirty dancing: "Couples leave nothing to the imagination as they perform erotic contortions in all conceivable positions." He

quoted Landymar Omeir's disgust: "... now they just mash up the pole." "Now," Rev. Budier agrees, "it is pure business."[109]

Antonia McCoy also comments on this situation, referring to the commercialization of the *palo de mayo* as it is currently used in Bluefields and along the Pacific coast to promote commerce and tourism.[110] She confirms that it is being designed as carnival, which is changing its original form and purpose as a result of influences imported from Limón, Costa Rica. Miss Lizzie's more conservative choreography did much to reunite the Creole population, which is not without its internal differences and tensions. Gordon explains such divides by discussing the presence of an educated class of Creoles in the decades prior to the advent of Sandinista rule: "Creole appropriation of the dominant ideology of Anglo racial and cultural superiority had another dissonant feature. Skin color and level of 'Africanity' were important bases of social hierarchy within Creole society itself. This is dramatized by the continued discursive differentiation between 'colored and Negro' Creoles. Color and culture were closely articulated with class and the basis of considerable divisiveness within the group."[111] Educated, well-positioned Creoles had lifestyles, values, religions, and traditions that mirrored Anglophone culture. They were well-off economically, had fairly light complexions, could be of mixed heritage, were Moravian churchgoers, and spoke English well. Parallel to this upper class were the lower classes of Creoles, among whom similar African and Afro-Caribbean traditions where preserved and widely practiced.[112]

Miss Lizzie's *palo de mayo* seemed designed to bridge the two divides by using formal choreography in synchrony with traditional Afro-Caribbean folk music and lyrics. Her adherence to the original designs did distance her staged renditions from the boisterous, grassroots, popular community events, which were marked by their "Africanity."[113] She did, however, preserve illustrations of the fertility ritual, very visible in the sensual dancing largely performed by the women to drumming and singing, in celebrations that surely evoked ecclesiastical condemnation.[114] Respect for this ancestral practice motivated Miss Lizzie to include it in her performances, even as she felt troubled by the way it impacted her efforts to unite and build her community—rightly so, for she worried about lewd interpretations on the rise in the Bluefields carnival.

While it falls under the rubric of what is deemed to be folklore or popular culture, this kind of display moves against feminist and literary activism that has always been concerned about the deep negative impact of all forms of female objectification. The exploitation of the gyrating female body takes us away from the more formal dance moves in Miss Lizzie's *palo de mayo* and opens the door to the debate surrounding the retention or rejection of certain cultural practices. Once again, the female body of dark hue becomes a site of interpretation and exploitation. A personal testimony is available from Shorlet Simmons, one of the dancers, who shows the difference between her love of the tradition and dance and the way she is contemplated and judged in this controversy: "It's not only me that's getting discriminated against that way because of being a black woman, because of the way we dance. They say the way we dance is like saying: 'Let's go to bed,' and that is not true. It is our way of dancing because we have the blood for music. I feel they envy the way we dance so that is why they talk so much about us."[115]

Miss Lizzie's resistance to any inappropriate co-opting of the female body means that her versions of the dances are "classic renditions" as opposed to popular backyard fetes or lively processions. The break from "colonial" patterns of representation seems to have shifted toward an increased sexualization of femininity into which women may or may not have bought. Modern-day displays of revelry are accosted and challenged because they seem to thrive on exploiting the female body, questionably with the collaboration of said subject—this, even as stalwarts such as Miss Lizzie and feminist activists decry the overall cumulative negative consequences, specifically in relation to Black female imaging. Trends and preferences among the younger generations continue to subsume the historical legacy of combating the long-term effects of such potentially denigrating images. As activists, concerned citizens, and community leaders (Miss Lizzie included), their challenge is to determine where wholesome enjoyment ends and indecency begins as well as to define issues of artistry and identity, especially as these relate to representations of the female body. The more conservative sectors of this coastal community struggle to accept the more libertine gyrations that attract today's youth.[116] The connections established between modern versions of the dance and women's freedom of expression seem to have overwhelmed the original argument that the wiser and older folk were making—that in the midst of modernity and political correctness (or convenience), the original art form has all but disappeared. Malespín Jirón offers insight into the deeper value of Miss Lizzie's enterprise as it relates to her community. He attaches a humanitarian aspect to her service, highlighting her efforts to use such activities to draw the region's youth away from potentially negative influences and distractions.[117] This enterprise has worked well as a tool for positive socialization and, more importantly, as a path to ensuring that the next generations develop a clear sense of their roots, their history, and the story of their beloved Bluefields.

CHAPTER 4

From "Mayaya las im key" to Creole Women's Writings

As part of her endeavor to broadcast the May Pole's legacy nationwide, Elizabeth Forbes Brooks (Miss Lizzie) mentions that she spent time writing about the meanings of the words and expressions in *palo de mayo* songs and translating some of them into Spanish. She confirms that every year, there were always new songs detailing what had transpired in the community. The devastating hurricane of October 1988 provoked a song the following May.[1] Some were used for dancing, while many others were only meant to be sung. These renditions may or may not be associated with a specific composer, as there are many older rhymes and songs that no single musician can claim; they belong to the collective, a situation that has led to adaptations, (mis)interpretations, and newer or Spanish versions within the rapidly changing world of modern pop and carnival music. Interestingly enough, such signals of national interest and appreciation have secured these songs' continuity, albeit not necessarily in the way Miss Lizzie envisioned.

Modifications to rhythms, the use of multiple languages (Creole, Spanish, English), and the introduction of other kinds of instruments are ongoing transformations that confirm the art's susceptibility to trending musical influences that naturally occur over time, many of which quickly fade and are subsequently replaced by others. They are measures of the spontaneous creativity and openness visible in an originally colonized people who did what they could to make this musical form their own. In music and poetry associated with the *palo de mayo*, one particularly striking constituent is Mayaya, goddess of spring, production, and fertility, to whom the local residents paid homage during the May festivities. Miss Lizzie referred to the "Mayaya Oh" song and called her "Maia," goddess of May and fertility.[2] Various musical renditions revere this goddess, and they seem to stem from deep-rooted communal practices. Older generations of Creole inhabitants, by way of oral storytelling and traditions, understand what led to Mayaya's veneration and lament this meaningful loss in community memory. Today, no rituals are performed, and if there is any mention of the goddess, it is exclusively for entertainment.[3]

Homage to the Goddess Mayaya in Music and Poetry

There is quite a bit of disaccord among those who are trying to understand the beginnings of Mayaya. One line of thought connected with antiquity establishes a correspondence with Maya (Maia), the Greco-Roman goddess and probable source of the name attributed to the month itself. In Greek legend, she is the wise old grandmother and midwife, originally worshipped as the goddess of the night sky, then later as the oldest of the Pleiades, or Seven Sisters (a cluster of stars). A surviving myth identifies her as the mother of the phallic god Hermes. The Romans associated this Greek version with their fire goddess of the same name, ruler of the forces of growth, warmth, and sexual passion. The festivals in homage to her were on the first day of her month, a ritual associated with the Christian practice of dedicating May to Mary, the queen of flowers.[4] Closer to home, in Nicaragua, Azizi Powell encourages the contemplation of Mayaya, the Nicaraguan derivative, as having deep (albeit hard to prove) African origins, arguing that the Greek goddess Maya (Maia) could have been modeled on Egyptian (African) mythical belief systems.[5] Differently, community scholars like Johnny Hodgson Deerings contemplate Mayaya's origins as Hispanic in nature, claiming that in Spain, a similar ritual existed with respect to a deity they called Maya or Maria Joven (Young Mary) who presided over the May festivity dedicated to the Virgin Mary, also known as the queen of May. While the roots of the manifestation are to some extent religious, overall, Hodgson Deerings seems to support Hugo Sujo Wilson in claiming that the traditional practice today in no way seems to align itself with any specific religious sect or propaganda, whether from Africa or Europe.[6]

We then hear from women's rights activist and scholar Antonia McCoy, whose article "El significado de Palo de Mayo" uses the original name, Maya, and connects rituals in her honor to enslaved ancestors who, mimicking the dances of their slave owners at their parties and gatherings, would have their own festivities that included dances around trees and wooden poles, a subtle form of ridicule and resistance against the cruelty and oppression of enslavement.[7] McCoy recognizes the existence of multiple versions of this story and remarks on a particular historical view that created a spontaneous connection among rituals of sowing and harvest, the earth's fertility, and the Afro-descendant female figure, a connection anchored in the Maya ritual performed during the first rains that ensured the earth's fertility and preparation for cultivation. Thomas Wayne Edison follows up by conferring maternal value on this deity, interested in establishing connections between Maya and other well-known deities in Cuba and Brazil associated with water, such as Yemayá.[8] Weighing in on the topic, in her interview with Alfonso Malespín Jirón, Miss Lizzie points to several versions surrounding the origins of *palo de mayo* and goes on to insist that her mother's ancestral line is the authentic one, for she was a direct descendant, belonging to one of the families that originally celebrated the ritual in homage to Mayaya.[9]

How does the literary universe react to this quest for understanding? Creole poetry builds on Mayaya's value as a central African-originating component that defines who they are as a people. Her name appears in poems, where she engages that space as idol and identity. On the one hand, there does not seem to be historically confirmable evidence that connects Mayaya to West African Yoruba and other spiritual practices that gave birth to Afro–Latin American equivalents such as vodun (Haiti), candomblé (Brazil), and regla de ocha (Cuba). Mayaya does not appear to present any of the spiritual dimensions that surround female orishas such as Yemayá or Oshun. On the other hand, history's inability to provide visible and concrete information contrasts with the way in which, from a literary perspective, the creation of interconnections among these female deities has proven to be a fruitful and stimulating development. Literature has tasked itself with compensating for the absences of traditional historical information while proving the need to read Afro-descendant histories using imaginative reconstructions.

Based on Miss Lizzie's version, festivities in homage to Mayaya always occurred in May or when the rains came, and the selection of the tree to be used as the pole was a specific process, since it had to be taken from their forest, possess tall branches and a smooth trunk, and could not bear fruit. The branches served to make spears and canoes, as they were lighter, while the trunk would be the object around which they danced.[10] The bare pole was then decorated with seasonal fruits—pineapples, guavas, mangoes, local apples—and as bits of fruit were attached, the singing and chanting to Mayaya began with the uttering of her name as dancers entered the circle around the tree. In a call-and-response pattern, participants danced and sang under the goddess's aura, recounting their lives, especially the difficulties. The art of the dance itself is important, for it follows a specific pattern. Flowers or fruits have been used to adorn the pole around which danced eight to twelve couples, each holding a ribbon that matched their outfit. Half of the dancers circled the pole in one direction while the other half danced in the opposite direction, with each dancer meticulously wrapping the pole with their ribbon as they crossed in front of each other, a choreography that allowed all the ribbons to be wrapped around the pole with precision. When all the ribbons where fully wrapped, dancers changed direction and unwrapped them.[11] They ended the celebrations with commitments of friendship and solidarity and proceeded to take their dancing into the streets in a procession that the old folks called Tulululu. This was a fertility rite of humans, the earth, the dancers' movements, the fruits, and the tree.[12]

Drawing on personal experiences and interviews, Deborah Robb Taylor and Sujo Wilson have lively and entertaining testimonial descriptions of the community events.[13] When interviewed, Pachanga, a former palo de mayo dancer who participated in the festivity, confirms that the ritual was circular; people gathered and formed one big human circle, leaving the middle for dancing couples. Participants were adults, including women in their fertile years, in keeping with the ritual to the land and homage to Mayaya. The steps and movements were a circular enactment; as the men entered the circle, trying to approach the women, they were rejected, their expressions of desire rescinded because the women displayed their unwillingness to share their fertility outside of wedlock. The ritual took place at night and lasted until close to dawn. As the night wore on, the music and enactment became more frenetic and frenzied, climaxing with the *Tulululu* steps somewhere around midnight. *Tulululu* was originally one of the most important dance steps. After the main circular festivities, the pole was removed, and a procession of musicians, dancers, and followers paraded through the streets, at times joining other neighborhood groups as they all danced and sang their way to the center of town. The main song, "Tulululu pass anda" [Tulululu pass under], has the status of a closing hymn in homage to the festivities. Hodgson Deerings provides a Creole version of the song:

Tu lu lu lu
Pass anda
Gial an buay de
Pass anda
Pass pass pass anda
Gial an buay de pass anda
Beholden gial. . . .

[Tu lu lu lu
Pass under
Girl and boy they
Pass under
Pass pass pass under
Girl and boy they pass under
Beholden girl . . .][14]

Dancers formed two lines facing each other, one line of men, the other women, everyone with their hands raised to form an arch and a tunnel. The couple at one end of the line danced through the tunnel (passing underneath) and took up a new position in their respective lines at the other end, thereby ensuring that the tunnel never ended. It was a contagious choreography that begged community involvement and officially closed the community *palo de mayo* celebration.[15]

Miss Lizzie was known for using popular songs in the *palo de mayo* dance sequences, as these were, in her view, authentic musical renditions of Creole daily life, their opinions, values, and experiences. These songs, many of which originated in the islands of the English-speaking Caribbean, are striking representations of the diverse confluences that comprise this heritage. A good example is the popular folk song "Mayaya las im key" or "Mayaya lasinki" [Mayaya lost her key]. Other versions—"Mayaya la sim ki," "Mayaya lass im key," "Mayaya la sin qui"—confirm its place in oral traditions; in other words, no one really knows or can agree about which of these written versions is original, correct, or legitimate, since these renditions are not necessarily connected to any single author or musician and are highly subject to adaptations, additions, and modifications.[16] The significance of the song is in its playful (ir)reverence to Mayaya. The key she lost potentially becomes symbolically relevant, for it is needed to open the door to the new season of spring,

associated with fertility and cultivation. There are other interpretations of the
lyrics. The idea of the woman losing her key is also popularly taken to mean that
what she really lost was her virginity, a meaning that is probably responsible for the
song's fame and explains its attraction for the performances and dancing masses
at carnival. The song can also be read as a problematic narrative about a woman
who loses a key given to her by her husband and who now fears he will kill her if
she does not find it.[17] While the story of a woman fearing for her life due to a lost
key begs contemplation (condemnation) of these implied stereotypical gender
roles—in this case, the abusive male versus the cowering female—it is a teaching
moment about domestic violence and male domination. At the same time, the
message gets swallowed up in the song's contagious rhythm and simple structure,
resulting in its popularity and numerous versions as singers switch out the lyrics
and insert anything that works.[18]

> Mayaya lass im key
> Mayaya Oh!
> Mayaya lass im key
> Mayaya Oh!
> A wan mi key fu go opin me do
> Mayaya Oh!
>
> [Mayaya lost her key
> Mayaya Oh!
> Mayaya lost her key
> Mayaya Oh!
> I want me (i.e., my) key for go open me door
> Mayaya Oh!][19]

Miss Lizzie offers an alternative interpretation in "Al son de Miss Lizzie," a
Bluefilms video production released in December 2011. In her documentary, not
uncommon with these folk songs, Miss Lizzie reveals a double meaning that adds
an extra layer to the tale and displays those less obvious cultural references to which
the verses really refer. For Miss Lizzie, "Mayaya las im key" means that Mayaya
lost her ability to bear children; she is infertile. It is a condition that both men and
women face, and her community found a way to symbolically refer to this situation
without directly speaking about it, their way of addressing the matter while preserving the privacy of the person(s) involved. This mechanism of indirect speech
is an important characteristic of these songs and transfers to the dance movements
as well. There can be distance between what one hears and the intended message.
This distance creates a protective circle around this culture, making it difficult for
outsiders to understand what is really being said, a strategy that also works well
for protecting children from the deeper nuances of adulthood and for sustaining
varying levels of secrecy and conspiracy as needed. The value of every song is in its
capacity to produce this multilayered effect. The ability of this particular melody

to produce so many meaningful options explains why it is such an important part of the *palo de mayo* legacy.

Differences exist between earlier (traditional) and more recent dance versions of the song. Sexual innuendos populate the more contemporary renditions and performances, a process whose end result is that the original messages of reverence to flora and fauna, harvesting, birth, rebirth, and productivity as they relate to the earth are subsumed. Existing beyond Miss Lizzie's displays, performances today may include provocative dance movements that clearly mirror the sex act and moves such as gyrating very close together, dancing between each other's legs, or males dancing with a cloth between their legs.[20] An examination of this song reveals its evolution in terms of enactment and value. It is one of many and becomes a tool for observing cultural shifts within the Creole way of life. The debate continues as to whether the current shifts have been positive or detrimental for the community's legacy and well-being. Sujo Wilson's interviews of the elderly, including one with Maximiliano Atily, indicate that "Mayaya las im key" was part of a legacy of leisure, relaxation, and village entertainment.[21] Townsfolk would gather or small groups would meet regularly to entertain themselves; they sang, clapped hands, and danced. Life was simpler back then, and they possessed none of the sophisticated instruments available today.

Atily does elaborate on the town's May Pole celebration in detail, and this is where he mentions their locally produced instruments—the donkey jawbone, the grater, and the tin can.[22] He describes the ring dance and game that went with the Mayaya song, the "Tulululu pass anda,"[23] the harvesting and decoration of a tree in preparation for the May Pole dancing and celebration, and the tradition's beverages of ginger beer, rice drink, and pinky-pinky. Hodgson Deerings explains the inevitability of the original British May Pole songs and dances ceding to Afro-Caribbean rhythms and instruments.[24] He places a lot of value on the *tambor de mano* [hand drum], provides details about local instruments, and adds that formal instruments such as the accordion, maracas, guitar, violin, mandolin, trumpet, and other drums were later introduced. In style and structure, May Pole was a community and family event that occurred thanks to the collective efforts of musicians, singers, dancers, and the public. According to Sujo Wilson, "Maypole was something decent. Nothing vulgar. It was for people who had discipline. Sometimes people were invited, but any well-behaved person could take part in the dancing."[25] No mention is made of actually dancing around the May Pole; instead, the focus is on the performing couples. The main objective seems to be establishing the differences between then and now in relation to the quality of dancing and decency. New elements represent a process of moral degeneration that is eroding the tradition from within, a view expressed by both Sujo Wilson and Miss Lizzie. They lament that the dances (and some songs) trending today are expressive of a vulgarity that has damaged the historical value of this Creole legacy, and they blame the popular expansion of this Creole-originated dance, profitable commercialization of their carnival traditions, and misinterpretations of what is, for them, a meaningful Afro-descendant legacy: "Partners were decently changed during the dance. They didn't use to hold each other nor do the vulgarities that they do today. It was a decent dance. Songs like 'Aunty Mama Gone Cowita' [Aunt Mama went to Cahuita], and 'Launche Ton Ova' [Boat capsized], were not Maypole Songs. Those songs were made afterward."[26] Sujo Wilson also addresses the blatant sexualized dancing within a discussion of class and generational gaps.[27] The elderly, whose main support consists of their memories of years past, object strongly to contemporary dance styles, for they are repulsed by the sensual movements and blatant lyrics that have replaced the older musical forms about customs and traditions. They are products of a Protestant formation and education that Sujo Wilson describes as "puritanic and snobbish," thereby finding such displays meaningless and abhorrent.[28] These debates point to differences between the older and younger community members in relation to decorum and correctness even as they confirm how parameters that determine such value systems have changed. The older generations seem worried for the whole community, while young folk are neutral and unconcerned, appear more individualistic, and worship modern-day images that are illustrative of material prosperity. It is clear that today's dance moves are having a greater impact on the female image, for while men also dance, more women than men perform, and they are the ones who take the trends forward and who probably are in the limelight as performers of moves that are points of contention. At the same time, these dances are not without context, for in the end, they are today's manifestations of those centuries-old ancestral fertility rituals associated with Mayaya and nature's bloom.

The transition from music and dance to poetry is a smooth one. Various poets use images and experiences of Creole existence to populate their works; indeed, these descriptive elements are reproductions of their lives, lands, and legacies. Their poems need to be read aloud, for they have a certain tempo and often include Creole English references, at times comprehensible only to those who understand their language. Their writing is a production symbolic of that in-between linguistic space they occupy. With the Pacific coast and Spanish legacy on one side of the country and the Caribbean Sea with its Anglophone island legacy on the other, this Creole poetic writing is unique in how it matches the complex way they have of describing who they truly are. Poetry airs their spirit of proud autonomy even as there is no doubting their clear commitment to Nicaragua, their motherland.

There seems to be uncertainty as to the authorship of poems such as "Mayaya perdió su llave" [Mayaya lost her key], the written version of the "Mayaya las im key" song, published in Poesía atlántica.[29] Its presence in this anthology reveals the thin line between written and spoken verse while serving as a gesture of deference to local customs and beliefs handed down through the generations. The footnote that accompanies this particular poem identifies Mayaya as symbolic of the Virgin Mary, the queen of May, a belief system in place since 1860 in the Pearl Lagoon area.[30] The name of the goddess and neologisms—for example, Mayo Ya—appear in a relatively large number of poems that treasure the native land and its traditions. Poetry reproduces the spirit of celebration that usually surrounds the deity by way of verses that are repetitive and sustain a beat. The festive mood of the poems emphasizes the atmosphere of entertainment generated by a fun-loving people. The Creole anthology is therefore a space for cultural preservation and a gathering of worthy literary depictions created by the community's poets. Creole, mestizo, and other *costeño* writers of the Atlantic coast celebrate the Mayaya/May phenomena in their verses.[31]

Alí Aláh's poem "Pimpóy bailóp" provides an interesting illustration of Mayaya's importance as ritual, rhythm, and music.[32] The poet engages the written word playfully as a way of capturing the dynamic nature of the moment when everyone is singing and dancing:

al rito-sinfín paloemayero:
"má-yáya-las-i-qui
  má-yáya-oóóh:

[to the endless May Pole ritual:
"Mayaya lost her key
  Mayaya Oh:][33]

Mayaya is also present in David McField's "Mayo," where experimentations with the goddess's name allow for slippages in and out of Spanish and English as well as associations with the month of May:

Mayaya Lasinki
Mayaya o
Maya, ya ya ya ya
Mayo llegó.

[Mayaya lost her key
Mayaya oh
Maya, ya ya ya ya
May arrived.][34]

Both José Santos Cermeño's "May Pole in Bluefields" and Carmen Merlo's "Otra vez ¡Mayo-Ya!" capture the passion and abandonment of ritualistic pleasures.[35] In terms of its structure and style, Santos Cermeño's "May Pole in Bluefields" is both poem and folk song.[36] The constant repetition of the verse "Mayaya lost the ky" attests to the poet's resolve to combine these two genres, maintain a simplicity of verse, and situate the deity within the sphere of oral tradition, where her iconic status and gender frame her as the generic representation of Creole women. Emblematic of this belief system, the poem starts by paying homage to the tree that has been selected to be part of the ritual. The rather sacrificial role that the tree plays is understood within a context of entertainment, for the tree serves human will. It has no choice, for it has been selected and decorated and will stand in the courtyard or patio as a participant and witness to mankind's intention—singing, drumming, frolicking, and drinking. The narrator speaks to the earthy and rustic aspects of *palo de mayo* in a way that allows us to understand the hypnotic effects of its rhythms, which drive the ritual and ensure full participation in the festivity. The following verses highlight the female body by referencing the loss of virginity, "lost the ky," and specific body parts—"Tus pechos dan olores de melon" [Your breasts give off scents of melon][37]—confirming that, as occurs in rituals of fertility, it becomes a site of stimulation and sensuality:

> (Mayaya lost the ky
> Mayayaón).
> Tus pechos dan olores
> de melón.
> (Mayaya lost the ky
> Mayayaón).
> Tus piernas hacen letras
> de crayon.
> (Mayaya lost the ky
> Mayayaón).
>
> [(Mayaya lost the key
> Mayayaón).
> Your breasts give off scents
> of melon.
> (Mayaya lost the key
> Mayayaón).
> Your legs make letters
> from crayon.
> (Mayaya lost the key
> Mayayaón).][38]

The poetic and musical structure of the verses is that of call-and-response, with a lead voice and chorus. The lyrical value is in the rhythm and movement driven along by simple, direct messages. What matters is the here and now—immediate pleasure and enjoyment of the tropical heat, rum, and music. Improvisation and crowd participation are central to the event, for the plan is to sustain the entertainment for as long as possible. Santos Cermeño's verses draw us toward the frolicking as the bodies in movement emerge in the glow of the fires. The narrating voice captures the mesmerizing moment, drawing us into the hypnotic effect of breasts and body contours as they move in and out of the light:

> Una pequeña lámpara
> daba su luz dorando
> pechos y redondeces
> negras, en un temblor
> de crepitantes leños

ardiendo en un infierno
de lujuriosos gestos,
al ritmo candenciosos
del son.

[A small lamp
gave off its light illuminating
breasts and Black
roundness, in a trembling/tremor/tremble of
crackling firewood
burning in an inferno
of lustful gestures
to the melodious rhythm
of the sound.][39]

In a similar manner, Merlo's "Otra vez ¡Mayo-Ya!" provides verses that dig deeper, retaking the messages of fertility and production to connect them with the erotic, stimulating nature of the ritual itself and the way the dancers totally give themselves over to the music, displayed in the sensuality of dancing bodies:

y al ritmo de los bailes eróticos
de la negrada con los "paña buays"
al son del "tu lu lu lu pasan."
Un refugio ante el peligro inminente
de contagiarte—bailar—
lleno de erotismo. ¡sabor y picardía!

[and to the rhythm of the erotic dances
of the Black folk with the *paña buays*
to the sound of the "Tulululu pass."
A refuge in the face of your imminent danger
of becoming infected—to dance—
full of eroticism. Flavor and naughtiness (sexual)!][40]

Merlo's verses declare that this is what Mayo-Ya is all about. It is a real entity with a life of its own, a month of dedication to the people and the earth, an ancestral legacy that is theirs but also now a national attraction, as many tourists arrive from the Pacific coast to enjoy it. The narrator describes it as a time of pleasure, a chance to forget all difficulties and challenges and, for a while, be who they truly are as a coastal people. Her message connects with the historical understanding of the legacy visible in Miss Lizzie's work in that the verses become a medium for marking the continuity that exists between the past and the present.

Eddy Alemán Porras's poem "Mayo es: Kupia kumi lasbaia wina kakalwra" belongs to this group, as it uses the Mayaya icon in the verses, this time with an emphasis on popular music bands and singers:

Beltrán Bustamante,
Tantó
y Los Siete Calientes
cantando y bailando
bailando y cantando:
"Mayaya la sinki
Mayaya oh!"
—Mayo Ya Llegó!—

[Beltrán Bustamante,
Tantó
and Los Siete Calientes
singing and dancing
dancing and singing:
"Mayaya lost her key
Mayaya oh!"
—May Has Already Arrived!—][41]

Optimistically, a Caribbean carnival setting blends with ethnic elements to invent words or raise images of a contagious party atmosphere, one in which Indigenous, Garifuna, and Creole peoples merge in a confluence of cultures, a diversity of ethnicities that compose today's Nicaragua—in the narrator's words, "Karibea/Nicarao."[42] The Mayaya rendition is played by popular bands, on the one hand, and community folk such as vendors and fishermen, on the other, a clear reflection of how it belongs to them all. Mayaya is central to songs, paintings, poetry, dances, and even the culinary arts, as it attests to the dynamic nature of the region's multilingual, multicultural, and multiethnic identity.

Carlos Rigby's "Si yo fuera Mayo" [If I were May] has a dynamic oral structure and seems to have been created for performance.[43] The poem reiterates the relationship of respect and appreciation between the people and their goddess; it reinforces her role as their protector who they summon through a ritual of chants, drumming, and dance.[44] The Mayaya image is interwoven with other components that display a deep understanding of the Creole people's love and dedication to Bluefields and the Caribbean coast. It follows the same pattern visible in other poems of incorporating the Mayaya concept for rhythmic and musical effect.[45] Rigby's poem is well designed in the way it appears as a compilation of life's images, beautiful but nevertheless representations of a harsh, difficult reality, which is the space from which *palo de mayo* will emerge. The Mayaya signifier emerges at the center of a labor protest movement to which the narrating voice gravitates in a clear display of solidarity. This alliance with the working class connects with Miss Lizzie's vision of the *palo de mayo* legacy as far more meaningful than mere entertainment; it is a path toward a deeper awareness of this community's wounds and tribulations, offering insight into the challenges they face and the solutions they deeply desire and need as a people. Verses do reflect the political tensions that remain among the *costeños*:

de tantos trabajadores
que aunque siendo tales
no todos comen pan
ni sudan de la frente
ni tendrán un aumento de sueldo
ni mucho menos nuevas promociones
hacia el antiguo oficio de hacer dinero
dentro de las marchas y protestas
por máyaya lasique má-yaya-o
con los pies de los policías
bailando sin querer:

[of so many workers
that even being who they are
do not all eat bread
nor sweat on their foreheads
nor will have an increase in wages
much less new promotions
toward the ancient profession of making money
within marches and protests
using Mayaya lost her key ma-yaya-oh
with policemen's feet
dancing spontaneously:][46]

The insertion of the Mayaya phenomenon within the precarious social context of harsh socioeconomic difficulty serves as a reminder of the spontaneous and natural connection between such renditions and the spaces from within which they emerge. The deity thereby serves as a medium for emphasizing that these spaces face their own challenges, and these songs inspired by her image, while they appear lighthearted, are reflective of specific experiences. The Mayaya song comes alive in a different way in McField's poem, moving beyond playful dance around a May Pole to assume a menacing, confrontational, spirited display of a people demanding what is rightfully theirs. In his article "Raza, conciencia de color y militancia negra en la literatura nicaragüense" [Race, color consciousness, and Black militancy in Nicaraguan literature], Carlos Castro Jo defines the commitment and consciousness that underpin writings by poets like McField and Rigby.[47] McField emerges as the militant poet, proud of his African roots, who uses his poetry against ethnic and cultural oppression. The symbolic spirit of Africa is the foundation upon which he builds his verses, placing the Afro-descendant subject at the center of his works and reiterating the vision of negritude (or Blackness) as representative of beauty as well as religious and political identity, all vital features of their nation's ethnoracial composition. Rigby's focus on history, homeland, *palo de mayo*, and daily life on the Atlantic coast is his way of expressing pride and love of Caribbean culture. He values the idea of Caribbean Creole culture as a confluence of Black and Indigenous influences, working into his verses the need to overcome racism and racial divides.[48]

A CARIBBEAN POETIC LEGACY: THE WOMEN WRITERS

Creole poetry refers to vibrant and concentrated traditions of primarily poetic production with themes of Caribbean-originated identity, usually associated with writers from Bluefields, with a few from other towns. Anthologies are written in English, Creole, and Spanish and speak primarily of life in Bluefields, *palo de mayo*, the month of May, Mayaya, Protestant-based religious expression (Moravian and Anglican), political autonomy, the Mayo-Ya carnival, Creole-Garifuna-Miskito identities, and proud Caribbean coastal origins. Short narratives, folktales, songs, rhymes, chants, and poetry compose the main cluster within a genre that is decades old and that, over time, has constructed itself exclusively on this heritage known for emphasizing its distinctiveness. While the boundaries of Creole writings are clear, they are not exclusive of Afro-descendants and do include writers and themes that showcase the Garifuna and Indigenous peoples and other coastal dwellers.

Even as Creole writers have been producing poems for generations, specific anthologies published since 1980 capture the cultural representations and sentiments that drive them as a people. Coinciding with the advent of the Sandinista revolutionary government, the 1980s saw a revived national interest in *palo de mayo* as an ever-increasing number of people arrived in Bluefields from the capital and other parts of the country to celebrate the event each May.[49] Since then, due to its popularity as well as the commerce and financial benefits it brings to town, the event has grown and solidified into the nation's carnival celebration. This interest has influenced other areas of cultural expression, including literary production, and has drawn attention to poetry by Creole writers. Today, there is Creole literature created, organized, and published by the writers and coastal dwellers themselves. The cost attached to publishing in this medium has pushed writers beyond anthologies, magazines, journals, newspapers, and pamphlets toward the internet, where there is no cost and their creative writing is more visible via Facebook and other social media platforms. This section explores the women's writings available in what I consider to be the four anthologies that are most representative of Creole poetic production.

Poesía atlántica (edited by Julio Valle-Castillo) came out in 1980 and may well be the first major anthology of the contemporary period produced under the Sandinista government. It confirms the strategic intentions of the state to be more cognizant of such diverse cultures. It is a politically correct, inclusive production commissioned by the Ministry of Culture, part of the Colección Popular de Literatura Nicaragüense [Popular collection of Nicaraguan literature] and dedicated to Indigenous, Creole, and mestizo writings in homage to the Caribbean coast. As the title indicates, its objective is multicultural, and its three main sections divide the Atlantic region's poetic production along ethnic lines both in terms of themes and in terms of writers. "Los cantos ancestrales" are songs and chants from among the Miskito, Rama, Suma, and other Indigenous peoples along with well-known *palo de mayo* songs. The second section, "Los cantos propios," features Creole writers whose poetic renditions center on the Afro-Nicaraguan legacy, especially as it relates to Bluefields and *palo de mayo*. "Los cantos propios" features three male Creole poets, David McField, Carlos Rigby, and Alí Aláh, as well as a worthy collection of poems by lawyer and well-known writer José Santos Cermeño, who was enamored of the Atlantic coast. The third section, "Los cantos deslumbrados," opens up to acclaimed mestizo poets whose writings speak to any aspect of the life and beauty of Bluefields and the Atlantic coast. The rhythmic and onomatopoeic nature of the Creole poems in this collection stylistically align with Nicolás Guillén's *negrista* poetry of the 1930s.[50] In his introduction, Lizandro Chávez Alfaro confirms the intention of the Sandinista government to recognize and pay homage to this cultural heterogeneity that was marginalized and segregated from the nation by the previous regime.[51] No Creole women writers are included in this anthology.

The year 1998 marks the publication of *Antología poética de la Costa Caribe de Nicaragua*, compiled by Eddy Alemán Porras and Franklin Brooks Vargas, the first anthology dedicated exclusively to writers from the Caribbean coast. The volume contains seventy poems by thirty-three poets, of whom ten are women. Two of the women self-identify as *costeña* and Creole, June Beer and Erna Loraine Narciso Walters, while three others identify as Garifuna. The anthology emerges from a group of Creole writers whose ultimate desire is to have their voices heard and record their Caribbean legacy through poetry. It comes as a rebirth after the cultural trauma experienced while processing political autonomy. Their literary production is specific in the way it seeks to describe their Caribbean experiences, the rise of the ancient Miskito kingdom, enslavement, Moravian religious indoctrination, and British colonial influences. Many verses dwell on the region—its landscape and natural beauty as well as the beauty of its Creole and Afro-descendant peoples and their practices. The poetry is written in English, Garifuna, Miskito, and Sumu.[52]

Bluefields en la sangre: Poesía del Caribe Sur Nicaragüense, also compiled by Alemán Porras and Brooks Vargas, will appear much later, in 2011, a collection of 169 poems by thirty-eight participants, of whom twelve are women. The volume features writers from La Fe, Pearl Lagoon, Kukra Hill, and Bluefields and presents itself as a work that seeks to reflect the ethnic diversity of the region's literary production.[53] The verses in this collection focus on this specific heritage as a way of reinforcing its difference, especially in the face of the broader spirit of nationalism that drives political agendas in Managua. The poetry is written in homage to the wonderful landscape, social gatherings, music, and respected personages. Underlying such praise and contemplation are a community's ongoing demands for greater justice and recognition of their cultural, economic, political, and gender-based uniqueness.[54]

Antología poética "Afrocarinica" also appeared in 2011, an endeavor specific to the town of Bluefields, organized by Angélica Brown Hendricks. This is a compilation of Creole and Afro-Nicaraguan poets written in Creole, English, and Spanish. In spirit and intention, the anthology is unapologetic and offers the poems in their original versions with no accompanying translations if written in English or Creole. Writers present a brief biography in which they declare their ethnic background—Creole, Garifuna, mestiza, and so on. By way of their poetry, we learn that they are bilingual and trilingual, and their verses claim and display this multicultural identity as a way of capturing the heritage of which Bluefields is so proud. It is a volume of twelve writers in total; seven are female poets, of whom six self-identify as Creole and one as Garifuna. Taylor confirms that this publication was an initiative of the Equipo de Trabajo en Asuntos Afrodescendientes [ETAA; Working Team on Afro-descendant Affairs] of Bluefields Indian and Caribbean University (BICU), a small endeavor to support new perspectives and strategic visibility for the region's Afro-descendant populations, its natural resources, and its potential.[55] The anthology emphasizes diversity in languages and customs, bringing a message of the region's multiethnic and plurilingual nature. Poems employ local components from coconuts and seafood to *palo de mayo*, the Crab Soup Festival, and the Garifuna way of life.

The attention these publications received—book launchings, public events, government recognition—reveal strategic plans by the government to recognize the rights of the nation's minority populations.[56] Within these textual spaces, the ideological premise is the same. Poetry facilitates the movement of oral language and traditions into the written space, allowing for ancestral beliefs associated with Black and Indigenous cultures to find their resonance in a more fulfilling way while serving as a device that makes visible compliance with mandates and policies such as those of regional autonomy and proud cultural patrimony. "Es por ello que estas composiciones o creaciones literarias ancestrales . . . desde sus fuentes originales son motivo de estudio, fuente de consulta, ensanchamiento de nuestro patrimonio cultural, así como motivo de orgullo local, regional y nacional" [It is because of this that these compositions or ancestral literary creations . . . from their original sources are subjects of study, reference sources, the broadening of our cultural patrimony as well as a source of local, regional, and national pride].[57]

The legacy of poetic writing is far older than the actual production of entire anthologies. By the late 1990s, poets such as June Beer, Carlos Rigby, David McField, Hugh Allan Budier Bryan, Sidney Francis Martin, and Byron Hodgson were making a name for themselves; they continue to be well-known poets, and their writings clearly reflect a deliberate cultivation of literary forms that register proud Creoleness. They are seasoned poets who have been writing for decades, each having developed their own eclectic, variegated style of verse in three languages. There have been vibrant moments, and they formed a writers' association called the Asociación de Poetas "Alí Aláh" ["Alí Alláh" Poets Association].[58] Writers have produced individual anthologies; McField's *Dios es negro: Poemas* (1967) is an example of verses expressive of the ideology of negritude. *Leyendas de la Costa Atlántica* (2003) reveals deep-rooted oral traditions, superstitions and beliefs, and myths and tales that appear in storytelling format.[59] Carlos Castro Jo's discussion places the topic of such writers and their works within a larger conversation on national production and confirms some of the shortfalls in relation to diversity and literary depictions in Nicaragua. He identifies insensitive portrayals among certain (non-Creole) Nicaraguan writers who have developed themes about the Indigenous peoples and Afro-descendants and whose ideas and poetic images mirror problematic perceptions, reproduce superficial ideas, and reveal the general lack of cultural appreciation that marks this society.[60] At the same time, he points out that this approach is not always true and calls attention to writings on themes related to the cultural phenomena of the coast without focusing on skin color.[61] He confirms that works by mestizo writers are about enriching aspects of Caribbean coastal culture, including Manuel Martínez, Alí Aláh, Santos Cermeño, and Lizandro Chávez Alfaro, even if they themselves are not originally a part of this heritage.[62] He does recognize the intrinsic claim on this legacy that is very visible, for example, in the militant style of poets such as McField and Rigby.[63]

Rossman Tejada discusses the more recent emergence of Caribbean Nicaraguan women poets and their subsequently delayed recognition within the national space in particular as well as the Hispanic world of literary writing in general.[64] There are writers who have been producing since 1975. While June Beer (1935–86) continues to be the best known, others have been published, especially Socorro Woods Downs, Carmen Andira Watson Díaz (Andira Watson), Angela Chow, Annette Fenton, Yolanda Rossman, Deborah Robb Taylor (Deborah Robb), Loveth Martínez (her name is also written as Lovette Martínez), Grace Kelly, Nydia Taylor, Erna Lorraine Narciso Walters, and Carla R. James.[65] June Beer is widely discussed as representative of Caribbean Creole writing and appears as part of the national canon, while these women writers have also made a name for themselves and have left their mark as Nicaraguan and Caribbean writers. They tend to be primarily poets whose writings are available online and in anthologies. They work the multiple lines of their heritage, simultaneously inserting themselves into their writings and their works into the nation even as said nation is oftentimes, at best, ambivalent to their presence. They do not seem to have many individual publications; rather, their writings are available in locally produced anthologies and in the quarterly publication *WANI: Revista del Caribe Nicaragüense*, a literary and cultural production of the Centro de Investigación y Documentación de la Costa Atlántica [CIDCA; Center for Research and Documentation of the Atlantic Coast] of Bluefields Indian and Caribbean University. Unpublished research monographs are part of the collection at the Universidad de las Regiones Autónomas de la Costa Caribe Nicaragüense (URACCAN) library in Bluefields, two of which focus on Creole women writers.[66]

In general terms, their production is not exclusively woman-centered or feminist in nature even as their identity as Creole women is a poetic theme and their writing displays a gender-based consciousness. Their verses proudly support the universal agenda of paying homage to a Caribbean coastal identity whose uniqueness is under constant scrutiny and evaluation. The defining trait is that they will write in English and/or Creole (not necessarily in Spanish), and they display a clear

dedication to themes that are specific to their world on the Caribbean coast, including ethnolinguistic diversity, autonomy, Bluefields, the tropical rainforest region,
the month of May, and religious faith. They are diverse and eclectic in their artistic
and narrative views even as one can perceive a certain synchrony in relation to the
Creole cause, ideological agenda, and purpose, motivated by the same agenda and
enthusiasm that drives Miss Lizzie.

The women writers in Alemán Porras and Brooks Vargas's *Antología poética
de la Costa Caribe de Nicaragua* design themes around their heritage, cultivate
nationalism, and help define what it means to be Nicaraguan quite apart from a
Sandinista identity. Several poems address gender-specific concerns of a social
and political nature or favor displays unique to the female experience while they
continue to share the same value systems and principles of pride in Creole identity as we have observed in Miss Lizzie. An important measure of their poetic
endeavors is the way their adherence to revolutionary ideals coexists favorably
with their immense pride and love for autonomy and Creole identity. They are fully
aware that such difference is theirs and not really a part of the cultural norms of
the dominant group located primarily in the Pacific region. June Beer's poetry in
English and Creole lines up with Miss Lizzie's *palo de mayo* performances in the
way they advocate for greater flexibility when it comes to descriptions of national
identity.[67] The performances match verses that insist on inclusiveness and true
representations of citizenship. Beer's "Poema de amor" calls attention and pays
homage to the original ethnic groups of the Caribbean coast in a spirited patriotic
poem that envisions them as Nicaraguan, "hijos de Sandino," or Sandino's sons
and daughters.[68] Similarly, Erna Loraine Narciso Walters's "How Much Have You
Invested? / ¿Cuánto has invertido?" reflects the central political theme of their
absolute commitment to preserving their autonomy:

> It gives you such a sense of pride
> when you mention Autonomy's name
> but how much have you invested
> to make your legal claim?
>
> It's time to rise Coast Brothers,
> and really do your part;
> don't wait until tomorrow
> but quickly make a start.[69]

Recognition of the region's autonomous status is an achievement gained with
sacrifice and loss that begs appreciation; it is the kind of loss the narrator urges
her community to embrace, understand, and build upon. Ileana Vanessa Lacayo
Ortiz, a mestiza writer from Bluefields, sustains the theme of Caribbean and
Atlantic legacy by reiterating their community's pride in self-governance in her
poem "Autonomía."[70] In poetry, self-governance is a sacred idea that underpins
the verses, reflective of its place in their origins as a people who identify as both
Caribbean and Nicaraguan.

The theme of autonomy encompasses all aspects of their lives in the region. Similarly, Isabel Estrada Colindres, self-identifying as a Garifuna woman, is inextricably tied to places like La Fe and Bluefields, as indicated in "La fe," written in English and Spanish.[71] Her loving gaze and tone match those of Garifuna poet Fermín González López, whose "The Lagoon / La laguna" draws attention to the municipality of Pearl Lagoon and dwells on the beauty of the lagoon and surrounding lands, valued as "the backbone of my home."[72] Irene Vidaurre Campos's "Costa Atlántica" coincides with this gaze on the land that she too idealizes in a poem composed solely of names of flora, fauna, fruits, the waters, and ethnicities found only in that region.[73] Identifying as a mestiza writer from Managua, her "¡Rica y empobrecida tierra mía!" [My rich and impoverished land!] comes in strong tones of joy and condemnation as the narrating voice traces the abuse and exploitation of her beloved land due to colonialism and national political processes while remaining in awe of its splendor and durability and the resilience of its diverse peoples.[74] She celebrates the legalization of autonomy while recognizing that it came at a price and is not always respected. The tones of these verses are accusatory yet protective and loving as the author resolves to safeguard her impoverished yet rich and beloved land from what it still has to face. This particular poem is revealing of the spirit that underlies much of Creole regional poetry, a spirit of ambivalence when it comes to defining their role within the nation as well as in terms of their relationship with the political establishment on the Pacific coast.

The women writers in Alemán Porras and Brooks Vargas's *Bluefields en la sangre* offer images they extract from daily life, a way of illustrating what autonomy means to them. Lesbia González Fornos's "Rondón es también. Pero que bien: ¡Autonomía!," Erna Narciso's "Autonomía," and Lovette Martínez's "Rundown/ Rondón" and "It Is Autonomy / Es autonomía" continue to manifest just how valuable and proud they are of this political and cultural status.[75] Political acknowledgment of their uniqueness and their own understanding of what it means to be Creole are important messages in their verses. Autonomy means many things. It represents their dishes, especially *rondón*, made with coconut, plantains, bananas, yams, potatoes, and meats cooked together in a delicious soup. It is in their songs, dances, and mannerisms. Autonomy holds them to higher standards personally, within their community, and in their interactions with other coastal peoples. It demands that Creoles, Garifunas, Indigenous peoples, and mestizos work in unity. Autonomy through verse demands an end to injustice, discrimination, and exclusion. In poetry, it signifies their history and the way they fought for and defended their land. It depicts their environment, nature, and natural resources. Autonomy is about their power, purpose, and strength sustained through tremendous diversity. This is a powerful and emotional theme, and many poets design their verses to include this message.

Portrayals of their land, region, and home are an important characteristic of the *Antología poética "Afrocarinica."* Verses pay homage to the natural beauty of the land, a central theme as seen in Annette Olivia Fenton Tom's "Poem XVI Pearl Lagoon" and Brenda Elena Green Wilson's "Nuestra tierra."[76] The town and municipality bear the same name as the largest coastal lagoon, Pearl Lagoon, located in the South Caribbean Coast Autonomous Region, and it is indeed a scenic place, home to a small, isolated community. Here is a place of tropical wonder where the multicolored flora and fauna match the multicultural peoples who inhabit the land. Green Wilson's verses are equally idealistic, glorifying the region they call home; the earth filled with riches, natural beauty, and enchantment; the place of their ancestors and their traditions. Human life is simple; the few needs are all met by nature as the local dwellers fish, sell their produce, and cook the very tasty *rondón*. The exuberant descriptions feed the general spirit of pride in the region's pristine nature and in the fact that it is all theirs, a spirit that harmonizes with all of this writing.

Antología poética "Afrocarinica" presents writers whose roots and verses are Caribbean and Creole. Erna Loraine Narciso Walters, Doris Merlin Forbes, Annette Olivia Fenton Tom, Brenda Elena Green Wilson, Isabel Estrada Colindres, Lovette Angélica Martínez Downs, and Joan Sinclair create verses, many in English, about love, life, God and faith, and situations within their community. In keeping with the Miss Lizzie legacy developed in this essay, customs and traditions are valued, as is the idea of preserving and understanding their history. Narciso Walters, for example, self-identifying as Creole, describes a past era in "Those Good Old Days," a poetic expression that mirrors the views of older folk like Miss Lizzie and Sujo Wilson, who see bygone days as containing value systems and customs that could well serve today's generations.[77] Life was not easy, but it was simpler; there were jobs, food to eat, clothes to wear, and a few schools where discipline and excellence in learning were priorities. The glorification of these earlier times, when today's elderly folk were children, is a nostalgic reaction that resists current value systems, as they are so different, reflective of a loss of certain types of knowledge and practices. Their poetry mirrors Miss Lizzie's vision of these changes as detrimental to their cultural wisdom and ancestry. In her interview, she identifies several reasons, including a lack of established and trustworthy historical records that inform about the true contours of *palo de mayo* and the effects of poverty that Blacks face constantly in Bluefields.[78]

As one of the more contemporary anthologies, *Antología poética "Afrocarinica"* includes the theme of the female character. Self-describing as a Creole *costeña* poet, Green Wilson is proud of her identity and ancestral roots as confirmed in "Soy costeña y ¿qué?" and "Identity."[79] Her verses coincide with those of Martínez Downs in "Black on Top," "I'm Proud," and "Time Is Now" in the way they treasure and develop their own forms of ethnic identity combined with pride in being Caribbean and autonomous.[80] The verses are enthusiastic and proud, registering an awareness of this distinction in a positive and defiant way. "Soy costeña y ¿qué?" is a strategic title, meaning "I am a coastal woman, and so what?"[81] It represents Green Wilson's way of firing back in the face of discrimination and adversity. She chooses to immerse herself in the joy of being who she is—Black, Caribbean, and *costeña*—and is full of energy, ready to chase away all sadness and share her enthusiasm and vitality. Similarly, in "Identity," the author encourages a noble stance and direct confrontation to achieve the acceptance and respect that is hers by right. The messages are simple and direct—teaching moments on how to be successful, how to think, how to act, and how to counteract the debilitating effects of discrimination. Green Wilson accepts her skin color, loves her race, and is particularly direct in her expectations of others, for, as she puts it, "I am black and no one can turn that back."[82] This is who she is, a person full of pride, self-esteem, and love of self who expects no less than respect and recognition from others. She is smart and capable and takes delight in herself as beautiful and worthy. Women's writings reveal acute awareness of the many challenges women face even as the female persona transmits messages of pride in identity and urges greater unity within the community.

The anthology *Bluefields en la sangre* reflects on experiences specific to women. Isabel Estrada Colindres's "Strong Wuman / Mujer fuerte" and Brenda Green's "Soy costeña" pay homage to the Creole and the coastal woman, whose strength, resilience, language, and pride of identity mark her in a specific way.[83] Her presence, energy, and personality are deemed enriching, especially when it comes to relationships with men; she is the one who will make the difference, who will energize the encounter and make it more meaningful. In other words, she is the strong woman. This external configuration finds its internal complement in poetry such as Annette Fenton's "Poem XXIX / Poema XXIX" and "Poem XII / Poema XII."[84] Introspective verses reveal her thoughts, sensations, reactions, and emotions, intent on describing who she really is on the inside. The narrating voice is candid during these moments as she reveals her tumultuous feelings; she displays deep insecurities, fears, and needs alongside a desire to make the most of life even as she experiences sensations of achievement. She exists physically, but she also exists in her dreams, and it is in dreaming that she finds her true self:

> Looking a little deeper I sense,
> an extremely imaginative yet sensitive being
> Whose brain, heart, flesh and bone
> like porous matter absorbs it all;
> The love, the pain, the feelings that sustain.[85]

While dreaming, she has to face her most intense vulnerabilities, which is actually not a bad thing, since she exists in her skin as a physical being, and that protects her in the end. She can abandon those potential weaknesses and instead build herself up to become stronger and more self-assured. Her dreams are like journeys, processes of personal searching and self-discovery at the end of which she is transformed, for she can see and be better.

PART III

A Colombian Case Study

CHAPTER 5

Rituals of *Alegría* and *Ponchera*

THE ENTERPRISING *PALENQUERAS*

Literature by *palenquera* women writers is transforming the way the Colombian nation views these women of African ancestry who proudly claim the nation's *palenques* [maroon communities] as their historical legacy. They are producing works, especially poetry, to accompany and solidify processes that describe and idealize their origins and identity. Today, in Colombia's port city of Cartagena, there are notable differences between national perception and self-perception, a tangible dissimilarity between, on the one hand, exotic, tropical images of the *palenqueras* as colorful street vendors that Cartagena cultivates as part of its tourism agenda and, on the other, ancestral narratives of identity these women themselves produce. Palenque de San Basilio, *cimarronaje*, the mythical figure of María Lucrecia, the *lumbalú* ritual in homage to the dead, and the transcendental image of Catalina Loango are consecrated paths to understanding what it means to belong to this community. This story unfolds in the contemporary setting of Cartagena de Indias, located on the Atlantic and Caribbean coasts of Colombia and Palenque de San Basilio, one of the famous maroon settlements in the Spanish Americas. The process of *palenquera* iconization finds real and meaningful support in the four bilingual (*palenquero* and Spanish) anthologies central to this study, María Teresa Ramírez's *Flor de palenque*, *Abalenga*, and *Mabungú triunfo: Poemas bilingües, palenque-español* and Mirian Díaz Pérez's *Tejiendo palabras con libertad / Binda ndunblua ku bindanga*. Women who proudly identify as *palenqueras* adhere to the deeper meanings associated with *cimarronaje*, a term describing the phenomenon of fugitive slaves and their settlements; more importantly, it implies a vision of freedom as taken, a successful and triumphant collaborative act of resistance. Overall, *palenquero* communities of Colombia have a specific and distinct legacy that proudly represents them as the first truly free African descendants, a status they claim as indicative of consistent and long-term action on the part of enslaved captives in their efforts to access freedom, reclaim their rights as individuals, and reestablish the lives they had on the African continent.[1]

Ample scholarship about colonization and enslavement in relation to Cartagena de Indias as well as an increasing amount of interest in the experiences of enslaved, freed, and free women are important current trends. The urge is to fill gaps, recognizing the dearth of information in relation to the historical and cultural situation of African and Afro-descendant women in the Latin American region generally.[2] At the same time, it is proving easier to study women as enslaved subjects within the colonial system than develop a line of historical reflection about women who fought, rejected, and escaped bondage, choosing to take destiny in their own hands and flee into the unknown jungles. They chose to become *cimarronas* and *palenqueras*, seekers and instigators of their own freedom. This is the history that was rarely recorded, one that requires reconstruction with the help of oral memory, folklore, traditional practices, and literature.

THE *PALENQUE* AS COLOMBIA'S CARIBBEAN LEGACY

The *palenque*, immortalized in literature, emerges as a space that provides reconnections with ancestry and revitalization of energies, a retaking of what its inhabitants left behind in their homelands in Africa, and a chance at constructing their lives in a new space on their terms. The word refers to a settlement of peoples who consciously chose to flee from bondage during the colonial era. Nina de Friedemann describes it as the earliest liberation movement that challenged the authority of the Spanish Empire until the campaigns that ended in Colombia's independence in 1810.[3] The term has come to represent much more. As the *palenques* thrived into modernity, some became foundations for modern-day cities; they are now historical treasures, spaces of traditional, religious, ritual, medicinal, and cultural practices that are part of Africa's legacy in the Americas.[4] Driven by desperation and motivated by dreams of creating a home, these new settlers dug in using their original skill sets, techniques, and long-standing practices to build homes, cultivate the land, forge weapons and tools, and adapt to the new environment effectively in order to ensure their survival on difficult terrain. They must have been an eclectic group, bearers of different cultural traditions and knowledge along with other skills acquired from the Indigenous peoples and from their contacts with their Spanish overlords.[5] As a unified group, they relied on one another, brought together by the realization that their survival depended on such reliance and an enterprising spirit.

Ruth Betty Lozano Lerma indicates that the majority of Colombia's Black population currently resides in the cities of Cali, Medellín, Bogotá, Cartagena, and Barranquilla.[6] Peter Wade points out that the Caribbean coast does not have the largest concentration of Afro-Colombians; however, the majority of studies on Afro-Colombianness focus on the *palenquero* legacy located in that area.[7] As Francisco Adelmo Asprilla Mosquera states, "Los cimarrones de ayer somos los afrocolombianos de hoy" [We, the maroons of yesterday, are the Afro-Colombians of today] is a concrete affirmation defining what, for many, is the most important line of Black identity in Colombia, one built on marronage.[8] It represents a legitimate claim to a proud legacy of rebellions, battles, escapes, journeys, and liberation.

While association with Palenque de San Basilio makes this vision one that many see as specific to Cartagena and the settlements in that region, the ideals embedded in this identity are so powerful that they appear at the center of agendas, projects, and advocacy. Such commitment is visible in the Movimiento Nacional Cimarrón [National Maroon Movement], currently one of the leading caucuses in Bogotá today, under the leadership of Juan de Dios Mosquera Mosquera.[9]

While *palenque*, in a generic sense, materializes as a specific realm of resistance, it has adjusted to accompany current trends and perceptions of multiculturalism within a national space. As terminology, it operates as if unique to San Basilio de Palenque—given its privileged status as the original, surviving, authentic settlement—even as it is a word that pushes forward, serving today as a reference to wherever *palenqueros* congregate or dwell. The famous example is the Chambacú neighborhood. Located just beyond the Walled City—that is, Cartagena's historical center—by the 1960s, it had grown to become the country's largest slum, deemed an eyesore and targeted for removal. Before it was dismantled in 1971, Chambacú was considered the poorest neighborhood of Cartagena, home to many Afro-Colombian families. In popular imaginary, it was deemed dangerous, a view challenged by Manuel Zapata Olivella's famous novel, *Chambacú, corral de negros*, which restores the area's historical, symbolic value as the traditional Black neighborhood of Cartagena and, therefore, a vital ancestral legacy.[10] *Palenquera* activist and community leader Dorina Hernández spent her childhood there; indeed, she confirms that it was a place of unfavorable memories, where her father met a violent death and her mother, a market seller, struggled to support her and her siblings.[11]

Uprisings, rebellions, and *palenques* were serious threats to colonial hegemonic rule, especially during the second half of the eighteenth century. Violence in the form of rebellions commenced as early as the beginning of the sixteenth century, and by the middle to late 1700s, such aggression was widespread and had all the characteristics of civil war.[12] Kathryn McKnight provides a description of *palenques*:

> *Palenques*—elsewhere known as *quilombos*, mocambos, cumbes, ladeiras, and mambises (Price 1)—provided important spaces where African-descent peoples preserved and created new cultural and social practices that had their roots in Africa. Such processes were dynamic, historically specific, and varied from one *Maroon* settlement to another. A *palenque*'s demographics, the birthplaces of its members, and the historical events through which these residents had lived, all molded the community's social relationships and cultural expressions. *Palenques* did not exist in isolation, and thus these processes were also affected by the community's engagement with their European and Amerindian neighbors, the politics of nearby urban centers, and their interactions with free and enslaved Afro-Latinos outside the *palenque*.[13]

Historians refer to advanced levels of organization and coordination among various fugitive groups. Numerous and organized, they posed a constant threat to the stability of colonial power in the territory and instilled fear among landowners and local authorities.[14] Palenque de San Basilio, today viewed as an African territory in Colombia, would have been one of several such settlements on the Atlantic coast; however, today it stands at the forefront of them all, is the most famous and well-documented case, and continues to provide the most enduring insight into what it means to be *palenquero*.[15] What guarantees this *palenque*'s special place in history is its iconic leader, Benkos Biohó, and its status as the *primer pueblo libre de América* [first free town of America], gained in 1713, when an agreement was signed between the inhabitants and the then bishop of Cartagena, who pledged to halt military intervention if the residents stopped attacking nearby towns. Their "Himno de Palenque," the *palenque* national anthem, composed in the late 1980s, proudly references this victory.[16] There is no doubt that such a profile has stimulated the rise of a *palenquero* literary *écriture*, a development discussed in detail in the following chapter.

Palenque de San Basilio is located at the base of the foothills known as the Montes de María, about forty-three miles southeast of Cartagena, Colombia's Caribbean city. It is in the municipality of Mahates and department of Bolívar in the northern part of Colombia. In 2005, the United Nations Educational, Scientific and Cultural Organization (UNESCO) granted it the prestigious title of Obra Maestra del Patrimonio Oral e Intangible de la Humanidad [Masterpiece of the Oral and Intangible Heritage of Humanity] in recognition of its status as the first free town in the Americas, securing its place and that of its immortalized leader, Benkos Biohó, in world history and its eternal preservation within the national territory. Four attributes consolidated *palenquero* cultural uniqueness: their music and chants, their language, their *lumbalú* ritual, and their *kuagros*, all of which are recurring themes in literature.[17] Known for their autonomous spirit, they have always insisted on the right to self-governance and shared governance, especially as it pertains to administrative decision-making about their villages, their lands, their culture, their language, and their political representation.[18] Internal frictions and certain tensions with regional and central organs of the government severely hamper the flow of financial resources to the communities, while flaws and lack of consensus within the local government and state administration pose challenges to *palenquero* political representation and participation in decision-making processes that directly impact their lives.

San Basilio developed its own systems of values and customs, expanded its right to self-rule, blocked colonial and postcolonial authority, held off attacks and raids, and in contrast with other similar sites, retained its autonomy and linguistic distinctiveness. These successes define the coast as the region of *palenques*, and the place known for its "heritage of blackness."[19] Wade explains that the residents proudly proclaim their African ancestry as a state of being. This *palenque* emerges as a space that has always embraced and reproduced its African (and American) heritage; indeed, it is no accident that artistic production celebrates this settlement as consisting of enclaves of warriors, both male and female. Historical, literary, and artistic representations provide ongoing images of the settlement and its peoples, who occupied positions at the forefront as defenders of freedom, instigators of all forms of resistance—uprisings, escapes, battles, attacks. Their presence and determination proved influential, affecting political agendas and military decisions in the region.[20]

With a population of about four thousand inhabitants, Palenque de San Basilio continues to have both real and symbolic effects. A destination for historical and scholarly tourism, it capitalizes on its long-term value by preserving and exploiting the image of its ancestral hero and leader, Benkos Biohó (also known as Domingo Biohó). His image represents victory and glory, thereby allowing all subsequent endeavors and discourses to prosper simply by association. This *palenque* and its leader are influential in Colombia's Caribbean, serving the interests of Afro-descendant movements of ethnic vindication as well as national efforts regarding politicized agendas that have to do with equity, diversity, and citizens' rights.[21] "La memoria histórica de Palenque es libertaria porque su razón de ser como pueblo lo ha construido a partir de la defensa de su condición de colectividad libre, con una autonomía de territorio y de vida que ha permanecido vigente durante los cuatrocientos años de la vida palenquera" [*Palenque* historical memory is about freedom because their raison d'être as a people has built itself upon the defense of their condition of free collectivity, with an autonomy of life and territory that has remained in force throughout four hundred years of *palenquero* existence].[22]

Elisabeth Cunin observes a fusion between Black and *palenquero* identity, as the latter infers a presence above and beyond that of the *cimarrón* [fugitive slave]. She claims that on the Caribbean coast, including Cartagena, the word *palenquero* is taken as referring specifically to an inhabitant originating from Palenque de San Basilio, whether they continue to live there or in the city of Cartagena. She views this as a narrowing in interpretation, a move toward a more authentic and exclusive vision of the space and history it represents: "El Palenque de San Basilio no es percibido como un palenque cualquiera, sino como El Palenque, única expresión verdadera de la gesta heroica del cimarrón" [The Palenque de San Basilio is perceived not as any *palenque* but rather as The Palenque, the only true expression of the *cimarrón*'s heroic gesture].[23] This specificity serves to sustain a sense of historical worth and influence. As Colombians, they define their identity distinctively at the same time that, when positioned with the diverse entourage of Afro-descendant communities (Afro-descendants, Afro-Colombians, Blacks, *raizales*, and Caribbean Colombians), they manifest a distinctiveness as lead actors by virtue of having left their mark on the history of the Black populace and also on the nation as a whole.[24]

Claims to this identity are pretty dynamic given that many Afro-Colombian women, *palenqueras* included, now transit a wide range of professions and positions. Further, within the realm of advocacy, Afro-descendant women are professionals of consciousness, in possession of a diverse range of ideological agendas through which they establish effective networks at the local, regional, and international levels. As activists, writers, educators, and scholars, their experiences, testimonies, and narratives are greater in number and therefore more available in the public domain; they continue to share, record, and publish information about their heritage and identity with great pride. In terms of the domain I refer to as *palenquera* literature, this identity can be assumed by anyone; one of the writers, María Teresa Ramírez, is not *palenquera* by birth even though she writes poetry in the language. María Mercedes Jaramillo describes her production as hybrid texts that create bridges to the ancestral world.[25] On the other hand, poet and educator Mirian Díaz Pérez self-identifies as a *palenquera* born in the urban *palenque* of Barranquilla, as does well-known community advocate Dorina Hernández. Activist, educator, and community leader, Hernández is very vocal in her support of ongoing efforts to preserve Palenque de San Basilio, even as her people fight for justice, recognition, and integration at all levels.

Cunin notes that consensus among historians about the geographical locations, founding, and fate of these settlements on the Caribbean coast is difficult. By contrast, San Basilio's inhabitants are very clear about their origin, antecedents, and historical chronology.[26] They pay homage to Benkos Biohó, whose image is well exploited, appearing even in literary works that idealize him and build on his legacy—his escape from slavery and rise to becoming the king of Arcabuco. He remains Colombia's greatest *cimarrón* and is an indelible part of his people's memory, appearing in poems, legends, stories, songs, and oral histories that narrate an epic past and those customs and traditions that mark this people.[27] The ever-expanding research on Biohó has done much to shift perspectives and has brought African peoples into the arena as instigators and griots of history. Targeted research is being done on the role women played in the escapes, confrontations, and battles. Kidnapped and enslaved in 1596 along the coast of Guinea-Bissau, West Africa, Biohó; his wife, Wiwa; their daughter, Orika; and son, Sando-Biohó endured the Middle Passage into Nueva Granada (today's Colombia), disembarking at the Port of Cartagena. They were transported on the same slave ship, although shackled separately, for it was customary to separate the men from the women and children. As leaders in their original communities (Biohó having claimed royal privilege), their spirit of rebellion and thirst for freedom must have been fierce as they struggled to regain control of their lives and sought to overcome bondage and suffering. With regard to female participation, we are left to imagine and reconstruct women's participation in these battles. Wiwa and Orika no doubt would have conspired to overthrow their captors; unfortunately, their actions remain unknown.[28]

In 1599, Biohó escaped enslavement, and in 1600, he started to appear in historical documents as a resistance fighter and the mastermind behind rebellions. He established the first free *palenque*, La Matuna, close to Cartagena, and expanded the settlement's population by freeing slaves and engaging in constant battle. La Matuna was well organized, with its own military and social and political infrastructure. A strategy of war was to burn the settlement and move to another location.[29] Biohó stole and made weaponry for battle, displaying great leadership and constituting a successful antislavery movement in the Caribbean zone around Cartagena. He went on to organize maroon sites, established zones and settlements of militarized resistance, and laid the foundations for political agreements with the colonizers. In 1606, he signed an agreement with governor Gerónimo de Suazo that officially recognized La Matuna's autonomy. The events surrounding his capture are unclear, and he was executed by hanging on March 16, 1621.[30] His legacy lives on, visible in the form of a large statue located in Palenque de San Basilio's central square. His fist raised toward the sky in a stance of defiance, he breaks the chains and reaches upward as if to grasp at freedom, a meaningful representation within the realms of Black history and visual arts in the Americas. He now straddles the worlds of history and myth, fiction and reality as a legendary figure, revolutionary icon, and founding father of Afro-Colombianness and *palenquero* identity. Zapata Olivella writes, "Benkos Biojo es un inmortal y como todos los mortales, alimentando en vida por las sombras de los ancestros" [Benkos Biohó is an immortal being and, like all mortals, in life, nourished by the shadows of his ancestors].[31] Warrior, military strategist, and politician, Biohó's bravery and victories guaranteed freedom, autonomy, and early recognition for his people, a feat that earned him a place as one of the founders of Colombia and national recognition as an inspirational figure. He is immortalized in their oral traditions, kept alive in narratives passed down through the generations in the form of epic recounts, children's stories, traditional songs, and chants.[32] The "Himno de Palenque," composed in the 1980s, pays him homage as the heroic leader of the *primer pueblo libre de América*.[33] After her husband's capture and execution in 1621, Wiwa, her children, and other survivors carried on his work and established the *palenques* of San Miguel, Sierra María, and San Basilio in the Bolívar department.[34]

De Friedemann recounts the "Leyenda de Arcos" [Legend of Arcos], an early twentieth-century pseudohistorical narrative woven by Camilo Delgado, former member of the Centro de Historia de Cartagena [Cartagena's Center of History]. Under the pseudonym of Dr. Arcos, Delgado compiled, wrote, and published several volumes known as *Historia, leyendas y tradiciones de Cartagena* [History, legends, and traditions of Cartagena].[35] The "Legend of Arcos" is a romantic tale involving Biohó's daughter, Orika, who fell in love with her enslaver's son, Don Francisco, shortly before fleeing with her family to escape slavery. She later tries to flee with her lover; however, she is recaptured, and Don Francisco is killed in the confrontation. Orika's father is unforgiving, and upon returning home, she submits to a ceremonial ritual during which she drinks a special potion prepared by the medicine man that would determine her culpability or innocence. Feeling the lethal effects of the poison, she succumbs to the potion and dies while the crowd shouts in support of the verdict. Meanwhile, led by her invincible father, the warriors claim victory after victory.[36]

This narrative emerges within the space of Cartagena's society, a stratified one dominated by whites and mestizos, original designers of the legends and histories about slavery and Afro-descendants. Such accounts and records are the results of interpretations, changes, transcriptions, and repetitions taken from notes and records kept by slave owners and other members of the predominantly white, educated ruling class. This explains the romanticized nature of the story as well as the difficulty historians face in confirming its veracity.[37] What is still missing and understudied is the role women played in this military and political activity. Who were they and what place or leadership roles did they occupy, especially in Palenque de San Basilio? Although it is a conglomerate of women and men, envisioning women as freedom fighters remains a challenge. Historical research is slowly uncovering archival references to these figures, citing, for example, Leonor, a queen, and Polonia, a heroine. The task of combing through archival documents in order to find and understand the roles that leading Afro-Colombian women may have played in history is now taking place. Natalia Silva Prada has researched Leonor, who ruled over a maroon site called El Limón, in existence during the seventeenth century, probably during the 1630s, in Nueva Granada. Queen Leonor bore two sons and lived as part of a community of about seventy inhabitants from various African nations and origins.[38] There is also some information about Polonia, the leader of Malambo, Bolívar, who in 1581 led a group of 150 *palenque-ros* into victorious battle against one Captain Pedro Ordóñez Ceballos.[39] Fabio Teolindo Perea Hinestroza's Afro-Colombian dictionary includes references to *cimarronas* Agustina and Felicita Campos.[40] *Palenquera* community leaders and scholars Teresa Cassiani Herrera and Rutsely Simarra Obeso write of the distinct experiences of African women who were enslaved and are convinced that they had to develop their own strategies to protect their lives, families, and ancestral legacies.[41] Such strategies started with a decision to become a maroon, racing away from Spanish oppression into hostile zones, toward new life and hope in freedom, taking with them their ideas and memories while looking forward to re-creating a free and independent version of Africa in the Americas.

Literary imaging is a recent phenomenon, resulting from increased Black consciousness after the 1970s. Cunin speaks to this new awareness among Afro-Colombians and indicates that the consolidation of a discourse of identity emerged during the early 1980s, part of a thrust toward greater inclusion in Colombian society.[42] Ramiro Delgado and colleagues speak of an awakening that occurred during the 1980s and the first part of the 1990s, a period marked by a drive for cultural affirmation—all part of contemporary initiatives to preserve and defend Afro-descendant legacies.[43] The emergence of a clear recognition of their ethnicity occurred with the advent of the 1991 constitution and Law 70. An important measure was the valuing of Afro-Colombian history with moves to protect and secure the longevity of the language by integrating both areas into the school curriculum, an ongoing mission that is not without its challenges. The community suffers from a lack of development and a sense of abandonment. There are clear signs of the struggles they face: poverty, lack of public infrastructure, illiteracy, and migration from the community. At the same time, it is a place of deep communal ties and traditions, an inner strength to which residents cling in spite of the sensation of having been forgotten by the state.[44]

Palenque de San Basilio is not located close to the city; it requires about a forty- to fifty-minute drive by taxi. Most inhabitants travel by bus, which takes longer. This distance increases a sense of difference, disconnection, and isolation. At the same time, the valuing of their distinct heritage relies on the meaningfulness of a separate and distinct social and ethnocultural group within Colombia. They are direct descendants of the original community, a fact they proudly confirm in their long-term resistance to slavery, colonization, and the debilitating effects of acculturation to the predominant Hispanic, miscegenated culture. This expression of self-worth and historical value directly counteracts the totality of the Spanish colonizing process and is a constant reminder of the community's triumph over subjugation. Their pride in their heritage is seen in their popularized conversion of the community's name from Palenque de San Basilio to San Basilio de Palenque, their way of saying that San Basilio is theirs and not the other way around. The unofficial change in the name reveals their bold, confident nature and coincides with the broader intention of this chapter, which is to arrive at a greater understanding of the *palenqueras'* universe and how their experiences connect to the broader context of Afro-Colombian community activism, Colombian attempts at affirmative action, the legacy of Afro-Colombianness, and issues at the intersection of race, gender, and society. This shift from the original historical name that matched Spanish colonial rule (where, given the nature of Spanish language structure, it seems that the *palenque* belongs to San Basilio) to the second option, San Basilio de Palenque (in which case, the *palenque* takes ownership of San Basilio) parallels the idea of intentionality that is very visible today in the projects and writings of Afro-Colombian and *palenquera* women. A blend of pride and denunciation captures the spirit of this social space and the writings that have emerged so far. Today, their world is rapidly changing, and it is within this inevitability that leaders and representatives denounce major problems greatly affecting their prosperity, productivity, and civil rights at all levels.

In Cartagena, *palenquera* identity seems to be specifically associated with women who are from San Basilio. The tone of Dorina Hernández's testimony is a display of pride and dignity. A recognized community leader, Hernández speaks about her identity and San Basilio de Palenque not in isolation but rather as part of a broader geographical space and historical experience.[45] As she declares, *palenque* "pasó a identificar la rebeldía y el pensamiento libertario de los esclavos que se liberaron del yugo español. El cimarronaje pasó a ser todo un pensamiento de libertad y respeto de la dignidad negra" [came to represent rebelliousness and the liberty mindset of the slaves who freed themselves from the Spanish yoke. Marronage became a whole way of thinking about freedom and respect for the dignity of Blacks].[46] In her testimony, Hernández declares that women fought alongside men, and together they won and guaranteed the founding of the first free settlement of the Americas under the guidance of Benkos Biohó. They fought fiercely—so much so that they forced the Spanish Crown into a peace agreement that recognized their sovereignty and prevented further attacks. San Basilio thus stands as the first territory ever ceded to Blacks, and its value is in this embattled legacy. It possesses its own language, system of government, community leaders, societies, and rituals, all of which are marks of its identity. The pride and sense of self are deep historical constructs. It emerges as an evolved version of *cimarrón*, a contemporary state of being, more meaningful in the way it guaranteed the status of freedom for all future generations.[47]

Hernández confirms that she is acutely conscious of her legacy because it was handed down to her by her forebearers. The successful spirit of resistance among her ancestors meant that they never accepted the condition of enslavement: "Nuestros abuelos siempre nos dicen que sus ancestros nunca fueron esclavos" [Our grandparents always tell us that their ancestors were never slaves].[48] *Palenques* exist because of a universal, assertive rejection of the condition of slavery and manifestations of absolute belief in personal freedom and free will.[49] Their logical explanation finds true meaning in their early resistance to the Spanish imposition from which they fled and against which they fought and died, eventually winning the right to lead their own lives in freedom. Hernández describes how she, like her people, thinks differently: "No tenemos mente ni conciencia de esclavos, porque forjamos nuestro pueblo sobre la base de la libertad" [We have neither the minds nor the awareness of slaves because we shaped our people on the basis of freedom].[50] This historical self-confidence is what underpins her social consciousness and activism.

Developments that include alternative portrayals of *palenqueras* in culture and literature find inspiration in San Basilio as the originating sacred space. These new directions include a gender-based perspective that strongly supports all endeavors striving for the well-being of the communities. The main areas are community organization, the defense of collective territories, and cultural preservation.[51] This renewed spirit inserts itself in contemporary trends of activism, state policies, and the celebration of the multiple Afro-descendant legacies that exist in Colombia today. Such transformation is very different from the experiences of segregation and racial discrimination that Hernández's testimony describes from her childhood years growing up in the *palenque* and in Cartagena. For example, she especially recalls suffering as a speaker of an unfamiliar language and as an Afro-descendant child in the school system.[52] Simultaneously, today's activism in Colombia has ensured the emergence of effective female leadership that, by way of international organizing, academic self-improvement, and effective political lobbying, is working to change problematic popular perceptions of the *palenqueras*, all within the broader processes of modernizing the way that Colombia envisions the role and potential of its Afro-descendant peoples.

In Homage to Cartagena's *Palenquera*

One cannot miss the cry of street vendors as they approach, presenting their produce to passersby: "Alegría, alegría, con coco y anis" [Joy, joy, with coconut and aniseed].[53] It is a female voice, at times rhythmic, in singsong fashion, reminding us that appreciating African legacy in Cartagena demands our focus on the *palenqueras*: "Para encarnar 'lo negro' en Cartagena toca ser mujer" [to embody "Blackness" in Cartagena, one has to be a woman].[54]

Writers perform, recite, and read poetry aloud in *palenquero* and Spanish, a strategy they have adopted to intrigue their audiences and transform the way their national culture imagines their universe. Their verses describe and display pride and resistance even as they invite their readers in to build deeper connections and understanding of what it really means to be a woman writer with a confluence of belief systems, traditions, histories of conflicts and achievements, myths, and legends whose formations are deep in the past. These authors reach out, constantly striving for greater readership, very much aware of the transforming potential of their writings and the ongoing uphill battle for recognition as women and Afro-descendants.

This identity is inextricably tied to the city of Cartagena de Indias. As Colombia's Caribbean city, it bears all the signs of that region's colonial legacy. Roshini Kempadoo describes Caribbean landscapes as "tropical sites . . . perceived as colonial projects associated with European metropolitan ownership."[55] Their structure is a product of that system of land use and production, a colonial imposition that has determined all subsequent arrangements and relations of labor and government. On Paseo del Pescador Avenue, located at the entrance to the Bocagrande neighborhood, is a monument in the form of a bronze statue done by Hernando Pereira Brieva that was commissioned by the Peace for Colombia Foundation in 2008 and donated to the *palenqueras*.[56] Mounted on a pedestal, the artist sought to reproduce the posture, attire, and merchandise of *palenqueras*; the statue bears a basket on her head and is poised as if walking. The plaque reads, "La mujer trabajadora, símbolo de la afrocolombianidad" [The hardworking (it could also mean "working" or "working-class") woman, symbol of Afro-Colombianness].

In Cartagena today, the roles of the *palenqueras* directly influence the display and marketing of the city's history, landscape, commerce, and tourist industry.[57] They serve fundamentally as a propaganda piece in support of this urban space called Colombia's Caribbean paradise, a categorical imaging that has become intrinsic to the worldview of Cartagena as a romantic tropical getaway.[58] This projection has taken its toll, since it has become the measure by which they are judged and identified. The fixed cultural image is that of Black women usually adorned in long, wide, flowing skirts, the dominant colors being blue, red, and yellow, matching those of the Colombian flag. They may wear their hair under colorful turbans; completing the display is a large aluminum bowl known as a *ponchera*, filled with tropical fruits—mangos, papayas, bananas, oranges, pineapples, and watermelons—placed on their heads as they walk. Homemade sweets, with ingredients such as grated coconut, maize, guava, milk, aniseed, and sesame seeds, are also for sale. The delicacy called *alegría* [joy], made with coconut, sugar, and aniseed, is the hallmark of their cooking. Sometimes they wear necklaces or may even have a flower stuck behind the ear or under the turban. Their strident voices announce their approach as they amble through the city center and tourist zones selling their products.

Poet Mirian Díaz Pérez confirms that independent of the issue related to cultural representations and images, as women, they have always preferred bright, multicolored adornments (*vestirse alegre*); indeed, they consider it an intrinsic part of their personality. The only time they use subdued colors is during periods of mourning. Society has been known to condemn this style of dress as *escandalosa* [scandalous], unsophisticated, and low class. *Palenqueras* faced criticism from within their community and beyond and tolerated a lot of negative social commentary; derogatory expressions revealed underlying homophobia and led to baseless presumptions about *palenqueras* and also about women who chose to dress in this manner. A common insult became "Pareces palenquera" [You look like a *palenquera*]. At first, in the face of such stigma, many, Díaz Pérez included, were deeply affected by this negative message and abandoned this style of dress and avoided bright colors altogether, especially in the urban spaces to which they often migrated in search of economic opportunities. Now, in the midst of heightened social consciousness, affirmative action measures, and increased support for diversity, they embrace it. Further, Díaz Pérez indicates that the *delantal* [apron] is a practical addition, as many women are cooking and selling delicacies. The long, wide skirts, or *polleras*, and *pañueletas* [head wraps] that represent many *palenqueras*' daily attire have been subsequently hijacked and incorporated into the city's marketing strategies to promote tourism. Díaz Pérez confirms this as a situation of identity appropriation combined with a deliberate dismissal of the ancestral value implicated in this attire. *Palenqueras*' heritage, creativity, and business agenda are not a part of this citywide action plan, while their attire and physical attributes, deemed highly marketable, suffer exploitative intrusions for which they receive credit or compensation.[59]

Uniquely of African ancestry and *palenquero* language speakers with bright attire matched by the colors of their fruits, with a smooth, effortless gait and *poncheras* artfully balanced on their heads, *palenqueras* at times contrast with the city, whose bustling nature and sophisticated business zones make them appear even more out of place. However, they have become the chosen representations of their race and ethnicity in Cartagena's public arenas and thus form part of the imagery of Cartagena as a tropical paradise, a situation that reflects Colombia's racialized interpretation of the motherland. They are the closest elaboration of Africa in Cartagena, an aesthetic lodged exclusively in appearances. These female subjects have become easily available replicas with added color and in designs that enhance the tropical Caribbean space that Cartagena prides itself on being.

Ruth Betty Lozano Lerma and Doris Lamus Canavate reflect on the economic implications of *palenqueras*' trade as grassroots saleswomen. What dominates is a widespread superficial perception of them as working-class street merchants whose daily earnings provide limited economic security. To a certain degree, their situation of economic difficulty persists, in part due to society's incapacity to envision them as enterprising, astute negotiators of financial transactions—indeed, as businesswomen.[60] The reality is that while the business potential is there, higher sales and profit margins remain a challenge; their enterprising spirit does not always translate into prosperity and good returns. In addition, they all compete in public spaces filled with many other kinds of vendors also targeting tourists. Long days and their vulnerability as Black women, often alone in the streets, are additional difficulties they have to face. As they remain all day in the streets, they are targeted by the police who patrol the tourist zones of the Old City and the beaches.

Their images appear in many forms and spheres of representation, all potentially quite lucrative—paintings, murals, dolls, small statues, photographs, documentaries, films, and television. Besides these visual representations, they are expected to make appearances or be visible at performances, receptions, and state functions, oftentimes as representations of an exotic and tropical Colombia. Auspicious occasions demand their appearances: "Venía el rey de España, entonces se llama a las palenqueras, le ponen un vestido, un disfraz, le pintan la porcelana, y allí está la palenquera" [The king of Spain was coming, so they call the *palenqueras*; they put a dress on her, a costume, make up her face, and there you have her, the *palenquera*].[61] In her dissertation, Yadmilla Bauzá-Vargas interviews *palenquera* Crista Salgado, who clarifies *palenqueras*' contradictory status and mixed feelings, especially after UNESCO declared Palenque de San Basilio a Masterpiece of the Oral and Intangible Heritage of Humanity.[62] Salgado describes feeling constantly exploited for political agendas by city officials. As a *palenquera*, she feels objectified—just an element in a display that includes the beaches, *murallas* [city walls], Old City, and tourist resorts. In this artificial mirage, *palenqueras* have little or no value, a status that conflicts with their self-image as the true founders of the city's commerce: "La lectura de los cartageneros y el resto de Colombia sobre las palenqueras, las coloca como parte del paisaje colonial que junto a las murallas de Cartagena conforman de igual manera objetos culturales decorativos, como los arcos, las columnas y los balcones que construyen la arquitectura de la colonización" [The manner in which residents of Cartagena and the rest of Colombia read the *palenqueras* makes them part of the colonial landscape, in that, together with the walls of Cartagena, they are cultural decorative objects, like the arches, the columns, and the balconies that comprise the architecture of colonization].[63] Sidestepping the traumatic experiences of African arrival and settlement in Cartagena, the lively and enterprising tones of tourism's agenda have no problem paying homage to the visual aspect of this female phenomenon, selling it as evidence of Colombia's rich colonial and racial heritage.[64] Within mainstream culture, this human presence functions as a tool for consumption and profit, whether political or financial. *Palenqueras*' value as human subjects is in relation to the goods and services associated with their bodies, the latter in constant motion given their obligation to make appearances dressed in bright, patriotic colors, thereby guaranteeing their usefulness and legitimacy. They constitute a business transaction; the tourist will gaze at them, take photographs, and upload them to the internet. They will appear in paintings, murals, and writings. In the city, images are prominent, on sale, and visible everywhere, including in souvenirs, paintings (like those of María Cristina Hoyos), promotional posters and fliers, tourist guides, and other products. They *are* Cartagena.

Here are subjects whose images suffer all kinds of appropriations—systematically envisioned as objects of commerce rather than as businesswomen in their own

right or occasionally subjected to sensual fabrications and portrayals in misrepre-
sentations that undercut the dignified history of which they are so proud. Then we
encounter those proposals that mean well but are ideological agendas that serve
political interests or gestures of benevolence. The Fundación Paz por Colombia
[Peace for Colombia Foundation], in collaboration with Cartagena's mayor and
town council, adopted *palenqueras* as the symbol for peace in Colombia, a worthy
gesture that, in its aim to be inclusive and in the interest of Colombia's profile as
a harmonious society, seemed to erase the heterogeneous nature of their historical
trajectory and that of *palenques* within this nation. This strategic move was meant
to support policies of multiculturalism. In the end, this is another reductive version
of what they, as *palenqueras*, are not; the message of peace relays a totally opposite
version of their relationship with the motherland even as it muffles their proud
legacy as warriors who, to date, are emblematic of processes of resistance to the
extreme violence resulting from the strife and displacement that they, as Afro-
Colombian women, continue to face. While they self-define as part of a proud,
strong, and vital lineage, their country does not fully appreciate their meaningfulness, at least not really, given that the Afro-descendant identity is customarily
associated with victimization and suffering.[65]

Having created this connection, the foundation selected to adorn their web
page with images of a *palenquera* posing alongside a white fashion contestant in a
bikini. Two other images displayed white and mulatto women adorned in colorful,
sensual costumes designed to emphasize their shapely bodies, with attire on their
heads mimicking *poncheras*. The foundation had clearly bought into the marketing
imagery used to boost the city's economy. The economic discourse of the tourism
agenda is also responsible in its marking of every similar female figure, submitting
her to static, problematic formulations riddled with sexist and racist implications:
"A menudo se las puede observar mientras pasean por las calles cartageneras,
moviendo sus caderas con sus largos faldones floreados o del color de su bandera:
amarillo, azul y rojo y su cabello envuelto con un pañuelo" [Often one can observe
them as they stroll through the streets of Cartagena, their hips swaying with their
long flowered or flag-colored skirts: yellow, blue, and red, and their heads wrapped
in cloth].[66] Such online commentary supports the billion-dollar economic and
marketing enterprise contrived to paint Colombia as a romantic getaway and sets
up such women as potential objects of desire, embedded into claims of tropical
paradise that Cartagena proudly uses to sell itself.[67] Interestingly, as Cunin indicates, this distorted engagement of culture and identity fits the ideological agenda
of the state, for which the projection of a multicultural and multiethnic society in
harmonious coexistence is strategic.[68]

In Cartagena's streets, *palenqueras* stand out; they are darker-hued Black female
subjects who engage with their environment using visual means even as, within this
urban landscape of city inhabitants and tourists, they are liable to vanish in processes of objectification and invisibility that reveal little appreciation of their roles
as seasoned entrepreneurs and generators of income using the ancestral know-how
of their foremothers and forefathers. "En África, el mercado y la mujer constituían

un cuerpo indivisible, el mercado era el terreno de la mujer y su más importante agencia dentro de la comunidad" [In Africa, the market and the woman were an indivisible entity; the market was the woman's territory and her most important sphere of operation within the community].[69]

Palenqueras potentially symbolize transplanted African women, mirroring those on the African continent who wear traditional dress, carry children on their backs, pound yams, fetch water, gather firewood, carry heavy baskets of food on their heads in perfect balance, take care of their family homes, and in some cases, are responsible for planting crops. These subjects merge, provoke a gendering of transatlantic memory, and culminate as vivid reminders of Latin America's undisputed African ancestry by way of the striking visuals *palenqueras* create as they walk the city, perfectly balancing large, heavy bowls or trays on their turbaned heads. This feature, visible in West African market sellers today in cities like Lagos and Ile-Ife, is an integral part of the *palenqueras*' daily routine.[70] There are, however, differences. Unlike the stereotypically charged imaging of traditional African women, *palenqueras* do not appear as mothers in the city spaces; their children are not with them in the streets, nor are infants tied to their backs. During the day, they walk and sell their products individually or congregate with other women vendors.

Bauzá-Vargas speaks to this as a tradition of the Yoruba peoples of West Africa, where women dominate in matters of business and bartering, remnants of which seem to have survived, especially within Palenque de San Basilio.[71] Nina de Friedemann's extensive research enriches our understanding of how these roles persist in Colombia to date. During the 1970s, when access to the *palenque* depended on a narrow dirt road, the "bus de las mujeres" [women's bus] was the only available public transportation, and these women boarded the bus at 4:00 a.m. every day to market their fruits and vegetables in the neighboring towns and city, returning home at sunset. Sometimes, there were no buses, and they had to resort to mules, horses, and donkeys to move around.[72]

These are not downtrodden figures; on the contrary, they are pillars of the tourism industry who smile for the cameras, are resourceful figures, and provide good services. They appear everywhere in the Casco Histórico [Historical Center] or the Ciudad Amurallada [Walled City], the heart of Cartagena's Old City and central tourism zone. They amble through Bolivar Park and the Santo Domingo Square. They are sure to pass by the cathedral and the San Pedro de Claver Church; some *palenqueras* will also work the beaches of Bocagrande, although those on the beaches may not always appear in typical dress.[73] When not on the move, they sit on the pavement, alone or in groups, selling produce grown on the acres of land they own and cultivate. This part of their lives remains unseen. The day starts very early because the only bus from San Basilio de Palenque to the city of Cartagena departs before dawn. They spend the day selling fruits and homemade sweets, thereafter riding the bus home any time after 3:00 p.m. This leaves almost no time for family, children, or the home. They are truly businesswomen, belonging to the countryside and the city, proudly aware of this added advantage and their ancestral heritage.

The societal focus on appearances limits perception and a deeper understanding of the exploitative nature of the city's commerce in relation to such women, even as they have bought into the business angle of such attire. Is there personal enrichment or adequate compensation? What benefits do they gain for being constantly in the limelight? They are Cartagena's icons, an intrinsic part of the way the city represents itself worldwide and a phenomenon of its tourism without necessarily being allowed to benefit from the lucrative intake of that industry. As a complement to the public space, images are plastered all over the World Wide Web, mostly without permission, since it is taken for granted that such reproductions are legitimate and favor the city's tourism plan, thereby effectively leaving no room for disputes regarding ownership or copyright.

In Cartagena, a spontaneous connection exists between this Afro-descendant subject and the drumming, songs, and dances that provide entertainment and represent their customs and daily practices. Besides performances in the city, nationally recognized celebrations take place every October in San Basilio de Palenque, especially the Festival de Tambores y Expresiones Culturales del Palenque [Festival of Palenque Drums and Cultural Expressions].[74] The festival presents dances, rituals, medicinal practices, forms of healing, beliefs, and oral traditions related to the Bantu language. African-originated cloth, head wraps, attire, dishes, and hairstyles are also featured. Storytelling and ancestral know-how are forms of community engagement that guarantee the continuity of connections between older and younger generations.[75]

This vision stands in contrast with the city streets that *palenqueras* navigate daily. The current focus on sequestering *palenquera* images for financial gain results in cultural insensitivity and irreverence; it involves the manipulation of a differential Black female body in what is still predominantly a mestizo-Hispanic space. Alfonso Cassiani discusses two cities: "En Cartagena y Mompox, históricamente, se hallan más arraigadas las prácticas racistas, seguidas de las capitales o zonas urbanas donde, además de discriminar, la explotación se da en términos laborales, culturales, turísticos" [Historically, in Cartagena and Mompox, racist practices are more ingrained, followed by the capitals or urban zones where, besides discrimination, exploitation occurs in the culture sector, the labor sector, and tourism].[76] Community leader, scholar, and advocate Rutsely Simarra Obeso has also spoken out against the situation of vulnerability and abuse generated in public spaces. These mothers, students, and wives, women of all ages, face severe economic instability and extreme poverty and suffer ill-treatment from all fronts as they work in the streets. Within tourist zones like the Walled City and the beaches, the *palenquera*'s race and socioeconomic background provoke an othering, rendering her an outsider and therefore a possible threat.[77]

As a teacher and leader, Dorina Hernández educates her students about the challenges they will continue to face in society, instilling an awareness of their proud legacy and efforts at inclusion and political correctness today. She speaks of a hierarchical structure in Cartagena that places her people at the bottom of the social ladder due to their ethnicity, language, and burial rituals, which few outside of their community understand. Many question the drumming, dancing, singing, and apparently joyful demonstrations that accompany a passing: "Pensar que el ritual fúnebre del palenquero, en el cual hay canciones y bailes, expresa alegría, goce y felicidad es desconocer que hay otras posibilidades de expresiones que tienen sus propias lógicas y valores comprensibles, solamente al interior de las culturas que los practican" [To think that the *palenquero* burial ritual, in which there are songs and dances, expresses joy, pleasure, and happiness, is to be unaware that there are other possibilities of expression that have their own logic and values comprehensible only within the cultures that practice them].[78] *Palenqueras'* status as independent individuals speaks to a meaningful self-perception that transcends the static visual of Black women in folkloric garb. Such perception is distinct from the tendency to assign minimal value to their professional trade or to treat them as premodern bearers of traditional practices. In the eyes of society, they remain at the margins of modernity; indeed, as Hernández points out, some citizens recommend that they may be better served by joining service-related employment, such as working in supermarkets or serving behind counters.[79]

Speeches and proclamations by local politicians, industrialists, and businessmen reveal their overall satisfaction with the financial and economic gains *palenqueras* accumulate, made possible by the aggressive marketing of these women as products of an enticing vacation destination. Their physical attributes, appearances, and enterprising spirit run parallel to their role as advocators of their patrimony or as protectors of their identity and of the *palenque* spaces they call home. Home is worth protecting, since it preserves their customs and traditions, sources of inspiration that feed their ongoing dedication to activism, advocacy, and literary writings: "La mujer Palenquera, vendedora de frutas y verduras en los mercados y calles, es presentada como fundadora del sistema de microempresas, punto de encuentro entre la tradición, el neoliberalismo y el desarrollo, que representa una buena parte de la economía colombiana" [The *palenquera* woman, seller of fruits and vegetables in the markets and streets, is presented as founder of the system of microbusinesses, point of convergence between tradition, neoliberalism, and development that represent a good part of the Colombian economy].[80]

Palenqueras are campaigning to claim ownership as producers, organizers, and promoters of their undertakings, from inception to sale. Professionally, they play multiple roles—farmer, property owner, head of household, cook, manager, saleswoman, businesswoman, and cultural entrepreneur. In order to guarantee the quality and respectability of their final product, they must hold the reins, providing the guidance and leadership necessary for success. These women have been working to organize themselves into a cooperative.[81] They are challenging city officials to guarantee their rights and are in the process of receiving greater recognition today.[82] Women like Dorina Hernández are leading the way to make the *palenquera* a viable trademark from which they will profit. This cause is growing exponentially, motivating them to treasure their ancestry and have increased confidence in their abilities. Their efforts have resulted in positive changes, earning them legal rights to their public spaces of business in 2011 and 2012.[83] This heightened sense of self-value is the result of education and information within their community and their spheres of social activism, as such spaces have proven to be supportive of their efforts at self-advocacy and of the politics of national development. Positive government responses align with recommendations from the United Nations and other international organizations such as the World Bank, which, responding to the International Decade for People of African Descent (2015–24), have urged countries of the region to reverse the legacy of discrimination and invisibility with respect to African and Indigenous peoples.[84]

At the same time, in light of the established commercial structure, it is hard to envision *palenqueras* as disassociated from this frame of reference. Claudia Mosquera Rosero-Labbé invites us to dwell on the expression *lugar de memoria* [place of memory] as a way of reconfiguring cultural expectations about these subjects and their connection with meaningful origins such as San Basilio de Palenque. She proposes a reenvisioning that would protect such women from the confines of socioeconomic and race-based expectations:

> Podría serlo si se *des-naturalizara* este duro oficio en ellas: me gustaría ver a otras mujeres de otros tonos de piel realizándolo para *des-racializarlo*; me gustaría ver representaciones pictóricas en las que aparecieran palenqueras en otros oficios o profesiones asociadas a distintos grupos sociales y culturales.

> [It could be so if one were to *de-naturalize* this harsh trade in them: I would like to see other women of other skin tones performing this trade so that it could be *de-racialized*; I would like to see pictorial representations where *palenqueras* appear in other trades or professions associated with different social and cultural groups.][85]

For community leaders and teachers like Dorina Hernández, this phenomenon is further evidence that Cartagena is one of the Colombian cities where racism is most evident.[86] The entity that, over time, has recognized, challenged, and spoken out against such institutional stereotyping has been the *palenqueras* movement, through the voices of leaders such as Rutsely Simarra Obeso, Teresa Cassiani, and Dorina Hernández.

Hernández identifies the important project of recovering the dignity of women who have been converted into profit-making objects.[87] Simarra Obeso drives home the need for new perceptions about the depth of her people's historical and linguistic worth through her research and essays focusing on women, history, and language in San Basilio de Palenque. Cassiani and Hernández are passionate teachers who have bought into ethnoeducation in order to transform communities through literacy projects and education while battling those measures and points of view that disturb society's understanding and appreciation of their legacy. They both treasure their ancestral achievements, are working to have them recognized and incorporated into education policies, and are deeply critical of the ongoing marginalizing and discriminatory trends.[88] Hernández speaks out against the way *palenqueras*, bearing their *poncheras* on their heads, are not in control of what happens to the thousands of photographs taken of them. The system—that is, Cartagena's tourism enterprise—is quite culpable, as it reproduces the women's images in the same ways it does the famous city walls, beaches, and blue sea.

Palenqueras are the producers, inventors, and designers of fresh fruits, packaged fruits, and sugary sweetmeats even as no systemic support is in place to ensure that they prosper from the use of these food and human advertisements, images, and sales. In recent years, they have unionized and created an organization called Asociación de Productores Agropecuarios, Dulces Tradicionales y Servicios Etnoturístico de Palenque [ASOPRADUSE; Palenque Producers Association for Agriculture, Traditional Sweets, and Ethnotourism] in collaboration with rural agricultural producers and businesses that provide ethnotourism services.[89] Recognizing an opportunity, some stores and supermarket chains are entering into contractual arrangements in order to purchase their products and sell them in packages that display their images. While they are now reaching a bigger market, these developments have not necessarily made them wealthy; they continue to be underpaid for an idea and a product that enriches their city and the hotel industry. Hernández uses the term *dignity* in her campaign and calls on the system to be more respectful of *palenqueras'* rights: "El trabajo de las palenqueras viene de unos saberes tradicionales y debe hacerse más dignamente" [The *palenqueras'* work derives from traditional forms of knowledge and should be performed with greater dignity].[90] She urges women to expand beyond rudimentary levels of enterprise and achieve greater operational sophistication.[91] Lamus Canavate has observed improvements over time and constructs a direct connection between the positive impact of the women's organization called the Asociación de Mujeres Afrodescendientes y del Caribe Graciela Cha-Inés [Graciela Cha-Inés Association of Afro-Descendant and Caribbean Women] and the creation of small cooperatives or enterprises by the sellers themselves.[92]

Hernández expresses the view that while widespread campaigning and activism sustain attention regarding the rights of Afro-descendants at all levels of society and across the country, the same cannot be said for women's rights; in fact, she is convinced that women's problems have, to a large extent, been abandoned within Afro-Colombian communities in part because Afro-consciousness movements have dedicated their energies primarily to racial identity.[93] Women are less organized, and many are unclear about benefits such as their access to higher education, their rights in the workplace, and their participation as citizens at all levels of society. Hernández confirms that while many men and women like her are tuned into the politics surrounding race and ethnicity, they are not as informed or enlightened in situations of gender inequality or discrimination. Many male leaders at the front of Black activism in the country continue to display disrespect for their female counterparts at work and at home and general disregard for the problems that women face daily; they continue to see women as sensual, as objects for male pleasure. Hernández confronts the way that Afro-Colombian leadership is willing to work fiercely toward ethnic and human rights yet seems unable and unwilling to extend the same value to Black women: "Nuestros compañeros, bajo el pretexto de que las costumbres son un asunto cultural, frecuentemente pisotean los derechos de las mujeres negras" [Our male companions, using as a pretext that customs are a cultural matter, frequently trample on the rights of Black women].[94] She laments the fact that both sexes often face the same problems, though many do not perceive this to be so. Men often do not support the Black female struggle, even as benefits bestowed on them come at a cost to women. She urges everyone to see gender not singularly in association with women but also in terms of their universal struggle as a community.

An Identity in Crisis? A *Palenquera*'s Testimony

Hernández's views are an integral part of this discussion for the way they provide an understanding of how she perceives her identity, her legacy, and her personal sense of self-worth. Her perceptions differ from the ways in which society tends to appreciate the community and traditions of women. Overall, few people understand who the *palenqueras* really are or the greater significance behind their way of life. Hernández is valuable for her understanding of issues and her intentions to defend the rights and land claims of her people. Her distinguished contribution is also visible in her connection with community rituals, beliefs, music, and religious practices. She clarifies the intrinsic and meaningful affiliation between ethnicity and heritage: "Una persona mestiza puede tener un hijo en Palenque, pero si vive con los palenqueros, si piensa, come y habla como Palenquero, es una persona Palenquera y culturalmente es una persona negra—incluso si tiene la piel blanca" [A mestizo person can have a child in the *palenque*, but if he lives with the *palenqueros*, thinks, eats, and speaks like a *palenquero*, he is *palenquero* and is culturally a Black person, even if his skin is white].[95] Even as Hernández's discourse centralizes Afro-Colombian ancestry, she does so consciously, counteracting cultural norms such as the tendency to self-identify as mulatto rather than Afro-Colombian or to ignore the racial discrimination that is so ingrained in the society.[96]

Palenqueras have had to seek ways to subvert the intense process of othering and, like other Afro-Colombian women, have mapped out strategies for community and personal advancement through education and feminist-based alliances.[97] The three main elements of identity formation continue to be the *palenquero* language, a deep sense of ethnic collectivity, and strategic organizing; these principles exist at the base of Hernández's current projects of activism and development. Their intrinsic value is in their language and in the idea of their origins in San Basilio de Palenque as a space that has never been conquered or dominated. Today, their language stands out as the most valuable linguistic legacy from Africa in Hispanic America. This means that the preservation of this legacy is crucial if the community is to survive. Hernández recalls a wise message from one of the community elders: "Uno de los abuelitos del Palenque nos dijo una vez: 'Cuando un pueblo pierde su lengua, ese pueblo está perdido'" [One of the grandfathers of the *palenque* once told us: "When a people lose their language, that people is lost"].[98]

Thanks to the tireless efforts by leaders such as Hernández, the only school in San Basilio de Palenque offers language classes, a testament to its widespread usefulness within that space and beyond, which has led to government support of similar ethnoeducational projects in Black communities within the Bolívar department (the province where San Basilio is located) and across the nation.[99] Special consideration by the state has led to the approval of a specific curriculum in schools that includes courses and teachings about traditional cultural practices. Instruction that explores African and *palenquero* origins, history, and rituals complements *palenquero* language studies, and students are encouraged to do their own research, a move that continues to bear fruit. Today, some of the leading historical, linguistic, and anthropological researchers are themselves from the community.[100] Hernández, herself a well-known and respected leader, has worked with Grupo Cultural de Palenque [Palenque Cultural Group] and was involved in designing and implementing a new curriculum based on ethnoeducation, a new direction in the country's approach to educating its diverse Indigenous and Afro-Colombian populations that would respect and develop their cultural identities. Ethnoeducation is rooted in the 1991 constitution, which consecrated Colombia as a pluralist nation. Its precepts were carried forward in Law 70 of August 1993, valued for breaking down barriers that may exist between *palenqueros* and Afro-Colombian communities and other ethnic groups in the country.[101] "Se parte del concepto de pedagogías propias entendidas como los dispositivos del mundo cultural del pueblo, mediante el cual se socializan los referentes identitarios, se mantiene viva la memoria histórica y la colectividad actúa como sujeto de derecho" [It starts with the concept of specific pedagogies understood to be devices within the cultural world of the people, by which means the various identities socialize themselves, maintain historical memory alive, and the collective acts as the legitimate subject].[102]

Thanks to the *palenque*'s ability to preserve its proud legacy and to efforts of community leaders like Hernández, the perpetuation of the language and oral culture of this people is somewhat secure. Over time, many bridges have been built between the city of Cartagena's administrative and educational system and San Basilio de Palenque. The ensuing ethnocultural consciousness and support of the school is ensuring that the language, history, and culture of the *palenque* are being passed down to the community's children. Hernández confirms that classes, recreational activities, sports, competitions, theater, and language games are among the ongoing community projects designed to reinstate pride in this linguistic legacy.[103] She recalls that the theatrical group had once presented a play as a way of sensitizing everyone to aspects of their lives, thereby providing greater awareness and offering a space for public displays that bring attention to difficult discussions such as disrespect and discrimination in public spaces. Theater has proved an effective way to first instill participants with pride in their language, traditions, and customs; then display their language and history; and finally, sensitize the public to the long-term impact of ingrained discriminatory practices.[104] This testimony subverts the preferred assumption of a mere street seller, pointing instead to life-changing projects of which she is a part. The most important endeavor is education, and many now take the path to the university where they use the opportunity to become involved in organizations and create networks beyond the *palenque*. This is a multilayered effort that begins within the *palenque* and expands outward, situating the residents' cause as part of a national movement of political processes that since the 1980s has been engaging such communities across the country. While these are heterogeneous struggles, their basis is pride in their legacy as an African-originated free people. The sources of inspiration vary depending on the social struggle; while, as is the case of Hernández, motivation and incentive may have come from a pride in their heritage, for others, their involvement in social activism began in left-wing movements.[105]

Besides the concrete project of valuing an education in their own language, women continue to use strategies they learned and developed in their home communities to help them deal with the difficulties and challenges of living in urban spaces like Cartagena and Barranquilla. A natural connection exists between traditional groups known as *kuagros* and the Afro-Colombian women's organization the Asociación de Mujeres Afrodescendientes y del Caribe Graciela Cha-Inés. It is here that we can observe the preservation of original values such as a firm belief in the well-being of the community and the indelible connection between the land and history.[106]

From *Kuagros* to the Asociación de Mujeres Afrodescendientes y del Caribe Graciela Cha-Inés

Literature pays homage to all aspects of *palenquero* life by capturing what is unique to that setting. Under constant threat of dismantlement, history indicates that the maroons designed a plan to guarantee the survival of their settlements, which led to the establishment of the social unit known as the *kuagro*. Given the value of the community over the individual, the *kuagro* takes center stage as the unifying plan.[107] It is, by definition, a focused group whose members share a certain characteristic; it was invented by the maroons as a strategy for communication and bonding, crucial when it came to defending the communes against attacks. Today, *kuagros* continue to exist, providing a medium for socialization and a way of building and sustaining strong and active relations beyond the family unit. They provide orientation, building individual awareness of being part of a larger, more complex entity with its own structure and forms of engagement.[108] The *kuagro* is the *palenque*'s way of setting up its social and political structure so that the whole community organizes and takes care of itself; indeed, many value such social groups for the sense of solidarity they transmit. They offer support and assistance when needed, and their main purpose is to build a sense of belonging by way of a sisterhood or brotherhood. They provide instruction on community values and customs, support for resolving conflicts, and religious or material assistance during illness or death. Their formation is motivated by any kind of familial or social connection, and this is a bond that is never undone.[109] A *kuagro* can take any form;

for example, it can comprise a group of people who share a specific job or occupation.[110] *Kuagros* serve different generations, different age groups, and different gender identities. Integrants gain knowledge together, learning skills and trusting one another to build bonds of sisterhood, brotherhood, respect, cooperation, and friendship that last a lifetime.[111] Older generations provide knowledge and guidance to younger generations, a process that has created a deep sense of belonging to a collective, a sensation of solidarity that endures. Participants acknowledge their connection to one another in tangible ways, especially through acts of kindness and sharing. An important part of the *kuagro* is a readiness to render financial assistance as needed, whether for a young couple about to be married or a family enduring illness or death.

Hernández's testimony includes mention of her grandfather and mother, who were serious *kuagro* leaders and members. Growing up, Hernández learned to appreciate firsthand the value of this tradition, especially in the way it ensures an effective network and sense of collectivity. Further, her description of the system indicates that women are never excluded, seen as secondary, or barred from assuming leadership or participating in activities such as the *peleas* [fights]. Hernández's role model was her mother, whose service to her community and role as breadwinner of her family ensured her place as leader of a large *kuagro*.[112] A spirit of rivalry and competitiveness among *kuagros* is encouraged, albeit in a positive way, as members work on endeavors that would confirm the superior abilities of their group. Pérez Tejedor confirms that confrontations can range from dance and love to fist fights.[113] Rivalries among *kuagros* are their way of sustaining this ancestral legacy and are maintained symbolically and through actual fistfights that are viewed as positive energies and are organized to build strength, resilience, and bonds rather than provoke bodily harm.[114] Hernández also mentions the fights because while they are a tradition of entertainment today, they were an important form of preparation for the defense of the *palenque* during colonial times.[115] Today, the battle for supremacy among the different *kuagros* involves both men and women. It is a display of physical strength and prowess without weapons of any kind; indeed, such a need would be looked down upon. Winning the fight brings great prestige in a setting that has for centuries constructed its sense of identity on defeating its enemies. The value of this legacy is in its long-term effect on women and implications for the expectations they have for themselves as well as what they deem to be their role and place in society: "La hermandad Palenquera de los kuagros y la práctica tradicional de las peleas en Palenque han ayudado mucho para que las mujeres seamos matronas combativas y trabajadoras. Las mujeres Palenqueras no aceptamos que en Cartagena la gente nos llegue a irrespetar" [The *palenquera* sisterhood of the *kuagros* and the traditional practice of the fights in the *palenque* have really helped women be combative and hardworking matrons. We, *palenquera* women, will not put up with disrespect from the people in Cartagena].[116]

Thanks to the social structure of the *kuagros*, the legacy of dignity and sisterhood among *palenqueras* runs deep, a natural part of their internal system of confidential relationships. Lamus Canavate confirms the kinds of endeavors and convictions in alliance with activism that have encouraged female leadership to argue and defend positions regarding the roles and politics of identity specific to the needs of Black women.[117] The historical trajectory of the *palenque* itself, whose survival depended on everyone's participation in its defense, produced a spirit of egalitarianism based on the belief that women were equally competent and able to deal with any confrontational and (physically) challenging situation. It is with this in mind that we can contemplate the Asociación de Mujeres Afrodescendientes y del Caribe Graciela Cha-Inés as a *palenquera* movement that stands as a contemporary version or adaptation of such deep-rooted alliances and commitment. This association can be approached as an extension of the *kuagro*, a sisterhood whose structure bears elements of the past while conforming to the nature and demands of society today.

Created in 1992 in Cartagena, the Graciela Cha-Inés Association is an organization of women who identify as *palenqueras*. While other similar women's organizations in Colombia thrive, this entity is unique, since it is the single unit that identifies particularly with women who proudly trace their roots, origins, homes, and livelihood to Palenque de San Basilio. Its headquarters were originally located in the heart of the historical center of Cartagena, housed alongside the Corporación para el Desarrollo de las Comunidades Afrocaribeñas Jorge Artel [Jorge Artel Corporation for the Development of Afro-Caribbean Communities] and the Instituto de Educación e Investigación Manuel Olivella Zapata [Manuel Olivella Zapata Education and Research Institute]. The single organization dedicated to Black women in the area presented its raison d'être as "por la visibilización, el posicionamiento, la identidad y la equidad de la mujer afrodescendiente y del Caribe" [to promote the visibility, positioning, identity, and equity of the Afro-descendant and Caribbean woman].[118] It was legally registered in 2002, and in 2007, it attained judicial and legal status as an officially recognized entity for women within the Proceso de Comunidades Negras [PCN; Process of Black Communities]. The PCN is a branch of the Movimiento Social Afrocolombiano [Afro-Colombian Social Movement], designed with the purpose of studying, reflecting, debating, and acting on the traumas of inequality and exclusion that Blacks face in Colombia.[119]

Graciela Cha-Inés in the association's name renders homage to matriarchs Graciela Salgado and Cha Inés Ortega, bearers of the *palenque* heritage and oral traditions. Salgado was a *tamborera*, or the central singer within the *lumbalú* burial ritual, and a member of the famous group of singers who call themselves the Alegres Ambulancias, known for their performances of the *bullerengue* dance.[120] *Cha Inés* [Tía Inés (Aunt Ines)] is in homage to an elderly woman, respected for her deep knowledge of their history and culture, a true guardian of the San Basilio legacy.[121] Clara Inés Guerrero García comments on the stature and distinction of such female guardians in *palenquero* society:

La memoria ancestral africana ha impregnado a su descendencia en América de una solidaridad característica y de un sentido de protección con ternura y firmeza, notorio sobre todo en las matronas, sin importar su oficio o condición social. . . . Su ética solidaria impregna su sentido común y las normas se aplican según la religión, la política o el sentido de la legalidad.

[African ancestral memory has impregnated its lineage in America with a characteristic solidarity and a sense of protection that comes with warmth and firmness, evident above all in the older women, irrespective of their trade or social condition. . . . Their ethic of solidarity permeates their common sense and they apply the norms based on religion, politics or the law.][122]

The association has a clear mandate: "La reivindicación de los derechos de las mujeres y las jóvenes afro-descendientes en Cartagena y la región caribe colombiana, propiciando actividades que respondan a la reafirmación de nuestra identidad cultural con perspectiva de género, a través de proyectos de etnodesarrollo e incidencia públicas de mujeres" [The asserting of rights for women and young girls of African descent in Cartagena and the Colombian Caribbean region by fostering activities that respond to the reaffirmation our gender-specific cultural identity through ethnodevelopment projects and public advocacy related to women].[123] Its designated tasks include the commercial activities and rights of *palenqueras* in Cartagena as well as the difficult circumstances of women and their families, displaced victims of armed conflict in the department of Bolívar and areas of the Pacific coast. Association members defend their position and speak out against the challenges they face in the city and surrounding region.[124] The leadership and members have proven their commitment to working with women to revert the negative impact of violence and sexual abuse.[125] One of the association's major community outreach projects is *por una vida libre de violencia* [for a life free from violence] that has as its specific agenda the construction of an autonomous process of organization for and by women even as it also targets Afro-Colombian youth, both male and female, in an endeavor to shed light on their specific situation while developing strategies to counteract their vulnerability and unfamiliarity with their rights. In November 2009, the association became a member of the Red Nacional de Mujeres Afrocolombianas Kambirí [Kambirí National Network of Afro-Colombian Women], the umbrella organization of the national Black women's movement, headquartered in Medellín, that holds a national congress every three years. Reparations, land rights, sexism, and violence are important topics of concern for the movement today.[126]

Rutsely Simarra Obeso, community leader, feminist, and activist, has served as the association's director. Very active in the community as a writer, researcher, and leader, she knows firsthand the needs and problems of the women who live there and in Cartagena. She has come to realize just how little the inhabitants of Cartagena actually know about her people and works to reverse this situation by expanding knowledge, appreciation, and understanding of the internal dynamics of this space. The organization is conscious of the need to sensitize the community at all levels and connect with local authorities to insist on measures that would transform the current state of affairs. As part of their projects, association members work on collective memory, compiling and preserving all kinds of materials that represent the *palenque* peoples. They educate all *palenqueros* and their descendants about the historical value of what they represent. A significant result is the published study of the lexicon, *Lengua ri Palenge: Jende suto ta chitiá; Léxico de la lengua palenquera*, compiled by Rutsely Simarra Obeso, Regina Miranda Reyes, and Juana Pabla Pérez Tejedor.

The Graciela Cha-Inés Association appears alongside other such entities and offices that identify with the heritage, activism, and politics in Cartagena. They are the Secretaria de Educación y Cultura de Bolívar Programa de Etnoeducación [Bolívar Secretary of Education and Culture Program of Ethnoeducation], Institución Educativa Técnica Agropecuaria Benkos Biohó de San Basilio de Palenque [San Basilio de Palenque Benkos Biohó Agricultural, Technical, and Educational Institute], Instituto de Educación e Investigación Manuel Olivella Zapata [Manuel Olivella Zapata Education and Research Institute], Equipo de Etnoeducación Bolívar [Bolívar Ethnoeducation Team], Consejo Comunitario de San Basilio de Palenque Ma Kankamana [Ma Kankamana San Basilio de Palenque Community Council], Corporación Festival de Tambores y Expresiones Culturales de Palenque [Corporation for Drums and Palenque Cultural Expressions Festival], Kuagro Juvenil Benkos Ku Suto [Benkos Ku Suto Youth Kuagro], Escuela de Danzas y Música Tradicionales Batata [Batata School of Traditional Dance and Music], and Corporación para el Desarrollo de las Comunidades Afrocaribeñas "Jorge Artel" [Jorge Artel Corporation for the Development of Afro-Caribbean Communities]. They represent an agglomeration that speaks to an active network designed to promote events, raise funds, develop all kinds of projects, and take measures to preserve the legacy for the future.[127] Within this structure, the Graciela Cha-Inés Association is the unit lobbying on their behalf, simultaneously providing the tools and ideological space for these women to focus on their interests, develop their projects, and negotiate their terms on equal footing.[128]

PALENQUERA HEROINES: WHERE HISTORY AND LEGEND CONVERGE

The concrete historical legacy of which *palenqueros* are very proud is complemented by mythical and spiritual beliefs connecting the community with their roots in Africa, with those who have died, and with their ancestors. An important part of their ancestral belief system finds resonance through two mythical figures, María Lucrecia and Catalina Loango.[129] These two myths coexist within the *palenquero* communal belief system, in which *palenqueros* share everything in life through the *kuagro* and in death through the *lumbalú* ritual. The mythical origins of this manifestation rest with María Lucrecia, whose sacrifice allowed them to establish spiritual ties with their ancestors.[130] Their world starts with the inhabitants of San Basilio de Palenque in place, a settlement of houses, families and crops with an established way of life. The tale is that one day, the inhabitants realized that they lacked a heaven or eternal place that was a replica of their *palenque*, a dwelling place to which their souls could transcend, for up to that point in time, there had been no deaths in this new life in the *palenque*. They gazed toward the heavens and observed that the spirits of their dead warrior maroons did not reside there; instead, their place of rest was in the faraway ancestral land. The souls of the dead who had previously participated in the marronage warfare had been returned to that distant land, unknown to them, called Africa. They approached Saint Peter and requested that upon death, they be allowed to dwell in heaven as a way of having representation, given that it was closer to what they now called home. They requested a *palenquero* settlement beyond life. Saint Peter agreed on one condition—namely, that the community provide a deceased person. The person chosen for death was a woman who had many children; however, someone had to kill her, which created a problem, as no one was brave enough to commit the act. Then someone with courage appeared, a woman called María Lucrecia, who shockingly took matters into her own hands and dealt a lethal blow to the woman with the large family. From that moment on, as the guardian of death, she would guide the deceased to their final resting place.[131] Thanks to her sacrifice, they are blessed with a heaven of their own, thereby comforted by the thought of a place beyond this life that reunites them with their ancestors.[132] The traumatic and difficult responsibilities that the two women in this legend (the victim and the perpetrator) assume are a testament to the crucial roles women play in the formation and perpetuation of belief systems.

The legend of Catalina Loango is well connected with the *lumbalú*, an ancient custom that appears as a theme in *palenquera* poetry. Armin Schwegler identifies *lumbalú* to mean "voice," derived from a Kikongo word originally meaning "melancholy, memory, recollection."[133] Rodríguez follows this line, indicating that the word may have originated in Bantu territory on the African continent.[134] Described by Schwegler as a magical-religious ritual, it is what remains of Bantu (and maybe other) beliefs and practices originally from West Africa.[135] Over time, it has become ceremonial and is a space for the deceased, the spirits of those who have passed on—musicians, drummers, singers, and the entire community, including children—thereby permitting its transmission through the generations. Mourners, family members, and those belonging to the deceased's *kuagro* gather, suspending all daily activities. Relatives and friends who live far away return to the *palenque* to participate in the ritual that continues for nine days after the burial.[136] In this space, everyone has a particular role—old, young, women, and men. The drumming is central and serves as a way to establish a connection with the spirit world, allowing the chants, which are often renditions from women known as *las cantadoras*, to reach beyond this life.[137] These religious and ceremonial incantations bring forth the stories of their ancestors and work to summon into their midst their progenitors, spirits, and deities. Schwegler provides us with examples of the chants in *palenquero*, a small sample of which is presented here alongside the Spanish and English translations:

chi ma nlongo	(soy de) los del Congo
chi ma (ri) Luango	(soy) los Luango
Chi mar i Luango ri Angola	De los Luango de Angola

[I am from those of the Congo
I belong to the Luango people
The Luango people of Angola][138]

*   *   *   *   *

Katalina Luango (I)

Lumbalú #1; cantado por Catalina Salgado (1913–)

e, <ña María Katalina, {de} Luango> e, chimbumbe e, olelelelo, elilelelilelo,
kaposanto;
   e, chimbumba negra Luango, e, chimbumbe
      olelelelo, elilelelilelo, kaposanto;
   e, kanoa a koé río Lamb', e; María Luango;
      olelelelo, elilelelilelo, kaposanto.[139]

Traducción de "Katalina Loango" (I)

eh, Doña María Catalina, de Loango, eh, "chimbumbe"
[= encanto, "diablito"] eh,
   olelelelo, elilelelilelo, caposanto [= cementerio];
eh, chimbumba [= ¿encantada?] negra de Loango, eh
"chimbumbe,"
   olelelelo, elilelelilelo, camposanto;
eh, la canoa se ha ido por el río Lamba [= el muerto está
viajando al otro mundo, eh; María Loango;
   olelelelo, elilelelilelo, caposanto.

[Translation of "Katalina Loango" (I)

Lumbalú #1; sung by Catalina Salgado (1913–)
hey, Mrs. Maria Catalina, from Loango, hey, "chimbumbe"
(= enchantment, "little devil") hey
   olelelelo, elilelelilelo, caposanto (= cementery);
hey, chimbumba (= enchanted? bewitched?) Black woman from Loango, hey
"chimbumbe,"
   olelelelo, elilelelilelo, camposanto;
hey, the canoe has gone down the Lamba river (= the deceased is
traveling to the other world, hey; Maria Loango;
   olelelelo, elilelelilelo, camposanto.][140]

The structure and style of these oral traditions find resonance in the poetic renditions by *palenquera* women writers who seek to capture the mood and rhythms
of the moment. Many chants are sacred and sung only by important matriarchs,
senior women of the communities, and high-ranking members of the *kuagros*. They
reflect the pain and melancholy of the moment.[141] As de Friedemann describes,

Cuando en Palenque de San Basilio se menciona al lumbalú, se evoca un ritual sagrado con ritmo, melodía, sentimiento e imágenes que avivan una cosmovisión de profundidades acuáticas, espacios terrenales y parajes de imaginería fantástica. Es en la poética de los cantos de lumbalú donde se han precisado huellas sociales y lingüísticas de ancestro africano.

[When *lumbalú* is mentioned in Palenque de San Basilio, it evokes a sacred ritual of rhythm, melody, emotion, and images that conjure up a worldview of deep underwater realms, earthly spaces, and fantastic imagery settings. It is in the poetic structure of the *lumbalú* chants that social and linguistic footprints of African ancestry have been specifically identified.][142]

Oral tradition is at the center of such practices; as a people, their capacity to endure relies on the preservation of their language. Numerous narratives bring to life characters and components of African memory. These oral narratives continue to be told as part of a process of education, appreciation, and cultural understanding as to why, for example, *lumbalú* is so important to the community.

The Catalina Loango narrative is well known and one of the best illustrations of a lasting oral tradition that is both mythical and historical in nature. She is an undeniable part of *palenquero* history and will continue in perpetuity, symbolic of community values. Rodríguez views the Loango story as one passed down through the ages and interprets it as a form of teaching and advisement, instructing the community about its roots and the consequences of certain decisions.[143] Its value is in its objective, weighed far beyond Catalina, who is but another woman of the village. She is not outstanding, brave, or special in any way but has a transforming experience. In this case, her apparent lack of judgment serves as a lesson for all subsequent generations. Rather than an act of bravery or heroism, here is a tale of human misjudgment and error that appears to be a teaching moment even as, by force of Catalina's extreme distress, she emerged as the instigator who opened the door to connect this world with the next, thereby allowing her people proximity with loved ones who have passed on.

Every time the story is told, a new version is created by the storyteller, who is always drawing on oral memory. This mythical tale that belongs to *palenquero* oral traditions lives on in the virtual world of the internet today, as it continues to be told and retold.[144] Guerrero García retells the version told by Tía Cato [Aunt Cato], a famous *lumbalú* singer who was said to be a direct descendant of Catalina Loango.[145] This version is a love story between the beautiful Catalina and a fish known in those parts as *barburito*. The fish is a disguise for a *moján*, an evil spirit of the waters who dwells deep in the river in an underground world that is, in fact, an inverted *palenque*—supposedly a kind of replica of the world aboveground. It is a dark and negative place where everyone walks backward, no one eats salt, new arrivals are poorly treated by family members, and *chimbumbe*, an atmosphere of spells and enchantments, reigns.[146]

One day while on the banks of the river, Catalina is captured and taken into this underworld by the evil spirit, or *moján*. Three days later, she eats salt and becomes part of this world, transforming into a *mojana*. From this moment, she visits the village every time someone dies to guide them into the underworld. Attempts are made to retrieve her to no avail. The first time she emerges to sing at a wake in her *mojana* form, the villagers try to keep her by tying her up; however, she escapes. Tía Cato's version goes on to say that before being captured, her role in the community was as a *lumbalú* singer. Guiding the dead into the afterlife was her trade; therefore, it was natural for her to continue in this role. In the end, she will never return to her original body and soul, and her suffering spirit continues to attend wakes at night.[147]

Yadmilla Bauzá-Vargas provides another version in which the protagonist's full name is Catalina Loango Salgado. One day at noon, the young, beautiful, possibly virgin Catalina went to the creek to perform the usual chores of fishing, washing, and collecting water and never returned. She would sing while performing her chores and while at the creek; possibly, on the day she was taken, she noticed a fish playing at her feet and was enchanted by it. Rather than return to the village with the other girls, she chose to remain at the creek, which is when she may have been coerced by the fish, which was really a spirit. She was taken by a *moán* (spelled differently in this version), a mystical being, who dragged her into the depths of the creek to a world made of gold. The villagers could hear her cry out from beneath the waters, where she remained trapped. Eventually, they stopped looking for her, and for a while, she did not return to the *palenque*.

One day, she begged her captor to let her return to sing at her mother's wake, thus arriving at her mother's home at midnight to express her sorrow, singing in a strange language. The ritual had already begun with the sacred drum, choral chants, dancing, and alcohol. Her sudden appearance, strange chanting, and dancing added spiritual force and allowed for the presence of ancestral spirits among them. She danced the *chimbumbe*, or dance of death, and recounted her story from the day of her capture, which was when the mourners realized she was no longer of this world. She remained the required nine nights at her mother's wake, singing death chants, after which she disappeared. She returned when another relative died, and the villagers tied her up and took her to the local priest with the hope that holy water would free her from the spell; however, her *moán* appeared and demanded her release. She is said to appear at every wake to perform her chants and dance of death at the *lumbalú* ritual, always narrating her story of capture. One day, someone died and she did not return; she was never seen again. Speculations reign—she remains enchanted by her *moán*, the girls call for her at the creek, and she emerges to tell them she cannot come, so they leave feeling sorry for her misfortune. Henceforth, a female soloist assumes her role in the ritual, singing the chants for the dance of death.[148]

Dorina Hernández's version of this myth is slightly different. Catalina Loango decides to go to the river at a time of the day when it is not permitted to be there. She is disobedient, and when she arrives, she comes upon a beautiful goldfish that fascinates her. The other women warn her to stay away from it, but she ignores them, driven by her fascination with the creature. It so happens that the goldfish is in fact a *moján* that grabs her and takes her to the bottom of the river. The villagers look everywhere for her, but in vain. From that day on, the legend goes that Catalina Loango starts to emerge from the depths of the river every time someone in the *palenque* dies to sing the *lumbalú* and partake in the burial ritual. Sometimes the villagers go so far as to tie her up in the church using the priest's vestment, but she never stays. Eventually, she stops appearing altogether, entering the realm of legend. Hernández describes this as a "mito de control social" [myth of social control], a tool for comportment and decorum, a way of alerting the women of the community as to what they should not do—namely, fixate on the male physical appearance or the male body, since not everything that glitters is gold.[149] In relationships, women should look for other qualities in men beyond physical attractiveness.[150] Hernández refers to the role that the reconstitution of this legend plays in the *palenque* today in terms of sustaining a deep and irrefutable sense of self and African legacy. Children are told the story, and it remains as a teaching tool, a lesson for men and, more importantly, women.

Bauzá-Vargas connects this legend to its African archetype, originating in the former African kingdoms of Calabar and Loango, located in today's territories of Nigeria and the Democratic Republic of the Congo. She also constructs parallels with a mythical woman, Sikaneka from Efor, who, upon gaining the power of the word, is promptly sacrificed and sinks to the ancestral world beneath the river.[151] Differences have emerged between African and American legends; for example, an important distinction is that the Catalina Loango myth sits at the intersection of race, gender, colonization, and *cimarronaje*, situations belonging to the Afro-descendant female experience in the Americas. Bauzá-Vargas identifies it as a narrative specific to the construction of a *cimarrona* identity.[152] Her tale is one of trauma, escape, struggle, and survival at the same time that it is a woman's story about her people, language, customs, territories, and deep and lasting connection to Palenque de San Basilio and its rituals: "La mujer proveedora del agua, del sustento, de los quehaceres, como son acarrear agua, pescar y lavar la ropa, y de las funciones de 'ordenar' todo, implícitas en inaugurar la vida y, finalmente, despedir la muerte, como la solista del Lumbalú" [The woman provides water, sustenance; performs chores, such as fetching water, fishing, and washing clothes; and executes the tasks of "organizing" everything, inherent in welcoming life and, finally, bidding farewell to death, like the *lumbalú* soloist].[153]

The legend seems to reenact Catalina's condition of submission, for she is taken by the *moán*, or water spirit, in the same way that she is historically forced to submit to the colonizing forces and the Spanish conqueror. At the same time, this is a legend that speaks to the survival of African belief, albeit in adapted form; today, it remains a striking story that belongs to Palenque de San Basilio. The legend, by design, builds on the American discourse of European colonial oppression (the *moán*), then subsequently expands by converting the ultimate victim (Catalina) into the catalyst that ensures the perpetuation of one of the most African-inspired rituals remaining today. The presence of the *palenque* space as resistance and as Africa transplanted in the Americas ensured the preservation and redesign of such a myth. From myth comes literary portrayal, evident in the bilingual poem "Retorno / Ku gogbé," a poetic version of Catalina's story told by the orisha Elégua to the recently resuscitated Benkos Biohó.[154] This mythical tale serves as another example of how stories (histories) have survived for centuries in spite of the colonial processes of subjugation and repression. Catalina emerges as the long-suffering woman, a clear representation of the power structure established between the captured Black female and the white male colonizing establishment. Her female body has become a discursive site—her youth, imagined attractiveness, carefree spirit, and eternal sacrificial burden are the material upon which to design an alternative historical perspective. Whether curse or blessing, her eternal emergence from the waters provides the means for her life story to endure as oral memory repeated innumerable times through the chants, thereby creating an indelible connection with the lives and legacies of women and men who originally took the initiative and fled.[155]

The creation of a *palenquera*-centered iconic legacy is therefore solidified in two ways: first, by affirming the significance of the *kuagro*, *lumbalú* ritual, and María Lucrecia and Catalina Loango legends, and second, as is presented in the following chapter, by working the spheres of literary representation whose verses confer iconic glory on this community of women.

CHAPTER 6

Palenquera Writings

A TWENTY-FIRST-CENTURY MOVEMENT

Palenquera literature thrives as a subsection of Afro-Colombian women's writings and constitutes a movement that is relatively recent. In Colombia, few critical studies engage with this body of work. Margarita Krakusin comments on its lack of local support and recognition, pointing out that these writers remain largely unknown locally and internationally.[1] In 1999, Laurence Prescott confirmed that works by Afro-Colombian women writers needed scholarly attention. He identified seven writers—Teresa Martínez Arce de Varela Restrepo, Luz Colombia de González, Edelma Zapata Pérez, Colombia Truque Vélez, Sonia Nadhezda Truque, Yvonne América Truque, and Maura Valentina González Quiñonez—who wrote under the pseudonym Perla de Ébano. His research indicated that Teresa Martínez Arce de Varela Restrepo published her first novel, *Guerra y amor*, in 1947 and may have been the first Black woman in Colombia to do so.[2]

THE GENRE OF BLACK WOMEN'S WRITINGS IN COLOMBIA

National recognition of the existence of a tradition of literary writing among these women is a twenty-first-century movement tied to the politics of greater advocacy for Afro-descendants and several government cultural and artistic projects designed to celebrate Colombia's ethnoracial diversity. Two important collections are *¡Negras somos! Antología de 21 mujeres poetas afrocolombianas de la región Pacífica* and *Antología de mujeres poetas afrocolombianas*, volume 16.[3] The latter is part of a major project initiated by the Ministry of Culture, which in 2010 published a collection of eighteen volumes called the *Biblioteca afrocolombiana de literatura* [Afro-Colombian Library of Literature]. Volume 16 is dedicated exclusively to women poets, including a collection of fifty-eight writers from different generations and geographical regions.[4] In 2011, leading poet Mary Grueso Romero commented on the lack of value placed on Black female poetic voicing due to their location and operation in other canonical spaces: "Primero por ser escritoras negras que no han tenido oportunidades para mostrar su quehacer literario, y segundo por ser mujeres y negras; esta suma nos ha condenado a la marginalidad, al silencio, a la invisibilidad total y sobre todo a la subvaloración de nuestro sentir" [First, for being Black women writers who have not had opportunities to show their literary work and second, for being women and Black; this summation has condemned us to marginality, silence, total invisibility and, above all, the devaluation of our poetic expression and feeling].[5]

The Afro-Colombian woman writer enjoys improved (although still limited) visibility today due to recent publications of anthologies dedicated exclusively to this genre of writing. Indeed, this was not always the case, as even though there were earlier writers, they remained unknown. Francineide Santos Palmeira refers to Lucrecia Panchano, whose publications date back to the 1960s; María Teresa Ramírez, who published *La noche de mi piel* in 1988; and Jenny de la Torre Córdoba, whose *Sonata en exilio* came out in 2007.[6] Santos Palmeira's research indicates that only two of the many anthologies published during the twentieth century include Black women writers: Óscar Echeverri Mejía and Alfonso Bonilla Naar's *Antología: 21 años de poesía colombiana, 1942–1963* and Teresa Rozo Moorhouse's *Diosas en bronce: Poesía contemporánea de la mujer colombiana*, which include works by Ana Milena Lucumí, Sonia Solarte, Yvonne América Truque, and María Teresa Ramírez.[7] In addition, Hortensia Alaix de Valencia's *La palabra poética del afrocolombiano* features María Teresa Ramírez, Mary Grueso Romero, and Edelma Zapata. Today, most writers are vigorously working to publish their individual anthologies or appear in poetry collections that feature various writers from all over Colombia. Evidence of their dedication and talent emerge in the literary productions of María Teresa Ramírez, Mary Grueso Romero, and María Elcina Valencia, outstanding practitioners in the art of poetic representation of the Afro-Colombian legacy. Their recognition, recitations, and publications in spaces such as the Rayo Museum in the town of Roldanillo and the Colombian Academy of Language solidify their dominance in the space of creative writing today.[8]

As Santos Palmeira explains, "O fato das histórias literárias e as antologias colombianas não abordarem a produção das escritoras afro-colombianas não significa que elas não existam ou que haja apenas três ou quatro" [The fact that literary histories and Colombian anthologies do not give attention/speak to the production of Afro-Colombian women writers does not mean that these do not exist, or that there are only three or four].[9] They are a part of scholarly studies that focus on Black female production in Spanish and Portuguese and are appearing in papers that address and analyze the phenomenon in a comparative way, with a transatlantic gaze across the Americas and beyond.[10] Today, by way of the state-sponsored publication, *Antología de mujeres poetas afrocolombianas*, which has 590 pages and presents some fifty-seven poets, we can confirm the initiatives being taken by the state to increase the visibility of these writers within the national territory.[11] The challenge for these writers continues to be obtaining financial support for publishing their works. Indeed, the three matriarchs continue to struggle with this, even as they have managed to publish their anthologies. María Elcina Valencia Córdoba has published *Todos somos culpables* [We are all guilty], *Susurro de palmeras* [Whisper of palms], *Rutas de autonomía y caminos de identidad* [Routes of autonomy and pathways of identity], *Analogías y anhelos* [Analogies and longings], and *Pentagrama de pasión* [Pentagram of passion].[12] Mary Grueso Romero has published *Ese otro yo que sí soy yo* [That other I and yes I am], *El mar y tú* [The sea and you], *Del baúl a la escuela* [From trunk to school], *Negra soy* [I am a Black woman], *La muñeca negra* [The black doll], and *La niña en el espejo* [The child (girl) in the mirror].[13] María Teresa Ramírez has published *La noche de mi piel* [Night of my skin], *Flor de palenque* [Palenque flower], *Abalenga* [Star], *Mabungú triunfo: Poemas bilingües, palenque-español* [Triumph: Bilingual poems, Palenque-Spanish], and *Mabungú triunfo: Cosmogonía africana*, volume 2.

The trend of segmenting the Afro-descendant experience in Colombia—the Pacific experience versus the Atlantic or by way of references such as *raizal, palenquero*, and Caribbean—speaks to those markers that influence how individual writers self-identify or define their poetic content. In this case, geography matters—for example, whether the writer is from the Pacific coast, the Atlantic coast, or the island of San Andrés. Such detail has value in terms of history and heritage, since many writers find inspiration in their place of birth. Geographical location and legacy determine production and professional interests even as writers present similar motivations in terms of their sources of inspiration, which include history, identity, Africa, enslavement, Blackness, invisibility, and social condition.

The construction of a formal literary space is dependent on our ability to encounter publications that express their universe. *Palenquero* literature (by male and female writers), while probably in existence as long as its people, is a recent development in terms of an accessible set of published works. It seems to have consolidated as primarily a twenty-first-century production that transcends the ethnicity and geographical location of the writers themselves. This century is also witnessing an increase in cultural and literary studies by *palenqueros* and other researchers, confirming the value of this legacy and added interest in reevaluating its history.[14]

Another important characteristic is that the texts can be bilingual, published in *palenquero* and Spanish. Words and expressions emerge, providing meaning, musicality, rhythm, and most importantly, political statements that reject the anterior positioning of the previous generation, members of whom had learned to deny their identity and avoid using their language. Writers and literary collaborators are currently producing literature through books; blogs and Facebook; rustic, eco-friendly volumes such as the ones produced by the Rayo Museum; performances; and calendars—any oral, paper-based, or electronic format that is amenable to display and dispersion, preferably at a lower cost. This eclectic approach represents a revival and is a testament to the creative and dynamic routes that writers are taking to produce and share their works. Elders or storytellers have always used the spoken word to share teachings and advise younger generations, facilitating the transmission of their practices, rules, skills, myths, and religious doctrines so as to ensure the continuing existence of the collective. Literature is at the heart of their ability to bond as a group, for it ensures continuing dialogue and interaction.[15]

The origins and pasts of these writers are so vital for defining who they are today that while they use current modern channels of communication and transmission of information, they treasure traditional gatherings and forms of expression. *Lumbalú* chants, the *himno municipal* [municipal anthem] that speaks of their past, songs about love and daily life, adult tales, family stories, and children's games are among the various forms of cultural transmission and resistance.[16] Poetry is an integral part of oral narrating and storytelling, as it can function as a tool of recitation and remembrance. It facilitates access to their history and descriptions of their daily lives. Indeed, *palenquero* poetry has been able to capture and sustain their spirit of marronage and attributes profound, universal dimensions to San Basilio de Palenque, making it a space of life, wonder, and magic.

Several works have been published with sponsorship from state entities and collaborating publishing houses. The Bololó Lungumbe Collection (2012) is the most prominent series, a ten-book project of which two are *palenquero* works: *Libertad Kaddume* [Freedom], compiled by Bernardino Pérez Miranda, a collection of narratives about *palenqueros*; and *Letras palenqueras, la profunda necesidad de nombrar: Ma letra ri palengue* [Palenquero letters, the deep need to name], an anthology of poems by Sebastian Salgado, Faustino Torres, and Uriel Cassiani.[17] The collection also includes a publication on male and female heroes, a children's novel, an anthology of Afro-Colombian short stories and fables, and a dictionary. Uriel Cassiani and María Teresa Ramírez stand out among writers who have published since the late eighties. Mirian Díaz Pérez, Ereilis Navarro Cáceres, and Solmery Cásseres Estrada have also joined this emerging poetic expression.[18] Allegiance to *palenquera* identity through literature rests in the writing itself, where content and design find inspiration in the historical legacy and spirit of active commitment visible in stellar figures such as Dorina Hernández and Rutsely Simarra Obeso.

Such female-driven discourse is always connected to activities related to the quotidian and various social projects and agendas that inspire these women to challenge society's structures that may not be working for them. Each writer has her own style, even as they are bonded by idyllic imagery or emotional displays of spaces, traditions, and customs—perhaps a poetic strategy for cultural reinforcement and reinvigoration. Idealism is a component writers use as they narrate the broad range of their experiences as a people by way of a woman-centered perspective. The increasing number of publications in the twenty-first century is testament to the way they treasure practices such as the *lumbalú* ritual and the distress of thinking that it may one day disappear. The historical awareness and emotional expression underlying this kind of literary production endows it with existential value, making it a process of documenting those elements of deep significance. In the end, these writings are serving to strengthen the ethnicity's future.

In light of the valuable legacy of the *palenquero* language, publications in support of its preservation have taken center stage as well. *Palenquera* writers and educators Solmery Cásseres Estrada and Rutsely Simarra Obeso are authors of the two dictionaries of terminology and expressions coming out of the community.

Cásseres Estrada is the first *palenquera* to produce a dictionary. The *Diccionario de la lengua afropalenquera-español* [Dictionary of the Afro-Palenquero-Spanish language] registers her commitment to her people and stands as a compilation by a community leader with the necessary linguistic and historical information passed down to her as an inheritance, a knowledge rooted in struggles for freedom. She wrote with the objective of presenting a vital living language that transcends several centuries. It remains an important record of their ancestry and is now available for future generations. A researcher, poet, folklorist, and educator with a degree in the social sciences, Cásseres Estrada is one of those steering the ethnoeducation project in Cartagena. She is a member of several women's movements including the Red Nacional de Mujeres Afrocolombianas [National Network of Afro-Colombian Women] and the Movimiento Étnico de Mujeres Negras de Colombia [Black Women's Ethnic Movement of Colombia].[19] Simarra Obeso, a director of the Asociación de Mujeres Afrodescendientes y del Caribe Graciela Cha-Inés [Graciela Cha-Inés Association of Afro-Descendant and Caribbean Women], produced the 2008 lexicon *Lengua ri Palenge: Jende suto ta chitiá; Léxico de la lengua palenquera.*[20] The compilation was a task involving all ethnoentities that identify as *palenqueros*, the state, and local experts. These dictionaries provide support for literary agendas, especially those that prioritize production in the *palenquero* language. Writings by Mirian Díaz Pérez and María Teresa Ramírez clearly display this agenda.

María Teresa Ramírez: Biography and Anthologies

María Teresa Ramírez was born June 17, 1944, in the town of Corinto in the department of Cauca on the Pacific coast. Political conflict forced her family to migrate to the coastal seaport city of Buenaventura, Colombia's main port on the Pacific coast, and it was there that she first came into contact with *palenquero*-speaking peoples. Graduating from the Universidad del Valle with a degree in history and philosophy, she worked for many years as a schoolteacher in the department of Cauca. Her career as a writer, primarily of poetry, started when she was very young and rose to new heights in 1988, stimulated by an encounter in the town of Roldanillo with renowned painter and plastic artist Omar Rayo and his wife, Águeda Pizarro Rayo, the latter a famous writer and connoisseur of the arts, both of whom urged her to write, publish, and share her poetry. She became famous for her passionate poetic renditions at the annual conferences for Colombian women poets held at the Rayo Museum, for which she received the title of *Huracana de la poesía* [Poetry's Hurricane].[21] Ramírez continues to participate in these conferences, a space she uses to recite her poetry in a display that reveals an understanding of the art she learned from oral traditions in the Pacific. She assumes the professional role of a *declamadora* [oral performer], an Afro-Colombian female griot who uses dramatic enactment while reciting from memory her own verses as well as poems from other famous writers. Her introduction to *Flor de palenque* gives details about her art, building bridges between knowledge about writing poetry, creativity, and acting. She would *declamar* [perform] many verses by memory and became known for her recitals of poets such as Helcías Martán Góngora, Oscar Echeverri Mejía, and Nicolás Guillén (the latter she found particularly inspiring).[22] As she says, "Mi trabajo va más allá de los textos tradicionales, se fundamenta en vivencias físicas y espirituales, donde la sensibilidad poética me ha permitido llevar a lo largo y a lo ancho de la Patria mis versos, para despertar actitudes positivas en negros, blancos, indígenas y mestizos" [My work is more than traditional texts; it is based on physical and spiritual experiences, in which poetic sensitivity has allowed me to take my verses to the length and breadth of my fatherland in order to waken positive attitudes among Blacks, whites, Indigenous peoples, and mestizos].[23]

Ramírez has several poems in which she incorporates oral techniques, rhythms, onomatopoeia, and *jitanjáforas*, some inspired by Nicolás Guillén's poetry. They serve to re-create the African and Afro-Colombian settings that underpin her verses. Defined as words and expressions that are often invented with no meaning, Ramírez confirms that she uses *jitanjáforas* for their performative and rhythmic value as well as for their stylistic resources that complement her lyrical intentions.[24] Here is an example:

Orúnla, Orunla
En tus tablas de madera
el destino escrito esta
Eia, eia, eleyay, Orúnla, Orúnla.

[Orúnla, orunla
on your wooden boards
is destiny written
Eia, eia, eleyay, orúnla, orúnla.][25]

Ramírez's anthologies—*La noche de mi piel* (1988), *Flor de palenque* (2008), *Abalenga* (2008), *Mabungú triunfo: Poemas bilingües* (2013), and *Mabungú triunfo: Cosmogonía africana*, volume 2 (2016)—are testimonies to her process of becoming a *palenquera* poet. *Abalenga* and *Mabungú triunfo: Poemas bilingües* are bilingual collections. Her poetry is also available in three anthologies: (1) *¡Negras somos! Antología de 21 mujeres poetas afrocolombianas*, (2) *Antología de mujeres poetas afrocolombianas*, and (3) *Poemas matriax: Antología de poetas afrocolombianas*.[26] The idea for the title *La noche de mi piel* was inspired by her participation in literary events at the Rayo Museum. In a poem bearing the same name, fleeing *cimarronas* move at night, a beautiful setting with the sky covered in stars, full of hope and expectation as they make their way toward a new identity, having broken the chains of bondage and escaped into the mountains. The verses transmit the idea of freedom not as gift bestowed but rather as a state of mind or a condition they appropriate by way of initiative and action, via escape and flight. At the same time, each must decide how and why this night is beautiful.

With regard to her anthology *Abalenga*, Ramírez reminisces about connecting with all things *palenque* as a process of gradual aesthetic commitment to the language and to learning about her African ancestry. She describes an encounter with Cásseres Estrada, who at the time was presenting her latest publication, *Diccionario de la lengua afropalenquera-español*. Ramírez opened it, and the very first words were "Cielo cobierto de estrellas y luceros" [Sky covered with stars and lights].[27] Finally, *Mabungú* [Triumph] is not meant to represent a windfall or sudden accomplishment; rather, it speaks to gains and successes achieved over time, with effort and dedication—indeed, a more difficult kind of achievement.[28] María Mercedes Jaramillo mentions that the words *abalenga* and *mabungú* are direct references to ancestry and its legacy. It is in *Abalenga, Flor de palenque,* and *Mabungú triunfo: Poemas bilingües* that we observe the emergence of the legacy in vivid poetic renditions, this coming from a writer not born in San Basilio de Palenque but who claims such Afro-Colombian roots and heritage as her own.[29] She has developed a deeper understanding through immersion in language and poetic creativity. Her ideological position is striking for the way it potentially criticizes, even dissolves the regional and geographical distinctions that define and maybe even divide Afro-Colombianness.

Ramírez confirms her passion for poetry. Poetry as performance is an extension of storytelling and those oral traditions that mark her origins and are an indelible part of her profile as a writer. In her introduction to *Flor de palenque*, she describes poetry as creation, recitations, and performances. Jaramillo appreciates Ramírez's infatuation with dramatization and confirms that she has become famous as a performer of her verses. The poems present a blend of elements that attest to her multiple linguistic and poetic influences, particularly Cuban poet Nicolás Guillén. Her difference is in the performative nature of her work and the intentional Africanization of her writing as it pertains to the *palenque* space and her multi-layered presentation of Black female experiences. Associations between the female body and rhythm that are controversial in *negrista* verses change direction as the *palenquera* becomes the bearer of Ramírez's people's legacy. Her aesthetic agenda is to move poetry from paper to performance, and to accomplish this objective, *palenquero* language, rituals, and rhythms are crucial for the theatrical atmosphere and effect she seeks to create through verse. *Jitanjáforas* and rhythmic imagery serve multiple functions in these verses, including dance movements, invented or real chants and evocations, music, and percussion. They are inspired by the language, and her sources of information include names, events, and aspects of daily life. Her verses are designed for oral exposition, and as I sat and listened to her, the striking nuances of her oral heritage came to light. The rise and fall of syllables, the placing of stress, the elongation or shortening of the vowels created emotion, atmosphere, and rhythm—all special effects that are lost on paper.[30]

Ramírez is interesting in the way she invents new and exciting forms of Black writing in *Flor de palenque* and *Mabungú triunfo: Poemas bilingües*. She is *palenquera* by commitment, and her poems reveal a deep appreciation of all aspects of being *palenquera*, especially their history, language, and rituals. She also brings a female perspective to numerous aspects of language and identity constructs. At the same time, her verses coincide with her convictions about who she is as a person, her roots and ancestral obligations. She is a "muje timbo" [very Black woman].[31] In her poem, this expression is used by the narrator to define herself as a dark-skinned woman, an integral part of her ideological position and poetic voice within a space that expresses absolute pride in such subjectivity.[32] Her publications are a major contribution, as they make up for the dearth of literary examples featuring this female, especially from the Black female perspective. Today, many studies about San Basilio de Palenque are linguistic analyses about the language that address the dilemma of its relationship with Spanish. At the same time, the *palenque* space becomes universal; indeed, Ramírez's gaze is extensive, touching on various forms of the human condition. Love, childhood, wealth, poverty, even happiness emerge as forms of existence that are intrinsic to this space; the anthology is bilingual, a narrative strategy and a way of confirming that as *palenqueras*, they too experience the same emotions and experiences as everyone else.

Abalenga

Abalenga is a collection of poems dedicated to Ramírez's ancestors and to all *palenqueros* who lit the fires of freedom.[33] The night's beauty, escape, and liberty serve to create layers of meaning and purpose at the core of the anthology. The narrating voice glorifies nature and displays it as supportive of the extreme measures taken by these women and men. Ramírez writes an introduction that uncovers her intentions with regard to this anthology.[34] "El Palenquero, fuego de libertad" [The *Palenquero*, fire of freedom], the title of her introduction, is fierce, indicative of the spirit and intention of the verses within. She justifies this bilingual anthology, articulating *palenquero* as one of the Indigenous languages of Colombia, rooted in linguistic components belonging to enslaved Africans. She connects *palenquero* to a specific African experience that started on the home continent and imagines the language taking shape gradually, from the moment of capture, to the agonizing Middle Passage journey endured only by the comforting presence of the Yoruba deities or orishas, and ending in solidified form in enslavement, rebellion, escape, and the fires these freedom seekers used to guide them through the darkness of the night and the deep forests, to their new home.[35] She projects the *palenque* as a part of the hilly landscape of Afro-America, a new formation representative of Africa that emerged under different names across the region—"ladeiras, mocambos, cumbes, rochelas, patucos, kilombos y manieles."[36] She contemplates African origin as indicative of multiple geographical locations, traceable by words, last names, and other references in her anthology, perhaps in homage to those ancestors who lit the initial fires of freedom. In *Abalenga*, the narrating voice aligns with the writer herself, who artistically and ideologically establishes her identity as *palenquera*.[37]

"Abalenga," the cornerstone of this anthology, is the first poem in which verses describe a group of *cimarrones* as they flee under the cover of night. The poem thrives on two levels of meaning. On one level, the tranquilizing nature of the words in *palenquero* and Spanish—"la noche es hermosa" [the night is beautiful]— provides a soft, mellow cover that keeps the mood of the verses from spiraling into overwhelming harshness. Their flight is calm, even joyful, as they retain a sense of security that comes from being together. They were enslaved laborers together, and now, under the beautiful night sky, they forge ahead as companions, always moving forward. On a second level, the verses seem to design the personality of the *cimarron*, creating a spirit of rebelliousness and a self-assertion in direct contrast to displays of fear or apprehension that often accompany scenes of enslavement and colonization in narratives, poems, and films. This poem is marked by a total lack of tension in the air. What is suggested is long-term planning and execution:

> Mi gente
> nosotros, hábiles
> trabajadores
> dueños de nosotros mismos,
> el látigo . . . nunca más.

> [My people
> we, skilled
> workers
> our own bosses,
> the whip . . . never more.][38]

The tone of defiance is established very early: "El látigo . . . nunca más." This particular tone emerges in each poem, offering a glimpse into what life was like for enslaved women and men.

Flor de palenque

As one of Ramírez's earlier collections, *Flor de palenque* sets the stage for *Mabungú triunfo: Poemas bilingües*, and while it does not deny the narrator's other heritages, it attests to what she describes as her phase of discovering and embracing her African ancestry and negritude. In her introduction to this volume, she greets Iansan, the Yoruba orisha of storms, sensuality, and passion with whom she identifies, an affiliation she credits to her own impetuous and enthusiastic temperament. A major characteristic of these verses is that they are meant to be performed. *Palenque* as a construct here is different from her subsequent anthology, since its poems do present two versions, one in Spanish and another that reproduces speech patterns and oral legacies of Blacks in the Pacific. This is a characteristic of her writing, one she started in *La noche de mi piel*. Within this setting, *palenque* symbolizes Blackness, Africa, the orishas, the drum and its rituals, racial identities, and the art of performing and writing poetry. She was drawn to Black writing; greatly influenced by the language, historical intention, and social realism in Guillén's Afro-Cuban poetry; and brought this spirit of rhythm and protest into her writing.[39]

"Tambor lumbalú para Guillén" pays homage to Guillén by way of his own *lumbalú* ceremony. Verses seem to capture the Black historical experience as it relates to Cuba and the Americas.[40] Africa as an idealized space together with its multiple ethnicities gives way to the American trauma of the Middle Passage and the plantation life of enslavement; it is a Cuban experience of mutilation, difficulty, loss, resistance, and rediscovery. The sound of the drum and the advent of the *palenques* transition toward rhythm and music (reminiscent of Guillén's Afro-Cuban lyricism) in verses in which Ramírez merges *el son cubano*, rumba, and maraca with the legacy of marronage, the orishas, and the saints. This collection contains several poems that remind us of Ramírez's Cuban *negrista* influences confirmed in *jitanjáforas*, such as "songo songo," "sensem-ayá," and "mayombe."[41] She creates percussion sounds and tempo with others— "¡Tumba timbero, tumbá, tumba," "¡Cunúname, cunúname¡," "¡Tam . . . tam . . . tum . . . tim . . . ," and "¡Tarumba¡ ¡Tamba¡"[42] Widely used in her poems, they are an effective resource for this professional female griot. Overall, her array of themes, the poetic idealization of the African world, and feminist conscious verses confirm her intention to contemplate matters of race, gender, and sexuality through verse.

Mabungú triunfo: Poemas bilingües, palenque-español

This anthology has as its subtitle *Poemas bilingües, palenque-español* [Bilingual poems: Palenque-Spanish] and highlights the specific nature of this study. Ramírez continues her work started in *Abalenga*. In *Mabungú triunfo: Poemas bilingües*, the *palenque* language is on an equal footing with Spanish. Poems are presented first in *palenquero*, then in Spanish, and the wide variety of themes prioritize elements encountered within that universe—Benkos Biohó, Yoruba deities, childhood experiences, Black female dignity, slavery, and love. The Spanish versions allow readers access to *palenquero* life, even as not everything is translated (or translatable)— perhaps as a way of emphasizing that this is a unique space into which readers must migrate willingly. Ramírez's action of assuming this identity confirms her belief in its central role within Afro-Colombian literary movements. The production of an anthology in their language aligns with ethnoeducational projects and campaigns of cultural specificity, an effective way of reiterating that this too is what it means to be Colombian.

MIRIAN DÍAZ PÉREZ: BIOGRAPHY AND ANTHOLOGY

Mirian Díaz Pérez's first bilingual anthology came out in 2013 with the title *Tejiendo palabras con libertad / Binda ndunblua ku bindanga* [Knitting words with freedom] and is dedicated to her people. Some of her writings are also available in Felipe Quetzalcoatl Quintanilla and Juan Guillermo Sánchez Martínez's *Indigenous Message on Water*.[43] She is, by profession, an ethnoeducator in the Institución Educativa Distrital San José [San José District Educational Institution] in Barranquilla. She also teaches at the Universidad del Atlántico [Atlantic University], having earned a degree in elementary education specializing in public administration and pedagogical sciences. Díaz Pérez went on to complete a master's in education.

Díaz Pérez self-identifies as a *palenquera* from the urban *palenque* of Barran-quilla.[44] Her parents had moved to the city, and while Díaz Pérez was still very young, she worked to help support her family. They made homemade delicacies and sold them in the streets. At a tender age, she realized that she did not want to do this forever, perceived the importance of an education, and with such dedication to her studies was able to build a career for herself. She was educated in a school run by nuns in the neighborhood of Bajo Valle and then went on to complete high school at the Carlos Meisel School, at which point she became aware of the uniqueness of her roots as well as conscious of the duties and rights of her people. She recalls reciting her writings in Spanish, keeping to herself those written in her mother tongue; indeed, during her adolescence and as a young woman, she avoided speaking *palenquero* in public for fear that her friends would make fun of her. Growing up, she recalls that her parents did not allow her to use it, fearing discrimination from her predominantly white friends and classmates who made fun of *palenqueros*. In those days, they spoke it in secret or at home within the family. She grew up in this ambiguous setting of noting the language's real value among her people and its marginalization everywhere else. Times changed, and she grew to appreciate and proudly claim this ancestry. She would later join the first Movimiento de Negritudes del Atlántico [Atlantic Negritude Movement], contributing to the meetings by reading the bilingual stories and poems she composed. The meetings provided her with the perfect space and audience to begin sharing her work, and she eventually became a central figure in the organization of the movement's literary encounters.[45]

Díaz Pérez started to write as a child, initially in *palenquero*. "Maldita enfermedad / Inkusi Sukutengue" is a poem in her collection that she originally learned from her father, who used to compose songs when she was a child.[46] Those verses provided solace at a time of considerable difficulty and challenges. She describes her production as nonconformist to rules of poetic production, more a reflection of customs and emotions expressed spontaneously. She works to capture those aspects that are specific to this ethnicity in verses that display them and preserve them in their authentic form; the *lumbalú* ritual is especially important. Her verses seek to narrate and describe the lives of her people; indeed, this insistence on publishing verses in *palenquero* is an ideological statement of self-affirmation, a way to strengthen their cultural relevance in a space that has historically rejected them.

She continues to give back to her community in the form of stories, myths, and legends, a way of providing the younger generations in particular with a deeper sense of pride and greater knowledge of their history and spirituality. She applies her skills as an educator, and her active involvement in institutional matters such as public policies draws attention to the specific circumstances of her people. This is now her life's work: she is currently a member of the Asociación de Etnoeducadores del Atlántico [ADETA; Atlantic Ethnoeducators Association] and vice president of the Association of Notable Black, Afro-Colombian, *Raizales*, and *Palenquera* Women.[47]

Díaz Pérez's role as a writer allows her to engage these educational and intercultural processes. She is particularly motivated by possibilities for the intellectual development of young Afro-descendants within the educational environment. As Raúl Gómez Afanador states, "Mirian nos presenta un buen trabajo, donde arrancamos con poemas de amor, interactuamos con una bella oda a los amigos que se fueron, apreciamos y distinguimos a quienes han estudiado el terruño y gritamos la influencia de nuestra raza" [Mirian presents us with a good work, where we start off with love poems, interact with a beautiful ode to friends who have passed away, appreciate and distinguish those who have studied the land, and shout the influence of our race].[48] Gómez Afanador observes that Díaz Pérez's poetic renditions can be placed alongside those of Mary Grueso Romero and María Teresa Ramírez in the way they cultivate an Afro-feminine discourse and speak of an ethnic space from their perspective as Black women writers.[49] The anthology becomes a politicized production in the way its design enforces the strategy of interculturalism, within which developments such as ethnoeducation emphasize the value of such heritage and reiterate its central (not peripheral) role in the nation.

Díaz Pérez's introduction to her work recalls a time when her people's legacy was not the prestigious national patrimony that it is today. Recognition at the level of the state came in direct response to the United Nations Educational, Scientific and Cultural Organization (UNESCO) declaration regarding San Basilio de Palenque, paving the way for policies to guarantee the preservation and strengthening of their language and culture. She reminds readers that her lineage had to ensure its own preservation, a feat that was only possible because of its experiences of resistance and endurance accumulated over time. Today, she witnesses an increasing trend toward erosion, forgetting, and abandonment of traditional knowledge that is affecting the clear line of identity her people have always sustained. Nowhere is this more evident than in their language, which explains the reason for her anthology. These verses are more than poems; they are the authentic oral expression of her people. Diaz Pérez discusses this issue in the introduction to her anthology:

> Teniendo en cuenta que la oralidad se ha convertido en el medio más utilizado a través del tiempo para la construcción de saberes, es importante resaltar que ésta nos permite difundir a las generaciones presentes y futuras, conocimientos, usos y costumbres. A través de ella algunos pueblos han podido conservar y mantener su identidad cultural, lo cual permite fortalecer lazos sociales y estructuras comunitarias.

> [Bearing in mind that orality has over time become the most used medium for the construction of wisdom, it is important to highlight that it allows us to spread knowledge, habits, and customs to present and future generations. Thanks to it, some people have been able to preserve and maintain their cultural identity, which allows for the strengthening of social bonds and community structures.][50]

Tejiendo palabras con libertad / Binda ndunblua ku bindanga [Knitting words with freedom] stresses the usage of the mother tongue and the positive results to be gained from promoting intercultural relations, thereby allowing differing subjects to learn more about one another and grow in respect and appreciation. Díaz Pérez's anthology is also working against the dearth of such material, for, as she confirms, available educational publications and textbooks are still lacking in terms of the quantity and quality of knowledge about Africa and Afro-Colombianness. The situating of *palenquero* versions of her poems alongside the Spanish ruptures the dominance of the latter language, places attention on this new kind of published literary format and its African-originated storytellers, and sets the stage for another kind of literary personage and performance within the Colombian space.[51] One of the most striking poems in her collection is "A esos grandes escritores / Pa ma katriaró ngande" [To those great writers], notable for the way it pays homage to the legacy of Afro-Colombian writing and thought.[52] She summons *palenquero* collaborators, writers, intellectuals, artists, and perpetuators of a specific legacy of which she is a part. In verse, she seems to line them up as inheritors, the true sons and daughters of the figure she describes as the king of rebels, son of Yemayá and Shango, the one without whom there would be no history—Benkos Biohó.

BENKOS BIOHÓ: AN AFRICAN KING IN AMERICA

Both Ramírez and Díaz Pérez cast Benkos Biohó in a glorified role as the ultimate heroic leader of these communities. As Ramírez pens in *Abalenga*, "En el lomo encabritado de Afro-América los palenques se denominaron: ladeiras, mocambos, cumbes, rochelas, patucos, kilombos y manieles. El primer cimarrón rey en América fue Benkos Biojó" [On the emerging slope of Afro-America, runaway slave communities were called *ladeiras*, *mocambos*, *cumbes*, *rochelas*, *patucos*, *kilombos*, and *manieles*. The first maroon king in America was Benkos Biohó].[53]

A poetic illustrator of this universe, Ramírez designs Biohó as the medium for transmitting the more meaningful messages and long-term agendas that underpin several poems in her anthologies. He emerges as a product of a long and powerfully inspiring legacy that he inherited, without which he would not have been able to achieve lasting fame and glory. He is idealized as an individual, endowed with attributes beyond human capacity, and appears as a phenomenon with ongoing impact. For these women writers, the process of glorifying Biohó and the *palenque* as symbols of their roots starts with the lyrical descriptions of the originating continent. Verses pay homage to African places, personages, deities, and events connected with a millennial past that slowly transitions toward the experiences of Africans in the Americas, thereafter settling into *palenque* images. Creations of Africa are randomly selected and can be sweeping, not specific, and idealistic in tone. Particularly important are the roles memory and spirituality play in designing paths of resistance.

There occurs an appropriation and Africanization of the national space, an impression created by the presence of this particular leadership; this is another version of their country's past, one that characterizes Colombia as an extension of the old continent. In Ramírez's *Flor de palenque*, the poems "Addis Ababa (nueva flor)" [Addis Ababa (new flower)], "Alma africana" [African soul], and "Ancestral sabor a lágrimas" [Ancestral taste of tears] display this direct yet ample connection to Africa, seeing it as inspirational for their rebellions and escape plans.[54] "Diaspora ario gende mi / Diáspora adiós mi gente" [Diaspora farewell my people], "Ancestral sabor a lágrimas," [Ancestral taste of tears], and "Adiós mi gente"

[Farewell my people] incorporate sentiments of sorrow, lamentations due to a profound sense of loss and separation from the motherland engrained forever in the memory of the narrating voices that cannot escape such trauma, for there are constant reminders everywhere and always—African peoples, drums, the sea, the whip, and tears.[55] In *Tejiendo palabras con libertad*, Díaz Pérez's poem "Soy / I a sé" [I am] clearly aligns the narrator's identity with those of various African peoples.[56] The expression "soy de Palenque" is popular, regularly used to self-identify, and in these verses, the *palenquera* identity is not derivative but rather equivalent to people situated on the old continent, including Bantus, Carabalís, Lucumís, and Yorubas.[57] This same spirit is in "Juntos/Jundo," where the narrator declares, "Yo soy del Congo de Angola / a mi me trajo una ola" [I am from the Congo of Angola / a wave brought me].[58]

Benkos Biohó, San Basilio, and *palenque* are inseparable as symbolic references to origins. Here is a manifestation that represents ancestrality, the home, the source, and the foundation of their heritage. It mirrors Africa as the narrator longingly tries to remember, replicate, or even return there. "Ma posa palenke / Las casas palenqueras" [Palenquero houses], "Diaspora ario gende mi / Diáspora adiós mi gente" [Diaspora farewell my people], and "San Basilio" attest to the eclectic nature of strategic symbols and the way history feeds into Ramírez's poetry.[59] Tofeme, Malambo, Cruz de Masinga, Guarné, and Tadó are *palenque* sites.[60] Arará, Kuniri, Keke, Uru, Muanga, and Ucambo are Ramírez's way of identifying the people of Africa, representations of all those who established diasporas. "Gunga Sumbi / Gunga Zumbi" and "Barule" pay homage to Brazil's Black hero, Zumbi of Palmares, and Barule, king of the Tadó *palenque*, located in the Chocó region of Colombia.[61] The legacy of Catalina Loango is indirectly visible in "Loyo ri la riba / Los arroyos de arriba" and "Loyo ri la bajo / Los arroyos de abajo," idyllic reminders of natural habitats and the central role brooks and streams play in their daily lives as well as their emotional and spiritual well-being.[62]

The idea of a strong ethnic grouping that overcame European domination and rejected foreign and European presence or influence is central to the poem "Kuagro/Compañeros."[63] The persona makes it quite clear that this experience belongs to those women and men whose painful historical trajectory was overcome by a legacy of collectivity and united struggle. They were able to defeat adversity because they fought and prospered together:

Los Palenqueros
con brazo fuerte lucharon
florece . . . florece
palenque.

[The *palenqueros*
with strong arms fought
flourishes . . . flourishes
palenque.][64]

The narrator emphasizes the lines of separation that were drawn between them and their oppressors: "Extranjero no, no, / europeo no, no" [Foreigner no, no, / European no, no]; however, she determined that the only way forward was to move beyond history's deep wounds and build a new home for themselves.[65]

"Lumba a Benkos Biojó / Oda a Benkos Biojó" is an ode that describes Biohó as the artifice of their freedom, the savior who tore them away from torture and death, who urged them to flee and fight, and who, as their Elégua, ultimately showed them the way.[66] He changed the direction of their lives, even for the most vulnerable, the children, the youth, and the elderly. The poem "Domingo Biojó" continues in this vein, for he is the embodiment of freedom and stands tall, overshadowing and protective as their king and orisha.[67] Similarly, in Díaz Pérez's "A esos grandes escritores / Pa ma katriaró ngande," he stands tall as a maker of history.[68] In this poem, Pérez pays homage to the nation's great writers and intellectuals, starting with the Afro-Colombians. Aquiles Escalante, Manuel Zapata Olivella, Delia Zapata, Juan Zapata Olivella, Germán Espinosa, Antonio Prada, and Abel Ávila are especially valuable for their strategic productions. Antonio Prada wrote Biohó into history, and Abel Ávila is a true ally and friend; nonetheless, it is Biohó, son of Yemayá and Shango, who is worthy of the pedestal, for without him, there would have been no history. This warrior king is *palenquero* memory. Poetic reverence also appears in Díaz Pérez's "Para el rey del Arcabuco / Pa ma loango ri arkabuko" and "Miserable/Sapokusuela," where the narrating voice acknowledges Biohó's bravery and sacrifice, expressing great pride to be a descendant of such a worthy lineage.[69]

Díaz Pérez inaugurates her bilingual anthology by paying homage to Elégua, who shows the way, and to Biohó, her ancestral monarch. In Díaz Pérez's writings, Biohó is central to the establishment of a poetic legacy of *palenquero* identity, especially in his role as an ancestor who dwells in the realm of the orishas:

A ti, Elegguá,
que abres las puertas
de entrada y de salida.

A Benkos Biohó,
"el rey del Arcabuco."

[To you, Elégua,
may you open the doors
of entry and departure.

To Benkos Biohó
"the king of the Swamps."][70]

"Retorno / Ku gogbé" [Return] and "Para el rey del Arcabuco / Pa ma loango ri arkabuko" [For the king of the swamps] depict him as infinitely legendary.[71] "Retorno / Ku gogbé" also establishes a connection between Biohó and Elégua, his father and protector, whom Biohó summons in the form of prayer, begging for life, guidance, and protection in the midst of darkness and difficulty. Elégua must also guide Biohó in his leadership role as a seeker of freedom. He urges Biohó to embrace the land, to find strength in it. "Retorno / Ku gogbé" is a dialogue in which Biohó—a father figure to his people, son of Elégua, and master of freedom—begs for Elégua's permission to gaze on the land for which he fought and died.[72] Verses describe past times of need and difficulty built into the historical legacy of their existence, as they fought to build their lives on a difficult, unforgiving land. Unfortunately, Biohó is deeply saddened by what he sees and, in dialogue with the orisha, laments the fact that everything he knew has disappeared. His fortress—the village with its huts, utensils, wells, streams, and flowing waters—is no more, wiped out by time:

> Oh! rebelde Bekos Biohó
> Oh! barón tan admirado
> El paso y andar del tiempo
> Todo eso ya lo ha borrado.

> [Oh! Rebellious Benkos Biohó
> Oh! So admired baron
> The passage and march of time
> Have all erased him.][73]

On seven different occasions, Biohó returned, and on one such journey, he met Catalina Loango. He thereby constructs an association between loss and the figure of Catalina Loango, whose very presence introduces death:

> Ella viene de repente
> más no se deja tocar
> cuando se muere su gente
> sus lecos puedo escuchar.

> [She comes suddenly
> but allows no one to touch here
> when one of her people dies
> her chants I can hear.][74]

Biohó is intrigued. He wishes to know more about this woman and is told her tragic story and mythical legacy of capture, imprisonment, and interminable destiny to appear at wakes. Now Catalina is gone, Biohó's warriors are no more, and his people speak another language. The invocation of Catalina reminds him of those brave warriors who fought at his side, and he strives to understand what is happening to his people today. The verses express sorrow as Biohó begs Elégua to take back the shadows, distress, and difficulty, to remove them from his sight, for he can no longer bear them. He is devastated—feels betrayed, rejected, lost in memory and time, his name now meaningless. He had fought for freedom, for life, and now he wishes to cry in anguish, to be left alone to contemplate what he sees as a divided legacy. Biohó is disillusioned, traumatized, and decides to leave. His name divided, scattered, even erased, he swears never to return to this life. "Retorno" is both fictional and historical, for it immortalizes Biohó and highlights the past while displaying the challenges they face today.

POETIC CONFIGURATIONS OF THE ORISHAS

The threads that hold this fragile yet determined community together create hidden connections among individuals, whether ancestral or living, and these bonds are visible during sentimental and ritual moments. Collective memory is sacred, and daily life incorporates spirituality in a meaningful, concrete way. Communication with the world of spirits takes place through their contact with and accumulated understanding of nature; nature itself is full of meaning, messages, and secrets that they store as memory and use to increase their sentiments of proud autonomy. Contact with the land builds wisdom and understanding that guide in life and serves as their counselor as they transition to the world beyond, a belief particularly visible in their rituals of death, and these, as with ancestral memory, are nurtured and fiercely protected by older women.[75] Evidence indicates that their beliefs seem to include forms of polytheistic deity worship similar to vodun in Haiti, Santeria and *regla de ocha* in Cuba, and candomblé in Brazil. Why do these illustrations appear in their poetry? Literary inventions and mythical-spiritual beliefs are driving such trends as they serve to identify different kinds of protection associated with their ancestors, spirits, *curanderos* [spiritual healers], and rituals of African traditions. The presence of deities in poems speaks to a contemporary transregional movement of religious and cultural influences that are proving to be stimulating for literary discourses and faith-based movements of all kinds. Belief in African-based religious expression, social activism, and Afro-aesthetic movements in Colombia serves as motivation and explains why writers continue to adopt and import these forms; they have made them an integral part of their own belief systems and celebrate them as a way of connecting with Afro-descendant systems in Haiti, Cuba, and Brazil, places that have proven to be influential in the solidification of African religions in the Americas. The centrality of Africanness is not exclusive, meaning that verses display ideas of syncretism as well.

During the 1980s, Ramírez met poet *declamador* Diego Álvarez (who uses the artistic and ethnic name Sabás Mandinga) from Cartago, who she describes as a prophet of Black poetry, well versed in African heritage. Through his teachings and guidance, she learned about African ancestral and Yoruba beliefs. In *Flor de palenque*, the poem "¿Quién te trujo? / ¿Quién te trajo?" reads as a eulogy in his honor.[76] It was an important moment for Ramírez, since before, she would avoid such matters, a process she describes as camouflage, a self-imposed whitening provoked by the dominant cultural preferences in her society. As a child growing up in Buenaventura, she listened to songs and music from Cuba that spoke of orishas, including Babaluaye and Shango, and was inspired later in life to do her own reading and research, discovering that Africa has its own marvelous history and cosmogony, myths and legends—a new learning that fueled her desire to learn *palenquero*.[77] Besides Ramírez, Díaz Pérez also displays these influences in her poetry; she has two poems, "Juntos/Jundo" and "Miserable/Sapokusuela," in which the narrating voices interpret the idea of unity in differences.[78] Blacks and whites are together in the same space as equals; however, they are not the same. They have different historical trajectories, hair, emotions, and names. In "Juntos," Díaz Pérez writes, "Santa Bárbara es a ti / lo que es Changó para mí" [Saint Barbara is for you / what Shango is for me].[79] The narrator is emphatic about her spirituality and lineage, for she considers herself to be daughter of the king (Benkos Biohó), a proud ethnic descent. In "Miserable," she rejects baptism and yearns to see the land of her forebears, Africa.[80]

Several poems in Ramírez's *Mabungú triunfo: Poemas bilingües* manifest the classic components of African-based spirituality, creating an atmosphere of mysticism and wonder. The verses make reference to two kinds of deities, or orishas: those associated with Yoruba derived beliefs (Oshun, Ogun, Elégua, Obatalá, Yemayá, and Shango) and others specific to the *palenquero* legacy (Lemba, Oninga, Babalú, Odudúa, and Iku). The pantheon of deities that appears supports greater causes that have to do with both the community and worthy individuals. The use of deities is a contemporary poetic technique, fruit of society's increasing association and familiarity with Cuban, Brazilian, and Haitian belief systems and their adoption in Colombia. Worshippers summon their orishas during moments of veneration, whether ceremonial or routine, and they do so in order to pay them homage or seek their protection. Odudúa and Obtalá-Babá appear during crises, as their people call to them in moments of great need, while the other deities are worshipped.[81] The belief system is dynamic and ranges from the central value of the drum as provocateur and medium to the world of the supernatural and the fantastic, including belief in the power of witches, as seen in the poem "Bangasunga/ Apasionada."[82] In "Yemayá Kalunga / Yemayá, diosa del mar," this mother-like figure bears children and canoes on her shoulders and her back, and she is summoned and greeted as the sister of Shango by all who see themselves as her children.[83] The spirit world is invoked as a way of confirming worshippers' adherence to and belief in unseen elements within the natural world.

Elégua, deity and guider of the pathways appearing in "Lumba a Benkos Biojó / Oda a Benkos Biojó," provides spiritual support for the historical battle in which the *palenque* must engage if it is to be free.[84] This poem summarizes maroon resistance and is dedicated to Biohó as the great warrior and leader, yet even he must pay homage to the gods and to Elégua, revered as the deity who showed the maroons the way to freedom, a feat he managed to achieve by turning history inside out. Biohó is the artifice of freedom enjoyed by all—children, adolescents, grandparents, Blacks, and Indians. He continues to represent leadership, liberty, and belief. The poem "Domingo Biojó" projects said warrior as an orisha worthy of veneration.[85] Originally Bantú, Kongo, and Arará, he arrives in the Americas and immediately loses his African identity. His slave owner gives him a Spanish name,

Domingo, an imposition intended to erase any previous forms of existence and a devastating yet significant act that determines his path and presence through and beyond slavery into the archives of history.[86] Biohó's African origin and role as a proud warrior and defender of his people coexists with this Spanish identity even as the former has greater value. In the poem, he is both ancestor and deity, and his people pray for him as he dwells among their ancestors under Elégua's protection.

Elégua, the Yoruba deity, or orisha, is valuable in this anthology, appearing in crucial moments of history and personal decision-making. The manifestation of this orisha continues in the poem "Bolá, reboliá / Vuela, rebolotea," for he is the powerful entity who is capable of controlling the narrator's destiny, especially her relationship with others.[87] The presence of Elégua in the verses reveals the fatalistic view that this deity is, in fact, the decisive force manipulating their lives and decisions:

> Elégua trenza nuestras vidas
> en las casas palenqueras,
> en las casas de los negros.
>
> [Elégua weaves our lives
> in *palenquero* homes,
> in Black people's homes.][88]

This is a striking image, as over time, the narrator describes how Elégua shapes destinies. He is a nonthreatening omnipresence in the home, a welcoming guide who is greeted, blessed, and respected.[89] Similarly, in "Gunga Zumbi," a poem of epic dimensions, the narrator pays homage to the greatest Brazilian *quilombo* leader, Zumbi, and declares with absolute certainty that Elégua is the dependable presence at his side who will guide him along in the direction he is meant to follow.[90] As with other moments in the text, the narrator presents the deity in a positive and uplifting light and as an integral part of the proud *palenqueros'* lives.[91] The image of this deity as a protector in heaven and on earth is reinforced in "Omar ngungú / Omar, artista creador" and "Chupungún," the latter a poem directed toward enslaved individuals who served as hunters of fugitive slaves.[92] The imagery moves back and forth between describing the trauma of those who are trying to escape bondage and condemning the actions of their enslaved companions who are hunting them down. The narrating voice accuses the hunters of having lost their way. This poem is particularly revealing of Elégua's role, for in this case, he is not the runaways' savior but a guiding presence. The scene is emotional, for the fugitives are desperate and without hope, a people begging their god to free them and lead them to their mystical home in heaven.

The Yoruba tradition of claiming to be sons and daughters of orishas is visible in "Omar ngungú / Omar, artista creador," a poem that pays homage to renowned artist Omar Rayo, whose talent makes him worthy of the title "Shango's favorite son."[93] Rayo's art is housed in the Rayo Museum, located in the town of Roldanillo in Valle del Cauca. His name lines up in significance with this deity, for *ngungú/ rayo* means "ray of light," which, by association, connects to the domain of lightning and explains the poetic strategy of calling him "son of Shango."[94] This deity's significance is in his continuity as one of the sacred entities that sustains the connection between Africa and America in Colombia's national space. Ramírez's poem honors Rayo and his wife, Águeda Pizarro Rayo, who nurtured and supported Ramírez's development as a poet. Famous feminist poet, writer, critic, and patron of the arts, Águeda Pizarro Rayo appears to have power over words, and by virtue of this combined artistry, the narrating voice of "Omar ngungú / Omar, artista creador" invokes other supreme deities—Oshun, Orun, and Elégua—to strengthen this poetic homage. The message of Shango's liberating and transforming power is an enduring part of *palenque* history, also visible in the poem "Barule."[95] Barule, king of a *palenque* located in Tadó around 1728, is victorious in battle thanks to the way Shango illuminated his path. Along with his brothers and warriors, Barule battled long and hard, always under the protection of the orishas. Barule and his people resisted; they rebelled, they fought, they tore off the restraints of enslavement, and they fled. "Changó fue sol, en su camino" [Shango was sun, in his path], and numerous battles later, free from bondage, they danced victoriously to the sound of the drum.[96]

Yoruba deities emerge in the verses as part of the poetic reconstruction of their ancestral universe. The gods reveal the inner workings of mysticism and belief. Shango, orisha of thunder, lightning, justice, virility, dance, and fire, is evoked in "Posa Kasangalanga / En casa de brujos" [In the house of witches]. He appears during rituals of magic and witchcraft, emerging as lightning, light, fire, and dance.[97] This is a world of ancient and mysterious practices, medicinal knowledge, spells, and belief in the forces of good and evil. In his ethnographic essay, Armin Schwegler reveals a social structure in which close ties remain between traditional life, local power, and *brujería* [witchcraft].[98] Belief in the survival of the spirits of their ancestors and in the ability of certain community members to control and influence this unknown world institutionalized the figure of the *nganga*—the witch doctor, spiritual protector, medicine man, or magician. His knowledge of the drums, magic potions, poisons, cures, ancestral chants, and evocations of the spirits are seen as inherited. In this house of witches, mystery reigns, and Shango's affiliation with lightning and fire explains why he was summoned using the medium of the drums to partake in ceremonial proceedings:

Tocan el viejo tambor del recuerdo
tranzan . . . trenzan recuerdos
ancestrales
tocando el antiguo
tambor inolvidable.

[They play the old drum from memory
They enter into a trance . . . they weave ancestral

memories
playing the old
unforgettable drum.][99]

The drumming becomes explosive and heightens tensions and expectation in the poem.

Ramírez clearly names the orishas, ancestors, and spirits Lemba, Oninga, Babalú, Tofeme, Mawue, Malambo, Odudúa, and Iku in her poetry.[100] They are mythical beings, some ex-warriors, worshipped as protectors and sought out in times of need for the wisdom they provide. In the poem "Lemba," this spirit of the streams and brooks is summoned and honored in his domain.[101] He is venerated for his dominion over water as a life-giving necessity; he is a protector, a provider of guidance and nourishment, and a powerful purifying force known to cast spells by shouting and crying.[102] Lemba emerges as a source of life, cleansing, and daily sustenance, especially for women, whose daily task it is to fetch water. The women spend hours at the water's edge washing, cleaning, singing, and socializing. This is their exclusive space, symbolic of their roles in daily life, and the place from which will emerge the famous myth of Catalina Loango.

The presence of two female orishas, Babalú and Oninga, in Ramírez's "Las hijas de Oninga" provokes postures of reverence as the verses capture community beliefs and appreciation, especially for Oninga, and construct an atmosphere in keeping with this orisha's personality.[103] Oninga is identified as the goddess of the night, and moonlight, fireflies, and the stars are her daughters, whom she loves and protects. Sensations of warmth and connection permeate this poem. Night as a potentially ominous darkness is not a configuration here; rather, it is embraced and enjoyed while the references to moonlight, fireflies, and stars, which only appear in the dark, bring joy and lightness that are comforting. In a similar vein, the poem "Babalú" pays homage to a spirit who was formerly a proud and beautiful female fighter.[104] The realm of the spirits, the ancestral world, and history come together in this warrior and leader. The transition from worthy human existence to the ancestral realm to, finally, the realm of the gods is central to the Yoruba belief structure, as is the way these beings retain a concrete connection with believers. Babalú is revered by Afro-Colombian and Indigenous women, a true daughter of Yoruba ethnicity who guides her people by communicating with their spiritual leaders. These deities are first and foremost protectors of their faithful followers; Oninga offers reassurance in the darkness, while Babalú is a leader and fighter, "capitana en el barco de la vida" [captain in the boat of life].[105] Both are destined to serve their worshippers throughout life's perilous journeys. The appearance of orishas specific to *palenquero* spaces confirms the transformative nature of their legacy and the mechanisms activated to keep African-originated traditions alive. Lemba, Oninga, and Babalú are exclusive to this space and unique in their ability to represent connections with the past—original identity, victories, heroes, and rituals. Within their spiritual legacy, the orisha realm is sacred even as it is open and accessible to faithful followers and provides for the smooth transition of their heroes into the spiritual realm.

THE *PALENQUERA*: A HETEROGENEOUS PORTRAYAL

Díaz Pérez's verses cultivate poetic exoticism, never shying away from an open admiration of the female body. She pays homage to such representation in the initial verses that inaugurate her anthology, mentioning a woman called Danitza, "la dueña de la exótica belleza de la mujer africana" [owner of the exotic beauty of the African woman].[106] "Mujer Palenquera / Ñakunga ri palengge," the second poem in the anthology, captures the contemporary physical image and seeks to represent it in captivating terms.[107] The narrator's words seem to indicate a moment of self-aggrandizement, a glorification of her body as universally unique, filled with its own potency:

> Que fémina tan candente
> su piel arde intensamente
> un fuego que sólo paren
> las mujeres de Palenque.

> [Such incandescent womanhood
> her skin burns intensely
> a fire that only *palenque* women
> can put out.][108]

Her skin is as dark as night, her smile radiating joy as she appears with her *ponchera* to sell her merchandise of confectionaries and fruits. The spirit of the poem is celebratory, embracing this female figure as a wonderful and endearing presence while cultivating a sense of ancestral pride in her clear African legacy and proud stance. This identity-affirming tone continues in "Soy / I a sé" as the revelation of a nationalistic pride in being African-Colombian; the *palenquera* extends into the African continent, idealistically embracing diverse representations and peoples that largely drive the Afro–Latin American sense of self.[109] She is Mandinga, Bantu, Carabalí, Maasai, Dinka, Lucumí, and Yoruba. The narrator's consciousness is woman-centered even as she expresses a vision of being part of something bigger than any one individual.

"Muje timbo / Mujer bien negra" focuses on her appearance and describes it as a blessing.[110] Here is a celebration of physical features, this time as a provocation the protagonist herself encourages:

> Bendigo este color negro en mí.
> Mi cabello,
> mi pelo es duro,
> soy sincera,
> sin mascaras.

[I bless this Black color in me.
My hair,
my hair is hard,
I am sincere,
without masks.][111]

The female protagonist self-describes as beautiful. She is proud of her dark complexion and kinky hair and ready to display, not disguise, these attributes to the world. Her pride is absolute, and the verses play with rhythmic chants and the repetition of the word *negra* to sustain the focus on the narrator's intention to express her total self-confidence and belief in the deeper value of her physical state and beauty.[112] She calls herself "doncella negra hermosa" [beautiful Black damsel], envisions her dark complexion as a blessing, and demonstrates happiness by way of chants in homage to what she calls the "color negro en mí" [Black color in me].[113] Her proclamation is punctuated by a rhythmic chant of joy and appreciation: "¡Oh malembé! / ¡Ya malembé! / O lei le le."[114]

As a complement to Mirian Pérez's poetry, María Teresa Ramírez's anthology touches on the global and variegated nature of identity, there are poetic moments that capture what the narrator perceives to be the essence of the *palenquera*'s universe. There are no limits to who she can be; in poetry, she emerges as a passionate lover, a symbol of Mother Nature, a prostitute, a witch, a mother, a warrior, a rich woman, a poor woman, a seller, a farmer, and an expert at braiding hair.[115] The poem "Vida buena pa' conquistar" [A good life to conquer] repeatedly evokes the expression "Mañana madre" [morning mother] in homage to Mother Nature, without whose intervention and protection the community could not survive.[116] The verses describe the quotidian as sacred ritual and historical legacy. The narrating voice immerses itself in the space and seeks to display it as alive and well, without fantasy or romance; rather, it is more of a direct and sincere representation of the multiple dimensions to this way of life that is often unfamiliar to the outsider.

Ramírez comments on stories about rich men and poor men in Colombia that inspired her to create one about women. "Komae galipotano—Komae kusube / Comadre rica y comadre pobre" [Rich sister and poor sister] is a story inspired by women's lived experiences.[117] It confronts ignorance and misunderstanding, challenging a lack of comprehension with regard to the difficulties that the *comadre pobre* or poor woman faces. The word *comadre* is significant, for it could mean "sister," "friend," "neighbor," or "close collaborator." Here is a story within a poem, a wise tale with a message about the consequences of misunderstanding and animosity as displayed by the *comadre rica* [rich woman]. The poem is structured for oral delivery and possesses rhythm and musicality, achieved by the pace of the short, fast verses and the employment of *jitanjáforas* and rhythmic phrases to keep the light and playful tone in place. The *comadre rica* is clueless about what it means to be a *comadre pobre*. Poverty means working hard to earn a living; the *comadre pobre* must clean rice, wash, cook, and sweep. She then has to cook the famous homemade delicacy, *alegría* [joy], stirring in the coconut, aniseed, and spices, for this is one of her main sources of income. She works hard at home and in the fields, has many children, and is somewhat resigned to her fate. Then her luck turns, for one day she stumbles upon an old traditional pot that she shows to her rich neighbor, who laughs at her and calls her crazy—bewitched, having consumed "bilongo y maranguango" [magic potions]. The pot turns out to be quite valuable and is subsequently purchased by a foreigner, and now the poor woman is wealthy. However, she does not behave like the rich woman, who eventually dies of jealousy and bitterness. Instead, the previously poor woman is kind and loving and uses her newfound fortune to help others. The poem itself is instructional, a teaching tool that reveals the value of kindness and a sense of community.

The dynamic portrayal continues in "Changaina / Mujer de vida alegre," where the narrator destabilizes pejorative nuances in words that are specific to women's roles.[118] In Colombia, "mujer de vida alegre" [a fun-loving woman] is a nice way of saying *puta* [prostitute]. *Changaina* means "prostitute" and could also mean "woman." Her public image is devastating, for she is abused and described as shameful, lost, and useless. Jealous women, "mujeres amargas," call her a spider, a sorceress who targets and entraps their husbands.[119] The verses create a rift between public opinion and self-perception, especially for the bitter women for whom the prostitute is a threat. Who is she? What is she like? She is cheerful, surprisingly pleasant, vivacious, and keeps herself clean.[120] She loves a party, knows how to have fun, likes to sing, is wise on matters of the heart, and is apt in the art of male entertainment and love making—for a fee, of course. She is always elegant, *pinchada* [proud], and brave like "el pájaro chamaría," a popular name for a small, fierce bird that does not back down from a fight.[121] The ultimate intention is to undermine popular opinions about immorality and expose biases against women, who are often condemned unfairly. An open and rounded portrayal works in her favor. No attempt is made to shelter her, nor is there any interest in painting her as angelic or perfect. She seems full of life, free-spirited, expressive, and responsible for her own actions. The narrator uses the expression *mujer de vida alegre* [woman who likes to have fun] to describe her, while others shout and call her names.[122] The narrating persona describes a woman who hugs men, goes wherever she wishes, and understands that she has to put up with other women who do not understand her and who even condemn her. For these women, she is a threat, and they condemn her verbally, calling her a shameless prostitute and publically humiliating her, for she is dangerous:

> Las mujeres amargas, no le hablen
> Le dicen: araña, enredadora
> Ella sabe hechizar a los hombres.
>
> [The bitter women, they do not speak to her
> They call her spider, troublemaker
> She knows how to bewitch men.][123]

The reaction of the village women contrasts with the position of the narrator, who plays with the idea of the woman's independence and free spirit, calling her "orgullosa, / siempre huele sabroso" [proud, / she always smells nice (delicious)].[124] For the narrator, she has to be brave to do what she does.

"Añuñia/Estresada" is a revelation of female vulnerability as a state of being that results from a life fully lived.[125] The poem seems to capture the persona at her lowest point, beaten down by failed dreams, life, love, and excesses. She is defeated, her heart battered by unsuccessful love affairs and dashed illusions; her soul is creased, daunted. She admits to her faults of being arrogant, distrustful, overly sensitive, and morbid; she did not take life seriously and paid the price. She used to be very well-off, describing the experience as stressful and suffocating. Seeking answers, she visited a shaman, who confirmed that her destiny would be arduous, punctuated by great moments of passion, yet she seemed destined to resist and fight back to the death. Years later, she is crippled in one leg, life weighs on her, and love is no longer there; however, with a positive disposition, she seems to still have a fighting spirit and is not ready to throw in the towel: "Batallando con firmeza / no me dejaré caer" [Fighting with conviction / I will not allow myself to fall].[126]

"Llanto yumulunga" is a beautifully designed poem that identifies the *palenquera* and engages her as an initiator of endeavors who appears everywhere.[127] She is present in areas beyond her *palenque* home; the city is hers, as this too is where she belongs, where she dwells today. The opening verses talk of light, maybe sunlight as it shines down, illuminating some spots, missing others. It's also heat, in a symbolic way, representative of life and death. Children in the street play a game called *la gallina ciega* [the blind chicken] as she walks by, this woman who is an eternal symbol of the tropics, selling her sweets made of pulp, sugar, and sour fruit, the latter perhaps symptomatic of the bitter, punishing legacy of slavery. She carries the residuals of her past and is constantly seeking out the formative moments of her spirit, symbolically represented in the poem as "el botón de una rosa, / mutilado en la sentina de la *Nao* negrera" [the rosebud / crushed in the bilge of a passing slave ship].[128] All this as she ambles through the streets, passing high walls that are like watchtowers of blood and stone—permanent fixtures there for future generations to observe as they come and go. As she saunters by, the wind brings the smell of palm trees, and on the way, she hears the cries of the *ekobio* [Black folk] as they bear the burden of historical infamy.[129]

In the end, poetry transcends history, making this female protagonist the pivotal point from which all movement and action emerges. This woman-centered message is especially clear in "Soy Palenque."[130] In an expressive gesture of conviction and self-confidence, the protagonist takes control of her destiny and decides to proclaim her own self-identity. She is not going to the *palenque*; she is the *palenque*. She seems to suffer from, even reject, the process of having to flee. Instead, she stands and defines her roles—woman, moon, lover, sun, mother, and earth—and addresses her male companion, shouting at him for being blind and egoistic and ignoring her. She is coming to terms with her own legacy, perceiving her inner strength and endurance even as she realizes her exploitation, in which she was an accomplice. Now she is different; she has obtained a new positioning that opens her mind and allows her to discern her self-imposed destructiveness as a woman and mother who was always sharing and giving of herself, always resigned, submissive, prayerful. It was as if she were nothing. In this *cimarrón* silence, she shouted; however, no one heard. No more, for now she frees her voice, unleashes her emotion, and forces him to listen:

Desencadenando mi voz y mi
hacer, aconteciendo, cabalgando
junto a ti
en la dura cerviz de la historia.

[Unchaining my voice and my
doing, happening, galloping
next to you
on the hard cervix of history.][131]

LUMBALÚ AS POETRY

Ramírez's "Ma moná minú / Los huérfanos" provides the space from which the *lumbalú* ritual emerges.[132] The narrating voice takes us into the moment of death in the community and reveals what happens when loved ones have passed. In this reenactment, the dead are not mentioned or called by name; rather, the focus is on the survivors who must now mourn their loss. They are *huérfanos* [orphans] who must pay homage to their parents who have died by singing in the dance of the dead. Members of the family, blood brothers and sisters, godparents, friends, soul mates, neighbors, and anyone who is a companion gather in support of the orphans, and as a community, they must now sing and dance in homage and remembrance. The narrator urges all those who are orphaned to lash out, weep loudly in despair, and express the sorrow that threatens to consume them. Crying is a way to calm the soul, especially after losing one's parents. It is a crying from the soul that only the orphan can hear and feel, even as the mothers who have died remain embedded in memory. The figures of dead mothers take over, for they are the very center of a child's universe. They are wise and love their children unquestioningly, no matter what. They are as strong as the oak tree in the hurricane, sincere, open, and direct; their words come like fresh water from the fountain. *Palenqueros* summon their orishas Odudúa (god of mercy) and Iku (goddess of death) to provide solace, protection, and guidance in their moment of need. Sorrow and wailing are overcome by ritualistic chanting and dance as the deceased transcend into the ancestral world. The mourners' sentiments of loss and pain change to hope in realizing that their parents will always be there as their guiding spirits, and surely they will be reunited in the future.

Lumbalú has a significant role to play in Díaz Pérez's poetry as well. She cultivates the idea of death as a community phenomenon and represents it as central to *palenquero* identity. "Diciembre / Me ri rioso," "Maldita enfermedad / Inkusi Sukutengue," "Africa habla / Afrika se chitiá," "La muerte de Evaristo / Ebarito a lungá," "Tambor/Batá," and "Las cosas de mi pueblo / Ma kusa ri tiela mi" speak to loss through death while trying to fathom the meaning and significance of life itself.[133] "Ritual fúnebre / Lumbalú" tells the story of Black Nicolasa, a woman who just lost her brother and is processing a *lumbalú* in his honor.[134] In the midst of her sorrow and tears, she chants, urging the drums to accompany the singing and dancing. The ritual is complete, for the community is there with her; the *kuagros* walk by her house as she adheres to tradition and completes the nine nights of prayers and grieving. Verses display emotional distress in the form of Black Nicolasa's wailing and lamentations—loud, visible, clear demonstrations of sorrow and pain. The emotionally charged atmosphere of the *lumbalú* drives this poem and reveals intimate details of family grief at the loss of a loved one within a compensating spiritual ambience that provides solace. Poetic interweaving is a constant in this kind of writing that works to describe this female presence by way of deep origins, ancient knowledge, and mythical belief.

Rituals of birth and death connect community members to one another and to the motherland in the poem "Africa habla / Afrika se chitiá"—this by way of the drums, or *batá*, the medium for entertainment and communication with their ancestors and orishas.[135] The narrating voice is celebrating her newborn, and the drums will help her family announce this joyous occasion. In the same poem, birth and death are equally acknowledged, for the *batá* will also play to prepare the space for the *lumbalú* in recognition of María Lalú's passing. The poem "Tambor/Batá" continues in the same vein as verses speak to the sacredness of the instrument that will always come alive under its owner's skillful guidance.[136] The *batá* allow the ancestors and their descendants on earth to connect with one another. They invite spirits and ancestors to descend and join the celebrations and rituals of their descendants. The drums will be heard in every corner of the community, for all must appear at the *lumbalú* and pay their respects. Ultimate symbols of strength and endurance, these instruments serve the people, reunite them, and sustain ancestral belief systems.

Conclusion

The following verses, taken from María Teresa Ramírez's "Llanto yumulunga," capture the spirit of this study. *Llanto yumulunga* means "painful crying," but these cries are also full of hope, which is why Ramírez chose this poem to close her anthology:

> Llanto yumulunga
> La luz juega en la ciudad,
> su juego claro-oscuro,
> juego caliente ¡vida-muerte!

> [Painful crying
> Light plays in the city
> its light-dark game
> an exciting game, life-death!][1]

Here is a description that displays contrasting sentiments. Like natural light, the light in the poem is playful, never constant; it goes and comes, creating moments with light and darkness, sometimes shadows, sometimes none. Parallel to this game of light is the idea of life and death, another phenomenon that is difficult to grasp, detail, and control. Instead of darkness and death, Ramírez prefers to focus on hope, light, and life, the sentiments that motivate her to keep writing and focus on her legacy.[2]

Like Ramírez's verses, this study navigates beyond polarities. For Afro-descendant female figures, silence and invisibility are a reality, even as their literary endeavors create moments of voicing and presence that are leaving their mark. Our ability to configure icons is dependent on ample knowledge of the social context of which they are a part, provided through testimonies and long-term confirmations, whether literary or mythical, real or imagined. Elizabeth Forbes Brooks (Miss Lizzie), the *palenqueras*, and the Ginés sisters are valuable for the way they have become dynamic figures, to a certain extent, endowed with institutional and foundational qualities. They are projected as sites where nation, sexuality, cultural memorialization, identity, diaspora, language, and gender converge. Each individual manages to speak out in spite of historical processes that detract from her ventures and achievements. Speaking out, in this case, is not merely vocal so that others can hear; it also can be configured as a process of taking the initiative, of producing, of leaving a mark on the culture and the nation in a way that reveals the source of that endeavor and leads right back to the originating female instigator.

While each case study is unique, as a whole, they serve to provide insight into some of the internal challenges each nation faces in terms of recognizing their illustrious women. The overall objective of this study is to offer a structural approach as to how to go about designing such a profile. I can confirm that subsequent studies cannot be unilineal; rather, they need to be multidimensional in order to capture the nuances of the person and the complexities of social relations to which she is committed. This leads to a deeper appreciation of what she has in mind, in what ways her actions are beneficial, and what can cause tensions or separations between her agenda and those of the larger circles to which she belongs—family, community, region, nation, and so on. It is a structured path that reduces the possibility for doubting or denying her glorification. Multiple literary and cultural voices are useful for revealing different angles of her story. More specifically, a focus on literary production by Afro-descendant women writers clarifies how they assume the role of creators of discourse and make it their own.

Talent in music set the Ginés sisters free and secured their nebulous presence in history and memory. They will continue to appear in the ongoing debates surrounding *el son cubano*. Whether real or imagined, the value of Micaela and Teodora Ginés's story is in its motivational features, in the way it has inspired gender-based scholarship and poetry. It is interesting that Cuba and the Dominican Republic register different processes and reactions to the possibility of the sisters' existence, legacy, and involvement in the establishment and expansion of the first settlements in both countries. During that time, when resources and skills were in short supply, one can imagine just how valuable these two musicians must have been, even though such value would have never been acknowledged or recorded within the colonizing structure being put in place—a structure that rendered them, their labor, and talents unworthy of measure or mention. Even if they might not have existed, we can reverse some of the historical process of erasure by saying that the trend of using African slaves to entertain the populace is well recorded. In the case of Cuba, which is proudly passionate about its status as a guardian of the *son*, there have been so many contemporary developments and so much self-questioning that the possibility of celebrating the legacy of these two sisters remains within the discursive domain of poetic verses. Poetry of the 1930s and 1940s, led by Nicolás Guillén's *Motivos de son*, initiates the legacy of homage and acknowledgment, both of which find consolidation in Aída Cartagena Portalatín's woman-centered poetic rewriting of the region's history.

Portalatín's African experiences and Afro-Dominican poetic renditions drive our ability to envision Teodora and Micaela as positioned at the beginning of the region's formation. They provide an alternative story about the experiences of enslaved females in a way that highlights their actions and endeavors as individuals, particularly in roles of production and development and in their use of their musical skills. The process of portraying these talented musicians cannot mitigate the devastating effects of the Middle Passage, the humiliation of being sold in a public square, or the final dehumanizing classification as a commodity. It can, however, provoke systemic adjustments, allowing for reconsiderations and new kinds of portraits, whether historical or literary. Portalatín's poem reaches back in time and pulls from historical silence and nonexistence the idea of these women, centralizing them in her nation's birth, growth, and expansion. Her embracing of negritude (or ancestral Blackness) and the story about these sisters is expressive of her desire to engage with this side of her ethnicity in spite of her nation's uneasy relationship with Afro-descendancy as an integral racial component of its peoples. Portalatín's poetic renditions, similar to María Teresa Ramírez and certain Bluefieldian poets, are driven by a question: Who am I? They are also driven by a desire to let the woman inside speak, perhaps on behalf of those long gone—especially those who never got a chance to do so.

Miss Lizzie's resuscitation of *palo de mayo* reminds her people of their uniqueness and adds to the legacy of Creolization that defines what it means to be Caribbean. Her choreography opened Nicaraguans to a world about which they were unaware. Its deep European origins as a pagan warm-weather feast traveled and transformed into deity worship in which Mayaya emerged as a Creole belief. *Palo de mayo* inspired a community, brought Caribbean-originated rhythms and music back into their consciousness, and over time, inspired a tradition of writing that guarantees its preservation. Miss Lizzie's professional successes, passion for dance, and evolution into community leadership took decades in a process of enrichment and consolidation throughout which she provided great advice, wisdom, and support for her community. She reset the foundation of her community even as such a move was disturbing to the postmodern society, for she was challenging her people to reflect on their origins and identity. The legacy she leaves in poetry, song, dance, and memoirs is acknowledged in her hometown, where the main library of the Universidad de las Regiones Autónomas de la Costa Caribe Nicaragüense (URACCAN) is named in her honor.

Palenquera writings work in support of the statue located in Cartagena. They reveal the underpinnings of a centuries-old legacy, thereby creating deeper appreciation and support for their commercial activities. Such *écriture* gives symbolic meaning to positions of confidence where we find not one but multiple women in various roles, including community leaders, teachers, activists, businesswomen, professors, and of course, writers. Assuming the identity of a *palenquera* poet has allowed these committed women to assume omniscient roles, as if they were the guardians and protectors of this legacy. Their poetry is more than lyrical and rhythmic verses; it is a space of cultural preservation and historical teaching, for it bears all the elements of their universe. The overall tone of this writing registers a preoccupation with the female condition, and it goes beyond this desire to feature her. A historically inherited focus continues in support of the survival and well-being of the group and its way of life. They write as inheritors of a proud legacy of self-freed Africans who challenged those in power, fought the system, and won their lives back in the new lands.

The focus on women writers and the Black female experience is central to constructing the vision of an inspirational and determined individual. She could be African, American, Caribbean, or Creole, identities she is free to claim as a writer and narrator. Critical studies on Afro–Latin American women's writings continue to accompany the literary production itself, one that is predominantly poetic. Literature makes a counterclaim and constructs the profile of an integral and forceful collaborator and leader who works in the name of justice and freedom. The contemporary shift is from the victimized to the rebel figure as many stories emerge of her deeds in the Spanish and Portuguese Americas. She resisted, revolted, rebelled, and fled to freedom in remote maroon settlements. She stood up to her white slave master and his family; survived torture, punishment, prison, and rape; worked hard, saved money, bought her freedom, and became the source of many untold stories. She rose from invisibility to become the leader of insurrections and, in some cases, her maroon community.

The literature at work in this study reveals one particular trend that helps writers sustain arguments of her existence and her feats while counteracting the debilitating effects of historical (textual) scholarship that cannot find supporting documentation. The trend is to take what may exist in rudimentary form and bring it to the forefront. The female figure that before was barely mentioned storms through the doors of verse and prose, taking up a prominent position at the center of controversy, community, government, and conflict. This fictional reenactment of historical female presence and action draws inspiration from the place or setting to which she belongs and about which she cares very much, a nurturing that, in the end, stimulates her community's belief in her greatness. The unreliability of text opens the door for myth, legend, and remembering. Equally important are cultural inventions and references based on stories passed down through the generations for which no written documents exist. The vivid imagination of a people is central to their self-construction and self-worth, and nowhere is this more important than in relation to the Afro-descendant woman. Mythical elaborations of her feats serve as forceful messages of value and achievement that are in use today to counteract her lack of historical presence in Latin America.

How do imagination and fiction support reality and proven historical initiatives or past bravery? Literature becomes a device that compensates for cultural shortfalls; it can go inside the Afro-descendant woman's story and understand it from her perspective. Defining heroism in relation to this figure continues to be challenging. Based on the situations presented here, it seems strategic to review the activities that have had a profound impact on her community. Such instances highlight her ability to take charge, be in control, define her space and intention, and execute change. Her individual characteristics become valuable, since oftentimes, from very early in life, a specific set of variables is responsible for the personality that emerges and brings about these ensuing societal transformations. She explores and builds relationships, displaying a natural capacity to push back against grave socioeconomic challenges and provoke change for the better. In the face of such overwhelming odds, what marks her is an ability to find ways to value herself and her community even within situations and societies that do not. Her view of herself is very different from the limiting and downtrodden perspective she can expect from her nation's history and the literary canon. We can confirm her participation in the construction of national discourses that are provocatively against the grain, actions that beg recognition. The beauty of the story is in her ability to think and act differently.

Writers create a discursive presence that can be brief or long-lasting; the female character lasts as long as we continue to read the verses in which she exists as a poetic version of the historical figure. Verses glorify her, ensuring that her portrait is always dynamic. The literary technique of bestowing iconic value to characters allows writers to interfere with reality and change the way things are so that instead of her being a mere part of some greater social process, she is at the helm of said process, has initiated the action, or is in some way reflective of a universal (feminine-driven) stance to which many of her peers adhere. In the end, a variety of spaces are available from which to construct icons. Creativity and talent in the arts and literature, political and military enterprises that become legendary in myths and historical accounts, the establishment of enterprises, foundational feats, and community-based, educational, and uplifting endeavors that have immediate positive outcomes are all possible areas of human achievement. Portrayals of needy women with precarious lifestyles or difficult circumstances are not always contrary to this profile. Her capabilities are infinite and become visible through effort, aspiration, and ambition. In the end, she only needs to believe in herself and in her ability to complete the undertaking.

Acknowledgments

I recall when the idea for this book came to me. It was during my visit to Cartagena, Colombia, in 2010, where I was attending the Second International Conference on Caribbean Studies (ICCS), organized by the University of Cartagena. While there, I noticed the statues that graced the network of streets and avenues, roundabouts, urban plots of green and flowers, the squares in front of cathedrals and churches, and gardens and parks. On horseback, the proud, authoritative Spanish figures—with the customary ponytailed hair or wigs, high-ranking army attire, and Caucasian features—were constant confirmations of the Castilian-led colonial foundation upon which Latin America's Spanish- and Portuguese-speaking countries were built. I realized I had spent many years traversing Latin American and European countries of Luso-Hispanic roots and gazed on too many of these male sculptures.

Then it hit me: Where are the statues of women in history? Any woman—any race or ethnicity. They were just not as visible. In particular, there were no Black women similarly featured. The few I found on my travels were smaller in size and not centrally positioned on grand avenues or boulevards, in main squares, or in front of majestic cathedrals. Further, they were never designed on tall, highly visible pedestals or as representations of combative glory, military status, or leadership; they tended to be shorter, placed at street level, of human height, specific to historical events, and not configured as broad national references. There are a few that pay homage to Hispanic and Indigenous women; there are almost none dedicated to women of African ancestry. From that initial question, this journey of discovery began, and I am deeply indebted to so many collaborators with whom I engaged directly for this book. Indirectly, there are so many others whose experiences, writings, and ideas remain crucial to my research.

Brazil

I'd like to give a special acknowledgment to the writers, scholars, and activists who are also my colleagues, friends, and collaborators situated across Brazil. While my book does not have a chapter on Brazil (I had originally planned and written one), it continues to be a fundamental source of academic inspiration for me. Brazilian scholarship on the Afro-descendant legacy in the Americas continues to dominate in volume and reach. For this book project, I am specifically indebted to scholarly writers of literature and academicians Conceição Evaristo, Miriam Alves, Márcio Barbosa, Henrique Cunha Jr., Cicera Nunes, Esmeralda Ribeiro, Mel Adun, Débora Almeida, Cristiane Sobral, Alzira Rufino, Selma da Silva, Maria Cecília Calaça, Zélia Amador, and Joselina da Silva.

I'd like to offer a special gesture of appreciation to Nalui (Ana Luiza Monteiro Alves), whose insight, intellectual savviness, and enthusiasm for life and justice continue to help me understand and value how Brazil's young generations of today are thinking and how committed they are to fighting for humanity and humanness. My colleagues who are a part of Artefatos da Cultura Negra no Ceará [Artifacts of Black Culture in Ceará] and the consórcio [consortium] are truly amazing, and I am extremely grateful to them for providing ongoing platforms of discussion and debate. I intentionally include in this section my appreciation for the dedicated North American researchers and colleagues Tanya Sanders, Sarah Ohmer, Rhonda Collier, and Lesley Feracho, whose writings, dialogues, and talks provide fuel for my own production. We all are committed scholars of Brazil.

Cuba

I cannot fully express my gratitude to Norma Guillard Limonta and Naima Guillard, whose support, dedication, and attention to the Cuba portion of this project helped me unearth the initial findings about the Ginés sisters and *el son cubano* that became the first two chapters. Their home, networks, and constant engagement in spite of daily challenges are truly a godsend, and they continue to provide me with a more profound understanding of Cuba. I extend my gratitude to Catherine Murphy and Julio Mitjans, whose creativity continues to be indispensable as intellectual stimulus for my own ideas. I give special thanks to Zuleica Romay, Lino Neira Betancourt, Bárbara Balbuena, Radamés Giro, Tomás Fernández Robaina, Oilda Hevia Lanier, Soleida Ríos, Georgina Herrera (1936–2021), Nancy Morejón, Gisela Arandia, Tomás Rodríguez, Julio Mitjans, Daisy Rubiera Castillo, Teresa Cárdenas, Alicia Valdés, Caridad Atencio, Rito Ramón Aroche, Roberto Zurbano, Lucila Insua Brindis, and Rosaida Ochoa Soto.

The organization known as Afrocubanas and the tireless efforts of its leadership to ensure a Black women's movement in Cuba have made Norma Guillard, Daisy Rubiera, and Gisela Arandia world-famous names that I respect and greatly admire. Since my initial encounters with such minds in the 1990s, I continue to draw on their narratives of culture and life as Black Cuban women committed to scholarship, justice, and literature.

THE DOMINICAN REPUBLIC

I was able to access the Archivo General de la Nación, located in Santo Domingo, thanks to the gracious attention of Carlos Andújar. This research space includes Afro-Dominican poet Blás Jiménez (1949–2009) and Rafael Jarvis Luiz. The Haitian-Dominican women NGO enterprises spearheaded by Sonia Pierre (1963–2011), the Afro-Dominican women's movement led by activists including Sergia Galván and Eulalia Jiménez, and women poets who self-identify as producers of Afro-Dominican and Caribbean writings are the spheres and experts to whom I am indebted. Many thanks.

NICARAGUA

I express my heartfelt appreciation to the committed members, esteemed professionals, writers, activists, and members of the Creole and Garifuna communities in Managua and Bluefields who welcomed me so warmly and fully supported my research needs. I am very happy to have met and engaged with representatives and writers who identify as Garifuna in addition to Creole women, Creole poets, and other members of the town of Bluefields. Indeed, these were memorable encounters. I say thank you to Mrs. Elizabeth Forbes Nelson and her family; *Rectora* of the Universidad de las Regiones Autónomas de la Costa Caribe Nicaragüense (URACCAN), Dr. Alta Hooker; Dorotea Wilson; Sidney Francis Martin; Brigette Budier; Allan Budier; Grace Kelly; and the students and faculty of URACCAN, Bluefields campus. I'd like to give special mention to two important community archivists, librarian Helen Fenton and historian Hugo Sujo Wilson, who were very valuable for their efforts at preserving the Creole community heritage. The poetry reading session with Creole and Garifuna poets Allan Budier, Joan Sinclair, and Isabel Estrada Colindres, which was organized to coincide with my visit to the university in Bluefields, was wonderful in the way the verses helped provide me with the literary narrative I needed for my manuscript.

COLOMBIA

Various writers, scholars, and activists from Bogotá, Cartagena, and Barranquilla are mentioned in the chapters dedicated to the Colombia case study. I acknowledge my debt to Rutsely Simarra Obeso, Guiomar Cuesta Escobar, María Teresa Ramírez, Angela Robledo, Dora Isabel Berdugo, Dorina Hernández, Juan Mosquera, Mary Grueso Romero, Mirian Díaz Pérez, Moises Pianeta, Solmery Casseres Estrada, Kairen María Gutiérrez Tejedor, and Uriel Cassiani.

Special Mention

There are individuals whose life work, community commitment, writings, and professional trajectory are inspiring and who, directly or indirectly, stimulated the writing of this book. I am grateful for the time, attention, and ideas I have received from Eulalia Bernard (1935–2021), Melva Lowe de Goodin, Courtney Wright, Maria Ramos Rosado, Ana Irma Lassén, Sueli Carneiro, Thelma Edwards, Carolyn Hodges, Shirley Campbell Barr, Magda Pollard, Odile Ferly, Nicole Roberts, Dawn Stinchcomb, Paulette Ramsay, La Vinia Jennings, Sonja Watson Stephenson, Viviane Manigat Jackson, and Glynis Hopkins Peters.

To my other collaborators whose names are not visible, I am deeply grateful for your support and attention over time.

Notes

INTRODUCTION

1. Georgina Herrera, "Oriki por las negras viejas de antes," in *Afrocubanas: Historia, pensamiento y prácticas culturales*, ed. Daisy Rubiera Castillo and Inés María Martiatu Terry (Havana: Editorial de Ciencias Sociales, 2011), 221. Unless otherwise indicated, all translations in this publication were made by the author.

2. Herrera, 219–24.

3. *Palenqueras* are women of African ancestry who to date dwell and belong to the remaining urban and rural towns and villages that were originally maroon settlements, or *palenques*. They are often associated almost exclusively with the Palenque de San Basilio, considered the most famous settlement established by their ancestors who fled and resisted enslavement.

4. Recent comparative studies include Marta Morena Vega, Marinieves Alba, and Yvette Modestín, eds., *Women Warriors of the Afro-Latina Diaspora* (Houston: Arte Público, 2012); Solimar Otero and Toyin Falola, eds., *Yemoja: Gender, Sexuality, and Creativity in the Latina/o and Afro-Atlantic Diasporas* (Albany: State University of New York Press, 2013); Paula Sanmartín, *Black Women as Custodians of History: Unsung Rebel Mothers in African American and Afro-Cuban Women's Writing* (Amherst, N.Y.: Cambia, 2014); Monique-Adelle Callahan, *Between the Lines: Literary Transnationalism and African American Poetics* (New York: Oxford University Press, 2011); and Vanessa K. Valdés, *Oshun's Daughters: The Search for Womanhood in the Americas* (Albany: State University of New York Press, 2014).

5. Sanmartín, *Black Women*, 116–18.

6. Sanmartín, 2.

7. Sanmartín, 116.

8. B. Christine Arce, *Mexico's Nobodies: The Cultural Legacy of the Soldadera and Afro-Mexican Women* (Albany: State University of New York Press, 2018), 92–93.

9. Callahan, *Between the Lines*, 29.

10. Jennifer Goett, *Black Autonomy: Race, Gender, and Afro-Nicaraguan Activism* (Redwood City, Calif.: Stanford University Press, 2017), 77.

11. Sanmartín, *Black Women*, 293.

12. Arce, *Mexico's Nobodies*, 38–39.

13. Sanmartín, *Black Women*, 2–4.

14. Also consult Dawn Duke, "Alzira Rufino's *A casa de cultura de mulher negra* as a Form of Female Empowerment: A Look at the Dynamics of a Black Women's Organization in Brazil Today," *Women's Studies International Forum* 26, no. 4 (July–August 2003): 357–68.

15. Alzira Rufino, Nilza Iraci, and Maria Rosa Pereira, *Mulher negra tem história* (Santos, Brazil: self-pub., 1986), 27.

16. Sara Más, "Revisitando un sueño," in *Magín: Tiempo de contar esta historia*, by Daisy Rubiera Castillo and Sonnia Moro (Havana: Ediciones Magín, 2015), 9.

17. Rubiera Castillo and Moro, *Magín*, 7.

18. Georgina Herrera, "Poetry, Prostitution, and Gender Esteem," in *Afro-Cuban Voices: On Race and Identity in Contemporary Cuba*, ed. Pedro Pérez Sarduy and Jean Stubbs (Gainesville: University Press of Florida, 2000), 121-22.

19. Rubiera Castillo and Moro, *Magín*, 20.

20. Rubiera Castillo and Moro, 17.

21. Rubiera Castillo and Moro, 17-18.

22. Rubiera Castillo's published essays include "La mujer de color en Cuba," in *Dos ensayos*, by Daisy Rubiera Castillo and Raúl Ruiz Miyares (Havana: Academia, 1996), 3-27; "El tiempo de la memoria," *La gaceta de Cuba* 1 (January–February 2005): 44-46; "La mujer en la santería o regla ocha: Género, mitos y realidad," in Rubiera Castillo and Martiatu Terry, *Afrocubanas*, 107-32; "Apuntes sobre la mujer negra cubana," *Cuban Studies* 42 (2011): 176-85; and "El discurso femenino negro de reivindicación (1888-1958)," in *Emergiendo del silencio: Mujeres negras en la historia de Cuba*, comp. Oilda Hevia Lanier and Daisy Rubiera Castillo (Havana: Editorial del Ciencias Sociales, 2016), 223-42.

23. Rubiera Castillo, "El tiempo de la memoria," 44-46. Her two other major book projects, *Afrocubanas* (with Inés María Martiatu Terry) and *Emergiendo del silencio* (with Oilda Hevia Lanier), maintain the characteristics of her paradigmatic agenda of historical recovery and bringing new perspectives to bear on history.

24. Rubiera Castillo, "El tiempo de la memoria," 44-46.

25. Daisy Rubiera Castillo, "Avivir la memoria: Desterrar el olvido," in Rubiera Castillo and Martiatu Terry, *Afrocubanas*, 11-12.

26. Herrera, "Oriki por las negras," 220.

27. Herrera, 224.

28. Daisy Rubiera Castillo and Georgina Herrera, *Golpeando la memoria: Testimonio de una poeta cubana afrodescendiente* (Havana: Unión, 2005), 220-21.

29. Rubiera Castillo and Herrera, 44.

30. Rubiera Castillo and Herrera, 44.

31. Yolanda Arroyo Pizarro, *Tongas, palenques y quilombos: Ensayos y columnas de afrore-sistencia* (self-pub., 2013), 23, 45, 81.

32. Mel Adun, "Zamani: Mulheres que contam, transforman e fazem história," in *A escritora afro-brasileira: Ativismo e arte literária*, org. Dawn Duke (Belo Horizonte, Brazil: Nandyala, 2016), 78-80. Also consult Carmen Faustino and Elizandra Souza, "Espalhando novas sementes," in *Pretextos de mulheres negras*, org. Carmen Faustino and Elizandra Souza (São Paulo: Coletivo Mjiba, 2013); and Mel Adun, preface to *Águas da cabaça*, by Elizandra Souza (São Paulo: Edição do Autor, 2012), 10-11.

33. Débora Almeida, "Se não for a minha história, eu não vou contar: Por uma representação negra," in Duke, *A escritora afro-brasileira*, 131-33.

34. Shirley Campbell, "Letras e vozes da diáspora negra," in *Griôs da diáspora negra*, org. Ana Flávia Magalhães Pinto, Chaia Dechen, and Jaqueline Fernandes (Brasília: Griô Produções, 2017), 23.

35. Henrique Marques Samyn, "A escrevivência como fundamento," *Mahin: Revista literária* 2, no. 3 (December 2020): 19, https://www.revistamahin.com.br (accessed January 2, 2021).

36. Marques Samyn, 19; Mateus Campos and Paula Bianchi, "Conceição Evaristo," *The Intercept Brasil*, August 30, 2018, https://theintercept.com/2018/08/30/conceicao-evaristo -escritora-negra-eleicao-abl/ (accessed March 23, 2021); "A premiada escritora negra, Conceição Evaristo," Literafro: O portal da literatura afro-brasileira, http://www.letras.ufmg.br/ literafro/noticias/1062-conceicao-evaristo-e-oficialmente-candidata-a-academia-brasileira-de -letras (accessed March 23, 2021).

37. Conceição Evaristo, "Gênero e etnia: Uma escre(vivência) de dupla face," in *Mulher no mundo: Etnia, marginalidade e diáspora*, ed. Nadilza Martins de Barros Moreira and Liane Schneider (João Pessoa, Brazil: Idéia, 2005), 52, 54.

38. Evaristo, 54.

39. Evaristo, 54.

40. Conceição Evaristo, *Becos da memória* (Belo Horizonte, Brazil: Mazza, 2006), 9.

41. Conceição Evaristo, *Insubmissas lágrimas de mulheres* (Belo Horizonte, Brazil: Nandyala, 2011), 9.

42. Evaristo, 9.

43. Evaristo's literary essays include "Luís Bernardo Honwana: Da afasia ao discurso insano em 'Nós matámos o Cão-Tinhoso,'" in *África & Brasil: Letras em laços*, ed. Maria do Carmo Sepúlveda and Maria Teresa Salgado (Rio de Janeiro: Atlântica, 2000), 227–39; "Da representação à auto-representação da mulher negra na literatura brasileira," *Revista palmares: Cultura afro-brasileira* 1, no. 1 (August 2005): 52–55; "Gênero e etnia," 201–12; "Da grafia-desenho de minha mãe, um dos lugares de nascimento de minha escrita," in *Representações performáticas brasileiras: Teorias, práticas e suas interfaces*, ed. Marcos Antônio Alexandre (Belo Horizonte, Brazil: Mazza, 2007), 16–21; "Chica que manda ou a Mulher que inventou o mar?," *Revista anuária de literatura* 18, no. 1 (2013): 137–60, https://periodicos.ufsc.br/index.php/literatura/article/view/2175-7917.2013v18nesp1p137/25244 (accessed June 20, 2019); and "O entrecruzar das margens—gênero e etnia: Apontamentos sobre a mulher negra na sociedade brasileira," in Duke, *A escritora afro-brasileira*, 100–110.

44. Evaristo, "Gênero e etnia," 201–12; Evaristo, "Da grafia-desenho," 16–21.

45. Evaristo, "Da grafia-desenho," 17–21.

46. Consult Aimé Césaire, *Return to My Native Land* (New York: Penguin, 1969), 52; Léopold Sédar Senghor, "Negritude: A Humanism of the Twentieth Century," in *Colonial Discourse and Post-colonial Theory: A Reader*, ed. Patrick Williams and Laura Chrisman (New York: Columbia University Press, 1994), 27–35; and Léon-Gontran Damas, *Pigments: Névralgies* (Paris: Présence africaine, 1972).

47. Arce, *Mexico's Nobodies*, 14.

48. Arce, 25–26.

49. Elizabeth Pérez, "Nobody's Mammy: Yemayá as Fierce Foremother in Afro-Cuban Religions," in Otero and Falola, *Yemoja*, 10.

50. Inés María Martiatu Terry, prologue to Rubiera Castillo and Martiatu Terry, *Afrocubanas*, 2.

51. *Womanist* is a term created by Alice Walker, first appearing in her short story "Coming Apart" (1979) and subsequently included in *In Search of Our Mothers' Gardens: Womanist Prose* (1983). Today it has mushroomed into a theoretical frame of reference within which to elaborate on the historical and contemporary trajectories of Black women globally.

52. Mayra Santos-Febres, *Sobre piel y papel* (San Juan: Ediciones Callejón, 2005), 63–67.

53. Santos-Febres, 65–66.

54. Santos-Febres, 66–67.

55. Santos-Febres, 72–75.

56. Santos-Febres, 72.

57. Santos-Febres, 73.

58. Santos-Febres, 73.

59. Santos-Febres, 75.

60. Santos-Febres, 12–27.

61. Santos-Febres, 140–60.

62. Santos-Febres, 159–60.

63. Miriam Alves, "O discurso temerário," in *Criação crioula nu elefante branco: I encontro de poetas e ficcionistas negros brasileiros*, org. Miriam Alves Cuti and Arnaldo Xavier (São Paulo: Secretaria de Estado da Cultura, 1987), 83.

64. See the following by Miriam Alves: "Axé Ogum," in *Reflexões: Sobre a literatura afro-brasileira*, org. Quilombhoje (São Paulo: Conselho de Participação e Desenvolvimento da Comunidade Negra, 1985), 58–67; "O discurso temerário"; "Enfim . . . nós: Por quê?," in *Enfim . . . nós / Finally . . . Us: Escritoras negras brasileiras contemporâneas / Contemporary Black Brazilian Women Writers*, ed. Miriam Alves, trans. Carolyn Richardson Durham

(Colorado Springs: Three Continental, 1995), 5–27; "*Cadernos Negros* (número 1): Estado de alerta no fogo cruzado," in *Poéticas afro-brasileiras*, org. Maria do Carmo Lanna Figueiredo and Maria Nazareth Soares Fonseca (Belo Horizonte, Brazil: PUCMinas, Mazza, 2002), 221–40; "Empunhando bandeira: Diálogo de poeta," in *A escrita de adé: Perspectivas teóricas dos estudos gays e lésbic@s no Brasil*, org. Rick Santos and Wilton Garcia (São Paulo: Xama, 2002), 153–61; "Invisibilidade e anonimato: Prefácio," in *Women Righting: Afro-Brazilian Women's Short Fiction / Mulheres escre-vendo: Uma antologia bilingüe de escritoras afro-brasileiras contemporâneas*, ed. Miriam Alves and Maria Helena Lima (London: Mango, 2005), 8–15; *BrasilAfro autorrevelado: Literatura brasileira contemporânea* (Belo Horizonte, Brazil: Nandyala, 2010); "As ações de resistência anônima das mulheres negras e os reflexos na escrita afro-feminina brasileira" (paper presented at the University of Tennessee, November 1, 2007); "A literatura negra feminina no Brasil: Pensando a existência," *Revista da IBPN* 3 (November 2010–February 2011): 181–89; and "A representação da morte nos contos de *Cadernos Negros* 34," in Duke, *A escritora afro-brasileira*, 180–91. The above essays come to mind and attest to her persistent and aggressive engagement with her sphere of endeavors.

65. Miriam Alves, "Miriam Alves," in *Cadernos Negros 8: Contos*, comp. Os Autores (São Paulo: Edição dos Autores, 1985), 13.

66. Alves, "A literatura negra feminina," 183.

67. Alves, *BrasilAfro autorrevelado*, 59.

68. Alves, 60–62.

69. Alves, 63–64.

70. Alves, 66.

71. Alves, 69.

72. Alves, 72–74.

73. I consider the elite four to be Conceição Evaristo, Miriam Alves, Esmeralda Ribeiro, and Geni Guimarães.

74. Esmeralda Ribeiro and Márcio Barbosa, introduction to *Cadernos Negros Black Notebooks: Contemporary Afro-Brazilian Literature / Literatura afro-brasileira contemporânea*, ed. Niyi Afolabi, Márcio Barbosa, and Esmeralda Ribeiro (Trenton, N.J.: Africa World Press, 2008), 3.

75. Esmeralda Ribeiro and Márcio Barbosa, "Apresentação," in *Cadernos Negros três décadas: Ensaios, poemas, contos*, org. Esmeralda Ribeiro and Márcio Barbosa (São Paulo: Quilombhoje, SEPPIR, 2008), 15.

76. Ribeiro and Barbosa, 15.

77. Esmeralda Ribeiro's essays include "Reflexão sobre literatura infanto-juvenil," in *Reflexões*, org. Quilombhoje (São Paulo: Conselho de Participação e Desenvolvimento da Comunidade Negra, 1985), 25–29; "A escritora negra e seu ato de escrever participando," in Cuti and Xavier, *Criação crioula*, 59–66; and "Dois textos para autocontemplar-se," in Duke, *A escritora afro-brasileira*, 156–65.

78. Ribeiro and Barbosa, introduction, 1–3. This introductory text appears in two special issues funded by the Brazilian Ministry of Culture.

79. Ribeiro, "A escritora negra," 59–66.

80. Ribeiro, 60.

81. Ribeiro, 61–62.

82. Ribeiro, 62.

83. Ribeiro, 62.

84. Ribeiro, "Dois textos," 156–65.

CHAPTER 1 — TEODORA AND MICAELA GINÉS

1. Robin D. Moore, *Nationalizing Blackness: Afrocubanismo and Artistic Revolution in Havana, 1920–1940* (Pittsburgh: University of Pittsburgh Press, 1997), 89. Moore comments on the fluidity of this musical genre. A precise definition is not possible, for it bears different names regionally (e.g., *changüí*, *sucu-sucu*). It is also a major art form that has evolved and produced other kinds of *son*-derived music, such as the recent *son-guajira*, *son-pregón*, *guaracha-son*, and *afro-son*.

2. James Robbins, "The Cuban 'Son' as Form, Genre, and Symbol," *Latin American Music Review* 2, no. 11 (Autumn–Winter 1990): 83; Karoline Bahrs, "El origen de sones afroantillanos: Perspectivas dominicanas con respecto al 'Son de la Ma' Teodora,'" *Latin American Music Review* 32, no. 2 (Fall–Winter 2011): 221–23.

3. Blas R. Jiménez, *Afrodominicano por elección, negro por nacimiento* (Santo Domingo: Manatí, 2008), 75.

4. Natalio Galan, *Cuba y sus sones* (Valencia, Spain: Pre-textos, 1983), 20.

5. Helio Orovio, *Diccionario de la música cubana biográfico y técnico*, 2nd ed. (Havana: Letras Cubanas, 1992), 209–10.

6. Orovio, 209–10.

7. Radamés Giro, *Diccionario enciclopédico de la música en Cuba*, vol. 4 (Havana: Letras Cubanas, 2007), 160–61.

8. See Mónica Mansour, *La poesía negrista* (Mexico: Era, 1973), 142–43; Moore, *Nationalizing Blackness*, 106; Giro, *Diccionario enciclopédico*, 163–64; and Giro, conversation with the author, May 18, 2017, in Havana, Cuba.

9. Danilo Orozco, "Nexos globales desde la música cubana con rejuegos de son y no son," *Boletímúsica*, no. 38 (October–December 2014): 56.

10. Orozco, 13.

11. Orozco, 56.

12. Orozco, 57.

13. See poems in Jorge Luis Morales, ed., *Poesía afroantillana y negrista: Puerto Rico, República Dominicana, Cuba* (Rio Piedras: Universidad de Puerto Rico, 1981); Nicolás Guillén, *Nicolás Guillén: Obra poética 1920–1958*, vol. 1 (Havana: Instituto Cubano del Libro, 1972); José Z. Tallet, *Orbita de Jose Z. Tallet*, ed. Helio Orovio (Havana: UNEAC, 1969); and Ramón Guirao, *Orbita de la poesía afrocubana 1928–1937* (Havana: Ucar, García y Cía, 1938).

14. Peter Manuel, "From Contradanza to *Son*: New Perspectives on the Prehistory of Cuban Popular Music," *Latin American Music Review* 30, no. 2 (Fall–Winter 2009): 185, 188; Elena Pérez Sanjurjo, *Historia de la música cubana* (Miami: La Moderna Poesía, 1986), 38; Emilio Grenet, *Popular Cuban Music* (Havana: Carasa, 1939), xxxvi. The musicologists who have confirmed Oriente as *son*'s place of origin include Manuel, Pérez Sanjurjo, and Grenet.

15. Rolando J. Rensoli Medina, *La Habana ciudad azul: Metrópolis cubana* (Havana: Ediciones Extramuros, 2015), 129–30. Rensoli Medina describes the military and administrative development of the two first settlements—Santiago de Cuba and La Habana—explaining their roles and eventual decision to make La Habana the capital of the colony.

16. Manuel, "From Contradanza to *Son*," 188.

17. Manuel, 185.

18. Manuel, 185.

19. Manuel, 189.

20. Manuel, 189–90.

21. Grenet, *Popular Cuban Music*, xxxvi.

22. Victoria Eli Rodríguez and Zoila Gómez García,. . . *haciendo música cubana* (Havana: Pueblo y Educación, 1989), 85–86; Argeliers León, *Del canto y el tiempo* (Havana: Letras Cubanas, 1984), 119. León confirms that the first three instruments that appeared among the people were the guitar (*guitarra*), the treble (*tiple*), and the chordophone (*bandurria*).

23. León, *Del canto*, 119.

24. Rodríguez and Gómez García,. . . *haciendo música cubana*, 85.

25. Robbins, "Cuban 'Son,'" 184–85; León, *Del canto*, 119–22.

26. Rodríguez and Gómez García,. . . *haciendo música cubana*, 83.

27. Manuel, "From Contradanza to *Son*," 185.

28. Orovio, *Diccionario de la música*, 13; Giro, *Diccionario enciclopédico*, 161.

29. Moore, *Nationalizing Blackness*, 89.

30. Giro, *Diccionario enciclopédico*, 161.

31. Rodríguez and Gómez García,. . . *haciendo música cubana*, 82.

32. Manuel, "From Contradanza to *Son*," 186–87; Robin D. Moore, *Music in the Hispanic Caribbean: Experiencing Music, Expressing Culture* (Oxford: Oxford University Press, 2010), 91.

33. León, *Del canto*, 113.

34. Orozco, "Nexos globales," 81.

35. Alejo Carpentier, *La música en Cuba* (Pánuco, Mexico: Fondo de Cultura Económica, 1946), 32.

36. Carpentier, 32.

37. Alejandro de la Fuente, *Havana and the Atlantic in the Sixteenth Century* (Chapel Hill: University of North Carolina Press, 2008), 154–56.

38. De la Fuente, 158–59.

39. De la Fuente, 173.

40. De la Fuente, 177.

41. De la Fuente, 181.

42. De la Fuente, 168, 170.

43. Carpentier, *La música en Cuba*, 34–35.

44. Carpentier, 35.

45. Carpentier, 35–36.

46. Carpentier, 36.

47. Cirilo Villaverde, *Cecilia Valdés: Novela de costumbres cubanas* (Mexico, Porrúa, 2006), 25, 38, 39, 120. Villaverde's canonical *costumbrista* novel, *Cecilia Valdés* (1839, 1882), is famous for its portrait of Cuba's colonial society. Set in the 1800s, it draws attention to musicians in Havana and makes reference to instrumentalists of color, both free and enslaved, who usually provided entertainment at dances and balls.

48. Moore, *Nationalizing Blackness*, 88.

49. Carpentier, *La música en Cuba*, 36.

50. Laureano Fuentes Matons, *Las artes en Santiago de Cuba: Apuntes históricos* (Santiago de Cuba: Establecimiento tipográfico de Juan E. Ravelo, 1893), 115; Orovio, *Diccionario de la música*, 210; Carpentier, *La música en Cuba*, 37.

51. Carpentier, *La música en Cuba*, 37.

52. Carpentier, 36; Moore, "Representations of Afro-Cuban Expressive Culture in the Writings of Fernando Ortiz," *Latin American Music Review* 15, no. 1 (Spring–Summer 1994): 36–37. In this essay, Moore discusses determinism and evolutionism as philosophical underpinnings at the base of cultural thought during the early twentieth century. The valuing of European artistic expression established and solidified itself upon convictions regarding the primitive and subordinate nature of all African endeavors, demoting them as foolish, savage, vulgar, and degenerate. Carpentier's definition of "primitivo antillano" adheres to such philosophical postulations even as it sets the stage for future analysis about Cuban identity as multiethnic in nature.

53. Carpentier, *La música en Cuba*, 36–37.

54. Carpentier, 38. The Andalusian *copla* is a popular song derived from a poetic form with the same name. It refers to a poem whose structure displays groups of four verses with eight syllables to each line. It was commonly adopted in Latin America. The word comes from the Latin word *copula*, meaning "link" or "union."

55. Carpentier, 38; B. Christine Arce, *Mexico's Nobodies: The Cultural Legacy of the Soldadera and Afro-Mexican Women* (Albany: State University of New York Press, 2018), 229–51. As an aside, Arce's *Mexico's Nobodies* includes a section on *son jarocho* as a hallmark of Afro-Mexican legacy in Mexico, its distinctive Afro-mestizo form, and rhythms that derive from African and Afro-Caribbean elements. She also discusses its nineteenth- and twentieth-century connections with the Cuban *son* by way of influences and musicians.

56. Carpentier, *La música en Cuba*, 39.

57. Carpentier, 39.

58. Flérida de Nolasco, *Santo Domingo en el folklore universal* (Ciudad Trujillo, Dominican Republic: Impresora Dominicana, 1956), 312.

59. Roberto González Echevarría, "Literature of the Hispanic Caribbean," *Latin American Literary Review* 8, no. 16 (Spring 1980): 7.

60. González Echevarría, 7–8.

61. González Echevarría, 8.

62. González Echevarría, 8.

63. González Echevarría, 10.

64. Vera Kutzinski, *Sugar's Secrets: Race and the Erotics of Cuban Nationalism* (Charlottesville: University Press of Virginia, 1993), 184–85.

65. Kutzinski, 184.

66. Kutzinski, 185.

67. Kutzinski, 185.

68. Carpentier, *La música en Cuba*, 39–40.

69. Carpentier, 40.

70. Carpentier, 41.

71. Carpentier, 37.

72. Eduardo Sánchez de Fuentes (1874–1944) was a Cuban composer and author of several publications on the history of Cuban folk music. He is said to have ignored the contributions of Africans to the formation of national music, emphasizing instead what he saw as Indigenous features. Subsequent historians seriously challenged this line of development, a process that has affected his credibility and prestige as one of the country's key researchers on the origins of Cuban music.

73. Carpentier, *La música en Cuba*, 38.

74. Carpentier, 38.

75. Alberto Muguercia y Muguercia, "Teodora Ginés ¿Mito o realidad histórica?," *Revista de la Biblioteca Nacional José Martí* 62, no. 3 (September–December 1971): 53–86. In this study, I will refer to this musicologist as Muguercia. In the endnotes, I will use Muguercia y Muguercia when referring to his publications.

76. Rodríguez and Gómez García,. . . *haciendo música cubana*, 81.

77. Juan Francisco Manzano, *Autobiografía* (Havana: Instituto del Libro Cubano, 1978); Miguel Barnet and Esteban Montejo, *Biografía de un cimarrón* (Havana: Instituto de Etnología y Folklore, 1966).

78. Antonio Gómez Sotolongo, "Muguercia y el fin de un mito," *Hoy*, May 15, 2004, http://hoy.com.do/muguercia-y-el-fin-de-un-mito-2/ (accessed January 2, 2014).

79. Fuentes Matons, *Las artes.*

80. Fuentes Matons, 113.

81. Fuentes Matons and Abelardo Estrada, *Las artes en Santiago en Cuba: Estudio de un libro, su autor y la órbita de ambos* (Havana: Letras Cubanas, 1981), 113; María Antonieta Henríquez, *Lo permanente en nuestra música* (Havana: Ediciones Museo de la Música, 2008), 26.

82. León's *Del canto* studies the origin and expansion of Cuban music, focusing on Hispanic and African influences. Also consult Raquel Llerandi and Luis Ángel Argüelles, Zoila Gómez García, Ana Ofelia Diez de Oñate, and Tomás Fernández Robaina in "Imaginarios: Aniversario 85 del nacimiento de Muguercia," *Librínsula: La revista de los libros*, http://librinsula.bnjm.cu/secciones/314/expedientes/314_exped_1.html (accessed May 23, 2014; page no longer extant).

83. Fuentes Matons, *Las artes*, 5–8.

84. Carpentier, *La música en Cuba*, 37; Orovio, *Diccionario de la música*, 210; Rodríguez and Gómez García,. . . *haciendo música cubana*, 82.

85. Muguercia y Muguercia, "Teodora Ginés," 53.

86. Muguercia y Muguercia, 53.

87. Muguercia y Muguercia, 53 (italic in the original).

88. Muguercia y Muguercia, 56.

89. Joaquín José García, *Protocolo de antigüedades, literatura, agricultura, industria, comercio, etc.*, vol. 1 (Havana: Imprenta de M. Soler, 1985), 297. The *vihuela* is a guitar-like string instrument from fifteenth- and sixteenth-century Spain, Portugal, and Italy, with six strings.

90. Muguercia y Muguercia, "Teodora Ginés," 118, 45, 159, 9–10, 5–8, 56.

91. Muguercia y Muguercia, 26–29, 7–8.

92. Muguercia y Muguercia, 58–59.

93. Arriving populations by then would have included enslaved Africans from Africa and from Spain, not to mention Spaniards from different regions of Spain and therefore not a cohesive group culturally.

94. Muguercia y Muguercia, "Teodora Ginés," 59.

95. Muguercia y Muguercia, 61.

96. Muguercia y Muguercia, 62.

97. Muguercia y Muguercia, 63.

98. Muguercia y Muguercia, 65.

99. Muguercia y Muguercia, 66–67.

100. Muguercia y Muguercia, 67.

101. Muguercia y Muguercia, 66–67.

102. Muguercia y Muguercia, 68.

103. Muguercia y Muguercia, 70–72.

104. Muguercia y Muguercia, 73.

105. Muguercia y Muguercia, 74.

106. Muguercia y Muguercia, 75.

107. Muguercia y Muguercia, 76.

108. Muguercia y Muguercia, 77.

109. Muguercia y Muguercia, 77.

110. Muguercia y Muguercia, 79.

111. Muguercia y Muguercia, 80.

112. Muguercia y Muguercia, 82–83.

113. Manuel, "From Contradanza to *Son*," 189–90. Manuel confirms that the *son* did in fact experience a revival and became popular in the twentieth century.

114. Muguercia y Muguercia, "Teodora Ginés," 83.

115. Muguercia y Muguercia, 83.

116. Henríquez's "Otras disquisiciones" is now available in Henríquez, *Lo permanente*.

CHAPTER 2 — THE INVENTION OF HISTORY THROUGH POETRY

1. Karoline Bahrs, "El origen de sones afroantillanos: Perspectivas dominicanas con respecto al 'Son de la Ma' Teodora,'" *Latin American Music Review* 32, no. 2 (Fall–Winter 2011): 223.

2. Carlos Andújar, *Identidad cultural y religiosidad popular* (Santo Domingo: Letra Gráfica, 2004); Carlos Andújar, *La presencia negra en Santo Domingo* (Santo Domingo: Letra Gráfica, 2011); Carlos Esteban Deive, *Los guerrilleros negros: Esclavos fugitivos y cimarrones en Santo Domingo* (Santo Domingo: Taller, 1997); Odalís G. Pérez, *La ideología rota: El derrumbe del pensamiento pseudonacionalista dominicano* (Santo Domingo: Manatí, 2002).

3. Blas R. Jiménez, *Afrodominicano por elección, negro por nacimiento* (Santo Domingo: Manatí, 2008); Celsa Albert Batista, *Mujer y esclavitud en Santo Domingo* (Santo Domingo: INDAASEL, 2003); Celsa Albert Batista, *Los africanos y nuestra isla (historia, cultura e identidad)* (Santo Domingo: INDAASEL, 2001); Pura Emeterio Rondón, *Estudios críticos de la literatura dominicana contemporánea* (Santo Domingo: Búho, 2005); Carlos Andújar, *De cultura y sociedad*, 2nd ed. (Santo Domingo: Letra Gráfica, 2004); Andújar, *La presencia negra*; Andújar, *Identidad cultural*. Self-identifying as a Black poet, Jiménez distances himself from the cultural tendency of African denial, thereby becoming this country's most vocal advocate of that ancestral line. Albert Batista, Rondón, and Andújar work on the notion of a nation of Afro-descendants even as they favor the idea of a national identity of mulattoness.

4. Aída Cartagena Portalatín, *Yania Tierra: Poema documento* (Washington, D.C.: Azul Editions, 1995).

5. Quoted in Dawn Duke, "Literatura afro-femenina en la República Dominicana ¿Una indefinitud que la define?," *Revista iberoamericana* 79, no. 243 (April–June 2013): 171–72.

6. Andújar, *De cultura y sociedad*, 73.

7. Andújar, 73–74.

8. Consult "Sebastián Lemba Calembo: Biografías dominicanas," www.mi-rd.com, last updated 2018, https://www.mi-rd.com/Interes/Historia/Sebastian-Lemba-Calembo.html

(accessed June 21, 2019); "Sebastián Lemba: El líder de la cimarronea," conectate.com, last updated September 25, 2020, https://www.conectate.com.do/articulo/sebastian-lemba -biografia-republica-dominicana/ (accessed June 21, 2019). Abdias do Nascimento (1959, 1979, 1980), Manuel Zapata Olivella (2007), Omar H. Ali (2014), and Miguel Barnet (1966) provide detailed, comprehensive writings on Zumbi, Benkos Biohó, and Esteban Montejo, respectively.

9. Flérida de Nolasco, *Santo Domingo en el folklore universal* (Ciudad Trujillo, Dominican Republic, Impresora Dominicana 1956), 311–20.

10. De Nolasco, 312.

11. De Nolasco, 313. Benigno Gutiérrez's *Arrume folklórico de todo el maíz* (Medellín, Colombia: Librería la Pluma de Ore, 1948) is a collection of typical musical renditions and popular narratives collected from rural peasants. They were very much a part of traditions associated with corn cultivation.

12. De Nolasco, 188–89.

13. De Nolasco, 312.

14. De Nolasco, 313.

15. Aída Cartagena Portalatín, "Las Ginés de Santo Domingo: Esclavas, negras, libertas y músicas," *El Urogallo* 6, nos. 35–36 (September–December 1975): 151.

16. Portalatín, 149.

17. Carlos Larrazábal Blanco, *Los negros y la esclavitud en Santo Domingo* (Santo Domingo: Julio D. Postigo e Hijos, 1967).

18. Portalatín, "Las Ginés de Santo Domingo," 149.

19. Portalatín, 149–50.

20. Portalatín, 150.

21. Albert Batista, *Los africanos*, 28. Also consult Dawn Duke, "From 'Yélida' to Movimiento de Mujeres Dominico-Haitianas: Gendering Problems of Whiteness in the Dominican Republic," in *At Home and Abroad: Historicizing Twentieth-Century Whiteness in Literature and Performance*, ed. La Vinia Delois Jennings (Knoxville: University of Tennessee Press, 2009), 83–84. It is a challenge to translate these terms. They are popular, indiscreet, discriminatory, even racial slurs for peoples of mixed race, products of varying degrees of Indigenous, African, and Spanish (from Spain) heritages. They are considerably used in the Dominican Republic and Cuba.

22. Blás Jiménez was particularly critical of the elitist nature of his country's nationalistic agenda, a path that has resulted in what he describes as a whitened version of history. The system reveals the consistent and deliberate exclusion of a fair and just representation of African and Afro-descendant legacies. He was convinced that the declaration of the Dominican Republic as a mulatto state may have facilitated such an agenda (*Afrodominicano por elección*, 26–27).

23. Albert Batista, *Los africanos*, 31–32.

24. Albert Batista, *Mujer y esclavitud*, 120.

25. Chiqui Vicioso, "Aída Cartagena Portalatín ¿El éxito según San . . . ?," in *Mujer y literatura*, ed. José Rafael Sosa (Santo Domingo: Editora Universitaria UASD, 1986), 79–85; Portalatín, *Yania Tierra*, 113.

26. Daisy Cocco de Filippis, introduction to *Sin otro profeta que su canto: Antología de poesía escrita por dominicanas*, ed. Daisy Cocco de Filippis (Santo Domingo: Taller, 1988), 14.

27. Vicioso, "Aída Cartagena Portalatín," 11.

28. Cocco de Filippis, introduction, 27; Vicioso, "Aída Cartagena Portalatín," 79–80.

29. David Howard, *Coloring the Nation: Race and Ethnicity in the Dominican Republic* (Oxford: Signal Books, 2001), 26–32. Also consult Mariana Past, "Problematic Cartographies: Hispaniola as Truncated Island in Aída Cartagena Portalatín's *Yania Tierra*," *Afro-Hispanic Review* 30, no. 2 (Fall 2011): 85–100; Duke, "From 'Yélida,'" 77–78. Howard argues that the roots of anti-Haitianism lie in Dominican-Haitian history specifically tied to the events related to the Haitian Revolution and the Haitian occupation of Santo Domingo that lasted from 1822 to 1844.

30. Joaquín Balaguer, *Historia de la literatura dominicana*, 7th ed. (Santo Domingo: Corripio, 1988), 297–303.

31. Portalatín, *Yania Tierra*, 12-13.

32. Clementina R. Adams, "Afro-Dominican Women Writers and Their Struggles against Patriarchy and Tradition," *Latin Americanist* 47, nos. 3-4 (December 2004): 8.

33. Adams, 9; Duke, "Literatura afro-femenina," 563.

34. Cocco de Filippis, introduction, 28; Aída Cartagena Portalatín, "Otoño negro," in *Dos siglos de literatura dominicana (S. XIX-XX): Poesía (II)*, ed. Manuel Rueda (Santo Domingo: Corripio, 1996), 195-96; Aída Cartagena Portalatín, *Obra poética completa (1955-1984)* (Santo Domingo: Búho, 2000), 207-8, 472-74, 475-77.

35. Aída Cartagena Portalatín, "La llamaban Aurora (Pasión por Donna Summer)," in *Tablero: Doce cuentos de lo popular a lo culto* (Santo Domingo: Taller, 1978), 11-17; Portalatín, "Otoño negro," 187-98.

36. Anthologies republished in Portalatín, *Obra poética completa*.

37. Chiqui Vicioso, "Prólogo: Ya no estás sola, Aída," in *Una mujer está sola*, by Aída Cartagena Portalatín (Santo Domingo: Ediciones Ferilibro, 2005), 14.

38. Vicioso, "Aída Cartagena Portalatín," Latin Art Museum, last updated April 16, 2019, http://www.latinartmuseum.com/portalatin.htm (accessed July 25, 2014).

39. Odalís Pérez, *Aída Cartagena Portalatín: De entero cuerpo* (Santo Domingo: Editora Universitaria UASD, 2007), 58.

40. Aída Cartagena Portalatín, *Culturas africanas rebeldes con causa* (Santo Domingo: Ediciones de la Biblioteca Nacional, 1986), inside cover.

41. Portalatín, 53.

42. Léopold Sédar Senghor, "Negritude: A Humanism of the Twentieth Century," in *Colonial Discourse and Post-colonial Theory: A Reader*, ed. Patrick Williams and Laura Chrisman (New York: Columbia University Press, 1994), 23.

43. Portalatín, *Culturas africanas*, 39-49.

44. Portalatín, 61-65.

45. Portalatín, 86-87.

46. Portalatín, 115.

47. Portalatín, 120.

48. Muguercia's name is spelled incorrectly in Portalatín's title and in her essay.

49. Portalatín, *Culturas africanas*, 123.

50. Portalatín, 124.

51. Portalatín, 125.

52. Portalatín, 125.

53. Portalatín, 125-26.

54. Portalatín, 126-28.

55. Cocco de Filippis, introduction, 15-16.

56. Nicole Roberts, "Racialised Identities, Caribbean Realities: Analysing Black Female Identity in Hispanic Caribbean Poetry," *Caribbean Review of Gender Studies* 1 (April 2007): 1-2.

57. Roberts, 4.

58. The English translations of this poem are taken from the 1995 bilingual edition.

59. Past, "Problematic Cartographies," 85.

60. Past, 87.

61. Kimberly Eisen Simmons, *Reconstructing Racial Identity and the African Past in the Dominican Republic* (Gainesville: University Press of Florida, 2009), 26-30; Howard, *Coloring the Nation*, 26-33; Dawn Stinchcomb, *The Development of Literary Blackness in the Dominican Republic* (Gainesville: University Press of Florida, 2004), 10-12; Silvio Torres-Saillant, "The Tribulations of Blackness: Stages in Dominican Racial Identity," *Latin American Perspectives* 25, no. 3 (May 1998): 130-31; Duke, "From 'Yélida,'" 65-66; Ernesto Sagás, *Race and Politics in the Dominican Republic* (Gainesville: University Press of Florida, 2000), 22-31; Eugenio Matibag, *Haitian-Dominican Counterpart: Nation, State, and Race on Hispaniola* (New York: Palgrave Macmillan, 2003), 99-104; Jiménez, *Afrodominicano por elección*, 20-27.

62. Past, "Problematic Cartographies," 86.

63. Past, 93.

64. Portalatín, *Yania Tierra*, 172–73.

65. Past, "Problematic Cartographies," 86–87.

66. Portalatín, *Yania Tierra*, 48.

67. Portalatín, 48–49.

68. Portalatín, 58, 64, 80, 168.

69. Portalatín, 70–71.

70. Portalatín, 78–79.

71. Portalatín, 70–71.

72. Portalatín, 70–71.

73. Portalatín, 72–73.

CHAPTER 3 — TRACING THE DANCE STEPS OF A "BRITISH" SUBJECT

1. Alfonso Malespín Jirón, *Bluefields en la memoria* (Bluefields, Nicaragua: URACCAN, 2003), 41.

2. Johnny Hodgson Deerings, *Orígenes de nuestro palo de mayo* (Managua: El Renacimiento, 2008), 17.

3. Edmund Gordon, *Disparate Diasporas: Identity and Politics in an African-Nicaraguan Community* (Austin: University of Texas Press, 1998), 15; Hugo Sujo Wilson, *Oral History of Bluefields / Historia oral de Bluefields* (Bluefields, Nicaragua: CIDCA-UCA, 1998), 10; Elizabeth Forbes Brooks, *Memorias de Miss Lizzie: Danzas, música y tradiciones de Bluefields* (Managua: GRAFITEX, 2011), 24.

4. Julio Valle-Castillo, ed., *Poesía atlántica* (Managua: Ministerio de Cultura, 1980); Víctor Obando Sancho, Ronald Brooks Saldaña, and Eddy Alemán Porras, eds., *Antología poética de la Costa Caribe de Nicaragua* (Managua: URACCAN, 1998); Angélica Brown Hendricks, coord., *Antología poética "Afrocarinica"* (Bluefields, Nicaragua: Bluefields Indian and Caribbean University, 2011); Eddy Alemán Porras and Franklin Brooks Vargas, comps., *Bluefields en la sangre: Poesía del Caribe Sur Nicaragüense* (Managua: 400 elefantes, 2011).

5. Malespín Jirón, *Bluefields en la memoria*, 15–17. Mrs. Rose, Reverend Allan Budier Ryan, José Sinclair, Doctor Henningston Omeir, David Bolaños Siu, to mention a few.

6. Malespín Jirón, 14–15.

7. Lizandro Chávez Alfaro, "Identidad y resistencia del 'criollo' en Nicaragua," *Cahiers du monde hispanique et luso-brésilien* 36 (1981): 89.

8. Gordon, *Disparate Diasporas*, 137–38. In this section, various terms refer to Creoles, including *coastal dwellers*, or *costeños*; *Blacks*; *Afro-descendants*; *Bluefieldians*; and *Caribbean peoples*. As Gordon describes, *costeño* can be fluid and political, for it is not exclusive to Afro-descendant Creoles. The most common Spanish versions are *criollo*, *costeño*, and *blufileño*. This range of terms speaks to their deep island roots and ethnic pride in their legacy of autonomy and Anglo-Caribbean heritage. Gordon confirms that historically, *Creole* referred to English and Creole language speakers of African descent as well as those of European and Indigenous roots who spoke these languages (40). Today, they are a Spanish-, English-, Caribbean English–, and Creole-speaking people who, in appearance and legacy, display substantial ethnic diversity (193).

9. Gordon, 137.

10. Autonomy Statute for the Regions of the Atlantic Coast of Nicaragua, Law no. 28 (September 7, 1987), CALPI, http://calpi.nativeweb.org/doc_3.html (accessed June 5, 2014); Jochen Mattern, *Autonomía regional en Nicaragua: Una aproximación descriptiva* (Managua: PROFODEM-GTZ/CSD, 2002), https://www.academia.edu/31109923/AUTONOM%C3 %8DA_REGIONAL_EN_NICARAGUA (accessed January 20, 2016); Carlos Vilas, "Revolutionary Change and Multi-ethnic Regions: The Sandinista Revolution and the Atlantic Coast," in *Ethnic Groups and the Nation State: The Case of the Atlantic Coast of Nicaragua*, ed. CIDCA / Development Study Unit (Stockholm: Stockholm University Press, 1987), 67; Edmund Gordon, "History, Identity, Consciousness, and Revolution: Afro-Nicaraguans and the Nicaraguan Revolution," in *Ethnic Groups and the Nation State: The Case of the Atlantic Coast of Nicaragua*, ed. CIDCA / Development Study Unit (Stockholm: Stockholm University Press, 1987), 145–56;

Socorro Woods Downs, *"I've Never Shared This with Anybody": Creole Women's Experience of Racial and Sexual Discrimination and Their Need for Self-Recovery* (Managua: URACCAN, 2005), 47. The "Autonomy Statute" was established under the Sandinista rule as the statute governing the region's autonomous status. Scholars have weighed in on the region's autonomy and the manner in which the government in Managua continues to exercise control over the Atlantic coast (Gordon, *Disparate Diasporas*, 203–52). Jochen Mattern views their autonomous status as very positive even as tensions with Managua exist given its tardiness in consolidating such status and its sluggish support of the region's development and modernization. A region of cultural and socioeconomic contrasts, it continues to trail behind the rest of the country as the poorest and least developed part of the nation, even as it is the most ethnically diverse. Woods Downs questions the validity of the region's legally recognized state of autonomy, finding it flawed in the way it has made no provisions for recognizing the specific needs of women. The assumption is that the exclaimer of multiethnicity will take care of everything.

11. Socorro Woods Downs and Courtney Desiree Morris, *"Land Is Power": Examining Race, Gender, and the Struggle for Land Rights on the Caribbean Coast of Nicaragua* (report for the Caribbean and Central American Research Council, Austin, Tex., June 2007), 6. Within the Caribbean coast of Nicaragua, we can identity six broad ethnic peoples or groupings: two Afro-descendant groups, the Garifuna and the Creoles; three major Indigenous groupings, the Miskito, the Rama, and the Mayagna (as well as other Indigenous ethnicities); and mestizos. Woods Downs refers to the Sumus, not the Mayagna, and uses the terms *mestizo* or *ladino* (42). Gordon has identified at least three lines of identity that many Creoles assume simultaneously: Blacks (in Spanish, *negros*), Creoles (referring to an Afro-descendant, Anglophone, Caribbean, and diasporic legacy), and Creole Indigenous (which is where the Spanish word *costeños*, meaning "coastal people," would appear [*Disparate Diasporas*, 192–93]).

12. Gordon, *Disparate Diasporas*, xi.

13. Germán Romero Vargas, *Las sociedades del Atlántico de Nicaragua en los siglos XVII y XVIII* (Managua: Fondo de Promoción Cultural, BANIC, 1995), 98–104, 290–96. Romero Vargas describes the historical presence of the British colonizers in the Nicaraguan coastal region. His discussion focuses on the establishment of the Providence Company in 1630, their interaction with the Indigenous peoples during the early 1700s, the very small community of British, the enslavement of Africans and Indigenous peoples, and the commercial and industrial activities in the region.

14. Luis Enrique Morales Alonso, "Presentation," in Forbes Brooks, *Memorias de Miss Lizzie*, 4.

15. Morales Alonso, 4.

16. Rayfield Hodgson Bobb, "Presentation," in Forbes Brooks, *Memorias de Miss Lizzie*, 5.

17. Forbes Brooks, *Memorias de Miss Lizzie*, 6.

18. Malespín Jirón, *Bluefields en la memoria*, 48.

19. Sujo Wilson, *Oral History of Bluefields*, 6.

20. Forbes Brooks, *Memorias de Miss Lizzie*, 7. The celebration of identity implied in the resuscitation of *palo de mayo* harmonizes with the existing intercultural and bilingual education system, designed by the state and the region's administrative representatives as a way to best cater to the needs of the region's ethnically heterogeneous populations. The debate about how to educate this multilingual, diverse region without detrimentally eroding its cultures is ongoing. See Felipe Stuart, ed., "Feature: Intercultural Bilingual Education," URACCAN, http://www/yorku.ca/cerlac/URACCAN/May97.html (accessed November 1, 2014; page no longer extant); Jane Freeland, "Intercultural-Bilingual Education for an Interethnic-Plurilingual Society? The Case of Nicaragua's Caribbean Coast," *Comparative Education* 39, no. 2 (May 2003): 243–48; Padmini Broomfield and Cynara Davies, "Costeño Voices: Oral History on Nicaragua's Caribbean Coast," *Oral History* 31, no. 1 (Spring 2003): 85, 88–89; Marva Spence Sharpe, "Educación en lengua criolla: Las actitudes de los educandos en la Costa Atlántica de Nicaragua," *InterSedes* 8 (2004): 3–6, www.redalyc.org/articulo .oa?id=66650815 (accessed February 17, 2012); and Myrna Cunningham Kain, *Anotaciones sobre el racismo por razones étnicas en Nicaragua* (lecture presented at the Centro para la Autonomía de los Pueblos Indígenas, Bilwi, RACCN, Nicaragua, November 2006), 78–81,

https://tbinternet.ohchr.org/Treaties/CERD/Shared%20Documents/NIC/INT_CERD_NGO
_NIC_72_9739_S.pdf (accessed February 17, 2012).

21. Chávez Alfaro, "Identidad y resistencia," 89.

22. Chávez Alfaro, 92.

23. Pierre Frühling et al., *Etnicidad y nación: El desarrollo de la autonomía de la Costa
Atlántica de Nicaragua (1987-2007)* (F&G, 2007), 25-27; David W. Jones and Carlyle A.
Glean, "The English-Speaking Communities of Honduras & Nicaragua," *Caribbean Quarterly* 17, no. 2 (June 1971): 53; Romero Vargas, *Las sociedades*, 93; Gordon, *Disparate Diasporas*, 4, 19-21; Woods Downs, *"I've Never Shared This,"* 43; Johnny Hodgson Deerings,
"May Pole History—Rescuing Our Culture," Bluefields Pulse, http://bluefieldspulse.com/
maypolehistoryrescuingourculture.htm (accessed May 7, 2015). Frühling et al. explain the
arrival and very successful evangelization campaign of the early Moravian missionaries. Jones
and Glean indicate that the Moravian missionaries' presence in the area was influenced by the
small community of German settlers who lived in a part of Bluefields called Prussian Town.
While they were initially more interested in converting the Indigenous peoples, they had more
success among the more affluent, fair-skinned Creoles and the Creole masses, who together
made up the congregation. Romero Vargas confirms that the arrival of Moravian missionaries
coincided with the decline of Miskito dominance and the rise in influence of the Creole community, especially in Bluefields. On May 2, 1847, the first two Moravian missionaries visited
Bluefields, and by 1849, they had settled in the town. Within five years, they built a church and
a pastoral residence and organized a school. The Moravian schools continue to be historically
recognized and respected on the Atlantic coast. Religious conversion went smoothly; the
Creole population was easier to work with than the Indigenous peoples, since Creoles already
understood English. Gordon narrates his own experiences living with a Creole family who
were devout Moravians.

24. Chávez Alfaro, "Identidad y resistencia," 93.

25. Chávez Alfaro, 93-94; Joe Bryan and Denis Wood, *Weaponizing Maps: Indigenous
Peoples and Counterinsurgency in the Americas* (New York: Guilford, 2015), 39; Sujo Wilson,
Oral History of Bluefields, 40-43, 48-51. Sujo Wilson confirms 1894 as the year of Bluefields's
incorporation into the state of Nicaragua. In *Oral History of Bluefields*, he describes this early
period, 1902-26, supported by firsthand accounts from elderly citizens.

26. Hodgson Deerings, *Orígenes*, 38.

27. Gordon links this Creole position to colonial religious doctrine and confirms the tendency among earlier Moravian missionaries to racially stereotype Creoles, viewing them as
practitioners of moral depravity, given to sexual extremes, excessive alcohol consumption, and
even heathenism (*Disparate Diasporas*, 47, 49).

28. Hodgson Deerings, *Orígenes*, 12-13.

29. Hodgson Deerings, 13.

30. Hodgson Deerings, 13-14.

31. Malespín Jirón, *Bluefields en la memoria*, 46-47.

32. Forbes Brooks, *Memorias de Miss Lizzie*, 7.

33. Forbes Brooks, 7.

34. The Universidad de las Regiones Autónomas de la Costa Caribe Nicaragüense [URACCAN; University of the Autonomous Regions of the Nicaraguan Caribbean Coast] was established in 1992. It has several campuses and proudly distinguishes itself as an institution with a
community intercultural agenda, best designed to serve its Creole, Garifuna, Indigenous, and
multiethnic students.

35. Information taken from the wall of the URACCAN Bluefields campus library during my
visit to Bluefields on March 22, 2012. Hodgson Deerings confirms that from the 1930s to the
1980s, Miss Lizzie, along with Mrs. Hilda Dixon, were major promoters and dance instructors
of the Ribbon Pole dance, or *baile de cinta* (*Orígenes*, 22).

36. Malespín Jirón, *Bluefields en la memoria*, 41-42.

37. Hodgson Deerings, *Orígenes*, 23. This is my speculation, but it may be a version of the
word *Scottish*.

38. Forbes Brooks, *Memorias de Miss Lizzie*, 11; Ivy Elizabeth Forbes Brooks, "Ivy Elizabeth (Lizzy Nelson) Forbes Brooks," in *The Times & Life of Bluefields: An Intergenerational Dialogue*, ed. Deborah Robb Taylor (Managua: Academia de Geografía e Historia de Nicaragua, 2005), 82, 84.

39. Robb Taylor, *Times & Life*, 277.

40. Malespín Jirón, *Bluefields en la memoria*, 41.

41. While reminiscing about the good old days, Sujo Wilson confirms the impact the centuries-old British system of education continues to have on the community. In the early days (probably the first decades of the twentieth century), the best teachers were Jamaican and schoolbooks were British, resulting in the acculturation of generations to English literary and cultural traditions (*Oral History of Bluefields*, 33).

42. Gordon, *Disparate Diasporas*, 69.

43. Robb Taylor, *Times & Life*, 311–18; Evett Keyla Herbbert Kelly and Itzel Thomas Hodgson, *Factores que inciden en la participación de las mujeres kriol en política del estado en la ciudad de Bluefields en el periodo 1998 al 2008* (Bluefields, Nicaragua: URACCAN, February 2010), 8.

44. Woods Downs, *"I've Never Shared This,"* 17. On the Caribbean coast, there are two areas within which women (Garifuna and Creole) encounter the greatest difficulty in terms of their recognition, participation as full citizens, and acceptance as equals or leaders: land rights (ownership) and running for public office (positions of political leadership). In-depth studies have been published by Woods Downs (2005), Woods and Morris (2007), and Herbbert Kelly and Thomas Hodgson (2010). Jennifer Goett's *Black Autonomy: Race, Gender, and Afro-Nicaraguan Activism* (Redwood City, Calif.: Stanford University Press, 2017) includes a chapter, "Sexual Violence and Autonomous Politics" (151–77), that closely analyzes the severe lasting negative impact of civil war and militarization of society on Creole women.

45. Woods Downs, *"I've Never Shared This,"* 20–24, 44. Besides race and gender biases, these studies always include the stigma associated with being Creole speakers and the process of othering implied therein, sustained by broad national impressions of a people who do not know to speak Spanish "properly" (61–62). See also Herbbert Kelly and Thomas Hodgson, *Factores que inciden*, 9.

46. Woods Downs, *"I've Never Shared This,"* 48–51.

47. Woods Downs, 71.

48. Herbbert Kelly and Thomas Hodgson, *Factores que inciden*, 21–22.

49. Herbbert Kelly and Thomas Hodgson, 30.

50. Pearl Lagoon, located in the South Caribbean Coast Autonomous Region of Nicaragua, houses the largest coastal lagoon, is considered a municipality, and is the name for a Creole village about twenty-two miles north of Bluefields. Gordon, *Disparate Diasporas*, 16.

51. Forbes Brooks, *Memorias de Miss Lizzie*, 9–10; Forbes Brooks, "Ivy Elizabeth," 81–82.

52. Wayne O'Neil and Maya Honda, "El inglés nicaragüense," *WANI: Una revista sobre la Costa Atlántica* 16 (October–December 1987): 55; Josef Hurtubise, "Poesía en inglés criollo nicaragüense," *WANI: Una revista sobre la Costa Atlántica* 16 (January–March 1995), 46. The expression *inglés estándar* [standard English] is very popular and continues to be used generally to establish the difference between, on the one hand, the language that, in places like Bluefields today, best reproduces the version imported by the colonizing British and, on the other, the Creole language that developed among enslaved Africans and their descendants living in colonies under British rule throughout history. Hurtubise divides Nicaraguan Creole poetry into two categories that align with the two language types—that is, standard English and Creole. He uses the word *populist* to describe poetic inventions associated with the latter language type without discussing the internal nuances of such categorization from within the community.

53. Jane Freeland, "Linguistic Rights and Language Survival in a Creole Space: Dilemmas for Nicaragua's Caribbean Coast Creoles," in *Language Rights and Language Survival: Sociolinguistic and Sociocultural Perspectives*, ed. Jane Freeland and Donna Patrick (Manchester, U.K.: St. Jerome, 2004), 111.

54. Sujo Wilson confirms the influences of Marcus Garvey's United Negro Improvement Association (UNIA), especially on the highly educated and renowned Creoles of the town during the 1920s. They were very active in this highly politicized endeavor that was the Back-to-Africa movement, connecting Bluefields to the Black Atlantic world in terms of UNIA's international influence while fueling their legacy of cultural difference and autonomy. The UNIA Hall, also called the Black Star Line, was located in Beholden and was the most important community center (*Oral History of Bluefields*, 60–61).

55. Gordon, *Disparate Diasporas*, 158; Forbes Brooks, *Memorias de Miss Lizzie*, 14, 39; Forbes Brooks, "Ivy Elizabeth," 82; Sujo Wilson, *Oral History of Bluefields*, 60–61. Gordon identifies five Creole movements active during the 1960s and 1970s: a group of pastors working to reform the Nicaraguan Moravian Church; the large progressive movement of intellectuals known as Organización Progresista Costeña [OPROCO; Organization in Pro of the Atlantic Coast]; an intellectual movement led by scholar Donovan Brautigam Beer to establish a Creole cultural difference; a group of students, declared Sandinistas; and the influential Southern Indigenous Creole Community (SICC) that focused on local politics (*Disparate Diasporas*, 151). Gordon fully describes OPROCO, a secular group of intellectuals (doctors, teachers, etc.), products of a Moravian education taught by nationalist Creole pastors. He does indicate that very few women were involved. From 1975 until the SICC movement's end, Miss Jenelee Hodgson was its president, an outstanding leader—a product of seminary schooling, the movement to nationalize the Moravian Church, and readings such as Fanon (155–66). She was an avid follower of Martin Luther King Jr. and the civil rights movement, reader of Afro-descendant Central American writers such as Quince Duncan, and participant in Angela Davis's activities and her Afro hairstyle (182–85). Gordon briefly mentions Angélica Brown, discussing her activism as a member of ISCC (228, 231). The disbandment of this activism is well recorded (235–39).

56. Forbes Brooks, *Memorias de Miss Lizzie*, 39.

57. Forbes Brooks, 14.

58. Forbes Brooks, 40.

59. Forbes Brooks, 46.

60. Forbes Brooks, 48–49.

61. June Beer, "Resurrection a' da wud" [Resurrection is the word], quoted in Hurtubise, "Poesía en inglés," 46. Hurtubise indicates that not all Creole writers were in support of the Sandinista revolutionary process. He credits the revolution with the literacy campaign in Creole, particularly the way it supported political and cultural autonomy for the region and the establishment of a program of bilingual education, all concrete measures that would have provided stimuli for this poetic movement.

62. Forbes Brooks, *Memorias de Miss Lizzie*, 46.

63. Forbes Brooks, "Ivy Elizabeth," 86; Sujo Wilson, *Oral History of Bluefields*, 85.

64. Courtney Desiree Morris, "Becoming Creole, Becoming Black: Migration, Diasporic Self-Making, and the Many Lives of Madame Maymie Leona Turpeau de Mena," *Women, Gender, and Families of Color* 4, no. 2 (Fall 2016): 171, 172.

65. Forbes Brooks, "Ivy Elizabeth," 84.

66. Forbes Brooks, *Memorias de Miss Lizzie*, 9–11; Forbes Brooks, "Ivy Elizabeth," 84; Gordon, *Disparate Diasporas*, 96–102.

67. Hodgson Deerings, *Orígenes*, 5.

68. Sujo Wilson, *Oral History of Bluefields*, 32, 82; Sujo Wilson, "Hacia una reincorporación justa y auténtica," in *La Costa Caribe nicaragüense: Desde sus orígenes hasta el siglo XXI*, ed. Jorge Eduardo Arellano (Managua: Academia de Geografía e Historia de Nicaragua, 2009), 67–72; Thomas Wayne Edison, "La cultura afro-caribeña vista en la poesía del *palo de mayo* en el poema *Si yo fuera mayo* por Carlos Rigby Moses," *WANI: Revista del Caribe Nicaragüense* 49 (April–June 2007): 23. The elderly citizens of Bluefields tell different stories about the creation of the town's neighborhoods and its inhabitants. For some, it was originally a town populated by Indigenous peoples. Others maintain that the ancestors of the Creoles are from Jamaica, Providence, and other Caribbean islands. While Beholden, Cotton Tree, and Old Bank are generally seen as the original neighborhoods, lively debate and rivalry remains as to which one is

the first and oldest. Equally entertaining are the stories about why these names were chosen. See Sujo Wilson, *Oral History of Bluefields*, 10–11; and Forbes Brooks, *Memorias de Miss Lizzie*, 24.

69. Hodgson Deerings, *Orígenes*, 17–18.

70. Anthony F. Aveni, *The Book of the Year: A Brief History of Our Seasonal Holidays* (Oxford: Oxford University Press, 2003), 84–85.

71. Aveni, 86.

72. Aveni, 86–90.

73. Aveni, 79–80.

74. Aveni, 81.

75. Aveni, 80–81.

76. Forbes Brooks, *Memorias de Miss Lizzie*, 10; Forbes Brooks, "Ivy Elizabeth," 82.

77. Malespín Jirón, *Bluefields en la memoria*, 43.

78. Aveni, *Book of the Year*, 81, 83.

79. Aveni, 83.

80. Aveni, 83.

81. Aveni, 83–86.

82. Today, CIDCA is called the Museo Histórico Cultural de la Costa Caribe BICU-CIDCA [Historical Cultural Museum of the Caribbean Coast BICU-CIDCA].

83. Hodgson Deerings, "May Pole History"; Hodgson Deerings, *Orígenes*, 18.

84. Hodgson Deerings, *Orígenes*, 8, 10.

85. Hodgson Deerings, 9.

86. Hodgson Deerings, 9.

87. Johnny Hodgson Deerings, "Orígenes de nuestro palo de mayo," *WANI: Revista del Caribe Nicaragüense* 57 (April–June 2009): 10–11. Edison complements Hodgson Deerings's idea by commenting on the social role that *palo de mayo* played under British rule as an emotional outlet that facilitated deep criticism of the Anglo-Saxon hegemonic structure ("La cultura afro-caribeña," 25). Also consult Hodgson Deerings, *Orígenes*, 24–33; Forbes Brooks, *Memorias de Miss Lizzie*, 17; and Antonia McCoy, "Significado del palo de mayo," *Revista Universitaria del Caribe* 8 (2002): 133.

88. Forbes Brooks, *Memorias de Miss Lizzie*, 13, 29.

89. Forbes Brooks, 14, 30.

90. Forbes Brooks, 10–11.

91. Bluefilms, "Al son de Miss Lizzie," July 4, 2012, YouTube video, 0:18:06, https://www.youtube.com/watch?v=HkTs-SfXGrU (accessed January 3, 2016).

92. Forbes Brooks, *Memorias de Miss Lizzie*, 12, 17.

93. Forbes Brooks, 17.

94. Forbes Brooks, 40.

95. Forbes Brooks, 39.

96. Hodgson Deerings, *Orígenes*, 15–16.

97. Forbes Brooks, "Ivy Elizabeth," 84.

98. Forbes Brooks, *Memorias de Miss Lizzie*, 30, 40; Forbes Brooks, "Ivy Elizabeth," 82–83.

99. Forbes Brooks, "Ivy Elizabeth," 83–84.

100. Hodgson Deerings, *Orígenes*, 19.

101. T. M. Scruggs, "Let's Enjoy as Nicaraguans: The Use of Music in the Construction of a Nicaraguan National Consciousness," *Ethnomusicology* 43, no. 2 (Spring–Summer 1999): 312.

102. Forbes Brooks, *Memorias de Miss Lizzie*, 32–35, 40.

103. Hodgson Deerings, *Orígenes*, 20–21.

104. Forbes Brooks, "Ivy Elizabeth," 86.

105. Forbes Brooks, 84–86.

106. Edison indicates that the *palo de mayo* festival changed from a popular local festivity to a more formal and larger celebration in 1980. The region's peoples were all invited to celebrate what became known as *¡Mayo Ya!*—a name that Rigby, as festival coordinator, proposed. From this moment, Bluefields became the home of Nicaragua's now world-famous Caribbean Carnival ("La cultura afro-caribeña," 23–24).

107. Malespín Jirón, *Bluefields en la memoria*, 17.

108. Sujo Wilson, *Oral History of Bluefields*, 85–86.

109. Robb Taylor, *Times & Life*, 312.

110. McCoy, "Significado del palo de mayo," 134.

111. Gordon, *Disparate Diasporas*, 47.

112. Gordon, 48, 67, 109–10; Goett, *Black Autonomy*, 30–31, 35–36. Goett presents a comprehensive discussion of Creole racial identity, conflicting views, and their legacy as a mixed-race people.

113. Gordon, *Disparate Diasporas*, 47.

114. Gordon, 49–50.

115. Robb Taylor, *Times & Life*, 323.

116. Edison, "La cultura afro-caribeña," 25.

117. Malespín Jirón, *Bluefields en la memoria*, 41.

CHAPTER 4 — FROM "MAYAYA LAS IM KEY"
TO CREOLE WOMEN'S WRITINGS

1. Elizabeth Forbes Brooks, *Memorias de Miss Lizzie: Danzas, música y tradiciones de Bluefields* (Managua: GRAFITEX, 2011), 14.

2. Forbes Brooks, 16.

3. Johnny Hodgson Deerings, *Orígenes de nuestro palo de mayo* (Managua: El Renacimiento, 2008), 8–10.

4. Patricia Monaghan, *The Book of Goddesses and Heroines* (New York: E. P. Dutton, 1981), 189.

5. Azizi Powell, "What Does Mayaya Lasinki Mean?," *Pancocojams* (blog), June 29, 2014, http://pancocojams.blogspot.com/2014/06/what-does-mayaya-lasinki-mean.html (accessed January 15, 2015).

6. Hodgson Deerings, *Orígenes*, 8–10.

7. Antonia McCoy, "Significado del palo de mayo," *Revista Universitaria del Caribe* 8 (2002): 131–32.

8. Thomas Wayne Edison, "La cultura afro-caribeña vista en la poesía del *palo de mayo* en el poema *Si yo fuera mayo* por Carlos Rigby Moses," *WANI: Revista del Caribe Nicaragüense* 49 (April–June 2007): 24.

9. Alfonso Malespín Jirón, *Bluefields en la memoria* (Bluefields, Nicaragua: URACCAN, 2003), 43.

10. Malespín Jirón, 43.

11. Edison, "La cultura afro-caribeña," 26.

12. Malespín Jirón, *Bluefields en la memoria*, 44.

13. Deborah Robb Taylor, ed., *The Times & Life of Bluefields: An Intergenerational Dialogue* (Managua: Academia de Geografía e Historia de Nicaragua, 2005), 82–87. Robb Taylor's *Times & Life* is a testimonial compilation of narratives in homage to her people. It is very revealing culturally and covers many details of Creole existence and thought. It is a collective production involving many worthy citizens of Bluefields who contributed their points of view and experiences.

14. Hodgson Deerings, *Orígenes*, 33.

15. Malespín Jirón, *Bluefields en la memoria*, 44–45; Hodgson Deerings, *Orígenes*, 16. Malespín Jirón describes that there were earlier afternoon festivities for children with games, storytelling, and a mini *palo de mayo*, during which they decorated and danced around a smaller pole. Hodgson Deerings confirms that activities for children and youth were during the day, in the afternoons, and they had their own choreography and games around the pole. Earlier children's rhymes included "London Bridge Is Falling Down." At the closing, they would bring the pole or tree down, and the children were allowed to grab at any fruit they could reach. These activities were among traditional practices that evolved over time. Today's younger generations are unfamiliar with the older songs and rhymes. There are fewer community gatherings and more staged and carnival performances, including the fact that

adaptations of the dances and music are performed in various parts of the country. Even among children, the emphasis is on gyrations with fewer displays of formal pole dancing or Miss Lizzie's *palo de mayo* choreography.

16. Wayne O'Neil and Maya Honda, "El inglés nicaragüense," *WANI: Una revista sobre la Costa Atlántica* 16 (October–December 1987): 54–60.

17. Edison, "La cultura afro-caribeña," 24–25.

18. Edison, 24–25. The recording available on YouTube is a good example. Chavalos_Org, "Mayaya Lasinki dimensión costeña concierto en vivo," February 24, 2010, YouTube video, 0:05:54, https://www.youtube.com/watch?v=JedH3X54seA (accessed January 15, 2015).

19. Hodgson Deerings, *Orígenes*, 26. See also Powell, "What Does Mayaya Lasinki Mean?"

20. Powell, "Mayaya Lasinki."

21. Hugo Sujo Wilson, *Oral History of Bluefields / Historia oral de Bluefields* (Bluefields, Nicaragua: CIDCA-UCA, 1998), 86.

22. Miss Lizzie's memoir presents a table of six instruments—tub, hand drum, grater, comb, rattle, and donkey jawbone—as well as a detailed explanation of the day-to-day materials used to invent them (Forbes Brooks, *Memorias de Miss Lizzie*, 29; McCoy, "Significado del palo de mayo," 133).

23. Sujo Wilson, *Oral History of Bluefields*, 86.

24. Hodgson Deerings, *Orígenes*, 14–15.

25. Sujo Wilson, *Oral History of Bluefields*, 86. Also available in Hodgson Deerings, *Orígenes*, 14.

26. Sujo Wilson, *Oral History of Bluefields*, 87.

27. Sujo Wilson, 85–87.

28. Sujo Wilson, 86.

29. Julio Valle-Castillo, ed., *Poesía atlántica* (Managua: Ministerio de Cultura, 1980), 32.

30. Valle-Castillo, 35.

31. Brenda Elena Green Wilson, "Maying Tide in Bluefields," in *Antología poética "Afrocari-nica,"* coord. Angélica Brown Hendricks (Bluefields, Nicaragua: Bluefields Indian and Caribbean University, 2011), 74–75; Ronald Brooks, "Llueve la vida," in *Antología poética de la Costa Caribe de Nicaragua*, ed. Víctor Obando Sancho, Ronald Brooks Saldaña, and Eddy Alemán Porras (Managua: URACCAN, 1998), 39–40; Carlos Rigby, "Si yo fuera Mayo," in *Bluefields en la sangre: Poesía del Caribe Sur Nicaragüense*, comp. Eddy Alemán Porras and Franklin Brooks Vargas (Managua: 400 elefantes, 2011), 77–78; David McField, "Mayo," in Alemán Porras and Brooks Vargas, *Bluefields en la sangre*, 46; Alí Aláh, "Pimpóy bailóp," in Obando Sancho, Brooks Saldaña, and Alemán Porras, *Antología poética*, 60–62; Carmen Merlo, "Otra vez ¡Mayo-Ya!," in Obando Sancho, Brooks Saldaña, and Alemán Porras, *Antología poética*, 92–93; Eddy Alemán Porrás, "Mayo es: Kupia kumi lasbaia wina kakalwra," in Alemán Porras and Brooks Vargas, *Bluefields en la sangre*, 155–58; Franklin Brooks Vargas, "Canción al negro/negra costeño/a," in Alemán Porras and Brooks Vargas, *Bluefields en la sangre*, 178–80; José Santos Cermeño, "Palos de Mayo en Bluefields," in Alemán Porras and Brooks Vargas, *Bluefields en la sangre*, 13–17; Santos Cermeño, "May Pole in Bluefields," in Alemán Porras and Brooks Vargas, *Bluefields en la sangre*, 20–23. All examples employ the name and the month of May as stylistic representations, for rhythmic and musical purposes, and as a cultural pronouncement of Creole belief and festivity.

32. Alí Aláh, "Pimpóy bailóp," in Obando Sancho, Brooks Saldaña, and Alemán Porras, *Antología poética*, 60–62.

33. Alí Aláh, 62.

34. Valle-Castillo, 46.

35. Valle-Castillo, 20–23, 92–93.

36. Valle-Castillo, 20–23.

37. Valle-Castillo, 21.

38. Santos Cermeño, "May Pole in Bluefields," 21.

39. Santos Cermeño, 20.

40. Santos Cermeño, 93.

41. Santos Cermeño, 156.

42. Santos Cermeño, 156.

43. Santos Cermeño, 77–78.

44. Carlos Alemán Ocampo, "Las lenguas del Caribe Nicaragüense," in *La Costa Caribe nicaragüense: Desde sus orígenes hasta el siglo XXI*, ed. Jorge Eduardo Arellano (Managua: Academia de Geografía e Historia de Nicaragua, 2009), 156.

45. Santos Cermeño, "May Pole in Bluefields," 42–44.

46. Santos Cermeño, 43–44.

47. Carlos Castro Jo, "Raza, conciencia de color y militancia negra en la literatura nicaragüense," *WANI: Una revista sobre la Costa Atlántica* 23 (April–June 2003): 29–30.

48. Castro Jo, 29–30. Edison provides a detailed discussion of Rigby's "Si yo fuera mayo" ("La cultura afro-caribeña," 21–32).

49. McCoy, "Significado del palo de mayo," 133.

50. Valle-Castillo, *Poesía atlántica*, 8–9.

51. Lizandro Chávez Alfaro, introduction to Valle-Castillo, *Poesía atlántica*, 15–16.

52. Lizandro Chávez Alfaro, prologue to Obando Sancho, Brooks Saldaña, and Alemán Porras, *Antología poética*, 11–15.

53. Víctor Obando Sancho, introduction to Alemán Porras and Brooks Vargas, *Bluefields en la sangre*, 3.

54. Alemán Porras and Brooks Vargas, *Bluefields en la sangre*, 5, 7.

55. Brown Hendricks, *Antología poética "Afrocarinica,"* 9.

56. Yolanda Rossman Tejada, "Aquí la palabra es arcoíris: La autonomía multicultural desde la poesía de escritoras costeñas," in *Mujeres en las literaturas indígenas y afrodescendientes en América Central*, ed. Consuelo Meza Márquez and Magda Zavala González (Aguascalientes, Mexico: Universidad Autónoma de Aguascalientes, 2015), 93.

57. Alemán Porras and Brooks Vargas, *Bluefields en la sangre*, 9.

58. Obando Sancho, Brooks Saldaña, and Alemán Porras, *Antología poética*, 99; Irene Vidaurre, "Biografía: Ronald Amadeo Brooks Saldaña (Q.E.P.D.)," in Brown Hendricks, *Antología poética "Afrocarinica,"* 12.

59. Deborah Robb et al., *Leyendas de la Costa Atlántica* (Managua: URACCAN, 2003).

60. Robb et al., 24–26.

61. Robb et al., 26.

62. Robb et al., 27.

63. Robb et al., 29–31.

64. Rossman Tejada, "Aquí la palabra," 92–93.

65. Alemán Porras and Brooks Vargas, *Bluefields en la sangre*; Sonja Stephenson Watson, *The Politics of Race in Panama: Afro-Hispanic and West Indian Literary Discourses of Contention* (Gainesville: University Press of Florida, 2014), 58; Rossman Tejada, "Una aproximación a la autonomía multicultural desde la poesía de escritoras costeñas" (MA thesis, URACCAN, Bilwi, Nicaragua, 2006), 41–42, 46–47; Rossman Tejada, "Aquí la palabra," 83–84; Magda Zavala González, "Para conocer a las poetas afrodescendientes centroamericanas," in Meza Márquez and Zavala González, *Mujeres en las literaturas*, 98–107; Consuelo Meza Márquez, "Memoria, identidad y utopía en la poesía de las escritoras afrocentroamericanas: Relatos de vida," in Meza Márquez and Zavala González, *Mujeres en las literaturas*, 121–22, 143–62. Throughout *Bluefields en la sangre*, Alemán Porras and Brooks Vargas present biographies of the writers that serve as introductions to their poetry.

66. The two monographs are Lillian Thomas Britton and Conrad Monroe Forbes, "Caracterización y análisis de la poesía de la poeta costeña creol Erna Narcisso Watters" (unpublished monograph, URACCAN, Bluefields, Nicaragua, December 2006); and Pedro Chavarria Lezama and Alice Ebanks Narcisso, "Estudio y antología de poetas de Bluefields en el período 1979–1996: Una contribución al conocimiento de la literatura de la Costa Atlántica" (unpublished monograph, UNAM Managua, Bluefields, Nicaragua, July 1997).

67. Dorothy E. Mosby, "'Nuevas nómadas': Negritud y ciudadanía en la literatura centroamericana," *Istmo: Revista virtual de estudios literarios y culturales centroamericanos* 16

(January–June 2008), http://istmo.denison.edu/n16/proyectos/mosby.html (accessed February 17, 2012).

68. Obando Sancho, Brooks Saldaña, and Alemán Porras, *Antología poética*, 19–20.

69. Erna Loraine Narcsiso Walters, "How Much Have You Invested? / ¿Cuánto has invertido?," in Obando Sancho, Brooks Saldaña, and Alemán Porras, *Antología poética*, 33–34.

70. Ileana Vanessa Lacayo Ortiz, "Autonomía," in Obando Sancho, Brooks Saldaña, and Alemán Porras, *Antología poética*, 119–20.

71. Isabel Estrada Colindres, "La fe," in Obando Sancho, Brooks Saldaña, and Alemán Porras, *Antología poética* 69–72.

72. Fermín González López, "La laguna," in Obando Sancho, Brooks Saldaña, and Alemán Porras, *Antología poética*, 77–78.

73. Irene Vidaurre Campos, "Costa Atlántica," in Obando Sancho, Brooks Saldaña, and Alemán Porras, *Antología poética*, 81.

74. Irene Vidaurre Campos, "¡Rica y empobrecida tierra mía!," in Obando Sancho, Brooks Saldaña, and Alemán Porras, *Antología poética*, 83–85.

75. Lesbia González Fornos, "Rondón es también. Pero que bien: ¡Autonomía!," in Alemán Porras and Brooks Vargas, *Bluefields en la sangre*, 59–60; Erna Narciso, "Autonomía," in Alemán Porras and Brooks Vargas, *Bluefields en la sangre*, 63; Lovette Martínez, "Rundown/Rondón," in Alemán Porras and Brooks Vargas, *Bluefields en la sangre*, 106–7; Lovette Martínez, "It Is Autonomy / Es autonomía," in Alemán Porras and Brooks Vargas, *Bluefields en la sangre*, 108–9.

76. Annette Olivia Fenton Tom, "Poem XVI Pearl Lagoon," in Brown Hendricks, *Antología poética "Afrocarinica,"* 64; Brenda Elena Green Wilson, "Nuestra tierra," in Brown Hendricks, *Antología poética "Afrocarinica,"* 76–77.

77. Erna Lorraine Narciso Walters, "Those Good Old Days," Brown Hendricks, *Antología poética "Afrocarinica,"* 44–45.

78. Malespín Jirón, *Bluefields en la memoria*, 48.

79. Brown Hendricks, *Antología poética "Afrocarinica,"* 73, 79.

80. Brown Hendricks, 89, 90, 91–92.

81. Brown Hendricks, 73.

82. Brown Hendricks, 79.

83. Alemán Porras and Brooks Vargas, *Bluefields en la sangre*, 120–22, 129.

84. Alemán Porras and Brooks Vargas, 225–27, 227–30.

85. Alemán Porras and Brooks Vargas, 227–30.

CHAPTER 5 — RITUALS OF *ALEGRÍA* AND *PONCHERA*

1. Arturo Rodríguez-Bobb, *Exclusión e integración del sujeto negro en Cartagena de Indias en perspectiva histórica* (Madrid: Iberoamericana, 2002), 134.

2. Moisés Munive Contreras, "Gozar de su cuerpo: El abuso sexual a las negras esclavas en el Caribe colombiano, Cartagena y Mompox, siglo XVIII," *Historia 02*, http://www.azc.uam .mx/publicaciones/tye/tye16/art_hist_02.html (accessed September 30, 2014; page no longer extant).

3. Nina de Friedemann, "San Basilio en el universo Kilombo-África y Palenque-América," in *Geografía humana de Colombia: Los afrocolombianos*, coord. Luz Adriana and Maya Restrepo, vol. 6 (Bogotá: Instituto Colombiano de Cultura Hispánica, 1998), 82.

4. Francisco Rodríguez, ed., *Palenque de San Basilio: Obra maestra del patrimonio intangible de la humanidad* (Bogotá: Ministerio de Cultura / Instituto Colombiano de Antropología e Historia, 2002), 11, https://repositorio.unicartagena.edu.co/handle/11227/7435 (accessed September 26, 2022).

5. Rodríguez-Bobb, *Exclusión e integración*, 136.

6. Ruth Betty Lozano Lerma, "Mujeres negras (sirvientas, putas, matronas): Una aproximación a la mujer negra en Colombia," *Revista de estudios latinoamericanos* 1, no. 49 (2010): 16, http://www.revistas.una.ac.cr/index.php/tdna/article/view/3720 (accessed March 11, 2010).

7. Peter Wade, *Blackness and Race Mixture: The Dynamics of Racial Identity in Colombia* (Baltimore, Md.: Johns Hopkins University Press, 1993), 87.

8. Francisco Adelmo Asprilla Mosquera, "Los afrodescendientes y el imaginario colectivo," in *La afrocolombianidad: Otra manera de pensar, sentir y valorar la diversidad*, ed. Francisco Adelmo Asprilla Mosquera, Miguel Hernández Valdez, and Vilma María Solano Oliveros (Barranquilla, Colombia: Organización Social de Comunidades Negras Ángela Davis, 2009), 146.

9. "Movimiento Nacional Cimarrón," Movimiento Nacional Cimarrón, http://www .movimientocimarron.org/; Doris Lamus Canavate, "El lugar político de las mujeres en el movimiento negro/afrocolombiano," *Reflexión Política* 10, no. 20 (June 2008): 247, 249–50, 252; Peter Wade, "Cultural Politics of Blackness in Colombia," *American Ethnologist* 22, no. 2 (May 1995): 342–44; Mauricio Pardo, "Iniciativa y cooptación: Tensiones en el movimiento afrocolombiano," in *150 años de la abolición de la esclavización en Colombia: Desde la marginalidad a la construcción de la nación*, ed. Ernesto Restrepo Tirado (Bogotá: Aguilar, 2003), 661–62; David de Ferranti et al., *Inequality in Latin America: Breaking with History?* (Washington, D.C.: World Bank, 2004), 78; Asprilla Mosquera, "Los afrodescendientes," 149; Charo Mina Rojas, *Defeating Invisibility: A Challenge for Afro-descendant Women in Colombia* (Colombia: Afro-descendant Women Human Rights Defender Project, PCN, April 2012), 2–3, http://www.afrocolombians.org/pdfs/Defeating%20Invisibility.pdf (accessed 16 June 2014).

One of two Black movement organizations created in 1970s, the Movimiento Nacional Cimarrón continues to exist, as noted on their website, appearing today as one of many movements while retaining its inspirational role. It can be viewed as groundbreaking and has been a space of activism for women and men, though not without some concerns regarding the lack of women in leadership, a situation that has no doubt inspired women to branch off and form their own movements.

Colombia has the second largest Afro-descendant population in Latin America. Blacks in Colombia today define themselves as Afro-descendants, Afro-Colombians, Blacks, *raizales*, Caribbean, and *palenqueros*, identities that are driven by historical experiences, political constructions, geographical locations, violence, and displacement. They are, broadly speaking, positive perceptions, differing from the prejudicial series of historical expressions bestowed on Africans under European colonization and slavery. The condition of *desplazamiento* [displacement] as a result of the ongoing violence connected with guerrilla warfare and the drug war has also become a marker of Afro-Colombianness.

10. Lucía Ortiz, "*Chambacú, corral de negros* de Manuel Zapata Olivella, un capítulo en la lucha por la libertad: *In memoriam*," *Inti: Revista de literatura hispánica*, nos. 63–64 (Spring–Fall 2006): 95–96.

11. Dorina Hernández, "Dorina Hernández," in *El despertar de las comunidades afrocolombianas*, ed. María Inés Martínez (Houston: LACASA, Centro de Investigaciones Sociales, 2012), 61–62.

12. Wade, *Blackness and Race Mixture*, 87–88.

13. Katherine Joy McKnight, "Elder, Slave, and Soldier: Maroon Voices from the Palenque del Limón, 1634," in *Afro-Latino Voices: Narratives from the Early Modern Ibero-Atlantic World, 1550–1812*, ed. Kathryn Joy McKnight and Leo J. Garofalo (Indianapolis: Hackett, 2009), 65.

14. Rodríguez-Bobb, *Exclusión e integración*, 133–34; Manuel Zapata Olivella, "Palenque, primer territorio libre de América," *Mundo*, June 20, 2007, 18; Teresa Cassiani Herrera and Rutsely Simarra Obeso, "Aproximaciones a la realidad de la mujer afro, construyendo el camino hacia una sólida proyección étnica, de género y cultural," *Tumbutú: Revista científica del sistema de investigación del Instituto Manuel Zapata Olivella* 3, no. 2 (July 2015): 49–60; Anthony McFarlane, "*Cimarrones* and *palenques*: Runaways and Resistance in Colonial Colombia," *Slavery & Abolition* 6, no. 3 (1985): 133.

The above authors study the phenomenon's early rise from about the late sixteenth century and expansion to the level of civil war by the eighteenth century. They confirm the *palenque* phenomenon as a constant pattern within the history of the nation. McFarlane comments that the high level of organized resistance forced Spanish authorities to recognize one powerful group of maroons that later became Palenque de San Basilio (*"Cimarrones* and *palenques,"* 135). He also confirms that while most maroons tend to be men, women (and children) have always been part of this phenomenon of resistance (141). Zapata Olivella identifies Benkos Biohó as a warrior who attacked the plantations, freeing men, women, and children. He credits their survival and longevity to the extensive secret networks they established, such as in ports, on boats, and with traffickers and pirates—this in spite of their location in the deep forest. Indeed, he confirms that enslaved women disobeyed authorities and sustained commercial ties with contrabandists and pirates despite the criminalization of commerce by slaves at the time ("Palenque, primer territorio libre," 19–20, 26).

15. Elisabeth Cunin, *Identidades a flor de piel: Lo "negro" entre apariencias y pertenencias; Mestizaje y categorías raciales en Cartagena (Colombia)* (Bogotá: IFEA-ICANH-Uniandes-Observatorio del Caribe Colombiano, 2003), 234, https://halshs.archives-ouvertes.fr/halshs -00291675 (accessed January 17, 2014).

16. Cunin, 235–36; Nina de Friedemann, *Ma Ngombe: Guerreros y ganaderos en palenque* (Bogotá: Carlos Valencia, 1987), 47–48; Nina de Friedemann and Carlos Patiño Rosselli, *Lengua y sociedad en el Palenque de San Basilio* (Bogotá: Instituto Caro y Cuervo, 1983), 37. De Friedemann attributes this designation of being the first free town to Roberto Arrázola, a member of the Academia de Historia de Cartagena who, in 1970, published a compilation of historical documents dating back to 1603–1799 under the title *Palenque, primer pueblo libre de América.* The documents were taken from the Archivo General de Indias in Seville and told the history of the *palenques,* rebellious Blacks, and their struggles under colonial rule in the province of Cartagena de Indias.

17. Rodríguez, *Palenque de San Basilio,* 11–13; Doris Lamus Canavate, "Relatos de vida de mujeres palenqueras en organizaciones del Caribe colombiano," in *Hijas de Muntu: Biografías críticas de mujeres afrodescendientes de América Latina,* ed. María Mercedes Jaramillo and Lucía Ortiz (Bogotá: Panamericana, 2011), 230; Juana Pabla Pérez Tejedor, "The Role of the Palenge Language in the Transmission of Afro-Palenquero Cultural Heritage," *Museum International* 60, no. 3 (2008): 71, http://www.academia.edu/6547529/The_Role_of_the_Palenge_Language _in_the_Transmission_of_Afro-Palenquero_Cultural_Heritage (accessed August 9, 2015); de Friedemann, "San Basilio," 85–86.

18. Hernández, "Dorina Hernández," 99.

19. Wade, *Blackness and Race Mixture,* 82.

20. Wade, 88.

21. Muteti Andrew Kyalo, "La comprensión de la muerte y de la vida eterna de los palenque-ros de San Basilio" (thesis, Pontificia Universidad Javeriana, Bogotá, Colombia, 2013), 19, 23–24; Clara Inés Guerrero García, "Memorias palenqueras de la libertad," Universidad Nacional de Colombia Digital Repositorio Institucional, 2013, https://repositorio.unal.edu .co/handle/unal/2862 (accessed September 26, 2022); Claudia Mosquera, Mauricio Pardo, and Odile Hoffmann, "Las trayectorias sociales e identitarias de los afrodescendientes," in *Afrodescendientes en las Américas: 150 años de la abolición de la esclavitud en Colombia,* ed. Claudia Mosquera, Mauricio Pardo, and Odile Hoffmann (Cartagena, Colombia: Universidad Nacional de Colombia, 2002), 40.

22. Guerrero García, "Memorias palenqueras," 379.

23. Cunin, *Identidades a flor,* 210.

24. Cunin, 209–10, 248.

25. María Mercedes Jaramillo, "María Teresa Ramírez: Heredera de Yemayá y Changó," in *Mabungú triunfo: Poemas bilingües, palenque-español,* 3rd ed., ed. María Teresa Ramírez (Bogotá: Apidama Ediciones, 2013), 8.

26. Cunin, *Identidades a flor,* 235.

27. Rodríguez, *Palenque de San Basilio,* 11–12.

28. Omar H. Ali, "Benkos Biohó: African Maroon Leadership in New Granada," in *Atlantic Biographies: Individuals and Peoples in the Atlantic World,* ed. Jeffrey A. Fortin and Mark Meuwese (Boston, Mass.: Brill, 2014), 263, 265–66.

29. Fabio Teolindo Perea Hinestroza, *Diccionario afrocolombiano: Afrorregionalismos, afroamericanismos y elementos de africanidad* (Chocó, Colombia: Corporación Autónoma Regional para el Desarrollo Sostenible del Chocó, 1996), 96.

30. Perea Hinestroza, 21; Zapata Olivella, "Palenque, primer territorio libre," 23; Guerrero García, "Memorias palenqueras," 367.

31. Zapata Olivella, "Palenque, primer territorio libre," 23.

32. Guerrero García, "Memorias palenqueras," 367. De Friedemann recounts these historical events in a narrative that seems to blend history and myth, resulting from her early anthropological investigations (*Ma Ngombe*, 46).

33. Cunin, *Identidades a flor*, 236.

34. Perea Hinestroza, *Diccionario afrocolombiano*, 20.

35. De Friedemann, *Ma Ngombe*, 43–49.

36. De Friedemann, 47–48.

37. De Friedemann, 43.

38. Natalia Silva Prada, "Leonor: Una reina palenquera de la gobernación de Cartagena de Indias," *Los reinos de las Indias en el Nuevo Mundo* (blog), April 9, 2013, https://losreinosdelasindias.hypotheses.org/559 (accessed September 26, 2022).

39. Ministerio de Cultura, "Polonia, heroína palenquera," in *Historias matrias: Mujeres negras en la historia* (Colombia: Ministerio de Cultura, República de Colombia), 3, https://www.mincultura.gov.co/SiteAssets/documentos/poblaciones/Mujeres%20negras%20en%20la%20historia.pdf (accessed March 8, 2014).

40. Perea Hinestroza, *Diccionario afrocolombiano*, 4, 28.

41. Cassiani Herrera and Simarra Obeso, "Aproximaciones a la realidad," 49.

42. Cunin, *Identidades a flor*, 224.

43. Ramiro Delgado et al., *Proceso de identificación y recomendaciones de salvaguardia (PIRS) de las manifestaciones asociadas al espacio de San Basilio de Palenque* (Cartagena de Indias, Colombia: Ministerio de Cultura, December 2007), http://www.google.es/?gws_rd=sslq=Proceso+de+identificaci%C3%B3n+y+recomendaciones+de+salvaguardia++%28PIRS%29 (accessed July 7, 2014).

44. Kyalo, "La comprensión," 20–21; Rafaela Vos Obeso, "La mujer en el Palenque de San Basilio," *Revista chichamaya* 2, no. 8 (July 24, 2012): 11, https://repositorio.unal.edu.co/handle/unal/54307 (accessed September 26, 2022).

45. Claudia Mosquera Rosero-Labbé, "La memoria del cimarronaje como patrimonio: Reparación simbólica para los afrocolombianos habitantes de San Basilio de Palenque," *Anaconda* 20 (May 2006): 18, http://www.google.es/?gws_rd=sslq=La+memoria+del+cimarronaje+como+patrimonio:++reparaci%C3%B3n+simb%C3%B3lica+ (accessed May 27, 2015).

46. Hernández, "Dorina Hernández," 56.

47. Maguemati Wabgou et al., *Movimiento social afrocolombiano, negro, raizal y palenquero* (Bogotá: Universidad Nacional de Colombia, 2012), 53–60; Hernández, "Dorina Hernández," 56; Rodríguez, *Palenque de San Basilio*, 26–27; Lamus Canavate, "Relatos de vida," 242. See above sources for analyses of historical notions of *cimarronaje* and organized freedom struggles as fundamental to the modern systems of Black activism today in Colombia.

48. Hernández, "Dorina Hernández," 57.

49. Mosquera, Pardo, and Hoffmann, "Las trayectorias sociales," 15.

50. Hernández, "Dorina Hernández," 57.

51. María Inés Martínez, preface to Martínez, *El despertar*, 37.

52. Hernández, "Dorina Hernández," 61, 63–64.

53. Los vecinos, "Palenquerita grito de alegría con coco y anís," April 4, 2015, YouTube video, 0:00:27, https://www.youtube.com/watch?v=10govXC--pc (accessed November 11, 2015); Kucha Suto Colectivo, "Las alegrías de las palenqueras," December 6, 2012, YouTube video, 0:10:00, https://www.youtube.com/watch?v=bG8xAYMuHu8 (accessed November 11, 2015). A song or cry of street vendors presenting their produce to passersby.

54. Cunin, *Identidades a flor*, 178.

55. Roshini Kempadoo, *Creole in the Archive: Imagery, Presence and the Location of the Caribbean Figure* (London: Rowman & Littlefield, 2016), 55.

56. "Monumento a las Palenqueras: Escultura en bronce de Hernando Pereira Brieva," Panoramio, http://www.panoramio.com/photo/4693537 (accessed March 11, 2010); Jerly Calvo Licero, "Palenqueras de Cartagena tendrán la oportunidad de crear una cooperativa para su bienestar," Fundación Paz por Colombia, http://www.pazporcolombia.org/article.php?sid=77 (accessed March 11, 2010; page no longer extant); "Homenaje a las palenqueras," Fundación Paz por Colombia, http://www.pazporcolombia.org/article.php?sid=45 (accessed March 11, 2010; page no longer extant).

57. Cynthia de Simone, "Palenqueras: Las vendedoras ambulantes más fotografiadas del Caribe," todoparaviajar.com, February 6, 2012, https://todoparaviajar.com/noticia/palenqueras-las-vendedoras-ambulantes-mas-fotografiadas-del-caribe- (accessed August 5, 2014).

58. Doris Lamus Canavate, "Negras, palenqueras y afrocartageneras: Construyendo un lugar contra la exclusión y la discriminación," *Reflexión Política* 12, no. 23 (June 2010): 235, http://revistas.unab.edu.co/index.php?journal=reflexion&page=article&op=view&path[]=926 (accessed February 4, 2014).

59. Mirian Díaz Pérez, conversation with the author, June 22, 2015.

60. Lozano Lerma, "Mujeres negras," 17.

61. Cunin, *Identidades a flor*, 179.

62. Yadmilla Bauzá-Vargas, "'Yo lo que sé de Catalina Loango . . .': Orality and Gender in the Caribbean" (PhD diss., University at Buffalo, Buffalo, N.Y., 1997), 46.

63. Bauzá-Vargas, 43.

64. Díaz Pérez, conversation; Ministerio de Cultura, "Todos los colores caben en nosotras: Palenqueras en Cartagena," in Ministerio de Cultura, *Historias matrias*, 15–16. Official state-sanctioned appropriation is evident in textual productions by the Ministry of Culture that tend to promote this cultural image, embedded in its discourse of Cartagena as tropical paradise and tourist destination.

65. "¡Yo soy afrocolombiana, soy promotora de paz!," *Palenques*, January 2014, 1. The trend of using the Afro-descendant subject as a tool for promoting discourses of peace and reconciliation is popular in the Black movement and within government entities.

66. "Homenaje a las palenqueras"; "En una calle de Cartagena: Palenqueras," *Espíritu naif* (blog), March 2013, http://espiritunaif.blogspot.com/2013/03/en-una-calle-de-cartagena-Palenqueras-3.html (accessed August 5, 2014); Rolando Alvarado, "Palenquera del Pacífico," Artelista, February 23, 2008, http://www.artelista.com/obra/2001121594272083-Palenqueradelpacifico.html (accessed August 5, 2014); Santiago Pinto Vega, *Las canoas del viento* (Bogotá: Instituto San Pablo Apostol, 2000).

67. Nadia V. Celis, "Bailando el Caribe: Corporalidad, identidad y ciudadanía en las plazas de Cartagena de Indias," *Caribbean Studies* 41, no. 1 (January–June 2013): 37. Celis mentions the sexualization of native bodies as part of the exoticism of colonially imposed discourses describing these tropical spaces that constitute the Caribbean. They continue today at the service and entertainment of visitors.

68. Cunin, *Identidades a flor*, 180.

69. Bauzá-Vargas, "'Yo lo que sé,'" 43.

70. From June to August 2013, I traveled to Nigeria. The marketplace was one of the many sites I visited repeatedly, and while there, I observed the phenomenon of these vendors who sold goods but also offered their services carrying loads that they artfully balanced on their heads.

71. Bauzá-Vargas, "'Yo lo que sé,'" 44.

72. De Friedemann and Patiño Rosselli, *Lengua y sociedad*, 21.

73. De Simone, "Palenqueras."

74. Alfonso Cassiani, "Las comunidades renacientes de la Costa Caribe continental," in Mosquera, Pardo, and Hoffmann, *Afrodescendientes en las Américas*, 580.

75. Rodríguez, *Palenque de San Basilio*, 19, 22.

76. Cassiani, "Las comunidades renacientes," 580.

77. Lamus Canavate, "Negras, palenqueras y afrocartageneras," 160.

78. Hernández, "Dorina Hernández," 64.

79. Hernández, 65.

80. Cunin, *Identidades a flor*, 238.

81. Calvo Licero, "Palenqueras de Cartagena," 1–2; Lamus Canavate, "Negras, palenqueras y afrocartageneras," 160–61.

82. Bauzá-Vargas confirms that these women have always organized themselves into business entities. She refers to an entity called the Microempresa Catalina Loango [Catalina Loango Microenterprise] belonging to a group of Palenquera vendors from the Mequejo neighborhood in Barranquilla ("'Yo lo que sé,'" 41).

83. Celis, "Bailando el Caribe," 32.

84. Rojas, *Defeating Invisibility*, 10; de Ferranti et al., *Inequality in Latin America*, 77–84.

85. Mosquera Rosero-Labbé, "La memoria del cimarronaje," 19–20.

86. Lamus Canavate, "Negras, palenqueras y afrocartageneras," 154, 157–58. Hernández also talks about her personal experiences and the racism she faced while holding public office. She presents the ongoing discrimination facing Black women in public venues such as beauty contests and discos ("Dorina Hernández," 105–7).

87. Hernández, "Dorina Hernández," 99–100.

88. Simarra Obeso, "La lengua palenquera: Una experiencia cosmovisionaria, significativa y creativa de los palenqueros descendientes de la diáspora africana en Colombia," *Revista anaconda*, https://www.humanas.unal.edu.co/colantropos/files/6914/7330/4008/Lengua_palenquera _Simarra.pdf (accessed September 26, 2022); Hernández, "Dorina Hernández," 105; Vos Obeso, "La mujer," 10–13; Dimas del Rosario de Ávila Torres and Rutsely Simarra Obeso, "*Ma-kuagro*: Elemento de la cultura palenquera y su incidencia en las prácticas pedagógicas en la Escuela San Basilio Palenque, Colombia," *Ciencia e interculturalidad* 11, no. 2 (July–December 2012): 88–99, http://www.lamjol.info/index.php/RCI/article/view/961 (accessed January 19, 2014); Rutsely Simarra Obeso, "Lengua ri Palenge: Suto tan chitiá / La lengua de Palenque: Contexto lingüístico, histórico y comunicativo," in *Las mujeres afrodescendientes y la cultura latino-americana: Identidad y desarrollo*, ed. Silvia Beatriz García Savino (Ciudad del Saber, Panama: Proyecto Regional "Población afrodescendiente de América Latina" del PNUD, 2009), 45–53; Lamus Canavate, "Relatos de vida," 231–34, 239.

89. Lamus Canavate, "Relatos de vida," 235; Lamus Canavate, "Negras, palenqueras y afro-cartageneras," 160.

90. Hernández, "Dorina Hernández," 100.

91. Hernández, 100.

92. Lamus Canavate, "Negras, palenqueras y afrocartageneras," 160.

93. Hernández, "Dorina Hernández," 100.

94. Hernández, 101.

95. Hernández, 69.

96. Hernández, 69–70.

97. Celis refers to the "Other denied," finding in her research on the topic two main targets, the India Catalina and the *palenquera* ("Bailando el Caribe," 38–39).

98. Hernández, "Dorina Hernández," 87.

99. Hernández, 54.

100. Pérez Tejedor, "Role of the Palenge," 76–77.

101. Dilia Robinson de Saavedra, "La política de etnoeducación afrocolombiana," in *I foro nacional de etnoeducación afrocolombiana*, ed. Ministerio de Educación Nacional (Bogotá: Ministerio de Educación Nacional, Imprenta Nacional, 2004), 13–14; Hernández, "Dorina Hernández," 54; Dorina Hernández Palomino, "La etnoeducación afrocolombiana: Elementos para la construcción de las experiencias institucionales-comunitarias," in Restrepo Tirado, *150 años*, 58–68; Dorina Hernández Palomino, preface to *Lengua ri Palenge: Jende suto ta chitiá; Léxico de la lengua palenquera*, comp. Rutsely Simarra Obeso, Regina Miranda Reyes, and Juana Pabla Pérez Tejedor (Cartagena, Colombia: Casa Editorial, 2008), 23–26; Wabgou

et al., *Movimiento social afrocolombiano*, 157–70, 211–12; Rubén Hernández C., "Identidad cultural palenquera, movimiento social afrocolombiano y democracia," *Reflexión Política* 16, no. 31 (June 2014): 107–8, http://www.redalyc.org/articulo.oa?id=11031312009 (accessed November 23, 2014); Mosquera, Pardo, and Hoffmann, "Las trayectorias sociales," 17–18; Kwame Dixon, "Transnational Black Social Movements in Latin America: Afro-Colombians and the Struggle for Human Rights," in *Latin American Social Movements in the Twenty-First Century: Resistance, Power, and Democracy*, ed. Richard Stahler-Sholk, Harry E. Vanden, and Glen David Kueker (Lanham, Md.: Rowman & Littlefield, 2008), 190–95.

Hernández Palomino has spoken extensively on the *Palenquera*'s condition and the effects of ethnoeducation on her community. The opening statement of Law 70, dated August 27, 1993, also known as the Ley de Comunidades Negras [Law of Black Communities], reads,

La presente ley tiene por objeto reconocer a las comunidades negras que han venido ocupando tierras baldías en las zonas rurales ribereñas de los ríos de la Cuenca del Pacífico, de acuerdo con sus prácticas tradicionales de producción, el derecho a la propiedad colectiva, de conformidad con lo dispuesto en los artículos siguientes. Así mismo tiene como propósito establecer mecanismos para la protección de la identidad cultural y de los derechos de las comunidades negras de Colombia como grupo étnico, y el fomento de su desarrollo económico y social, con el fin de garantizar que estas comunidades obtengan condiciones reales de igualdad de oportunidades frente al resto de la sociedad colombiana.

[The present law has as its objective to recognize the Black communities that occupy barren lands in the coastal, rural zones along the rivers in Cuenca del Pacífico, in accordance with their traditional methods of production, the right to collective property, in conformity with the following articles. Likewise, it has as its objective to establish mechanisms for the protection of the cultural identity and rights of the Black communities of Colombia as an ethnic group and the encouragement of their social and economic development, with the aim of guaranteeing that these communities obtain real conditions of equality of opportunity in relation to the rest of Colombian society.]

102. Hernández C., "Identidad cultural palenquera," 107.

103. Hernández, "Dorina Hernández," 67–68.

104. Hernández, 68.

105. Hernández, 67.

106. Del Rosario de Ávila Torres and Simarra Obeso, "*Ma-kuagro*," 9; Delgado et al., *Proceso de identificación*, 5–8; Nina de Friedemann and Jaime Arocha, "Colombia," in *No Longer Visible: Afro-Latin Americans Today*, ed. Minority Rights Group (London: Minority Rights Publication, 1995), 55; de Friedemann, "San Basilio," 85–86; Hernández C., "Identidad cultural palenquera," 96–98; John Lipski, *A History of Afro-Hispanic Language: Five Centuries, Five Continents* (Cambridge: Cambridge University Press, 2005), 235–40, 270–72; John Lipski, "Free at Last: From Bound Morpheme to Discourse Marker in Lengua ri Palenge (Palenquero Creole Spanish)," *Anthropological Linguistics* 54, no. 2 (Summer 2012): 101.

The *kuagro* (also spelled *cuagro*) is one of the legacies inherited from the days when the *palenques* were communities of maroons. It refers to a kind of brotherhood or sisterhood, a social group united under some kind of allegiance to life. The history of *palenques* confirms ritual battles or war games between *kuagros* as a way of allowing the communities to be warrior-ready. Today, they continue as a symbolic gesture and a way of sustaining a sense of community among *palenqueros*. They serve to defend their territory, offer support in times of difficulty, and maintain and consolidate cultural practices. The *kuagro* secures their language; burial rituals; traditional practices of production, gastronomy, and performance; storytelling traditions; and traditional medicine. Lipski is renowned for the depth and breadth of his linguistic research on the *palenquero* language.

107. Hernández C. and Guerrero García use the term *kuagro* to identify the male group and *cuadrillera* for the female group. See Hernández C., "Identidad cultural palenquera,"

96; and Clara Inés Guerrero García, "Memoria sagrada y espiritualidad en palenque," *La Revista* 3, 2013, https://laparada.uniandes.edu.co/index.php/la-revista/la-revista-3/los-tesos/la-otra-orilla-de-palenque (accessed October 27, 2014).

108. Rodríguez, *Palenque de San Basilio*, 32.

109. Delgado et al., *Proceso de identificación*, 6.

110. Rodríguez, *Palenque de San Basilio*, 33.

111. Pérez Tejedor, "Role of the Palenge," 73.

112. Pérez Tejedor, 62.

113. Pérez Tejedor, 33.

114. Delgado et al., *Proceso de identificación*, 6-7.

115. Hernández, "Dorina Hernández," 58-59; de Friedemann, "San Basilio," 85-86; de Friedemann and Patiño Rosselli, *Lengua y sociedad*, 50.

116. Hernández, "Dorina Hernández," 60.

117. Lamus Canavate, "Relatos de vida," 240.

118. This declaration was located on a poster found outside of the entity's headquarters in Cartagena.

119. Hernández C., "Identidad cultural palenquera," 102-3; Dixon, "Transnational Black Social Movements," 186-89, 191-92; Lamus Canavate, "Relatos de vida," 236-40; Lamus Canavate, "Negras, palenqueras y afrocartageneras," 159.

120. Lamus Canavate, "Relatos de vida," 241; Lamus Canavate, "Negras, palenqueras y afrocartageneras," 159. This is a fertility dance performed only by women that involves drums, hand-clapping, choral chanting, and singing. It is a ritual dance particularly performed when young women reach puberty.

121. Lamus Canavate, "Relatos de vida," 237-38.

122. Guerrero García, "Memorias palenqueras," 384.

123. *Asociación de mujeres afrodescendientes y del Caribe Graciela Cha-Ines*, pamphlet (Cartagena, Colombia: Asociación de mujeres afrodescendientes y del Caribe Graciela Cha-Ines, 2010); Hernández, "Dorina Hernández," 57.

124. Mosquera, Pardo, and Hoffmann, "Las trayectorias sociales," 39; Jaime Arocha, "Inclusion of Afro-Colombians: Unreachable National Goal?," *Latin American Perspectives* 25, no. 3 (May 1998): 80; Lamus Canavate, "Relatos de vida," 238; Lozano Lerma and Bibiana del Carmen Peñaranda Sepúlveda, "Memoria y reparación ¿Y de ser mujeres negras qué?" (presentation at the Seminario GEAS-CES, Cartagena de Indias, Colombia, October 18-20, 2005), 2, http://www.scribd.com/doc/19184719/memoria-y-reparacion-y-las-mujeres-negras-que (accessed October 9, 2014). The vulnerability of Afro-descendants to violence is well recorded. Situations include forced displacement from their lands, the seizing of ancestral territories, genocide, the imposition of hegemonic development, the destruction of their culture and nature, the debilitating effects of globalization, and crippling poverty.

125. Pérez Tejedor, "Role of the Palenge," 75. See also "Muere a los 83 años la artista del folclor colombiano Graciela Salgado," *El país*, September 14, 2013, https://www.elpais.com.co/entretenimiento/cultura/muere-a-los-83-anos-la-artista-del-folclor-colombiano-graciela-salgado.html (accessed September 26, 2022); Liliana Martínez Polo, "Nueve noches de lumbalú para Graciela Salgado," *El tiempo*, September 15, 2013, http://www.eltiempo.com/archivo/documento/CMS-13063819 (accessed October 6, 2014); Liliana Valencia, "Niñas palenqueras recuperan la tradición de las cantadoras: Liliana Valencia informa," May 19, 2013, YouTube video, 0:01:31, http://www.youtube.com/watch?v=f9tjOLbkYWA (accessed September 30, 2014).

126. Information taken from the Graciela Cha-Inés Association's pamphlet I received during my visit to their headquarters in Cartagena in March 2010. Additional details in Lozano Lerma and Peñaranda Sepúlveda, "Memoria y reparación," 1-8; Wabgou et al., *Movimiento social afrocolombiano*, 198, 201-3; and Lamus Canavate, "Negras, palenqueras y afrocartageneras," 157.

127. Cassiani, "Las comunidades renacientes," 580.

128. Lamus Canavate, "Negras, palenqueras y afrocartageneras," 158.

129. Rodríguez, *Palenque de San Basilio*, 16; Guerrero García, "Memorias palenqueras," 373-74.

130. Rodríguez, *Palenque de San Basilio*, 34; Pérez Tejedor, "Role of the Palenge," 74; Kyalo, "La comprensión," 35–38.

131. Delgado et al., *Proceso de identificación*, 8–14, 16–21; Guerrero García, "Memorias palenqueras," 373–74. Delgado et al. detail the various stages of the ritual and the manner in which it is sustained over time. They discuss the origins of the word, the value and meaning of the chants, the African legacy of the ceremony, and its current state.

132. Guerrero García, "Memorias palenqueras," 373–74.

133. Armin Schwegler, *"Chi ma 'kongo'": Lengua y rito ancestrales en el Palenque de San Basilio (Colombia)*, 2 vols. (Frankfurt: Vervuert Verlag, 1996), 3.

134. Rodríguez, *Palenque de San Basilio*, 35.

135. Schwegler, *"Chi ma 'kongo,'"* 58.

136. Rodríguez, *Palenque de San Basilio*, 32.

137. Schwegler, *"Chi ma 'kongo,'"* 145.

138. De Friedemann, *Ma Ngombe*, 91.

139. Schwegler has produced comprehensive linguistic studies about the *lumbalú* chants. This chant is shorter; however, he fully analyzes another called "Chimbumbe," as it more closely relates to the Catalina Loango myth (*"Chi ma 'kongo,'"* 582–93).

140. Schwegler, 178.

141. Rodríguez, *Palenque de San Basilio*, 32; de Friedemann and Arocha, "Colombia," 55–56.

142. De Friedemann, *Ma Ngombe*, 91.

143. Rodríguez, *Palenque de San Basilio*, 39.

144. Bauzá-Múscolo, "La leyenda de Catalina Loango," *Revista trimestral de estudios literarios* 7, no. 31 (October–December 2007): 1–3, https://www.scribd.com/document/480282835/CATALINA-LOANGO (accessed February 7, 2015).

145. Guerrero García, "Memoria sagrada y espiritualidad"; Teresa Saldarriaga, prod., *La tía Cato* (San Basilio de Palenque, Colombia: Yuma Vídeo Cine, 1994), documentary, 25 min., https://www.youtube.com/watch?v=jlIicgKm86k (accessed September 26, 2022).

146. Consult the *palenquero* singing, Palenque Records, "Chimbumbe—Graciela Salgado & Alegres Ambulancias," September 6, 2012, YouTube video, 0:03:42, https://www.youtube.com/watch?v=_VTcEleFyv8 (accessed August 5, 2015); Antonio Coello, *Chimbumbe* (Mexico: La Sombra Negra Producciones, 2008), http://www.obsidianatv.com/video/35/chimbumbe (accessed August 12, 2015).

147. Guerrero García, "Memoria sagrada y espiritualidad."

148. Bauzá-Vargas, "'Yo lo que sé,'" 55–59.

149. Hernández, "Dorina Hernández," 86.

150. Other versions of the myth are available in Schwegler, *"Chi ma 'kongo,'"* 582–83; and Rodríguez, *Palenque de San Basilio*, 30–31.

151. Bauzá-Vargas, "'Yo lo que sé,'" vi, 115.

152. Bauzá-Vargas, 51.

153. Bauzá-Vargas, vi.

154. Bauzá-Vargas, 43–48.

155. Bauzá-Vargas, 22, 113.

CHAPTER 6 — PALENQUERA WRITINGS

1. Margarita Krakusin, "Cuerpo y texto: El espacio femenino en la cultura afrocolombiana en María Teresa Ramírez, Mary Grueso Romero, Edela Zapata Pérez y Amalia Lú Posso Figueroa," in *"Chambacú, la historia la escribes tú": Ensayos sobre cultura afro-colombiana*, ed. Lucía Ortiz (Madrid: Iberoamericana, 2007), 198.

2. Laurence Prescott, "Perfil histórico del autor afrocolombiano: Problemas y perspectivas," *América negra* 12 (December 1996): 115–16; Laurence Prescott, "Evaluando el pasado, forjando el futuro: Estado y necesidades de la literatura afro-colombiana," *Revista iberoamericana* 65, nos. 188–89 (July–December 1999): 559; Francineide Santos Palmeira, "Escritoras na literatura afrocolombiana," *Estudios de literatura colombiana* 32 (January–June 2013): 91.

3. Guiomar Cuesta Escobar and Alfredo Ocampo Zamorano, comps., ¡Negras somos! Antología de 21 mujeres poetas afrocolombianas de la región Pacífica (Bogotá: Apidama Ediciones, 2013); Alfredo Ocampo Zamorano and Guiomar Cuesta Escobar, comps., Antología de mujeres poetas afrocolombianas, vol. 16 (Bogotá: Ministerio de Cultura, 2010).

4. Mónica María del Valle Idárraga, "Escenario edénico y naturaleza prístina en Sail Ahoy!!! ¡Vela a la vista!, y The Spirit of Persistence de Hazel Robinson Abrahams: Dos formas de recuperar una isla colonizada," Estudios de literatura colombiana 28 (January–June 2011): 22, http://aprendeenlinea.udea.edu.co/revistas/index.php/elc/article/view/10931/10006 (accessed July 9, 2014).

5. Germán Romero Vargas, Historia de la Costa Atlántica (Managua: CIDCA-UCA, 1996), 149.

6. Santos Palmeira, "Escritoras na literatura afrocolombiana," 88.

7. Santos Palmeira, 90.

8. Alain Lawo-Sukam, "Mary Grueso Romero y María Elcina Córdoba: Poetas de la identidad afro-colombiana," in Hijas de Muntu: Biografías críticas de mujeres afrodescendientes de América Latina, ed. María Mercedes Jaramillo and Lucía Ortiz (Bogotá: Panamericana, 2011), 170–71; María Mercedes Jaramillo, "María Teresa Ramírez y María de los Ángeles Popov: Herederas de Yemayá y de Changó," in Jaramillo and Ortiz, Hijas de Muntu, 191.

9. Santos Palmeira, "Escritoras na literatura afrocolombiana," 91.

10. Francineide Santos Palmeira, "Escritoras negras na América Latina" (presentation given at the XI Congresso Luso-Afro-Brasileiro de Ciências Sociais, Salvador, Bahia, Brazil, August 7–10, 2011), 5–6, http://www.google.es/?gws_rd=sslq=Escritoras+negras+na+Am %C3%A9rica+Latina (accessed January 22, 2015); Santos Palmeira, "Escritoras na literatura afrocolombiana," 92.

11. In 1996, Prescott was able to identify seven women writers of certain prominence even as their names never appeared in national literary historiographies ("Perfil histórico del autor," 115).

12. She has published under different names: Elcina Valencia, María Elcina Valencia, Elcina Valencia Córdoba, and María Elcina Valencia Córdoba.

13. Grueso Romero also produced the CD Mi gente, mi tierra y mi mar (Manizales, Colombia: Hoyos Editores, 2003).

14. Clara Inés Guerrero García, "Memorias palenqueras de la libertad," Universidad Nacional de Colombia Digital Repositorio Institucional, 2013, https://repositorio.unal.edu.co/handle/unal/2862 (accessed September 26, 2022).

15. Dorina Hernández discusses the long-term impact of negative perceptions of the palenquero language and how they were able to reverse that trend through education in the palenques and in broader society. Hernández, "Dorina Hernández," in El despertar de las comunidades afrocolombianas, ed. María Inés Martínez (Houston: LACASA, Centro de Investigaciones Sociales, 2012), 77–78, 83–85. Rutsely Simarra Obeso, Regina Miranda Reyes, and Juana Pabla Pérez Tejedor, comps., Lengua ri Palenge: Jende suto ta chitiá; Léxico de la lengua palenquera (Cartagena, Colombia: Casa Editorial, 2008), is one of various dictionary projects being conducted by palenquera women writers and linguists.

16. Guerrero García, "Memorias palenqueras," 381.

17. Prescott presents Sebastián Salgado Cásseres as one of the first contemporary palenquero writers to publish an anthology. Bajo un son de tambores came out in 1982. In 2011, Pérez Miranda published Chitieno lengua ku ma kuendo: Hablemos palenquero a través del cuento (Prescott, "Perfil histórico del autor," 117).

18. Ereilis Navarro Cáceres produced a calendar of poetry and Black hairstyles for women. She is the author (along with José Pallares Vega and Edy Luz Navarro Cásseres) of Origen y resistencia de los peinados afrodescendientes como estrategia pedagógica (Barranquilla, Colombia: Todo Arte Publicidad, 2014). In 2001, Solmery Cásseres Estrada published an anthology, Mis recuerdos (Cartagena de Indias, Colombia: Pluma de Mompox, 2001). Her poetry is also available in Ocampo Zamorano and Cuesta Escobar, Antología de mujeres.

19. Mirian Díaz Pérez, "Diccionario de la lengua afro-palenquera," El universal, August 15, 2010, http://www.eluniversal.com.co/suplementos/dominical/diccionario-de-la-lengua-afro-palenquera (accessed May 28, 2017).

20. Simarra Obeso, Miranda Reyes, and Pérez Tejedor, *Lengua ri Palenge.*

21. Águeda Pizarro Rayo, introduction to Ramírez, *La noche de mi piel*, by María Teresa Ramírez (Roldanillo Valle, Colombia: Ediciones Embalaje del Museo Rayo, 1988), xii.

22. María Teresa Ramírez, *Flor de palenque* (Bogotá: Artes Gráficas del Valle, 2008), 19–22; Pizarro Rayo, introduction, xii; Águeda Pizarro Rayo, prologue to Ramírez, *Flor de palenque*, 12; Águeda Pizarro Rayo, "María Teresa Ramírez—Almanegra: Abalenga," in *Abalenga*, by María Teresa Rámirez (Roldanillo Valle, Colombia: Museo Rayo, 2008), xii.

23. Ramírez, *Flor de palenque*, 16.

24. Jaramillo and Ortiz, *Hijas de Muntu*, 192; María Mercedes Jaramillo, "María Teresa Ramírez: Heredera de Yemayá y Changó," in *Mabungú triunfo: Poemas bilingües, palenque-español*, 3rd ed., ed. María Teresa Ramírez (Bogotá: Apidama, 2013), 19.

25. Ramírez, *Flor de palenque*, 43.

26. Secretaría de Cultura y Turismo de Cali, *Poemas matriax: Antología de poetas afrocolombianas* (Cali, Colombia: Artes Gráficas del Valle, 2012), 17; María Teresa Ramírez, conversation with the author, June 28, 2015. Ramírez received much support and encouragement from renowned artist Omar Rayo (1928–2010) and his wife, well-known writer Águeda Pizarro Rayo; they are owners of the Rayo Museum and directors of the annual Meeting of Colombian Women Poets, now in its thirty-third year, the major conference on women's literature in the country. Their poetry is published every year in a collection called *Universos*, part of the museum's accomplishments in the area of publications. In addition, Ediciones Embalaje is well known as a rustic, eco-friendly press that has proven to be very supportive of women writers. Ramírez credits Omar Rayo for giving the title to her first anthology, *La noche de mi piel.*

27. Solmery Cáseres Estrada, *Diccionario de la lengua afropalenquera-español* (Cartagena de Indias, Colombia: Pluma de Mompox, 2009), 15.

28. Ramírez, conversation with the author.

29. Jaramillo, "María Teresa Ramírez: Heredera," 8.

30. Ramírez, conversation with the author; Ramírez, *Flor de palenque*, 19; Jaramillo, "María Teresa Ramírez: Heredera," 9–11; Pizarro Rayo, "María Teresa Ramírez," xii.

31. Ramírez, *Mabungú triunfo: Poemas bilingües*, 42–43.

32. Ramírez, 42–43; "Mabungú, poesía en palenquero," *Extrovesia*, July 1, 2012, http://extroversia.universia.net.co/diadia/2012/noticias/actualidad/mabungu_poesia_en_Palenquero/actualidad/14803/103/104.html (accessed June 11, 2014; page no longer extant). "Muje timbo" and "Mujer bien negra" are titles to the same poem in *palenquero* and Spanish, respectively.

33. Ramírez, *Abalenga*, v.

34. Ramírez, 1.

35. Ramírez, 2.

36. Ramírez, 2–3. These terms are from different parts of Latin America and refer to the settlements created by Africans and Afro-descendants as they fled enslavement and built their own independent shelters and communities.

37. Ramírez, v; Pizarro Rayo, "María Teresa Ramírez," xvii.

38. Ramírez, *Abalenga*, 2.

39. Ramírez, *Flor de palenque*, 16; Pizarro Rayo, "María Teresa Ramírez," xii–xiii.

40. Ramírez, *Flor de palenque*, 29–30.

41. Ramírez, 33, 31, 45, 58, 50.

42. Ramírez, 24, 42, 55, 57.

43. Felipe Quetzalcoatl Quintanilla and Juan Guillermo Sánchez Martínez, *Indigenous Message on Water—Mensaje indígena de agua* (London, Ontario: Indigenous World Forum on Water and Peace, 2014).

44. *Palenqueros* have always migrated from their original homes in the countryside to urban centers. Urban *palenques* are neighborhoods with a concentration of such dwellers—in this case, in the city of Barranquilla.

45. Mirian Díaz Pérez, conversation with the author, June 22, 2015.

46. Mirian Díaz Pérez, *Tejiendo palabras con libertad / Binda ndunblua ku bindanga* (Barranquilla, Colombia: Santa Bárbara, 2013), 54–57.

47. This biographical information was taken from the inside cover page and inside back page of her anthology, available in a text written by María Victoria Herrera V.

48. Raúl Gómez Afanador, "No juzgo, sólo celebro—a manera de prólogo," in Díaz Pérez, *Tejiendo palabras con libertad*, 5.

49. Gómez Afanador, 7.

50. Díaz Pérez, *Tejiendo palabras con libertad*, 10-11.

51. Díaz Pérez, 12-13.

52. Díaz Pérez, 22-25.

53. Ramírez, *Abalenga*, ii-iii.

54. Ramírez, *Flor de palenque*, 39, 80, 110-11.

55. Ramírez, *Mabungú triunfo: Poemas bilingües*, 70-73; Ramírez, *Flor de palenque*, 110-11; Ramírez, *Abalenga*, 6.

56. Díaz Pérez, *Tejiendo palabras con libertad*, 49.

57. Díaz Pérez, 49.

58. Díaz Pérez, 72-73.

59. Ramírez, *Mabungú triunfo: Poemas bilingües*, 62-63, 70-73, 121, 123.

60. Ramírez, 63.

61. Ramírez, 80-83, 114-15.

62. Ramírez, 116-17, 118-19.

63. Ramírez, 34-35.

64. Ramírez, 35.

65. Ramírez, 35.

66. Ramírez, 50-51.

67. Ramírez, 52-53.

68. Díaz Pérez, *Tejiendo palabras con libertad*, 22-23.

69. Díaz Pérez, 64-65, 74-75.

70. Díaz Pérez, 15.

71. Díaz Pérez, 43-48, 64-65.

72. Díaz Pérez, 43-48.

73. Díaz Pérez, 43.

74. Díaz Pérez, 44.

75. Guerrero García, "Memorias palenqueras," 384.

76. María Teresa Ramírez, *Mabungú triunfo: Cosmogonía africana*, vol. 2 (Bogotá: Apidama Ediciones, 2016), 31-32.

77. Ramírez, conversation with the author; Ramírez, *Flor de palenque*, 15; Pizarro Rayo, prologue, 12; Jaramillo, "María Teresa Ramírez: Heredera," 10-11.

78. Díaz Pérez, *Tejiendo palabras con libertad*, 72-73, 74-75.

79. Díaz Pérez, 72.

80. Díaz Pérez, 74.

81. Díaz Pérez, 97, 131.

82. Ramírez, *Mabungú triunfo: Poemas bilingües*, 38-39.

83. Ramírez, 40-41.

84. Ramírez, 50-51.

85. Ramírez, 53.

86. Charo Mina Rojas, *Defeating Invisibility: A Challenge for Afro-descendant Women in Colombia* (Colombia: Afro-descendant Women Human Rights Defender Project, PCN, April 2012), 137, http://www.afrocolombians.org/pdfs/Defeating%20Invisibility.pdf (accessed 16 June 2014).

87. Ramírez, *Mabungú triunfo: Poemas bilingües*, 76-77.

88. Ramírez, 77.

89. Ramírez, 77.

90. Ramírez, 80-83.

91. Ramírez, 83.

92. Ramírez, 88-91, 110-13.

93. Ramírez, 88–89.

94. Ramírez, 89.

95. Ramírez, 114–15.

96. Ramírez, 115.

97. Ramírez, 60–61.

98. Armin Schwegler, *"Chi ma 'kongo'"*: *Lengua y rito ancestrales en el Palenque de San Basilio (Colombia)*, 2 vols. (Frankfurt: Vervuert Verlag, 1996), 490–91.

99. Ramírez, *Mabungú triunfo: Poemas bilingües*, 61.

100. Ramírez, 49, 63, 69, 87, 93, 97, 99.

101. Ramírez, 48–49.

102. Jaramillo, "María Teresa Ramírez: Heredera," 13.

103. Ramírez, *Mabungú triunfo: Poemas bilingües*, 68–69.

104. Ramírez, 92–93.

105. Ramírez, 93.

106. Díaz Pérez, *Tejiendo palabras con libertad*, 15.

107. Díaz Pérez, 18–19.

108. Díaz Pérez, 18.

109. Díaz Pérez, 49.

110. Díaz Pérez, 42–43.

111. Díaz Pérez, 43.

112. Díaz Pérez, 43.

113. Díaz Pérez, 43.

114. Díaz Pérez, 42–43.

115. Ramírez, *Mabungú triunfo: Poemas bilingües*, 38–39, 78–79, 56–57, 59, 60–61, 97, 35, 92–93, 104–9, 105, 107, 124–25.

116. Ramírez, 57.

117. Ramírez, 104–9.

118. Ramírez, 58–59.

119. Ramírez, 59.

120. Ramírez, 59.

121. Ramírez, 59.

122. Ramírez, 59.

123. Ramírez, 59.

124. Ramírez, 59.

125. Ramírez, 126–27.

126. Ramírez, 127.

127. Ramírez, 134–36.

128. Ramírez, 134.

129. Ramírez, 134.

130. Ramírez, *Flor de palenque*, 44. Also available in Secretaría de Cultura y Turismo de Cali, *Poemas matriax*, 21. This anthology is a collection of Afro-Colombian women poets sponsored by the local government of Cali.

131. Ramírez, *Flor de palenque*, 44.

132. Ramírez, *Mabungú triunfo: Poemas bilingües*, 94–99.

133. Díaz Pérez, *Tejiendo palabras con libertad*, 31–34, 54–57, 62–63, 66–67, 68–69, 70–71.

134. Díaz Pérez, 58–61.

135. Díaz Pérez, 62–63.

136. Díaz Pérez, 68–69.

CONCLUSION

1. María Teresa Ramírez, ed., *Mabungú triunfo: Poemas bilingües, palenque-español*, 3rd ed. (Bogotá: Apidama, 2013), 134.

2. María Teresa Ramírez, conversation with the author, June 28, 2015.

Bibliography

"Academia Colombiana de la lengua presentó Biblioteca de Escritoras Afrocolombianas." soydebuenaventura.com, May 2, 2014. https://www.soydebuenaventura.com/articulos/academia-colombiana-de-la-lengua-presento-biblioteca-de-escritoras-afrocolombianas (accessed July 18, 2014).

Adams, Clementina R. "Afro-Dominican Women Writers and Their Struggles against Patriarchy and Tradition." *Latin Americanist* 47, nos. 3–4 (December 2004): 7–28.

Adun, Mel. Preface to *Águas da cabaça*, by Elizandra Souza, 10–11. São Paulo: Edição do Autor, 2012.

———. "Zamani: Mulheres que contam, transforman e fazem história." In Duke, *A escritora afro-brasileira*, 78–85.

Aláh, Alí. "Pimpóy bailóp." In Obando Sancho, Brooks Saldaña, and Alemán Porras, *Antología poética*, 60–62.

Alaix de Valencia, Hortensia. *La palabra poética del afrocolombiano*. Bogotá: Litocencoa, 2001.

Alarcón, Norma. "Chicana's Feminist Literatures: A Re-vision through Malintzin, or Malintzin: Putting Flesh Back on the Object." In *This Bridge Called My Back: Writings by Radical Women of Color*, edited by Cherríe Moraga and Gloria Anzaldúa, 182–90. Waterton, Mass.: Persephone, 1981.

Albert Batista, Celsa. *Los africanos y nuestra isla (historia, cultura e identidad)*. Santo Domingo: INDAASEL, 2001.

———. *Mujer y esclavitud en Santo Domingo*. Santo Domingo: INDAASEL, 2003.

Alemán Porras, Eddy. "Mayo es: Kupia kumi lasbaia wina kakalwra." In Alemán Porras and Brooks Vargas, *Bluefields en la sangre*, 155–58.

Alemán Porras, Eddy, and Franklin Brooks Vargas, comps. *Bluefields en la sangre: Poesía del Caribe Sur Nicaragüense*. Managua: 400 elefantes, 2011.

Ali, Omar H. "Benkos Biohó: African Maroon Leadership in New Granada." In *Atlantic Biographies: Individuals and Peoples in the Atlantic World*, edited by Jeffrey A. Fortin and Mark Meuwese, 263–94. Boston, Mass.: Brill, 2014.

Almeida, Débora. "Se não for a minha história, eu não vou contar: Por uma representação negra." In Duke, *A escritora afro-brasileira*, 129–35.

Alvarado, Rolando. "Palenquera del Pacífico." Artelista, February 23, 2008. http://www.artelista.com/obra/2001121594272083-Palenqueradelpacifico.html (accessed August 5, 2014).

Alves, Miriam. "A literatura negra feminina no Brasil: Pensando a existência." *Revista da IBPN* 3 (November 2010–February 2011): 181–89.

———. "A representação da morte nos contos de *Cadernos Negros* 34." In Duke, *A escritora afro-brasileira*, 180–91.

———. "As ações de resistência anônima das mulheres negras e os reflexos na escrita afrofeminina brasileira." Paper presented at the University of Tennessee, November 1, 2007.

———. "Axé Ogum." In *Reflexões: Sobre a literatura afro-brasileira*, organized by Quilombhoje, 57–67. São Paulo: Conselho de Participação e Desenvolvimento da Comunidade Negra, 1985.

———. *BrasilAfro autorrevelado: Literatura brasileira contemporânea.* Belo Horizonte, Brazil: Nandyala, 2010.

———. "*Cadernos Negros* (número 1): Estado de alerta no fogo cruzado." In *Poéticas afrobrasileiras*, organized by Maria do Carmo Lanna Figueiredo and Maria Nazareth Soares Fonseca, 221–40. Belo Horizonte, Brazil: PUCMinas, Mazza, 2002.

———. "Empunhando bandeira: Diálogo de poeta." In *A escrita de adé: Perspectivas teóricas dos estudos gays e lésbic@s no Brasil*, organized by Rick Santos and Wilton Garcia, 153–61. São Paulo: Xama, 2002.

———. "Enfim . . . nós: Por quê?" In *Enfim . . . nós / Finally . . . Us: Escritoras negras brasileiras contemporâneas / Contemporary Black Brazilian Women Writers*, edited by Miriam Alves, translated by Carolyn Richardson Durham, 5–27. Colorado Springs: Three Continental, 1995.

———. "Invisibilidade e anonimato: Prefácio." In Alves and Helena Lima, *Women Righting*, 8–15.

———. "Miriam Alves." In *Cadernos Negros 8: Contos*, compiled by Os Autores, 13. São Paulo: Edição dos Autores, 1985.

———. "O discurso temerário." In Cuti and Xavier, *Criação crioula*, 83–86.

———. "Palavras jongadas de boca em boca." In Cuti and Xavier, *Criação crioula*, 11–30.

Alves, Miriam, and Maria Helena Lima, eds. *Women Righting: Afro-Brazilian Women's Short Fiction / Mulheres escre-vendo: Uma antologia bilingüe de escritoras afro-brasileiras contemporâneas.* London: Mango, 2005.

Andújar, Carlos. *De cultura y sociedad.* 2nd ed. Santo Domingo: Letra Gráfica, 2004.

———. *Identidad cultural y religiosidad popular.* Santo Domingo: Letra Gráfica, 2004.

———. *La presencia negra en Santo Domingo.* Santo Domingo: Letra Gráfica, 2011.

Anonymous. "Mayaya perdió su llave." In Valle-Castillo, *Poesía atlántica*, 32.

"A premiada escritora negra, Conceição Evaristo." Literafro: O portal da literatura afro-brasileira. http://www.letras.ufmg.br/literafro/noticias/1062-conceicao-evaristo-e -oficialmente-candidata-a-academia-brasileira-de-letras (accessed March 23, 2021).

Arce, B. Christine. *Mexico's Nobodies: The Cultural Legacy of the Soldadera and Afro-Mexican Women.* Albany: State University of New York Press, 2018.

Arellano, Jorge Eduardo. "Antecedentes históricos." In Arellano, *La Costa Caribe nicaragüense*, 19.

———, ed. *La Costa Caribe nicaragüense: Desde sus orígenes hasta el siglo XXI.* Managua: Academia de Geografía e Historia de Nicaragua, 2009.

———. "Pluma invitada." In Arellano, *La Costa Caribe nicaragüense*, 7–9.

———. "Poesía y narrativa." In Arellano, *La Costa Caribe nicaragüense*, 309–11.

———. "Tres lenguas étnicas de Nicaragua." In Arellano, *La Costa Caribe nicaragüense*, 158–82.

———. "Zelaya, los criollos de Bluefields y la anexión de la Mosquitia." In Arellano, *La Costa Caribe nicaragüense*, 73–82.

Arocha, Jaime. "Inclusion of Afro-Colombians: Unreachable National Goal?" *Latin American Perspectives* 25, no. 3 (May 1998): 70–89.

Arroyo Pizarro, Yolanda. *Caparazones*. Carolina, Puerto Rico: Publicaciones Boreales, 2010.

———. *Las negras*. Carolina, Puerto Rico: Boreales, 2012.

———. *Saeta, the Poems*. Carolina, Puerto Rico: Boreales, 2011.

———. *Tongas, palenques y quilombos: Ensayos y columnas de afroresistencia*. Self-published, 2013.

———. *Violeta*. Carolina, Puerto Rico: Boreales, 2013.

Asociación de mujeres afrodescendientes y del Caribe Graciela Cha-Ines. Pamphlet. Cartagena, Colombia: Asociación de mujeres afrodescendientes y del Caribe Graciela Cha-Ines, 2010.

Asprilla Mosquera, Francisco Adelmo. "Los afrodescendientes y el imaginario colectivo." In *La afrocolombianidad: Otra manera de pensar, sentir y valorar la diversidad*, edited by Francisco Adelmo Asprilla Mosquera, Miguel Hernández Valdez, and Vilma María Solano Oliveros, 146–50. Barranquilla, Colombia: Organización Social de Comunidades Negras Ángela Davis, 2009.

Autonomy Statute for the Regions of the Atlantic Coast of Nicaragua, Law no. 28 (September 7, 1987). CALPI. http://calpi.nativeweb.org/doc_3.html (accessed June 5, 2014).

Aveni, Anthony F. *The Book of the Year: A Brief History of Our Seasonal Holidays*. Oxford: Oxford University Press, 2003.

Bacardí Moreau, Emilio. *Crónicas de Santiago*. Vol. 1. Barcelona: Tipografía de Carbonell y Esteva, 1908.

Bachiller y Morales, Antonio. *Apuntes para la historia de las letras y de la instrucción pública en la isla de Cuba*. Vol. 2. Havana: Imp. Del Tiempo, 1860.

Bahrs, Karoline. "El origen de sones afroantillanos: Perspectivas dominicanas con respecto al 'Son de la Ma' Teodora.'" *Latin American Music Review* 32, no. 2 (Fall–Winter 2011): 218–39.

Balaguer, Joaquín. *Historia de la literatura dominicana*. 7th ed. Santo Domingo: Corripio, 1988.

Balutansky, Kathleen M., and Marie-Agnès Sourieau, eds. *Caribbean Creolization: Reflection on the Cultural Dynamics of Language, Literature, and Identity*. Gainesville: University Press of Florida, 1998.

Barnet, Miguel, and Esteban Montejo. *Biografía de un cimarrón*. Havana: Instituto de Etnología y Folklore, 1966.

Bauzá, Yamila. "La leyenda de Catalina Loango." *Etnoliteratura* (blog), May 13, 2009. http://etnoliteratura.blogspot.com/2009/05/la-matica-de-aji_13.html (accessed February 24, 2015).

Bauzá-Múscolo, Yadmilla. "La leyenda de Catalina Loango." *Revista trimestral de estudios literarios* 7, no. 31 (October–December 2007): 1–3. https://www.scribd.com/document/480282835/CATALINA-LOANGO (accessed February 24, 2015).

Bauzá-Vargas, Yadmilla. "'Yo lo que sé de Catalina Loango . . .': Orality and Gender in the Caribbean." PhD diss., University at Buffalo, Buffalo, N.Y., 1997.

Beckles, Hilary. *Centering Women: Gender Discourses in Caribbean Slave Society*. Kingston, Jamaica: Ian Randle, 1999.

Beer, June. "Poema de amor." In Obando Sancho, Brooks Saldaña, and Alemán Porras, *Antología poética*, 19–20.

Benítez-Rojo, Antonio. "Three Words toward Creolization." In Balutansky and Sourieau, *Caribbean Creolization*, 53–61.

Bernard, Eulalia. *Ciénaga*. San José, Costa Rica: Guayacán Centroamericana, 2006.

Bluefilms. "Al son de Miss Lizzie." July 4, 2012. YouTube video, 0:18:06. https://www
.youtube.com/watch?v=HkTs-SfXGrU (accessed January 3, 2016).

Borge, Tomás. "La primera propuesta de autonomía." In Arellano, *La Costa Caribe nicaragüense*, 142–43.

Brooks, Ronald. "Llueve la vida." In Obando Sancho, Brooks Saldaña, and Alemán Porras,
Antología poética, 39–40.

Brooks Saldaña, Ronald. "Silencio étnico." In Brown Hendricks, *Antología poética "Afrocarinica,"* 14.

Brooks Vargas, Franklin. "Canción al negro/negra costeño/a." In Alemán Porras and Brooks
Vargas, *Bluefields en la sangre*, 178–80.

Broomfield, Padmini, and Cynara Davies. "Costeño Voices: Oral History on Nicaragua's
Caribbean Coast." *Oral History* 31, no. 1 (Spring 2003): 85–94.

Brown Hendricks, Angélica, coord. *Antología poética "Afrocarinica."* Bluefields, Nicaragua:
Bluefields Indian and Caribbean University, 2011.

Bryan, Joe, and Denis Wood. *Weaponizing Maps: Indigenous Peoples and Counterinsurgency
in the Americas*. New York: Guilford, 2015.

Callahan, Monique-Adelle. *Between the Lines: Literary Transnationalism and African American Poetics*. New York: Oxford University Press, 2011.

Calvo Licero, Jerly. "Palenqueras de Cartagena tendrán la oportunidad de crear una cooperativa para su bienestar." Fundación Paz por Colombia. http://www.pazporcolombia.org/
article.php?sid=77 (accessed March 11, 2010; page no longer extant).

Campbell, Shirley. "Letras e vozes da diáspora negra." In *Griôs da diáspora negra*, organized
by Ana Flávia Magalhães Pinto, Chaia Dechen, and Jaqueline Fernandes, 20–31. Brasília:
Griô Produções, 2017.

Campos, Mateus, and Paula Bianchi. "Conceição Evaristo." *The Intercept Brasil*, August 30,
2018. https://theintercept.com/2018/08/30/conceicao-evaristo-escritora-negra-eleicao
-abl/ (accessed March 23, 2021).

Carpentier, Alejo. *La música en Cuba*. Pánuco, Mexico: Fondo de Cultura Económica,
1946.

Cásseres Estrada, Solmery. *Diccionario de la lengua afropalenquera-español*. Cartagena
de Indias, Colombia: Pluma de Mompox, 2009.

———. *Mis recuerdos*. Cartagena de Indias, Colombia: Pluma de Mompox, 2001.

Cassiani, Alfonso. "Las comunidades renacientes de la Costa Caribe continental." In Mosquera, Pardo, and Hoffmann, *Afrodescendientes en las Américas*, 573–94.

Cassiani Herrera, Alfonso. "San Basilio de Palenque: Historia de la resistencia 1599–1713."
In Restrepo Tirado, *150 años*, 70–91.

Cassiani Herrera, Teresa, and Rutsely Simarra Obeso. "Aproximaciones a la realidad de
la mujer afro, construyendo el camino hacia una sólida proyección étnica, de género y
cultural." *Tumbutú: Revista científica del sistema de investigación del Instituto Manuel
Zapata Olivella* 3, no. 2 (July 2015): 49–60.

Castro Jo, Carlos. "Raza, conciencia de color y militancia negra en la literatura nicaragüense." *WANI: Una revista sobre la Costa Atlántica* 23 (April–June 2003): 21–32.

Celis, Nadia V. "Bailando el Caribe: Corporalidad, identidad y ciudadanía en las plazas
de Cartagena de Indias." *Caribbean Studies* 41, no. 1 (January–June 2013): 27–61.

Césaire, Aimé. *Return to My Native Land*. New York: Penguin, 1969.

Chacón, Ninozka. *Perfume de luna*. Managua: URACCAN, 2003.

Chavalos_Org. "Mayaya Lasinki dimensión costeña concierto en vivo." February 24, 2010.
YouTube video, 0:05:54. https://www.youtube.com/watch?v=JedH3X54seA (accessed
January 15, 2015).

Chavarría Lezama, Pedro, and Alice Ebanks Narcisso. "Estudio y antología de poetas de Bluefields en el período 1979–1996: Una contribución al conocimiento de la literatura de la Costa Atlántica." Unpublished monograph, UNAM Managua, Bluefields, Nicaragua, July 1997.

Chávez Alfaro, Lizandro. "Identidad y resistencia del 'criollo' en Nicaragua." *Cahiers du monde hispanique et luso-brésilien* 36 (1981): 87–97.

———. Introduction to Valle-Castillo, *Poesía atlántica*, 11–16.

———. "La Costa Atlántica: Nombres y vértegras." In Arellano, *La Costa Caribe nicaragüense*, 11–17.

———. Prologue to Obando Sancho, Brooks Saldaña, and Alemán Porras, *Antología poética*, 11–15.

Cocco de Filippis, Daisy, ed. *Sin otro profeta que su canto: Antología de poesía escrita por dominicanas.* Santo Domingo: Taller, 1988.

Coello, Antonio. *Chimbumbe.* Mexico: La Sombra Negra Producciones, 2008. http://www.obsidianatv.com/video/35/chimbumbe (accessed August 12, 2015).

Conceição, Sônia Fátima da. "Obsessão." In *Cadernos Negros*, vol. 16, *Contos*, edited by Aristides Barbosa and Os Autores, 93–101. São Paulo: Edição dos Autores Quilombhoje Literatura, 1993.

Cuesta Escobar, Guiomar, and Alfredo Ocampo Zamorano, comps. *¡Negras somos! Antología de 21 mujeres poetas afrocolombianas de la región Pacífica.* Bogotá: Apidama Ediciones, 2013.

Cunin, Elisabeth. *Identidades a flor de piel: Lo "negro" entre apariencias y pertenencias; Mestizaje y categorías raciales en Cartagena (Colombia).* Bogotá: IFEA-ICANH-Uniandes-Observatorio del Caribe Colombiano, 2003. https://halshs.archives-ouvertes.fr/halshs-00291675 (accessed January 17, 2014).

Cunningham Kain, Myrna. "Anotaciones sobre el racismo por razones étnicas en Nicaragua." Lecture presented at the Centro para la Autonomía de los Pueblos Indígenas, Bilwi, RACCN, Nicaragua, November 2006. https://tbinternet.ohchr.org/Treaties/CERD/Shared%20Documents/NIC/INT_CERD_NGO_NIC_72_9739_S.pdf (accessed February 17, 2012).

Cuti, Miriam Alves, and Arnaldo Xavier, orgs. *Criação crioula nu elefante branco: I encontro de poetas e ficcionistas negros brasileiros.* São Paulo: Secretaria de Estado da Cultura, 1987.

Damas, Léon-Gontran. "La Negritude en question." In *Jeune Afrique: Critical Perspectives on Léon-Gontran Damas*, translated and edited by Keith Q. Warner, 13–19. Washington, DC: Three Continents, 1988.

———. *Pigments: Névralgies.* Paris: Présence africaine, 1972.

Danger, Matilde, and Delfina Rodríguez, comps. *Mariana Grajales.* Santiago de Cuba: Oriente, 1977.

Da Silva, Joselina. "'Mulher negra tem história': Os processos organizativos das feministas afro-brasileiras nos anos setenta e oitenta." In *Africanidade(s) e afrodescendência(s): Perspectivas para a formação de professores*, edited by Maria Aparecida Santos Correa Barreto, Patrícia Gomes Rufino Andrade, Henrique Antunes Cunha Júnior, and Alexsandro Rodrigues, 125–44. Espíritu Santo, Brazil: EDUFES, 2012.

Davies, Carole Boyce. "Introduction: Black Women Writing Worlds; Textual Production, Dominance, and the Critical Voice." In *Moving beyond Boundaries*, vol. 2, *Black Women's Diaspora*, edited by Carole Boyce Davies, 1–15. New York: New York University Press, 1995.

Deavila Pertuz, Orlando. "Una breve historia de Chambacú." *Chambacú* (blog), August 28, 2011. http://chambacu1971.blogspot.com/2011_08_01_archive.html (accessed September 13, 2014).

DeCosta-Willis, Miriam, ed. *Daughters of the Diaspora: Afra-Hispanic Writers*. Kingston, Jamaica: Ian Randle, 2003.

De Ferranti, David, Guillermo E. Perry, Francisco H. G. Ferreira, and Michael Walton. *Inequality in Latin America: Breaking with History?* Washington, DC: World Bank, 2004.

De Friedemann, Nina. *Ma Ngombe: Guerreros y ganaderos en palenque*. Bogotá: Carlos Valencia, 1987.

———. "San Basilio en el universo Kilombo-África y Palenque-América." In *Geografía humana de Colombia: Los afrocolombianos*, vol. 6, coordinated by Luz Adriana Maya Restrepo, 79–101. Bogotá: Instituto Colombiano de Cultura Hispánica, 1998.

De Friedemann, Nina, and Jaime Arocha. "Colombia." In *No Longer Visible: Afro-Latin Americans Today*, edited by Minority Rights Group, 47–76. London: Minority Rights Publication, 1995.

De Friedemann, Nina, and Carlos Patiño Rosselli. *Lengua y sociedad en el Palenque de San Basilio*. Bogotá: Instituto Caro y Cuervo, 1983.

Deive, Carlos Esteban. *Los guerrilleros negros: Esclavos fugitivos y cimarrones en Santo Domingo*. Santo Domingo: Taller, 1997.

De Jesus, Carolina Maria. *Diário de Bitita*. Rio de Janeiro: Nova Fronteira, 1986.

———. *Quarto de despejo: Diário de uma favelada*. São Paulo: Livraria Francisco Alves, 1960.

De la Fuente, Alejandro. *Havana and the Atlantic in the Sixteenth Century*. Chapel Hill: University of North Carolina Press, 2008.

De la Torre, José María. *Lo que fuimos y lo que somos, o La Habana antigua y moderna*. Havana: Impr. De Spencer, 1857.

Delgado, Ramiro, Luis Gerardo Martínez Miranda, Juana Pabla Pérez Tejedor, Jesús Natividad Pérez Palomino, Ana María Maldonado Ardila, and Cristina Daza Rodríguez. *Proceso de identificación y recomendaciones de salvaguardia (PIRS) de las manifestaciones asociadas al espacio de San Basilio de Palenque*. Cartagena de Indias, Colombia: Ministerio de Cultura, 2007. https://www.scribd.com/document/284380237/SW5mb3JtYWNpw7M gc29icmUgUGFsZW5xdWUtZ2VuZXJhbA-110280-1-3029-1-1 (accessed July 7, 2014).

Del Rosario de ávila Torres, Dimas, and Rutsely Simarra Obeso. "*Ma-kuagro*: Elemento de la cultura palenquera y su incidencia en las prácticas pedagógicas en la Escuela San Basilio Palenque, Colombia." *Ciencia e interculturalidad* 11, no. 2 (July–December 2012): 88–99. https://doi.org/10.5377/rci.v11i2.961 (accessed January 19, 2014).

del Valle Idárraga, Mónica María. "Escenario edénico y naturaleza prístina en *Sail Ahoy!!! ¡Vela a la vista!*, y *The Spirit of Persistence* de Hazel Robinson Abrahams: Dos formas de recuperar una isla colonizada." *Estudios de literatura colombiana* 28 (January–June 2011): 17–38. https://www.academia.edu/es/48387579/Escenario_ed%C3%A9nico_y_naturaleza _pr%C3%ADstina_en_Sail_Ahoy_Vela_a_la_vista_y_The_Spirit_of_Persistence_de _Hazel_Robinson_Abrahams_dos_formas_de_recuperar_una_isla_colonizada (accessed September 26, 2022).

Denis Rosario, Yvonne. *Capá prieto*. 2nd ed. San Juan: Isla Negra, 2010.

de Nolasco, Flérida. *Santo Domingo en el folklore universal*. Ciudad Trujillo, Dominican Republic: Impresora Dominicana, 1956.

de Simone, Cynthia. "Palenqueras: Las vendedoras ambulantes más fotografiadas del Caribe." todoparaviajar.com, February 6, 2012. https://todoparaviajar.com/noticia/palenqueras-las -vendedoras-ambulantes-mas-fotografiadas-del-caribe- (accessed August 5, 2014).

Díaz Pérez, Mirian. "Diccionario de la lengua afro-palenquera." *El universal*, August 15, 2010. http://www.eluniversal.com.co/suplementos/dominical/diccionario-de-la-lengua -afro-palenquera (accessed May 28, 2017).

———. *Tejiendo palabras con libertad / Binda ndunblua ku bindanga*. Barranquilla, Colombia: Santa Bárbara, 2013.

Dixon, Kwame. "Transnational Black Social Movements in Latin America: Afro-Colombians and the Struggle for Human Rights." In *Latin American Social Movements in the Twenty-First Century: Resistance, Power, and Democracy*, edited by Richard Stahler-Sholk, Harry E. Vanden, and Glen David Kueker, 181–95. Lanham, Md.: Rowman & Littlefield, 2008.

Duke, Dawn, org. *A escritora afro-brasileira: Ativismo e arte literária*. Belo Horizonte, Brazil: Nandyala, 2016.

———. "Alzira Rufino's *A casa de cultura de mulher negra* as a Form of Female Empowerment: A Look at the Dynamics of a Black Women's Organization in Brazil Today." *Women's Studies International Forum* 26, no. 4 (July–August 2003): 357–68.

———. "From 'Yélida' to Movimiento de Mujeres Dominico-Haitianas: Gendering Problems of Whiteness in the Dominican Republic." In *At Home and Abroad: Historicizing Twentieth-Century Whiteness in Literature and Performance*, edited by La Vinia Delois Jennings, 61–92. Knoxville: University of Tennessee Press, 2009.

———. *Literary Passion, Ideological Commitment: Toward a Legacy of Afro-Cuban and Afro-Brazilian Women Writers*. Lewisburg, Pa.: Bucknell Univesity Press, 2008.

———. "Literatura afro-femenina en la República Dominicana ¿Una indefinitud que la define?" *Revista iberoamericana* 79, no. 243 (April–June 2013): 559–76.

Echeverri Mejía, Óscar, and Alfonso Bonilla Naar, eds. *Antología: 21 años de poesía colombiana, 1942–1963*. Bogotá: Stella, 1964.

Edison, Thomas Wayne. "La cultura afro-caribeña vista en la poesía del *palo de mayo* en el poema *Si yo fuera mayo* por Carlos Rigby Moses." *WANI: Revista del Caribe Nicaragüense* 49 (April–June 2007): 21–32.

Eisen Simmons, Kimberly. *Reconstructing Racial Identity and the African Past in the Dominican Republic*. Gainesville: University Press of Florida, 2009.

"En una calle de Cartagena: Palenqueras." *Espíritu naif* (blog), March 2013. http://espiritunaif.blogspot.com/2013/03/en-una-calle-de-cartagena-Palenqueras-3.html (accessed August 5, 2014).

Estrada Colindres, Isabel. "La fe." In Obando Sancho, Brooks Saldaña, and Alemán Porras, *Antología poética*, 69–72.

———. "Strong Wuman / Mujer fuerte." In Alemán Porras and Brooks Vargas, *Bluefields en la sangre*, 120–22.

Evaristo, Conceição. "Apresentação." In *Olhares diversos: Narrativas lésbicas, contos*, organized by Edmeire Exaltação and Neusa das Dores Pereira, 5–7. Rio de Janeiro: Centro de Documentação e Informação Coisa de Mulher, 2008.

———. *Becos da memória*. Belo Horizonte, Brazil: Mazza, 2006.

———. "Chica que manda ou a Mulher que inventou o mar?" *Revista anuária de literatura* 18, no. 1 (2013): 137–60. https://periodicos.ufsc.br/index.php/literatura/article/view/2175-7917.2013v18nesp1p137/25244 (accessed June 20, 2019).

———. "Da grafia-desenho de minha mãe, um dos lugares de nascimento de minha escrita." In *Representações performáticas brasileiras: Teorias, práticas e suas interfaces*, edited by Marcos Antônio Alexandre, 16–21. Belo Horizonte, Brazil: Mazza, 2007.

———. "Da representação à auto-representação da mulher negra na literatura brasileira." *Revista palmares: Cultura afro-brasileira* 1, no. 1 (August 2005): 52–55.

———. "Gênero e etnia: Uma escre(vivência) de dupla face." In *Mulher no mundo: Etnia, marginalidade e diáspora*, edited by Nadilza Martins de Barros Moreira and Liane Schneider, 201–12. João Pessoa, Brazil: Idéia, 2005.

———. *Insubmissas lágrimas de mulheres*. Belo Horizonte, Brazil: Nandyala, 2011.

———. "Literatura negra: Uma voz quilombola na literatura brasileira." In *Um tigre na floresta de signos: Estudos sobre poesia e demandas sociais no Brasil*, edited by Edimilson de Almeida Pereira, 132–44. Belo Horizonte, Brazil: Mazza, 2010.

———. "Luís Bernardo Honwana: Da afasia ao discurso insano em 'Nós matámos o Cão-Tinhoso.'" In *África & Brasil: Letras em laços*, edited by Maria do Carmo Sepúlveda and Maria Teresa Salgado, 227–39. Rio de Janeiro: Atlântica, 2000.

———. "O entrecruzar das margens—gênero e etnia: Apontamentos sobre a mulher negra na sociedade brasileira." In Duke, *A escritora afro-brasileira*, 100–110.

———. "Prefácio: Em legítima defesa." In *Escritos de uma vida: Sueli Carneiro*, by Sueli Carneiro, 7–9. Belo Horizonte, Brazil: Letramento, 2018.

Evaristo, Conceição, and Josina Ma da Cunha. Introduction to *Oro obinrin: 1 prêmio literário e ensaístico sobre a condição da mulher negra*, organized by Andréia Lisboa de Souza de Criola and Conceição Evaristo, 17–20. Rio de Janeiro: Criola e Conceição, 1998.

Extrovesia. "Mabungú, poesía en palenquero." July 1, 2012. http://extroversia.universia.net /co/diadia/2012/noticias/actualidad/mabungu_poesia_en_Palenquero/actualidad/14803/ 103/104.html (accessed June 11, 2014; page no longer extant).

Faustino, Carmen, and Elizandra Souza. "Espalhando novas sementes." In *Pretextos de mulheres negras*, organized by Carmen Faustino and Elizandra Souza, 6–7. São Paulo: Coletivo Mjiba, 2013.

Fenton, Annette. "Poem XII / Poema XII." In Alemán Porras and Brooks Vargas, *Bluefields en la sangre*, 227–30.

———. "Poem XXIX / Poema XXIX." In Alemán Porras and Brooks Vargas, *Bluefields en la sangre*, 225–27.

Fenton Tom, Annette Olivia. "Poem XVI Pearl Lagoon." In Brown Hendricks, *Antología poética "Afrocarinica,"* 64.

Fenwick, M. J., ed. *Sisters of Calibán: A Multilingual Anthology of Contemporary Women Poets of the Caribbean*. Falls Church, Va.: Azul Editions, 1996.

Fernández Robaina, Tomás. "Sobre Alberto Muguercia." *Librínsula: La revista de los libros*. http://librinsula.bnjm.cu/secciones/314/expedientes/314_exped_1.html (accessed May 23, 2014; page no longer extant).

Forbes Brooks, Elizabeth. *Memorias de Miss Lizzie: Danzas, música y tradiciones de Blue-fields*. Managua: GRAFITEX, 2011.

Forbes Brooks, Ivy Elizabeth. "Ivy Elizabeth (Lizzy Nelson) Forbes Brooks." In Robb Taylor, *Times & Life*, 81–86.

Freeland, Jane. "Intercultural-Bilingual Education for an Interethnic-Plurilingual Society? The Case of Nicaragua's Caribbean Coast." *Comparative Education* 39, no. 2 (May 2003): 239–60.

———. "Linguistic Rights and Language Survival in a Creole Space: Dilemmas for Nicaragua's Caribbean Coast Creoles." In *Language Rights and Language Survival: Sociolinguistic and Sociocultural Perspectives*, edited by Jane Freeland and Donna Patrick, 103–37. Manchester, U.K.: St. Jerome, 2004.

Frühling, Pierre, José Miguel González Pérez, Hans Petter Buvollen, and Edelberto Torres-Rivas. *Etnicidad y nación: El desarrollo de la autonomía de la Costa Atlántica de Nicaragua (1987–2007)*. Guatemala: F&G, 2007.

Fuentes Matons, Laureano. *Las artes en Santiago de Cuba: Apuntes históricos*. Santiago de Cuba: Establecimiento tipográfico de Juan E. Ravelo, 1893.

Fuentes Matons, Laureano, and Abelardo Estrada. *Las artes en Santiago en Cuba: Estudio de un libro, su autor y la órbita de ambos*. Havana: Letras Cubanas, 1981.

Galan, Natalio. *Cuba y sus sones*. Valencia, Spain: Pre-textos, 1983.

García, Joaquín José. *Protocolo de antigüedades, literatura, agricultura, industria, comercio, etc.* Vol. 1. Havana: Imprenta de M. Soler, 1985.

García Savino, Silvia Beatriz, ed. *Derechos de la población afrodescendiente de América Latina: Desafíos para su implementación.* Panama: Proyecto Regional "Población afrodescendiente de América Latina," 2010.

Giro, Radamés. *Diccionario enciclopédico de la música en Cuba.* Vol. 4. Havana: Letras Cubanas, 2007.

Goett, Jennifer. *Black Autonomy: Race, Gender, and Afro-Nicaraguan Activism.* Redwood City, Calif.: Stanford University Press, 2017.

Gómez Afanador, Raúl. "No juzgo, sólo celebro—a manera de prólogo." In Díaz Pérez, *Tejiendo palabras con libertad,* 3–7.

Gómez Sotolongo, Antonio. "Muguercia y el fin de un mito." *Hoy,* May 15, 2004. http://hoy .com.do/muguercia-y-el-fin-de-un-mito-2/ (accessed January 2, 2014).

Gonçalves, Ana Maria. *Um defeito de cor.* Rio de Janeiro: Record, 2006.

González Echevarría, Roberto. "Literature of the Hispanic Caribbean." *Latin American Literary Review* 8, no. 16 (Spring 1980): 1–20.

González Fornos, Lesbia. "Rondón es también. Pero que bien: ¡Autonomía!" In Alemán Porras and Brooks Vargas, *Bluefields en la sangre,* 59–60.

González López, Fermín. "The Lagoon / La laguna." In Obando Sancho, Brooks Saldaña, and Alemán Porras, *Antología poética,* 75–78.

González Mandri, Flora María. *Guarding Cultural Memory: Afro-Cuban Women in Literature and the Arts.* Charlottesville: University of Virginia Press, 2006.

Gordon, Edmund. *Disparate Diasporas: Identity and Politics in an African-Nicaraguan Community.* Austin: University of Texas Press, 1998.

———. "History, Identity, Consciousness, and Revolution: Afro-Nicaraguans and the Nicaraguan Revolution." In *Ethnic Groups and the Nation State: The Case of the Atlantic Coast of Nicaragua,* edited by CIDCA / Development Study Unit, 135–68. Stockholm: Stockholm University Press, 1987.

Green Wilson, Brenda Elena. "Identity." In Brown Hendricks, *Antología poética "Afrocarinica,"* 79.

———. "Maying Tide in Bluefields." In Brown Hendricks, *Antología poética "Afrocarinica,"* 74–75.

———. "Nuestra tierra." In Brown Hendricks, *Antología poética "Afrocarinica,"* 76–77.

———. "Soy costeña y ¿qué?" In Brown Hendricks, *Antología poética "Afrocarinica,"* 73.

Grenet, Emilio. *Popular Cuban Music.* Havana: Carasa, 1939.

Grueso Romero, Mary. *Del baúl a la escuela: Antología literaria infantil.* Buenaventura, Colombia: Impresora Feriva, 2003.

———. *El mar y tú.* Buenaventura, Colombia: Impresora Feriva, 2003.

———. *Ese otro yo que sí soy yo: Poemas de amor y mar.* Buenaventura, Colombia: Marymar, 1997.

———. *La muñeca negra.* Bogotá: Apidama, Códice, 2013.

———. *La niña en el espejo.* Bogotá: Apidama, Códice, 2013.

———. *Mi gente, mi tierra y mi mar.* CD. Manizales, Colombia: Hoyos Editores, 2003.

———. *Negra soy: Poemas.* Rondanillo, Colombia: Talleres Editoriales del Museo Rayo, 2008.

———. "Voces negras en la poética femenina colombiana." In *Marginalia: Encuentros con la literatura,* compiled by Carlos A. Castrillón, 149–62. Armenia, Colombia: Centro de Publicaciones de la Universidad del Quindío, 2011.

Guerrero García, Clara Inés. "Memoria sagrada y espiritualidad en palenque." *La Revista 3*, 2013. https://laparada.uniandes.edu.co/index.php/la-revista/la-revista-3/los-tesos/la-otra -orilla-de-palenque (accessed October 27, 2014).

———. "Memorias palenqueras de la libertad." Universidad Nacional de Colombia Digital Repositorio Institucional, 2013. https://repositorio.unal.edu.co/handle/unal/2862 (accessed September 26, 2022).

Guillén, Nicolás. *Nicolás Guillén: Obra poética 1920–1958*. Vol. 1. Havana: Instituto Cubano del Libro, 1972.

Guirao, Ramón. *Orbita de la poesía afrocubana 1928–1937*. Havana: Ucar, García y Cía, 1938.

Gutiérrez, Benigno. *Arrume folklórico de todo el maíz*. Medellín, Colombia: Librería la Pluma de Ore, 1948.

Henríquez, María Antonieta. *Lo permanente en nuestra música*. Havana: Ediciones Museo de la Música, 2008.

Henríquez Ureña, Max. *Panorama histórico de la literatura cubana*. Vol. 1. Havana: Edición Revolucionaria, 1967.

Herbbert Kelly, Evett Keyla, and Itzel Thomas Hodgson. *Factores que inciden en la participación de las mujeres kriol en política del estado en la ciudad de Bluefields en el periodo 1998 al 2008*. Bluefields, Nicaragua: URACCAN, 2010.

Hernández, Dorina. "Dorina Hernández." In *El despertar de las comunidades afrocolombianas*, edited by María Inés Martínez, 54–108. Houston: LACASA, Centro de Investigaciones Sociales, 2012.

Hernández Balaguer, Pablo. *Catálogo de música de los archivos de la Catedral de Santiago de Cuba y del Museo Bacardí*. Havana: Biblioteca Nacional José Martí, 1961.

Hernández C., Rubén. "Identidad cultural palenquera, movimiento social afrocolombiano y democracia." *Reflexión Política* 16, no. 31 (June 2014): 94–113. http://www.redalyc.org/ articulo.oa?id=11031312009 (accessed November 23, 2014).

Hernández Palomino, Dorina. "La etnoeducación afrocolombiana: Elementos para la construcción de las experiencias institucionales-comunitarias." In Restrepo Tirado, *150 años*, 58–68.

———. Preface to Simarra Obeso, Miranda Reyes, and Pérez Tejedor, *Lengua ri Palenge*, 23–26.

Herrera, Georgina. *África*. Matanzas, Cuba: Ediciones Matanzas, 2006.

———. *Grande es el tiempo*. Havana: Unión, 1989.

———. *Granos de sol y luna*. Havana: Unión, 1978.

———. "Legítima cubanía en el pensamiento." *Unión: Revista de literatura y arte* 82 (2014): 4–7.

———. "Oriki por las negras viejas de antes." In Rubiera Castillo and Martiatu Terry, *Afrocubanas*, 219–24.

———. "Penúltimo sueño de Mariana." In *Wanilere teatro*, edited by Inés María Martiatu Terry, 277–315. Havana: Letras Cubanas, 2005.

———. "Poetry, Prostitution, and Gender Esteem." In *Afro-Cuban Voices: On Race and Identity in Contemporary Cuba*, edited by Pedro Pérez Sarduy and Jean Stubbs, 118–25. Gainesville: University Press of Florida, 2000.

Herrera V., María Victoria. "Mirian Díaz Pérez." In Díaz Pérez, *Tejiendo palabras con libertad*, back inside cover.

Heywood, Linda M. *Njinga of Angola: Africa's Warrior Queen*. Cambridge, Mass.: Harvard University Press, 2017.

Hodgson Bobb, Rayfield. "Presentation." In Forbes Brooks, *Memorias de Miss Lizzie*, 5.

Hodgson Deerings, Johnny. "May Pole History—Rescuing Our Culture." Bluefields Pulse. http://bluefieldspulse.com/maypolehistoryrescuingourculture.htm (accessed May 7, 2015).

————. *Orígenes de nuestro palo de mayo*. Managua: El Renacimiento, 2008.

————. "Orígenes de nuestro palo de mayo." *WANI: Revista del Caribe Nicaragüense* 57 (April–June 2009): 5–23.

"Homenaje a las palenqueras." Fundación Paz Por Colombia. http://www.pazporcolombia.org/article.php?sid=45 (accessed March 11, 2010; page no longer extant).

hooks, bell. *Ain't I a Woman? Black Women and Feminism*. New York: Routledge, 2015.

Howard, David. *Coloring the Nation: Race and Ethnicity in the Dominican Republic*. Oxford: Signal Books, 2001.

Hurtubise, Josef. "Poesía en inglés criollo nicaragüense." *WANI: Una revista sobre la Costa Atlántica* 16 (January–March 1995): 43–56.

"Imaginarios: Aniversario 85 del nacimiento de Muguercia." *Librínsula: La revista de los libros*. http://librinsula.bnjm.cu/secciones/314/expedientes/314_exped_1.html (accessed May 23, 2014; page no longer extant).

Jaramillo, María Mercedes. "María Teresa Ramírez: Heredera de Yemayá y Changó." In Ramírez, *Mabungú triunfo: Poemas bilingües*, 7–22.

————. "María Teresa Ramírez y María de los Ángeles Popov: Herederas de Yemayá y de Changó." In Jaramillo and Ortiz, *Hijas de Muntu*, 190–213.

Jaramillo, María Mercedes, and Lucía Ortiz, eds. *Hijas de Muntu: Biografías críticas de mujeres afrodescendientes de América Latina*. Bogotá: Panamericana, 2011.

Jelly-Schapiro, Joshua. "'Are We All Creoles Now?' Ethnicity and Nation in a Heterogeneous Caribbean Diaspora." In *Ethnicity, Class, and Nationalism: Caribbean and Extra-Caribbean Dimensions*, edited by Anton L. Allahar, 23–55. Lanham, Md.: Lexington Books, 2005.

Jiménez, Blas R. *Afrodominicano por elección, negro por nacimiento*. Santo Domingo: Manatí, 2008.

Jones, David W., and Carlyle A. Glean. "The English-Speaking Communities of Honduras & Nicaragua." *Caribbean Quarterly* 17, no. 2 (June 1971): 50–61.

Kempadoo, Roshini. *Creole in the Archive: Imagery, Presence and the Location of the Caribbean Figure*. London: Rowman & Littlefield, 2016.

Krakusin, Margarita. "Cuerpo y texto: El espacio femenino en la cultura afrocolombiana en María Teresa Ramírez, Mary Grueso Romero, Edela Zapata Pérez y Amalia Lú Posso Figueroa." In *"Chambucú, la historia la escribes tú": Ensayos sobre cultura afro-colombiana*, edited by Lucía Ortiz, 97–216. Madrid: Iberoamericana, 2007.

Kucha Suto Colectivo. "Las alegrías de las palenqueras." December 6, 2012. YouTube video, 0:10:00. https://www.youtube.com/watch?v=bG8xAYMuHu8 (accessed November 11, 2015).

Kutzinski, Vera M. *Sugar's Secrets: Race and the Erotics of Cuban Nationalism*. Charlottesville: University Press of Virginia, 1993.

Kyalo, Muteti Andrew. "La comprensión de la muerte y de la vida eterna de los palenqueros de San Basilio." Thesis, Pontificia Universidad Javeriana, Bogotá, Colombia, 2013.

Lacayo Ortiz, Ileana Vanessa. "Autonomía." In Obando Sancho, Brooks Saldaña, and Alemán Porras, *Antología poética*, 119–20.

Lamus Canavate, Doris. "El lugar político de las mujeres en el movimiento negro/afrocolombiano." *Reflexión Política* 10, no. 20 (June 2008): 236–57.

————. "Negras, palenqueras y afrocartageneras: Construyendo un lugar contra la exclusión y la discriminación." *Reflexión Política* 12, no. 23 (June 2010): 152–66. http://revistas

.unab.edu.co/index.php?journal=reflexion&page=article&op=view&path[]=926 (accessed February 4, 2014).

———. "Relatos de vida de mujeres palenqueras en organizaciones del Caribe colombiano." In Jaramillo and Ortiz, *Hijas de Muntu*, 229–44.

Landers, Jane G. *Atlantic Creoles in the Age of Revolutions*. Cambridge, Mass.: Harvard University Press, 2010.

Larrazábal Blanco, Carlos. *Los negros y la esclavitud en Santo Domingo*. Santo Domingo: Julio D. Postigo e Hijos, 1967.

Lawo-Sukam, Alain. "Mary Grueso Romero y María Elcina Córdoba: Poetas de la identidad afro-colombiana." In Jaramillo and Ortiz, *Hijas de Muntu*, 170–89.

León, Argeliers. *Del canto y el tiempo*. Havana: Letras Cubanas, 1984.

Lipski, John. "Free at Last: From Bound Morpheme to Discourse Marker in *Lengua ri Palenge* (Palenquero Creole Spanish)." *Anthropological Linguistics* 54, no. 2 (Summer 2012): 101–32.

———. *A History of Afro-Hispanic Language: Five Centuries, Five Continents*. Cambridge: Cambridge University Press, 2005.

López Prieto, Antonio. *Parnaso cubano*. Havana: Impr. Miguel de Villa, 1881.

Los vecinos. "Palenquerita grito de alegría con coco y anís." April 4, 2015. YouTube video, 0:00:27. https://www.youtube.com/watch?v=10govXC--pc (accessed November 11, 2015).

Lowe de Goodin, Melva. *De from Barbados a to Panamá*. Panama: Géminis, 1999.

Lozano Lerma, Ruth Betty. "Mujeres negras (sirvientas, putas, matronas): Una aproximación a la mujer negra en Colombia." *Revista de estudios latinoamericanos* 1, no. 49 (2010): 1–22. http://www.revistas.una.ac.cr/index.php/tdna/article/view/3720 (accessed March 11, 2010).

Lozano Lerma, Ruth Betty, and Bibiana del Carmen Peñaranda Sepúlveda. "Memoria y reparación ¿Y de ser mujeres negras qué?" Presentation at the Seminario GEAS-CES, Cartagena de Indias, Colombia, October 18–20, 2005, 1–8. http://www.scribd.com/doc/19184719/memoria-y-reparacion-y-las-mujeres-negras-que (accessed October 9, 2014).

Malespín Jirón, Alfonso. *Bluefields en la memoria*. Bluefields, Nicaragua: URACCAN, 2003.

Mansour, Mónica. *La poesía negrista*. Mexico: Era, 1973.

Manuel, Peter. "From Contradanza to *Son*: New Perspectives on the Prehistory of Cuban Popular Music." *Latin American Music Review* 30, no. 2 (Fall–Winter 2009): 184–212.

Manzano, Juan Francisco. *Autobiografía*. Havana: Instituto del Libro Cubano, 1978.

Marques Samyn, Henrique. "A escrevivência como fundamento." *Mahin: Revista literária* 2, no. 3 (December 2020): 12–19. https://www.revistamahin.com.br (accessed January 2, 2021).

Martiatu Terry, Inés María. Prologue to Rubiera Castillo and Martiatu Terry, *Afrocubanas*, 1–10.

Martínez, Lovette. "It Is Autonomy / Es autonomía." In Alemán Porras and Brooks Vargas, *Bluefields en la sangre*, 108–9.

———. "Rundown/Rondón." In Alemán Porras and Brooks Vargas, *Bluefields en la sangre*, 106–7.

Martínez, María Inés. Preface to *El despertar de las comunidades afrocolombianas*, edited by María Inés Martínez, 36–38. Houston: LACASA, Centro de Investigaciones Sociales, 2012.

Martínez Downs, Lovette Angélica. "Black on Top." In Brown Hendricks, *Antología poética "Afrocarinica,"* 89.

———. "I Am Proud." In Brown Hendricks, *Antología poética "Afrocarinica,"* 90.

———. "Time Is Now." In Brown Hendricks, *Antología poética "Afrocarinica,"* 91–92.

Martínez Polo, Liliana. "Nueve noches de lumbalú para Graciela Salgado." *El tiempo*, September 15, 2013. http://www.eltiempo.com/archivo/documento/CMS-13063819 (accessed October 6, 2014).

Más, Sara. "Revisitando un sueño." In Rubiera Castillo and Moro, *Magín*, 7–10.

Matibag, Eugenio. *Haitian-Dominican Counterpart: Nation, State, and Race on Hispaniola*. New York: Palgrave Macmillan, 2003.

Mattern, Jochen. *Autonomía regional en Nicaragua: Una aproximación descriptiva*. Managua: PROFODEM-GTZ/CSD, 2002. https://www.academia.edu/31109923/AUTONOM%C3%8DA_REGIONAL_EN_NICARAGUA (accessed January 20, 2016).

McCoy, Antonia. "Significado del palo de mayo." *Revista Universitaria del Caribe* 8 (2002): 131–34.

McFarlane, Anthony. "*Cimarrones* and *palenques*: Runaways and Resistance in Colonial Colombia." *Slavery & Abolition* 6, no. 3 (1985): 131–51.

McField, David. "Mayo." In Alemán Porras and Brooks Vargas, *Bluefields en la sangre*, 43–48.

McField, David R. *Dios es negro: Poemas*. Managua: Mundial, 1967.

McKnight, Kathryn Joy. "Elder, Slave, and Soldier: Maroon Voices from the Palenque del Limón, 1634." In *Afro-Latino Voices: Narratives from the Early Modern Ibero-Atlantic World, 1550–1812*, edited by Kathryn Joy McKnight and Leo J. Garofalo, 64–81. Indianapolis: Hackett, 2009.

Meireles, Cecília. *Poesias completas de Cecilia Meireles*. Vol. 5. Rio de Janeiro: Civilização Brasileira, 1974.

Merlo, Carmen. "Otra vez ¡Mayo-Ya!" In Obando Sancho, Brooks Saldaña, and Alemán Porras, *Antología poética*, 92–93.

Meza Márquez, Consuelo. "Memoria, identidad y utopía en la poesía de las escritoras afrocentroamericanas: Relatos de vida." In Meza Márquez and Zavala González, *Mujeres en las literaturas*, 119–86.

Meza Márquez, Consuelo, and Magda Zavala González, eds. *Mujeres en las literaturas indígenas y afrodescendientes en América Central*. Aguascalientes, Mexico: Universidad Autónoma de Aguascalientes, 2015.

Micklin, Anna T. "Negritude Movement." Black Past, June 29, 2008. https://www.blackpast.org/global-african-history/negritude-movement/ (accessed March 19, 2021).

Ministerio de Cultura. *Historias matrias: Mujeres negras en la historia*. Colombia: Ministerio de Cultura Dirección de Poblaciones, 2010. https://www.mincultura.gov.co/SiteAssets/documentos/poblaciones/Mujeres%20negras%20en%20la%20historia.pdf (accessed March 8, 2014).

———. "Polonia, heroína palenquera." In Ministerio de Cultura, *Historias matrias*, 3.

———. "Todos los colores caben en nosotras: Palenqueras en Cartagena." In Ministerio de Cultura, *Historias matrias*, 15–16.

Mitjans, Aurelio. *Estudio sobre el movimiento científico y literario de Cuba*. Havana: Imprenta de A. Alvarez, 1890.

Monaghan, Patricia. *The Book of Goddesses and Heroines*. New York: E. P. Dutton, 1981.

"Monumento a las Palenqueras: Escultura en bronce de Hernando Pereira Brieva." Panoramio. http://www.panoramio.com/photo/4693537 (accessed March 11, 2010).

Moore, Robin D. *Music in the Hispanic Caribbean: Experiencing Music, Expressing Culture*. Oxford: Oxford University Press, 2010.

———. *Nationalizing Blackness: Afrocubanismo and Artistic Revolution in Havana, 1920–1940*. Pittsburgh: University of Pittsburgh Press, 1997.

———. "Representations of Afro-Cuban Expressive Culture in the Writings of Fernando Ortiz." *Latin American Music Review* 15, no. 1 (Spring–Summer 1994): 32–54.

Morales, Jorge Luis, ed. *Poesía afroantillana y negrista: Puerto Rico, República Dominicana, Cuba.* Rio Piedras: Universidad de Puerto Rico, 1981.

Morales Alonso, Luis Enrique. "Presentation." In Forbes Brooks, *Memorias de Miss Lizzie,* 4.

Moreno, Marisel. "'Burlando la raza': La poesía de escritoras afrodominicanas en la diáspora." *Camino real* 3, no. 4 (2011): 169–92.

Moreno Vega, Marta, Marinieves Alba, and Yvette Modestin, eds. *Women Warriors of the Afro-Latina Diaspora.* Houston: Arte Público, 2012.

Morris, Courtney Desiree. "Becoming Creole, Becoming Black: Migration, Diasporic Self-Making, and the Many Lives of Madame Maymie Leona Turpeau de Mena." *Women, Gender, and Families of Color* 4, no. 2 (Fall 2016): 171–95.

Mosby, Dorothy E. "'Nuevas nómadas': Negritud y ciudadanía en la literatura centro-americana." *Istmo: Revista virtual de estudios literarios y culturales centroamericanos* 16 (January–June 2008). http://istmo.denison.edu/n16/proyectos/mosby.html (accessed February 17, 2012).

———. *Place, Language, and Identity in Afro–Costa Rican Literature.* Columbia: University of Missouri Press, 2003.

Mosquera, Claudia, Mauricio Pardo, and Odile Hoffmann, eds. *Afrodescendientes en las Américas: 150 años de la abolición de la esclavitud en Colombia.* Cartagena, Colombia: Universidad Nacional de Colombia, 2002.

———. "Las trayectorias sociales e identitarias de los afrodescendientes." In Mosquera, Pardo, and Hoffmann, *Afrodescendientes en las Américas,* 13–42.

Mosquera Rosero-Labbé, Claudia. "La memoria del cimarronaje como patrimonio: Reparación simbólica para los afrocolombianos habitantes de San Basilio de Palenque." *Anaconda* 20 (May 2006): 16–23. http://www.google.es/?gws_rd=sslq=La+memoria+del +cimarronaje+como+patrimonio:++reparaci%C3%B3n+simb%C3%B3lica+ (accessed May 27, 2015).

"Movimiento Nacional Cimarrón." Movimiento Nacional Cimarrón. http://www .movimientocimarron.org/ (accessed May 27, 2015).

"Muere a los 83 años la artista del folclor colombiano Graciela Salgado." *El país*, September 14, 2013. https://www.elpais.com.co/entretenimiento/cultura/muere-a-los-83-anos -la-artista-del-folclor-colombiano-graciela-salgado.html (accessed September 26, 2022).

Muguercia y Muguercia, Alberto. "Teodora Ginés ¿Mito o realidad histórica?" *Revista de la Biblioteca Nacional José Martí* 62, no. 3 (September–December 1971): 53–86.

Munive Contreras, Moisés. "Gozar de su cuerpo: El abuso sexual a las negras esclavas en el Caribe colombiano, Cartagena y Mompox, siglo XVIII." *Historia 02.* http://www.azc .uam.mx/publicaciones/tye/tye16/art_hist_02.html (accessed September 30, 2014; page no longer extant).

Narciso, Erna. "Autonomía." In Alemán Porras and Brooks Vargas, *Bluefields en la sangre,* 63.

Narciso Walters, Erna Loraine. "Those Good Old Days." In Brown Hendricks, *Antología poética "Afrocarinica,"* 44–45.

———. "How Much Have You Invested? / ¿Cuánto has invertido?" In Obando Sancho, Brooks Saldaña, and Alemán Porras, *Antología poética,* 33–34.

Nascimento, Abdias do. *O quilombismo.* Rio de Janeiro: Vozes, 1980.

———. *Sortilégio: Mistério negro.* Rio de Janeiro: Teatro Experimental do Negro, 1959.

———. *Sortilégio II: Mistério negro do Zumbi redivivo.* São Paulo: Paz e Terra, 1979.

Navarro Cáceres, Ereilis, José Pallares Vega, and Edy Luz Navarro Cásseres. *Origen y resistencia de los peinados afrodescendientes como estrategia pedagógica*. Barranquilla, Colombia: Todo Arte Publicidad, 2014.

Newton, Velma. *Los hombres del "Silver Roll": Migración antillana a Panamá 1850–1914*. Panama: Sociedad de Amigos del Museo Afroantillano de Panamá, 1984.

Obando Sancho, Víctor. Introduction to Alemán Porras and Brooks Vargas, *Bluefields en la sangre*, 3–7.

Obando Sancho, Víctor, Ronald Brooks Saldaña, and Eddy Alemán Porras, eds. *Antología poética de la Costa Caribe de Nicaragua*. Managua: URACCAN, 1998.

Ocampo, Carlos Alemán. "Cultura de poder: Literatura indígena y afrocaribeña en Nicaragua." *Revista Universitaria del Caribe* 27, no. 2 (2000): 149–76.

———. "Las lenguas del Caribe Nicaragüense." In Arellano, *La Costa Caribe nicaragüense*, 149–57.

Ocampo Zamorano, Alfredo, and Guiomar Cuesta Escobar, comps. *Antología de mujeres poetas afrocolombianas*. Vol. 16. Bogotá: Ministerio de Cultura, 2010.

O'Neil, Wayne, and Maya Honda. "El inglés nicaragüense." *WANI: Una revista sobre la Costa Atlántica* 16 (October–December 1987): 54–60.

Orovio, Helio. *Diccionario de la música cubana biográfico y técnico*. 2nd ed. Havana: Letras Cubanas, 1992.

Orozco, Danilo. "Nexos globales desde la música cubana con rejuegos de son y no son." *Boletímúsica*, no. 38 (October–December 2014): 17–94.

———. "Perfil sociocultural y modo son en la cultura cubana." *Boletímúsica*, no. 38 (October–December 2014): 3–16.

Ortiz, Lucía. "*Chambacú, corral de negros* de Manuel Zapata Olivella, un capítulo en la lucha por la libertad: *In memoriam*." *Inti: Revista de literatura hispánica*, nos. 63–64 (Spring–Fall 2006): 95–108.

Otero, Solimar, and Toyin Falola, eds. *Yemoja: Gender, Sexuality, and Creativity in the Latina/o and Afro-Atlantic Diasporas*. Albany: State University of New York Press, 2013.

Palenque Records. "Chimbumbe—Graciela Salgado & Alegres Ambulancias." September 6, 2012. YouTube video, 0:03:42. https://www.youtube.com/watch?v=_VTcEleFyv8 (accessed August 5, 2015).

Pardo, Mauricio. "Iniciativa y cooptación: Tensiones en el movimiento afrocolombiano." In Restrepo Tirado, *150 años*, 652–84.

Past, Mariana. "Problematic Cartographies: Hispaniola as Truncated Island in Aída Cartagena Portalatín's *Yania Tierra*." *Afro-Hispanic Review* 30, no. 2 (Fall 2011): 85–100.

Perea Hinestroza, Fabio Teolindo. *Diccionario afrocolombiano: Afrorregionalismos, afroamericanismos y elementos de africanidad*. Chocó, Colombia: Corporación Autónoma Regional para el Desarrollo Sostenible del Chocó, 1996.

Pérez, Elizabeth. "Nobody's Mammy: Yemayá as Fierce Foremother in Afro-Cuban Religions." In Otero and Falola, *Yemoja*, 9–41.

Pérez, Odalís G. *Aída Cartagena Portalatín: De entero cuerpo*. Santo Domingo: Editora Universitaria UASD, 2007.

———. *La ideología rota: El derrumbe del pensamiento pseudonacionalista dominicano*. Santo Domingo: Manatí, 2002.

Pérez Miranda, Bernardino. *Chitieno lengua ku ma kuendo: Hablemos palenquero a través del cuento*. Cartagena de Indias, Colombia: Ediciones Pluma de Mompox, 2011.

———, comp. *Libertad Kaddume*. Cartagena de Indias, Colombia: Corpoataole, 2012.

Pérez Sanjurjo, Elena. *Historia de la música cubana*. Miami: La Moderna Poesía, 1986.

Pérez Tejedor, Juana Pabla. "The Role of the Palenge Language in the Transmission of Afro-Palenquero Cultural Heritage." *Museum International* 60, no. 3 (2008): 71–79. http://www.academia.edu/6547529/The_Role_of_the_Palenge_Language_in_the_Transmission_of_Afro-Palenquero_Cultural_Heritage (accessed August 9, 2015).

Pinto Vega, Santiago. *Las canoas del viento*. Bogotá: Instituto San Pablo Apostol, 2000.

Pizarro Rayo, Águeda. "Almanegras." In Ramírez, *Abalenga*, vi–xi.

———. Introduction to Ramírez, *La noche de mi piel*, xii.

———. "María Teresa Ramírez—Almanegra: Abalenga." In Ramírez, *Abalenga*, xii–xxiii.

———. Prologue to Ramírez, *Flor de palenque*, 10–12.

Pombo, Rocha. Preface to *Histórias da nossa história*, by Viriato Corrêa, 9–24. Rio de Janeiro: Livraria Castillo, 1923.

Portalatín, Aída Cartagena. "Aída Cartagena Portalatín." In Sosa, *Mujer y literatura*, 113.

———. *Culturas africanas rebeldes con causa*. Santo Domingo: Ediciones de la Biblioteca Nacional, 1986.

———. "La llamaban Aurora (Pasión por Donna Summer)." In *Tablero: Doce cuentos de lo popular a lo culto*, 11–17. Santo Domingo: Taller, 1978.

———. "Las Ginés de Santo Domingo: Esclavas, negras, libertas y músicas." *El Urogallo* 6, nos. 35–36 (September–December 1975): 149–54.

———. *Obra poética completa (1955–1984)*. Santo Domingo: Búho, 2000.

———. "Otoño negro." In *Dos siglos de literatura dominicana (S. XIX–XX): Poesía (II)*, edited by Manuel Rueda, 187–98. Santo Domingo: Corripio, 1996.

———. *Víspera del sueño: Del sueño al mundo; Homenaje póstumo*. Santo Domingo: La Poesía Sorprendida, 1990.

———. *Yania Tierra: Poema documento*. Washington, D.C.: Azul Editions, 1995.

Powell, Azizi. "What Does Mayaya Lasinki Mean?" *Pancocojams* (blog), June 29, 2014. http://pancocojams.blogspot.com/2014/06/what-does-mayaya-lasinki-mean.html (accessed January 15, 2015).

Prescott, Laurence. "Evaluando el pasado, forjando el futuro: Estado y necesidades de la literatura afro-colombiana." *Revista iberoamericana* 65, nos. 188–89 (July–December 1999): 553–65.

———. "Perfil histórico del autor afrocolombiano: Problemas y perspectivas." *América negra* 12 (December 1996): 104–25.

Quetzalcoatl Quintanilla, Felipe, and Juan Guillermo Sánchez Martínez. *Indigenous Message on Water—Mensaje indígena de agua*. London, Ontario: Indigenous World Forum on Water and Peace, 2014.

Ramírez, María Teresa. *Abalenga*. Roldanillo Valle, Colombia: Museo Rayo, 2008.

———. *Flor de palenque*. Bogotá: Artes Gráficas del Valle, 2008.

———. *La noche de mi piel*. Roldanillo Valle, Colombia: Ediciones Embalaje del Museo Rayo, 1988.

———. *Mabungú triunfo: Cosmogonía africana*. Vol. 2. Bogotá: Apidama Ediciones, 2016.

———. *Mabungú triunfo: Poemas bilingües, palenque-español*. 3rd ed. Bogotá: Apidama Ediciones, 2013.

Ramírez, Serafín. *La Habana artística: Apuntes históricos*. Havana: Impr. del E. M. de la Capitanía General, 1891.

Ramos, Fábio Pestana, and Marcus Vinícius de Morais. *Eles formaram o Brasil*. São Paulo: Contexto, 2010.

Ramos, Helena. "Deborah Robb: Libérrima como el jazz." Asociación Nicaragüense de Escritoras ANIDE. http://www.escritorasnicaragua.org/criticas/44 (accessed April 20, 2015).

Rensoli Medina, Rolando J. *La Habana ciudad azul: Metrópolis cubana*. Havana: Ediciones Extramuros, 2015.

Restrepo Tirado, Ernesto, ed. *150 años de la abolición de la esclavización en Colombia: Desde la marginalidad a la construcción de la nación*. Bogotá: Aguilar, 2003.

Ribeiro, Esmeralda. "A escritora negra e seu ato de escrever participando." In Cuti and Xavier, *Criação crioula*, 59–66.

——. "Dois textos para autocontemplar-se." In Duke, *A escritora afro-brasileira*, 156–65.

——. "Reflexão sobre literatura infanto-juvenil." In *Reflexões*, organized by Quilombhoje, 25–29. São Paulo: Conselho de Participação e Desenvolvimento da Comunidade Negra, 1985.

Ribeiro, Esmeralda, and Márcio Barbosa. "Apresentação." In *Cadernos Negros três décadas: Ensaios, poemas, contos*, organized by Esmeralda Ribeiro and Márcio Barbosa, 15–16. São Paulo: Quilombhoje, SEPPIR, 2008.

——. Introduction to *Cadernos Negros Black Notebooks: Contemporary Afro-Brazilian Literature / Literatura afro-brasileira contemporânea*, edited by Niyi Afolabi, Márcio Barbosa, and Esmeralda Ribeiro, 1–3. Trenton, N.J.: Africa World Press, 2008.

Rigby, Carlos. "Si yo fuera mayo." In Alemán Porras and Brooks Vargas, *Bluefields en la sangre*, 77–78.

——. "Si yo fuera Mayo." In Obando Sancho, Brooks Saldaña, and Alemán Porras, *Antología poética*, 42–44.

Robb, Deborah, Víctor Obando Sancho, Hugo René Montalván, José Ramón Molina Vargas, Guillermo M. Monterrosa Z, and Zarifet Bermúdez Jureidini. *Leyendas de la Costa Atlántica*. Managua: URACCAN, 2003.

Robbins, James. "The Cuban 'Son' as Form, Genre, and Symbol." *Latin American Music Review* 2, no. 11 (Autumn–Winter 1990): 182–200.

Robb Taylor, Deborah, ed. *The Times & Life of Bluefields: An Intergenerational Dialogue*. Managua: Academia de Geografía e Historia de Nicaragua, 2005.

Roberts, Nicole. "Racialised Identities, Caribbean Realities: Analysing Black Female Identity in Hispanic Caribbean Poetry." *Caribbean Review of Gender Studies* 1 (April 2007): 1–18.

Robinson de Saavedra, Dilia. "La política de etnoeducación afrocolombiana." In *I foro nacional de etnoeducación afrocolombiana*, edited by Ministerio de Educación Nacional, 13–17. Bogotá: Ministerio de Educación Nacional, Imprenta Nacional, 2004.

Rodriguez, Francisco, ed. *Palenque de San Basilio: Obra maestra del patrimonio intangible de la humanidad*. Bogotá: Ministerio de Cultura / Instituto Colombiano de Antropología e Historia, 2002. https://repositorio.unicartagena.edu.co/handle/11227/7435 (accessed September 26, 2022).

Rodríguez, Victoria Eli, and Zoila Gómez García. . . . *haciendo música cubana*. Havana: Pueblo y Educación, 1989.

Rodríguez-Bobb, Arturo. *Exclusión e integración del sujeto negro en Cartagena de Indias en perspectiva histórica*. Madrid: Iberoamericana, 2002.

Rojas, Axel. *Cátedra de estudios afrocolombianos*. Popayán, Colombia: Taller Editorial Universidad del Cauca, 2008. https://www.academia.edu/28581799/Catedra_de_Estudios _Afrocolombianos_Aportes_para_maestros (accessed September 26, 2022).

Rojas, Charo Mina. *Defeating Invisibility: A Challenge for Afro-descendant Women in Colombia*. Colombia: Afro-descendant Women Human Rights Defenders Project, PCN, 2012. http://www.afrocolombians.org/pdfs/Defeating%20Invisibility.pdf (accessed June 16, 2014).

Romero Vargas, Germán. "El conflicto anglo-español en la Costa de Mosquitos." In Arellano, *La Costa Caribe nicaragüense*, 45–66.

———. *Historia de la Costa Atlántica*. Managua: CIDCA-UCA, 1996.

———. *Las sociedades del Atlántico de Nicaragua en los siglos XVII y XVIII*. Managua: Fondo de Promoción Cultural, BANIC, 1995.

Rondón, Pura Emeterio. *Estudios críticos de la literatura dominicana contemporánea*. Santo Domingo: Búho, 2005.

Rossman Tejada, Yolanda. "Aquí la palabra es arcoíris: La autonomía multicultural desde la poesía de escritoras costeñas." In Meza Márquez and Zavala González, *Mujeres en las literaturas*, 77–94.

———. "Una aproximación a la autonomía multicultural desde la poesía de escritoras costeñas." MA thesis, URACCAN, Bilwi, Nicaragua, 2006.

Rozo Moorhouse, Teresa, ed. *Diosas en bronce: Poesía contemporánea de la mujer colombiana*. Irvine, Calif.: Ediciones Latidos, 1995.

Rubiera Castillo, Daisy. "Apuntes sobre la mujer negra cubana." *Cuban Studies* 42 (2011): 176–85.

———. "Avivir la memoria: Desterrar el olvido." In Rubiera Castillo and Martiatu Terry, *Afrocubanas*, 11–13.

———. "El discurso femenino negro de reivindicación (1888–1958)." In *Emergiendo del silencio: Mujeres negras en la historia de Cuba*, compiled by Oilda Hevia Lanier and Daisy Rubiera Castillo, 223–42. Havana: Editorial del Ciencias Sociales, 2016.

———. "El tiempo de la memoria." *La gaceta de Cuba* 1 (January–February 2005): 44–46.

———. "La mujer de color en Cuba." In *Dos ensayos*, by Daisy Rubiera Castillo and Raúl Ruiz Miyares, 3–27. Havana: Academia, 1996.

———. "La mujer en la santería o regla ocha: Género, mitos y realidad." In Rubiera Castillo and Martiatu Terry, *Afrocubanas*, 107–32.

———. *Reyita, sencillamente: Testimonio de una negra cubana nonagenaria*. Havana: Instituto Cubano del Libro, PROLIBROS, 1996.

Rubiera Castillo, Daisy, and Georgina Herrera. *Golpeando la memoria: Testimonio de una poeta cubana afrodescendiente*. Havana: Unión, 2005.

Rubiera Castillo, Daisy, and Inés María Martiatu Terry, eds. *Afrocubanas: Historia, pensamiento y prácticas culturales*. Havana: Editorial de Ciencias Sociales, 2011.

Rubiera Castillo, Daisy, and Sonnia Moro. *Magín: Tiempo de contar esta historia*. Havana: Ediciones Magín, 2015.

Rufino, Alzira. *Eu, mulher negra, resisto*. Santos, Brazil: Ed. da Autora, 1988.

———. *Mulher negra: Uma perspectiva histórica*. Santos, Brazil: Alzira Rufino, 1987.

Rufino, Alzira, Nilza Iraci, and Maria Rosa Pereira. *Mulher negra tem história*. Santos, Brazil: Self-published, 1986.

Sagás, Ernesto. *Race and Politics in the Dominican Republic*. Gainesville: University Press of Florida, 2000.

Saldarriaga, Teresa, prod. *La tía Cato*. San Basilio de Palenque, Colombia: Yuma Vídeo Cine, 1994. Documentary, 25 min. https://www.youtube.com/watch?v=jlIicgKm86k (accessed September 26, 2022).

Salgado, Sebastian, Faustino Torres, and Uriel Cassiani. *Letras palenqueras, la profunda necesidad de nombrar: Ma letra ri palengue*. Cartagena de Indias, Colombia: Corpoataole, 2012.

Sanmartín, Paula. *Black Women as Custodians of History: Unsung Rebel Mothers in African American and Afro-Cuban Women's Writing*. Amherst, N.Y.: Cambria, 2014.

Santos Cermeño, José. "May Pole in Bluefields." In Alemán Porras and Brooks Vargas, *Bluefields en la sangre*, 20–23.

———. "Palos de Mayo en Bluefields." In Alemán Porras and Brooks Vargas, *Bluefields en la sangre*, 13–17.

Santos-Febres, Mayra. *Sobre piel y papel*. San Juan: Ediciones Callejón, 2005.

Santos Palmeira, Francineide. "Escritoras na literatura afrocolombiana." *Estudios de literatura colombiana* 32 (January–June 2013): 87–102.

———. "Escritoras negras na América Latina." Presentation given at the XI Congresso Luso-Afro-Brasileiro de Ciências Sociais, Salvador, Bahia, Brazil, August 7–10, 2011, 1–13. http://www.google.es/?gws_rd=sslq=Escritoras+negras+na+Am%C3%A9rica+Latina (accessed January 22, 2015).

Schmidt-Nowara, Christopher. *Slavery, Freedom, and Abolition in Latin America and the Atlantic World*. Albuquerque: University of New Mexico Press, 2011.

Schwegler, Armin. *"Chi ma 'kongo'": Lengua y rito ancestrales en el Palenque de San Basilio (Colombia)*. 2 vols. Frankfurt: Vervuert Verlag, 1996.

Scruggs, T. M. "Let's Enjoy as Nicaraguans: The Use of Music in the Construction of a Nicaraguan National Consciousness." *Ethnomusicology* 43, no. 2 (Spring–Summer 1999): 297–321.

"Sebastián Lemba: El líder de la cimarronea." conectate.com, last updated September 25, 2020. https://www.conectate.com.do/articulo/sebastian-lemba-biografia-republica-dominicana/ (accessed June 21, 2019).

"Sebastián Lemba Calembo: Biografías dominicanas." www.mi-rd.com, last updated 2018. https://www.mi-rd.com/Interes/Historia/Sebastian-Lemba-Calembo.html (accessed June 21, 2019).

Secretaría de Cultura y Turismo de Cali. *Poemas matriax: Antología de poetas afrocolombianas*. Cali, Colombia: Arte Gráficas del Valle, 2012.

Sédar Senghor, Léopold. "Negritude: A Humanism of the Twentieth Century." In *Colonial Discourse and Post-colonial Theory: A Reader*, edited by Patrick Williams and Laura Chrisman, 27–35. New York: Columbia University Press, 1994.

Silva Prada, Natalia. "Leonor: Una reina palenquera de la gobernación de Cartagena de Indias." *Los reinos de las Indias en el Nuevo Mundo* (blog), April 9, 2013. https://losreinosdelasindias.hypotheses.org/559 (accessed September 26, 2022).

Simarra Obeso, Rutsely. "La lengua palenquera: Una experiencia cosmovisionaria, significativa y creativa de los palenqueros descendientes de la diáspora africana en Colombia." *Revista anaconda*. https://www.humanas.unal.edu.co/colantropos/files/6914/7330/4008/Lengua_palenquera_Simarra.pdf (accessed September 26, 2022).

———. "Lengua ri Palenge: Suto tan chitiá / La lengua de Palenque: Contexto lingüístico, histórico y comunicativo." In *Las mujeres afrodescendientes y la cultura latinoamericana: Identidad y desarrollo*, edited by Silvia Beatriz García Savino, 45–53. Ciudad del Saber, Panama: Proyecto Regional "Población afrodescendiente de América Latina" del PNUD, 2009.

Simarra Obeso, Rutsely, Regina Miranda Reyes, and Juana Pabla Pérez Tejedor, comps. *Lengua ri Palenge: Jende suto ta chitiá; Léxico de la lengua palenquera*. Cartagena, Colombia: Casa Editorial, 2008.

Sosa, José Rafael, ed. *Mujer y literatura*. Santo Domingo: Editora Universitaria UASD, 1986.

Souza Saleme, Ruth. "*Cagüira: 'Tears of the Soul.'*" In *Cadernos Negros*, vol. 22, *Contos Afro-Brasileiros*, organized by Quilombhoje, 91–98. São Paulo: Okan, 1999.

Spence Sharpe, Marva. "Educación en lengua criolla: Las actitudes de los educandos en la Costa Atlántica de Nicaragua." *InterSedes* 8 (2004): 1–12. http://www.redalyc.org/articulo .oa?id=66650815 (accessed February 17, 2012).

Stephenson Watson, Sonja. *The Politics of Race in Panama: Afro-Hispanic and West Indian Literary Discourses of Contention.* Gainesville: University Press of Florida, 2014.

Stinchcomb, Dawn. *The Development of Literary Blackness in the Dominican Republic.* Gainesville: University Press of Florida, 2004.

Stuart, Felipe, ed. "Feature: Intercultural Bilingual Education." URACCAN. http://www/yorku .ca/cerlac/URACCAN/May97.html (accessed November 1, 2014; page no longer extant).

Sujo Wilson, Hugo. "Hacia una reincorporación justa y auténtica." In Arellano, *La Costa Caribe nicaragüense,* 67–72.

———. *Oral History of Bluefields / Historia oral de Bluefields.* Bluefields, Nicaragua: CIDCA-UCA, 1998.

Tallet, José Z. *Orbita de Jose Z. Tallet.* Edited by Helio Orovio. Havana: UNEAC, 1969.

Thomas Britton, Lillian, and Conrad Monroe Forbes. "Caracterización y análisis de la poesía de la poeta costeña creol Erna Narcisso Watters." Unpublished monograph, URACCAN, Bluefields, Nicaragua, December 2006.

Tinkam Crisanto, Karl. "Biografía." In Brown Hendricks, *Antología poética "Afrocarinica,"* 114–15.

———. "Soy quien soy." In Brown Hendricks, *Antología poética "Afrocarinica,"* 118–19.

Torres-Saillant, Silvio. "The Tribulations of Blackness: Stages in Dominican Racial Identity." *Latin American Perspectives* 25, no. 3 (May 1998): 126–46.

Valdés, Alicia. *Diccionario de mujeres notables en la música cubana.* Santiago de Cuba: Oriente, 2011.

Valdés, Vanessa K. *Oshun's Daughters: The Search for Womanhood in the Americas.* Albany: State University of New York Press, 2014.

Valencia, Liliana. "Niñas palenqueras recuperan la tradición de las cantadoras: Liliana Valencia informa." May 19, 2013. YouTube video, 0:01:31. http://www.youtube.com/ watch?v=f9tjOLbkYWA (accessed September 30, 2014).

Valencia Córdoba, María Elcina. *Analogías y anhelos.* Roldanillo, Colombia: Talleres Editoriales del Museo Rayo, 2008.

———. *Pentagrama de pasión.* Bogotá: Apidama, 2010.

———. *Rutas de autonomía y caminos de identidad: Poemas.* Buenaventura, Colombia: Impresos y diseños EVA, 2001.

———. *Susurro de palmeras: Poemas.* Buenaventura, Colombia: Litografía Palacio, 2001.

———. *Todos somos culpables: Cantos.* Roldanillo, Colombia: Talleres Editoriales del Museo Rayo, 1992.

Valle, Francisco. "Palo de mayo." In Arellano, *La Costa Caribe nicaragüense,* 274.

Valle-Castillo, Julio. "Criterio de edición." In Valle-Castillo, *Poesía atlántica,* 7–10.

———, ed. *Poesía atlántica.* Managua: Ministerio de Cultura, 1980.

Vicioso, Chiqui. "Aída Cartagena Portalatín." Latin Art Museum, last updated April 16, 2019. http://www.latinartmuseum.com/portalatin.htm (accessed 25 July 2014).

———. "Aída Cartagena Portalatín ¿El éxito según San . . . ?" In Sosa, *Mujer y literatura,* 79–85.

———. "Prólogo: Ya no estás sola, Aída." In *Una mujer está sola,* by Aída Cartagena Portalatín, 11–18. Santo Domingo: Ediciones Ferilibro, 2005.

Vidaurre, Irene. "Biografía: Ronald Amadeo Brooks Saldaña (Q.E.P.D.)." In Brown Hendricks, *Antología poética "Afrocarinica,"* 11–13.

Vidaurre Campos, Irene. "Costa Atlántica." In Obando Sancho, Brooks Saldaña, and Alemán Porras, *Antología poética*, 81.

———. "¡Rica y empobrecida tierra mía!" In Obando Sancho, Brooks Saldaña, and Alemán Porras, *Antología poética*, 83–85.

Vieira, Lia. *Chica da Silva: A mulher que inventou o mar.* Rio de Janeiro: OR Produtor Editorial Independente, 2001.

———. "Por que Nicinha não veio?" In *Cadernos Negros*, vol. 16, *Contos*, edited by Edição dos Autores, 63–64. São Paulo: Quilombhoje, 1993.

Vilas, Carlos. "Revolutionary Change and Multi-ethnic Regions: The Sandinista Revolution and the Atlantic Coast." In *Ethnic Groups and the Nation State: The Case of the Atlantic Coast of Nicaragua*, edited by CIDCA / Development Study Unit, 61–100. Stockholm: Stockholm University Press, 1987.

Villaverde, Cirilo. *Cecilia Valdés: Novela de costumbres cubanas.* Mexico: Porrúa, 2006.

Vos Obeso, Rafaela. "La mujer en el Palenque de San Basilio." *Revista chichamaya* 2, no. 8 (July 24, 2012): 10–13. https://repositorio.unal.edu.co/handle/unal/54307 (accessed September 26, 2022).

Wabgou, Maguemati, Jaime Arocha Rodríguez, Aiden José Salgado Cassiani, and Juan Alberto Carabalí Ospina. *Movimiento social afrocolombiano, negro, raizal y palenquero.* Bogotá: Universidad Nacional de Colombia, 2012.

Wade, Peter. *Blackness and Race Mixture: The Dynamics of Racial Identity in Colombia.* Baltimore, Md.: Johns Hopkins University Press, 1993.

———. "Cultural Politics of Blackness in Colombia." *American Ethnologist* 22, no. 2 (May 1995): 341–57.

———. "Understanding 'Blackness' and 'Africa' in Colombia: Music and the Politics of Culture." In *Afro-Atlantic Dialogues: Anthropology in the Diaspora*, edited by Kevin A. Yelvington, 351–78. Santa Fe, N.Mex.: School of American Research Press, 2006.

Walker, Alice. *The Complete Stories.* Phoenix: Orion, 2005.

———. *In Search of Our Mothers' Gardens: Womanist Prose.* San Diego: Harcourt Brace Jovanovich, 1983.

Watson, Andira. "Las reacciones de la sociedad frente a una literatura de mujeres indígenas y afrodescendientes: Una reflexión desde la literatura de mujeres de la Costa Caribe Nicaragüense." *WANI: Revista del Caribe Nicaragüense* 57 (April–June 2009): 51–59.

Wilson, Carlos Guillermo. "The Caribbean: Marvelous Craddle-Hammock and Painful Corucopia." In Balutansky and Sourieau, *Caribbean Creolization*, 36–43.

Woods Downs, Socorro. *"I've Never Shared This with Anybody": Creole Women's Experience of Racial and Sexual Discrimination and Their Need for Self-Recovery.* Managua: URACCAN, 2005.

Woods Downs, Socorro, and Courtney Desiree Morris. *"Land Is Power": Examining Race, Gender, and the Struggle for Land Rights on the Caribbean Coast of Nicaragua.* Report for the Caribbean and Central American Research Council, Austin, Tex., June 2007.

"¡Yo soy afrocolombiana, soy promotora de paz!" *Palenques*, January 2014, 1.

Zapata Olivella, Manuel. *Chambacú, corral de negros.* Medellín, Colombia: Bedout, 1967.

———. "Palenque, primer territorio libre de América." *Mundo*, June 20, 2007, 18–27.

Zavala González, Magda. "Para conocer a las poetas afrodescendientes centroamericanas." In Meza Márquez and Zavala González, *Mujeres en las literaturas*, 97–117.

Index

About the Author

Dawn Duke, professor of Spanish and Portuguese in the Department of Modern Foreign Languages and Literatures at the University of Tennessee, Knoxville, was awarded the Lindsay Young Professorship (2021–23) and is the current chair of the Portuguese program. A former chair of the Africana studies program, she is also affiliated faculty in the Latin American and Caribbean studies program. She is the author of *Literary Passion, Ideological Commitment: Toward a Legacy of Afro-Cuban and Afro-Brazilian Women Writers* (Bucknell University Press), editor of *A escritora afro-brasileira: Ativismo e arte literária*, and coeditor of *Celluloid Chains: Slavery in the Americas through Film*. She has also published more than twenty-two articles and chapters.